AF148036

Maria Antonietta Macciocchi

NLB

Letters from
inside the Italian Communist Party
to Louis Althusser

Lettere dall'interno del P.C.I. a Louis Althusser
first published by Feltrinelli, Milan, 1969;
second edition, with Appendix, published 1970
© Giangiacomo Feltrinelli Editore, 1969
This translation first published 1973
Translated from the Italian by Stephen M. Hellman
© NLB, 1973

NLB, 7 Carlisle Street, London W1

Designed by Gerald Cinamon
Typeset in Monotype Ehrhardt
Printed and bound by CPI Group (UK) Ltd, Croydon, CR0 4YY

Preface

In America, Germany, France and also in Italy, there were already clear warning signs of what was going to happen in 1968. The student movements had become widespread and active. The spiralling of the war in Vietnam was beginning to show the problems inherent in the thesis of coexistence on which US-USSR relations are based. The Cultural Revolution in China was in full swing. The pictures of Che's body were on the front pages of all the newspapers. The working class was uneasy in many countries, and the problem of the role and the very strategy of the large Communist Parties in the West was beginning to become evident.

It was the end of 1967, and I decided to accept the Party's offer to me to leave my position as *l'Unità*'s Paris correspondent, after five years in France, in order to return to Italy and work again inside the Party as a candidate for the 1968 general elections.

My major reason for accepting this offer was a desire and a need to find out the truth of what was going on in my country and my party. The only way I could fulfil this need was by getting involved in the party organization, acting again as a militant among hundreds of thousands of militants. It was this same need to find out the truth which led me to suggest, before leaving Paris, a project of correspondence to the Communist philosopher, Louis Althusser. I am bound to Althusser by a profound intellectual and political friendship, and I wanted to share this experience with him. Neither of us originally intended publication, as is clear from the letters themselves. They were simply to be a way of intellectually fixing and disciplining my impressions, the facts I discovered, and the questions raised by the situation. After Althusser's first letters, which open this collection, I began to write these 'letters from inside the PCI' from the very first day I arrived in Naples, after an absence of twenty years.

When the campaign ended, I found myself with 400 typed pages, consisting of his letters and mine. What was I now to do with them?

The kind of research on Naples which they contain had never been done before. Nor was there any reporting of this nature on the general condition of the Party – particularly in a moment like an electoral campaign, when the Party unleashes all of its energies, all of its inner tension, all of its ability to influence society. Such a moment allows the actions of the Party itself to contribute to an analysis of its conditions, its functions and its role. Its strengths and weaknesses come clearly to the fore. And the questions – be they stimulating or disturbing – that its militants are asking today in the period of profound development which Italian society is currently undergoing, also emerge clearly.

I therefore had to ask myself whether it was better to publish all this, or to give it to the Party so that, internally, attention could be given to a militant's experience and the issues raised by this experience. It took me some time to decide. I gave the manuscript to three comrades, two of them important leaders, for comments. One, from the generation of exiles under Fascism, was interested but prudent – he was worried about the image of the Party which emerged from my experience. Another, the same age as myself, was profoundly disturbed. The third, a young student barely over twenty years of age, insisted that I try to offer to as many people as possible, especially the younger generation, the testimony of a militant who, from *inside the Party*, asks herself the same questions that all revolutionaries are asking. So, finally, in agreement with Althusser, I decided to publish, in Italy and France, these 'letters from inside the PCI', together with his own to me.

I reached this decision primarily in reaction to the new situation which has arisen in Italy and all over the world. Both the crumbling of many recent hypotheses and the posing of new, dramatic problems for the strategy of Western Communist Parties tells me that the Italian Communist Party (which reflects within itself all the phenomena which are shaking society) must be seen with realistic eyes by all those who – even though they may follow very different routes – are travelling towards a common historical rendezvous. All are seeking the means, the forces, and the strategy capable of ensuring the transition to socialism in our societies – the societies of a capitalism which is advanced and at the same time decrepit, i.e. of what is often currently termed mature capitalism. Moreover, the PCI has never tried to avoid a discussion of its policies, because we have never been a sect, even if it has often been said that we are a church. We are – and we ought to be – a 'collective intellectual', and proof of this could be seen in the long, passionate and at times even bitter debate that characterized the phase prior to the Twelfth Congress in Bologna in February 1969, and, to a lesser degree, in the debate at the Congress itself.

These are letters from Naples because it was in Naples that my experience occurred. But the problems I discuss are not simply those of Naples. They are problems which affect all of Italy and the entire Party, at a time when the entire Party is preoccupied with the common need for an analysis and is passing through a common watershed. Certainly, in places where the P C I holds important positions of local power, such as Emilia-Romagna, Tuscany or Umbria, or other places where the social and political context is different from that of Naples, the general perspective would perhaps be different. For that reason, it would be of great interest to see the same problems viewed through these different lenses. Will someone do this? I hope so. For only from an *overall critical perspective* can *overall proposals* for the *entire party* emerge, proposals capable of ensuring that the PCI will assert its ability to be at the head of the masses at a time when the masses are increasingly showing their powerful capacity of intervention.

Althusser's letter on the 'May Events' (pp. 301ff.) and, perhaps especially, the one that preceded it (pp. 298ff.) represent, in my opinion, an important initial theoretical and political contribution from which to begin an analysis of the revolutionary party, in relation to the national society and to the international workers' movement. The answer to these letters, clearly, cannot be mine alone.

M.A.M.
April 1969

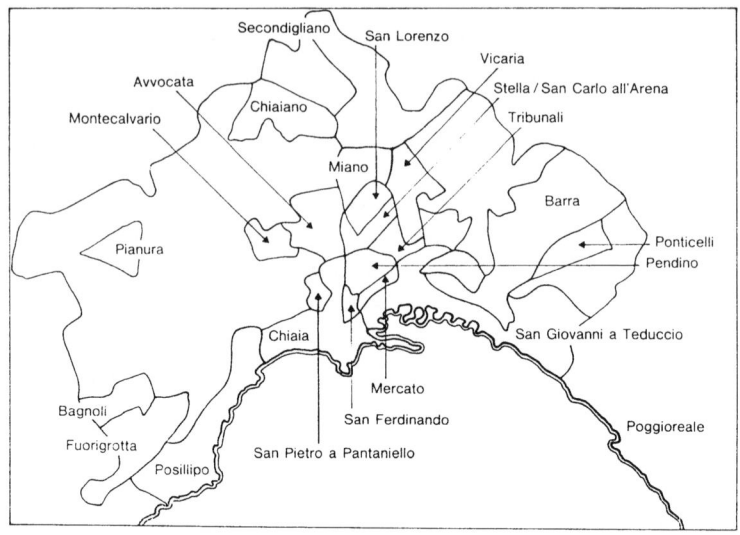

Naples : Electoral districts

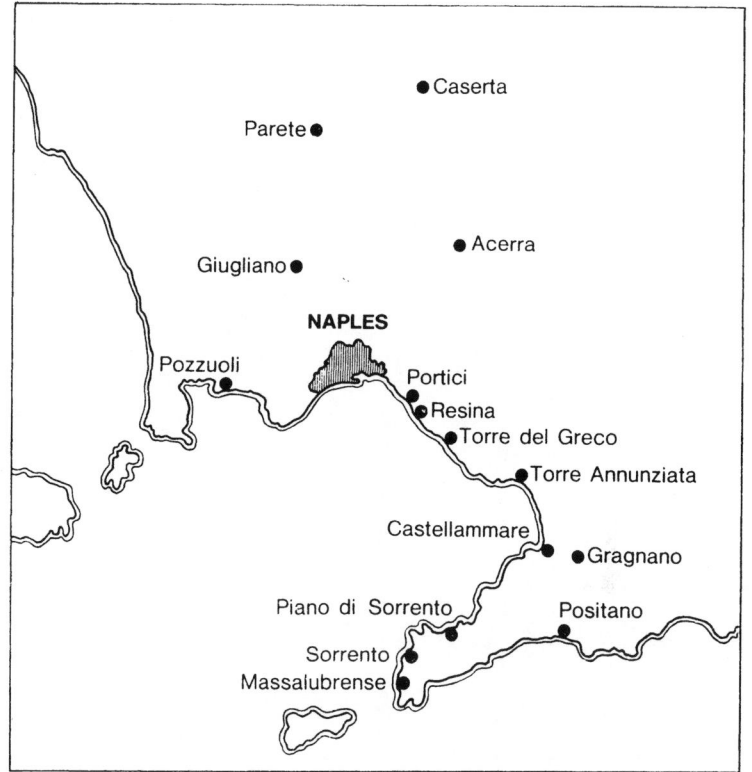

The Naples area

Organizational Chart of the Italian Communist Party

NATIONAL LEADERSHIP

Central Committee (171)
Central Control Commission (41) } ⟶ National Executive (20) } ⟶ { Political Bureau (7) } ⟶ { General Secretary
Secretariat (7) (+up to 2 deputies)

Editor-in-chief of *Unità*
Head of Parliamentary Group
Heads of Commissions:
Local administration; Social security;
Press and propaganda; Women;
Factories; Agrarian; Culture;
Middle classes; The South; Foreign Affairs

REGIONAL ORGANIZATIONS (20)

Regional Committees (or Federations) ⟶ Regional Secretariat ⟶ Regional Secretary

PROVINCIAL FEDERATIONS (109)

Federal Committees
Federal Control Commissions } ⟶ Provincial Executive ⟶ { Provincial political committee
and/or secretariat } ⟶ Provincial secretary

AREA COMMITTEES (64 City Committees, 750 Communal or Zonal Committees)

SECTIONS (10,884)

CELLS (24,838, of which 3,236 in factories)

MEMBERS (1,502,889)

Explanatory note

All figures are for 1968, when this book was written. The arrows indicate election.

The key organizational units below national level are the Provincial Federation and the Section. However, in big cities like Naples, the City Committee may also be important.

The Federation referred to throughout this book is the Provincial Federation of Naples. As its name suggests, it covers the entire province of Naples, which includes the capital city and eighty-eight other towns. In 1968 this Federation had 32,983 members, of whom 18,287 were in the city of Naples itself. The latter also has a City Committee, mentioned on several occasions in this book.

The Provincial Federation of Naples comprises 116 Sections, 28 of them in the city itself.

Letters

Dear M.A., *Paris, 3 February 1968*

I hope you received the telegram I sent when the *Unità* interview came out.[1] I was really thrilled by this great success. The work you did, and I can imagine the tenacity and patience which was required, was magnificent. I thank you profoundly. On Monday I bought the Sunday *Unità* in Paris, but there wasn't anything in it (it was the Milan edition, and I never imagined that there were differences between the Milan and Rome issues). So I said to myself: 'Hold on, there must be some minor problems . . . let's just wait and see.' Then, yesterday, I managed to find a copy at Montparnasse (it was sold out everywhere else) with the interview. The headlines and titles are *magnificent*, and the translation is excellent. The last two words are perfect. It's a journalistic and political masterpiece: when you open the paper it's impossible not to read the text, just from the point of view of the layout. I particularly hope that workers read it.

Two things interest me most of all:
1. if there are reactions from Italian workers, and if so how they are expressed;
2. the reactions of youth (i.e. students).

If you could give me your impressions about this, it would really help.

I also wanted to let you know that the Italian edition of *Reading Capital*, cut down to my articles and those of Balibar, will be coming out soon. It contains a very brief 'Italian' introduction – which specifies that later on we will correct both our terminology (which is too 'structuralist', and Marxism is not 'structuralism') and also my definition of philosophy – along with my letter to *Rinascita*.

1. On 1 February 1968 *Unità* published an interview with Louis Althusser by Maria Antonietta Macciocchi. This interview, entitled 'Philosophy as a Revolutionary Weapon', was published in English in *New Left Review*, no. 64, and included in Louis Althusser, *Lenin and Philosophy and Other Essays*, NLB, 1971. (Trans.)

Your information on your present situation, in all its details, is most interesting. I'll repeat here my complete agreement on our correspondence project and I'll also repeat that I see this project as a really important one.

In the broadest sense, the present period holds out infinite possibilities and resources. You have to know where they are, how they are often disguised, hidden, suffocated, etc. Then, too, remember that things are going to be happening very rapidly, and you must make your own imagination keep up with the flow of events as much as possible. Remember Zhdanov's watchword: 'Never underestimate the state of the *democratic* forces.' Just replace *democratic* with another adjective and the expression is very much to the point.

One of our problems is that even when we decide not to *underestimate*, we still end up pretty wide of the mark. We have been so conditioned to underestimate things that both our bodies and our spirits are wrapped in a Nessus's shirt. Even when we think we are overestimating, we still underestimate. The masses are potentially (potentially: in fact – but no one gives them the means) far *ahead* of 'us'. The whole issue is to know *in what sense*. We need to know this in an extremely precise way: exactly what sectors of the 'masses' are on the move, where, in what forms (which can be unknown, unexpected, without precedent). Once this is 'under control', the rest is child's play. But of course it's a game which doesn't leave much time for 'sleeping' any more. Think about it.

Louis

Dear M.A., *Paris, 11 March 1968*

I was happy to read of the latest developments in your letter of 8 March, especially the news that you have reached an important step in the 'pre-campaign campaign'. If I understand correctly, you have been 'elected' to the slate of candidates for the general elections. And this in spite of your bad reputation! That's already an accomplishment. Use this first step well.

First objective: to find out what is really going on among 'the people' (see Mao's 100 per cent Leninist definition at the beginning of his article, 'On the Correct Handling of Contradictions Among the People'). An electoral campaign can be a first (limited but real) step towards understanding what is happening among 'the people'. A campaign also provides a means of responding to the preliminary but absolutely essential question for every political undertaking: *What does 'the People' mean, today, in Italy?* Another way of putting it might be: What classes make up 'the people'? What fractions of classes are involved *beyond* the proletariat and poor peasants? How, today, are the poor peasants defined? Poor peasants: agricultural workers, hence agricultural proletariat, i.e. agricultural wage-labourers plus poor peasants who receive no wage or only a semi-wage. What are the limits of this social stratum? Where does the petty bourgeoisie begin among the peasants? What part of this peasant bourgeoisie sides with the workers? Can it side with the workers? This goes back to Lenin's question: at what point are we, and what forms does 'capitalist development' take in the countryside? The same questions have to be asked of the urban petty bourgeoisie.

As long as you can't answer the question: What, today, comprises the people in a given country (*today*, because the composition of the people varies historically; *in a given country*, because the composition of the people changes from place to place), you can't do anything in politics. Only by knowing what 'the people' means can you then develop: (1) a mass political line; (2) corresponding political actions. It should be understood that the analysis must also consider the forces of the class enemy, or the enemies of the people, and their policies. But if you *only* take the enemies of the people into account without knowing who the people are, what their forces are, what their resources and capabilities are, and what the masses 'want' (even if they can't 'say so' in a clear, consistent manner), you are at the enemy's mercy.

Making war (class struggle) cannot consist of passing your time reflecting exclusively on the forces and strategy of the adversary, but first of all consists of 'taking stock of your own forces' and choosing your own terrain and your own forms of struggle. Our forces are those of the people, and it is by beginning with them that you are able to perceive clearly the motives and schemes of the enemy. If you fail to make an accurate tally of your own forces and their resources, even with a good knowledge of the enemy you won't get very far. . . .

Louis

Dear Louis, *Naples, 28 March 1968*

Last Sunday, 24 March, I officially became a candidate of the Italian Communist Party for the general elections in the Naples–Caserta District. All of us were presented to the public at the same time on the stage of the Metropolitan Theatre of Naples.[1] There was quite a crowd jammed in there – the comrades said they hadn't seen anything like it for years. Their clothes were mostly old and shabby, but they listened intently and applauded the speeches generously. Only once in a while did a few of them in the front rows interrupt to hurl some flaming epithet, in dialect, at our opponents. One which particularly struck me was *'na monnezza* (*una mondezza* in Italian), which could be translated roughly as 's***'. I was quite bewildered by it all – what with the shouting, with trying to follow the speakers and get the feeling of what the issues were in this campaign, and above all because of the fear which enveloped me like a second skin. I wanted to say, 'Listen, I'm not up to this', or 'I don't have anything to do with all this', and then leave like a character out of Gombrowicz. But it wasn't like that at all. It's really banal: you know that. I've done so many things as a militant for the P C I, at one time or another. This has meant assuming the role of political organizer, propagandist, leader of women's groups, speaker, journalist, editor of political weeklies, and finally *Unità* correspondent in Paris. All this before now being plunged straight into the 'Deep South' of Italy.

I am what you French would call a 'parachuted' candidate. But this definition, when I considered it from my rented room at 55 Rue de

1. Italy has a multi-member district system of election, wherein the number of seats assigned each party is by proportional representation: if a party gets 50 per cent of the votes in a district, it receives half the seats of that district. The list, or slate, that the party presents, as in the above case, is equal to or greater than the total number of seats and hence obviously consists of many more candidates than will be elected. (Trans.)

Varenne, looking out over the Matignon Gardens, didn't bother me at all. On the contrary: this was the way for me to re-establish a relationship with the Party from the inside, in a Federation, at the base, in the most simple and direct manner. Hence I hardly worried about being 'parachuted in'. I think you will see what I mean if I go over the logic that led me to my current situation.

After five years of political journalism, Paris and its impotent Left and de Gaulle and Mitterand and Mollet and the endless, enervating wait for the emergence of the common platform of the Left which never came, all the secrets and hysterias of this petty world of politics where everyone was forever bent over in profound contemplation of his navel, was making me sick. All of the social, political, intellectual and cultural refinements I had absorbed had induced a sort of drunkenness.

I could list them all. In no particular order: the *gentilesse-politesse* of circumlocution and the ductile, Saussurified language whose subtleties I can by now follow, even though the cultivated Parisian swallows half of what he's saying. And the Odéon and the Comédie Française, and Malraux's 'monster' exhibitions at the Grand and Petit Palais, and receptions at the embassies and at the Quai d'Orsay, and the press conferences at the Ministry of Information given by the rotating Peyrefittes, and the meals – cultural events in the style of Brillat-Savarin, and the Autumn literary prizes, and the Café Flore with 'leftist' spokesmen lined up like mannequins from the Galeries Lafayette, and Lévi-Strauss and Lacan and Foucault, and the Godard of *La Chinoise*; and the *coiffeur* twice a week, and *L'Express* and *L'Observateur* and all this *impitoyable grandeur* that you have to blot out each night with a sleeping pill. But you have to stay alert to it continuously, sifting out what is *à la mode, export-import* and what it is all really worth. On the level of personal relations, as well, you have to go through the most tedious gymnastics imaginable to try to breach the privacy of the French, who – as the *nouveaux riches* of this commodity – have joined the English as its most brutal defenders. To enter a Frenchman's circle of friends is like trying to squeeze yourself on to a *carnet* which is already full up, because it still contains the names of the dead, the missing, and the transferred: nothing has been renewed for years. Finally, in spite of thousands of intricate links and protocols, you realize in the end that they are pathetically incapable of affection and incurably lonely.

I learned a lot of things – probably because I chose to view Paris as a virtue and not a vice – and nothing is more enriching, in spite of what is commonly believed, than to lead an ascetic life there. But I was beginning to feel like a person who had eaten partridge, and only partridge, in that fat consumer society.

As a Communist, since my goal in life is not to be a correspondent, it was when I realized that I had, in the course of five years, learned the trade of socialite that I also began to feel that I was running the risk of becoming *bureaucratized*, of falling into a routine. The decisive moment for me came between November and December 1967, between a conference of the General in the Banquet Hall of the Elysée Palace and a workers' assembly at Renault: the events were only two days apart.

The General, whom all (including Beuve-Mery of *Le Monde*) had agreed was exceptionally brilliant that day, making half the world dislocate its jaw laughing at his jokes about England and the Common Market, seemed to me like Methuselah in decrepit surroundings: the Elysian glories, the journalists laughing, and all the carefully prepared answers added to this. All that laughter made me think of jaw-bones rattling in death's heads, and in a way the most decrepit thing of all was the conceit, the arrogance of the French, fortunate enough to have such an intellectually refined, humorous man at the head of the Republic. It was all like one of those huge frescoes celebrating the splendours of the Trianon under Louis XVI. I wondered if maybe it wasn't time to oppose *Bolshevism* to '*Gaulle-shevism*'.

Two days later, at the Renault plant at Boulogne Billancourt, it was black as pitch by six in the evening, and pouring with rain. The workers, soaked to the skin in their overalls, filed into the union hall for a PCF meeting. They were brusque, bitter, laconic; their exhaustion, clearly evident, made them short-tempered and they wanted to leave. We were all crowded into this Turkish bath of damp clothes, crushed up against one another with the acrid smell of sweat hanging in the air. Underfoot were fags and packages and lunches brought by the workers, and these added to the total effect. You could sense truth there, jammed into these few square yards which seemed to create a microcosm that represented the world of the revolt against all mystifications.

It was this event, like others before it in the past, which suddenly made me see that I had a decision to make, and fast. Enough of this abstract work of research and comments and being isolated among other intellectuals. I had to return to reality, to my reality, in Italy. The proposal to be a Deputy, which I had originally rejected, came back to mind. You, too, had asked me, more than once, what there was for me to do in Paris in the future, and that too had set me to thinking. You and I, discussing this then – far from this Neapolitan theatre where I'm now spelling out this little history – were unable to see any alternative other than direct political involvement, to return to the masses. A purely political decision, reached by people uncontaminated by electoralism and, indeed, perfectly conscious of the crisis of parliamentary institutions in general.

At the time I thought – you often call me an *ingénue* – that while the Naples comrades might not have offered ritual sacrifices to celebrate my decision to return, at least they wouldn't be unhappy to see me. Well, perhaps the information that the Party leaders gave me was simply wrong; or perhaps they did not want to upset me; or maybe the decisive fact was that the leadership had decided to keep that particular Deputy's seat for a woman, since it had been held by another woman comrade from Naples for twenty years, and the woman happened to be me; or perhaps, as some told me, they really wanted to utilize whatever experience I had managed to acquire, covering the Common Market for five years, in the Foreign Affairs Commission of the Chamber of Deputies; or maybe it was just the simple, but decisive in its own way, fact that the new *Unità* correspondent, who had been waiting for two years to replace me, was there in Paris, suitcase in hand.

Put all these 'perhapses' and questions together and you have the reasons for my departure from Paris at dawn one morning in January. The city smelled of freshly-baked bread, a particularly feminine odour, mixed with that of café-au-lait: I left alone, because I couldn't hide my emotion and I didn't want to turn around at the last minute and end up like Lot's wife. I had convinced myself that they would be waiting eagerly for me in Rome. This was not quite correct; rather, there was courteous embarrassment. Instead of heading South, I had barely arrived at Fiumicino Airport than I found myself in the air again, press credentials from *l'Unità* still intact, on a flight to northern Europe to research some articles on European social democracy. Instead of Naples and the sea, I was in Stockholm, Oslo, Helsinki and Copenhagen that January of 1968, with the temperature hovering around zero the whole time.

It is hot here in the theatre, and my memories of the Nordic cold make the warmth back here in the last row of candidates on stage seem still more palpable. When I returned from that trip near the North Pole, my comrades told me that the Federal Committee of Naples, given the green light to decide democratically, had accepted my candidacy. They did this, of course, without my having set foot in Naples, but at least this way no one could say that I had hung around to influence the decision. I got the news of my acceptance from comrade P.V., who came to Rome to explain precisely and with a wealth of detail how matters stood. I was naïve enough to ask if there had been any opposition, and he said that it consisted only of a few malcontents, someone who would have liked the post himself, someone else who had lost his seat after twenty years in Parliament, etc., but nothing more than that. It was this news which made me write you that letter of 8 March, when I said there had been approval. But now I really don't know how things stand, because in Naples you find things out by circumlocution or circumvolution, always by word of mouth through fifteen different people before you finally come to someone who feels close enough to you to let you in on things. I tried to get hold of the regional secretary, who is also a member of the CC, but he didn't have the time, he said, to see me right then.

So I really don't know what is in store for me, not that it matters all that much. The Federation secretary – I've known him since his youth, when he was still a worker, and was glad to find out that he was now secretary – is a comrade who did a five-year course of political studies at Moscow. He asked me if, after the elections, I would be politically active in Naples; the question really shocked me because of course I am only here as the result of a *political choice*.

I am also becoming aware, as I study my surroundings, that I do not understand too much about the local 'deputy-élite', around which so many arguments, ambitions and disputes seem to centre. In Paris a deputy is like, say, an important journalist for *Le Monde* or *L'Humanité*. With inimitable delicacy I learned in France, I tried to make the comrade secretary of the Federation understand that he wasn't getting a dead weight. All this happened early in March when I first went to tell him that, if my candidacy was not well received in the Party, I would be happy to 'forget the whole matter', 'simply decamp', etc. But he said *no, no, no*: everything was going just fine, and the really important thing was to get the OK of the big sections – which

I got. As a result, they asked for my birth certificate for the electoral documents, plus my signature, and I was, from that moment, officially 'Candidate Macciocchi'. Not that I really know yet what 'candidate' means, against what or whom I'll have to measure myself, but for me this is a 'political choice' which I am going to follow through to the end: I am not going to be a candidate in the sense of being an electoral instrument, but am going to try to reverse the usual relationship and use my candidacy as a means of putting myself in contact with the people. I made this decision in Paris, and you remember our conversation: you said that an electoral campaign could be a first means of discovering what's happening among 'the people', and a way of beginning to answer the absolutely most important question for any attempt to engage in political activity: Who are the people, today, in Italy?

I think I have a good chance of discovering the 'dominant mentality' of the South, and of using this brief period of the elections to try to understand what 'the people' means today in Italy: of what classes it is composed, beyond the proletariat and poor peasantry; how far its revolutionary impact extends and to what degree we will be able to interpret it, or suppress it, and so on.

I have to remind myself continuously that I have not always worked with such *concrete* ideas. For many years I moved in a totally acritical way, armed only with an enthusiastic spirit. My political life, after I was a partisan in Rome, began right here in Naples in '44, which is why I now return here. I really have done everything since then.

In '46, to kill their lice, I helped wash Neapolitan kids' hair with kerosene before they were sent to the homes of Emilian and Tuscan sharecroppers. In '47, during the Peasants' Congress of the Mezzogiorno at Pozzuoli, I took part in the distribution of chickens which the peasants had brought as gifts for the people of Naples: we drove around with truckloads of chickens (already dead or dying from the trip), which we carried as gifts of solidarity to the hospitals, the orphanages and the jails. Of the many 'lives' I was tallying up on the stage of the Metropolitan, these in particular came rushing back, overwhelming me.

Now, back after twenty years, it is like growing two decades older all at once, suffering a sudden senility in twenty-four hours. In the midst of reflecting on all my transformations, on my chameleon-like adaptability, I am undergoing a minor sort of identity crisis, for I honestly don't know which role best characterizes me. What am I, exactly; a journalist, good at her trade, who can write indiscriminately from Paris, Stockholm, Moscow, or Algiers, who carries her house along with her like a snail, impervious of changes in latitude or climate – or a woman politicized to the very extremities of her nerve-endings, who can't live away from the political struggle; or maybe an intellectual torn from her studies and launched into the whirlwind of action by certain historical events, which began with the armed resistance against Fascism?

When I brush aside the smokescreens and rationalizations, I arrive, even from this candidates' platform, at only one conclusion: I am, like millions of others, a militant in a revolutionary movement. It is just that the sum total of my accomplishments, like those of my entire generation, is pathetically little. We have made neither 'The Revolution' nor 'Socialism', and we run the risk of getting sucked down in the quicksand of a smooth, cloying system, that of the dominant bourgeoisie and its ideology, which threaten us from every side. Back in Naples, I am reminded that the PCI, for capitalism, is part of the national panorama, taken for granted like the Bay or Vesuvius, to be marked with three stars in the ruling class's Michelin Guide: 'visit recommended'. But are things really like this? The bourgeoisie often miscalculates. When the *capolista*[2] of this electoral district began his speech with references to Vietnam, the audience seemed a lot younger all at once. Everyone jumped up with shouts of 'Death to Imperialism!', 'Socialism will win!', and one sensed a robust force rippling under the roof of the theatre, like a live muscle under skin. In your letter of 3 February, you wrote that the masses are 'terribly ahead' of us, you wrote of the infinite resources there are, and that things are going to happen quickly. . . .

Meanwhile, I am getting some crude impressions of the objective reality here, even if I don't yet have sociological data. If Naples had Argus's hundred eyes, her poverty would make her cry out of every one of them. The city is more decadent and diseased than it was twenty years ago. Capitalism, you see, has no interest in 'saving' her. It is like the story of the water in the towns of the South we were talking about one night at your apartment: men will get the water only

2. The *capolista* is the man who is the head of the list, and assured of election. At Naples this person is Giorgio Amendola, one of the most powerful leaders of the PCI and the acknowledged chief of the right wing. (Trans.)

when capitalism first decides that it needs the water to create some industry it wants or needs. Until then, entire regions will have to remain dry. In the same way, in Naples, our famous *voragini* may cave the streets in at any time, as happened on Thursday 21 March at Fuorigrotta: the forty-second slide in the centre of the city, a small, domestic, commonplace earthquake – and capitalism doesn't lift a finger, because the needs of its growth mechanism make it irrelevant if Naples collapses. Since the city is not really productive, it could just as well be petrified like Pompeii. The capitalist equilibrium here in Italy, in fact, is based on an organic interrelationship between growth and backwardness: poverty here is functional to well-being elsewhere. Per-capita income in the South is a third of that of the most advanced parts of the North. And the active population is only thirty per cent of the resident population!

From the theatre stage, bedecked with the tricolour and a bit of red, I looked out over this woebegotten crowd, with lined, worn and hungry faces. They waved dusty placards which seemed twenty years old, recalling another era. They had just one word on them, 'Work'. Work: the primordial aspiration. Old and young alike at Naples agree on this, since the city has the highest unemployed or non-employed population in Italy. I got my first statistical-sociological data (1967) on Naples from the Chamber of Commerce the day before yesterday. It is interesting to note in passing that these data, which are regularly kept up to date, can be found neither at Federation headquarters nor at the Chamber of Labour.

The data amazed me: I was afraid I didn't understand something. Naples has a population of 1,265,358; its province has 1,402,454 more. Out of this total of 2,667,812, the workforce is only *808,860*, of whom 770,668 are employed and, officially, 38,172 unemployed. The population not considered to be in the workforce, then, is 1,782,000. Hence the workforce is only 30.9 per cent of the population, which is lower than the South's mean (33.3 per cent) and is in fact the lowest figure in all of Italy (national average: 37.8 per cent). Between 1961 and 1967 the whole country's workforce fell 5 per cent, but Naples went down 9 per cent, nine more degrees of degradation. The inactive population is more than twice the size of the active population.

That's not all, either, for every index shows incredible drops from the beginning of '67 to the beginning of '68: there are 17 per cent more unemployed, 2.2 per cent less jobs, 27 per cent more minors in search of their first employment; 2.3 per cent fewer of the population got married, live births are down 4.4 per cent, deaths at birth are up 2.9 per cent. The entire demographic balance is, compared to 1967, 8.9 per cent lower.

Deaths: deaths due to cancer are down slightly, while there is a rise in deaths due to *mental diseases and diseases of the nervous system*, and also *infective and parasitical diseases*. People go crazy, in other words, or else they die from contagious illnesses which are closely related to the filth and lack of hygiene in the city. There are 400 official cases of viral hepatitis registered at the Cotugno Hospital, where they treat contagious illnesses, but at least ten times that many either take care of themselves or else get no care at all, and these victims all infect other people. The functionary at the Chamber of Commerce was thrilled with my *'sociological' interest*, because, he told me, in Naples the parties, unions and authorities are oblivious to statistics, and finally someone had arrived who broke his isolation as a researcher. Afterwards, he asked me if I were from Turin.

What is Naples? These figures are disturbingly similar to the American government's report on the social causes of the revolt of the Blacks in America: data of this type are blood relatives. But who is it that has spoken of the 'solution of the Southern Problem', of 'indus-trialization changing the face of the Mezzogiorno', and so on and so forth? I at once think back to all the incredible distortions arrived at as a result of economism, technocratism, planning, the 'theories of consumer society' and their neo-positivist implications. But in all this chaos, I can't for the life of me understand what the Party's orators mean when they refer to 'new majorities', 'structural reforms', 'positive solutions to the crisis', etc. Since arriving here I have been living in a state of shock, of trauma, pursued everywhere by the fetid odour of Naples' poverty. It's like Algiers or Cairo must be, I tell myself. But no one really seems to be aware of it. Our 'discourse' is a constructive one, it deals with future possibilities. But frankly, I don't see that we have such great alternatives to offer. And when I said this some comrades responded that this electoral campaign was to be part of a 'process of development', a 'stage of growth in the evolution of an organic strategy'. The answers of the Cumaean Sybil made more sense.

What can the common folk understand? Electoral predictions are uniformly gloomy here in the Party. We've become so conditioned to *underestimate* that even the pessimistic calculations that I've seen on the results of this election seem to me to err on the side of 'underestimation'. You were right to call it a Nessus's shirt.

Your question follows me, from far away: what is the People, *today, in a given country*, because the composition can change in different conditions and moments. Hence what, today, is *this* Neapolitan people, its sub-proletariat and its urban petty bourgeoisie; what part of it can join forces with the proletariat and poor peasants? I look beyond the dark, close-packed heads in the theatre and once again I feel a humiliating sense of ignorance and terror. 'The masses are, in terms of their capabilities, terribly ahead of us,' you wrote. How, once convinced of this, do you go about speaking to the masses, I keep wondering; how do you change a vague rhetoric into a vigorous revolutionary language people can understand?

I think we have enormous 'linguistic' problems, problems of 'rigour in our vocabulary'. The terms 'process', 'perspective', 'prospect', 'alternative', 'structural reforms', 'the reform strategy', and 'new majority', to name just a few, are all like rubber bands, and some other time I'll tell you about how they can be stretched in any direction, as much as one likes, until they signify almost anything. Let's just focus for the moment on one such word, *discorso*, or 'discussion, discourse, etc.', which you hear in an Italian Communist's every other sentence. The word can mean, beyond the strict sense of its derivation from *giving a speech*, the following: *report, examination, intervention, process of growth*, and so on. Your *discourse* can be unitary or divisive, collaborative or oppositional, hence it can mean something or its opposite. This kind of semantic garble, which expresses no precise concepts, ends up clouding our formulations beyond all communication – like when priests speak Latin – and obscures our revolutionary future.

The problem, hence, of *verbal rigour*. At the Faculty of Architecture at Rome, occupied by students, I found, on the blackboard of the Main Hall, the first revolutionary message aimed directly at language. I was really moved by it, since I thought I was alone when, in Paris, I first spoke to you about these semantic problems. I copied down the whole phrase, which goes like this: 'All speakers will refrain from pronouncing the following words: at the level of – instrumentalization – demystification – document – sensitize – DISCOURSE – structural moment – it is no accident that – to the extent that.'

During the February student rebellion, certain other words, at the same time, reappeared on the walls of schools in Florence, Bologna, Venice, and Rome: 'revolution – dictatorship of the proletariat – bourgeoisie – bourgeois – antagonistic class – the working class, the only objectively revolutionary class – proletarians – class struggle.' This, to me, is an aggressively revolutionary language, all the more so because certain words like 'revolution' or 'revolutionary' have not been seen for years in our political semantics. To read these words now really has a striking effect, as if you suddenly discover an integral piece of clothing you had long forgotten, or that the sun is shining and we're still carrying our umbrellas. Why is linguistic rigour necessary? I remember, word for word, your response in the *Unità* interview (this section never got published): 'In political, ideological and philosophical struggle, words are also either weapons and explosives or tranquillizers and poisons. The whole class struggle can, at times, be encapsulated in the battle for one word against another. Certain words fight like enemies. Others offer the opportunity for vacillation: they are the location of a decisive but as yet undecided battle.'

These are all absolutely basic political questions. Right now, I for one do not know where to start in order to eliminate 'the vacillation, and resolve the undecided battle'. So many problems are crowded into my head that I feel I have flocks of birds flapping around in there. I keep feeling the desire to flee that I have mentioned earlier, and I would like to be able, magically, to be back in Paris again. We could talk in your study, with those vivid geometric symbols on the blackboard that sometimes make me believe that theory can aspire to be as exact as certain sciences.

Here at Naples everyone is very much on his own, no one works in groups: at most you copy down things from books already written or speeches already given. There is no social and intellectual habit of meetings and discussions, everyone withdraws from collective life and into his own private little world. Since arriving I have only been invited out to dinner twice, both times by very old friends. I ask myself if it is I who have changed too much, including these last five years in France. I have too many 'rationalist' pretensions, and, today (with titanic conflicts being acted out in Italy and all over the world, between ruling and exploited classes, between imperialism and socialism) I feel – more than any historicist need to locate the phenomena I'm living in the present historical situation, so as to discover their objective theoretical content – an urgent need for rigour, for the maximum possible rationality and 'scientificity', in order to understand what to do politically; what the Party is; what the relationship is, today, between the Party and the masses. At the same time, these twenty years weigh on me and call for a revision, a political and historical examination of my total situation in which these 'humanist' and 'historicist' aspects are considered as well.

Isn't there a contradiction here? The aim is to create a link between philosophy-politics-science. How, then, do we get rid of this 'monkey' on our backs, which is the inability to fit our own tumultuous, exhilarating, and at times ambivalent past into a nice, concise formulation of the class struggle? Republic, unitary government, the collapse of antifascist unity, the frontal confrontation, a sputtering opposition, opposition inside the system, appeals for political unity, an alternative programme, structural reforms, an alternative model of development. As you say, 'You name it'. Then, in the international sphere, our successive 'stages' have been essentially the same as those of the foreign policy of the USSR: from Yalta to Khrushchev's 'coexistence', in a see-sawing continuity, or *renewal in continuity*, according to a typically Italian formula, which sometimes stresses acritical acceptance and at other times assumes a certain diplomatic distance.

The totally *new fact* on the political scene is that, when the young now declare themselves 'fed up with their fathers', they mean that they can no longer stand *this glorious historical baggage* that we make them carry, and which they rightly think subjugates them to the terms of *our* present policies and practices. They're sick of the ex-combatants that we seem to be, ready as we always are to march under the Triumphal Arch of our own sentiments: what pseudo-revolutionary narcissism! I'm as fed up with this as they are. And yet I am right in the middle of it all, I am a part of everything being attacked, and attacked for good reason. It is because of this set of circumstances that, from time to time, when you spoke more 'directly' to me than usual, *I stopped listening, I broke contact*, as you used to say. At the same time, however, I never let myself get sucked in bureaucratically, I always maintained a degree of rigour 'in ideas and in praxis'. But what purpose does all this serve, really? That's the political problem in a nutshell. We seem to be terribly out of date. All of us, or almost all of us. The revolt of the younger generation is a serious political symptom for us, too, not only for the system. But then I remember your last course for scientists at the Rue d'Ulm.[3] I remember the crowd of kids there who filled all the seats an hour before the lecture began, and I remember thinking then that you were one of the few, in Paris, who could talk to the students without having to fear being booed.

Digression on the student disturbances

I returned to Italy when the rebellion was just breaking out. The university youth, occupying the faculties, fighting with the police, holding out against the government for four months, had thrown the whole authoritarian, paternalistic, baronial system of teaching into a profound crisis. This represented a complete refusal of the university's dogmatic attempts to inculcate into the students the ideology of the bourgeois ruling class. But the students also linked the university struggle provocatively to the political struggle, with unbreakable, sacrosanct bonds. All of the figleaves which cover compromise, reformism and 'theoretical escapism' were torn away. It quickly became clear that there was a new political strategy of aggressive attack against capitalism in the making: for victory against imperialism in Vietnam, for the defeat of the Americans. It was not just a didactic, but a political – an exquisitely political – internationalist, anti-imperialist message which went out from this struggle. The students identify not only with Che Guevara and Castro, but also with Mao. Seeing this, one can only conclude that attempts to distort the Cultural Revolution in China or treat it as a grotesque aberration are the result of a sclerosis in European culture and political thought. It is evident that the Cultural Revolution has been contagious, and has taught young people in all countries imagination and revolutionary passion for new forms of struggle. Ideological class struggle, an integral part of the general class struggle, of politics, has become the theme of numerous new journals run by young people, which one finds completely sold out in the bookstores. At Paris, you were the one who pointed out to me the first copies of some, like *Lavoro politico, Quaderni rossi,* and *Quaderni piacentini.* The student generations in this 'New Course' are frantic in their need to analyse Marx, Lenin and Mao. This is really an unprecedented phenomenon for Italy, where Marxism, even when

3. Site of the École Normale Supérieure in Paris, where Althusser is Professor of Philosophy. (Trans.)

part of the philosophy curriculum of the preparatory schools, is handled with kid gloves by professors intimidated by God and by Croce. Moreover, even when the teachers call themselves Marxists, they are all too often 'vehicles of the dominant bourgeois ideology'.

So there is an enormous idealistic and ideological vacuum for which we Communists are also responsible: you can't replace Marxism with 'structural reforms'. And you can't replace Marx with the Resistance.

I don't see any real danger at present coming from the sociological composition of the movement (i.e. that the students are primarily petty-bourgeois in origin), mostly because that modicum of ideological rigour of which I spoke means that they recognize – and even write on walls – that it is the working class which is revolutionary; they will tell you that 'students are not an objectively revolutionary class', and so on. Much more typical of them is the slogan I saw written on the wall of the Faculty of Letters at Rome: 'Arm the workers and end this crap'. The real danger, at the present time, seems to me to lie in the 'Marcuseanization' of Marx, Lenin and Mao. In Italy, 30,000 copies of *One-Dimensional Man* have been sold, and only 4,000 of *For Marx*. It is this kind of thing that seems to be influencing the development of Marxist theoretical research and hence the development of a correct political struggle in Western Europe.

End of digression

I am changing course again, and we are back at the presentation of Communist candidates for the election of 19 May 1968. The end of the campaign meeting is like a skyrocket going off. You can sense something which must be *hope*, the desire for things to change, and hence a pressure which is objectively revolutionary. All the while, on the stage of the Metropolitan, I keep realizing that *I am different from the other candidates*. All these problems are boiling inside me and I sit in my candidate's chair as if on hot coals. The others, I can see, are different in this respect: they are relaxed, happy, and this, to them, seems to be a day when their real merit has been given a public airing. You might even say that they feel that today they have been consecrated.

Meanwhile, just one thing keeps pounding in my skull: Is it possible to use an electoral campaign to discover what is going on among the people?

If it is, let's move into the project we agreed on in Paris: I will tell you, a Communist philosopher, about my direct political experiences. But since I am anything but a philosopher, my phrasing may not seem very pertinent to your interests, not concise enough, knowledgeable enough, or honed to the proper sharpness. But what does a philosopher have to learn from a woman engaged in politics anyhow? I, however, have a pretty clear idea of how a philosopher-militant like you can help me put important political issues in their proper perspective.

Do you think there could be some 'interest' in a dialogue-correspondence between a philosopher who works at the most rigorous Marxist theoretical research, and a Communist who is in the midst of the reality of a struggle, a political contest, in a specific objective situation? You have taught me that Marxist philosophy nourishes itself on politics, that there is no revolutionary theory without class struggle. On what I have given you in this letter, can you tell me how to 'adjust my sights'? What are the 'theses' on which I ought to base my efforts? Among all the things I have been listing here in such disorganized fashion, which seem to you to be of primary interest, which secondary? On what points would you like me to work most systematically?

But the first question you must respond to is this: How can we 'work together' in these letters – given that philosophy is basically politics, according to Marx, Lenin, and Gramsci – and define 'very concrete' questions about the *class struggle* as it presents itself, *today*, *in Italy* and specifically in the South?

Maria Antonietta

Dear M.A.,   *Paris, 2 April 1968*

(1) It is agreed, then, that I will receive your letters on a day-to-day basis. But I really wish you would write them without any consideration of eventual publication. Labriola and Sorel, in their correspondence, became aware at a certain moment that they were writing letters which *one day would appear in print*. The result is not what one could call very satisfactory. We must write with the idea that we are writing for *one another*, not for publication. The idea of publishing could lead us into blind alleys.

(2) The most important things you can write to me are the precise, positive, material facts you learn: e.g., write about the women who earn sixty lire an hour. 'Impressions' are important, but above all it is the *facts* which count. It is essential to make facts known, recognize them, give them names (providing figures), etc. And this is also of direct theoretical importance. After all, you don't 'see' facts unless you have a 'point of view' or, as Lenin put it, a class-based viewpoint, which of course is always rich with theoretical content. Naturally this does not exclude your discussing this or that larger issue, or expressing whatever personal views you may have on given problems. But we need facts, data. See Marx: all his concrete chapters on the working day, etc.; and Lenin: the development of capitalism in Russia. These works are loaded with *facts*.

(3) I am too tired tonight to send detailed comments on your first letter. But I would like to make a few comments about *you*, the candidate. *As far as you are concerned, you must see things in a long-term perspective.* You have to be aware of just where you are in your work; what means are available to you; what the objective possibilities are, in the light of those means and of the situation of the workers' movement today in Italy.

You absolutely must find a *means* by which you can best utilize your electoral campaign – if possible, an original and effective one. Speeches are not very useful. You cannot learn anything from the people if you are talking to them. You have to learn things from them by listening directly. You should hold small meetings (above all *in the factories*), utilizing the organization of the Party. And make people, both inside and outside the Party, talk. Listen, and only speak afterwards. You have to come up with *an original electoral campaign.* I do not know what it will be like, I cannot invent it for you, but you will have to go deep into your own intelligence and imagination and also call on the workers' imagination to help you figure this out. For example: go and speak with the workers in cafeterias, or during their rest periods, etc. Away from public meetings. You should also make the older comrades speak, for they are the 'pupils of our eyes', those who have not become favoured leaders and who have preserved intact their acute sense of class identification. This you should do in the *cells* and *sections* of the base: you can also go there to discuss generally with the rank-and-file members, and ask how *they* would conduct a good electoral campaign.

So ask their opinion. This is all the more important in that you will be considered, at the beginning, as an 'imported' candidate, one parachuted into Naples at the insistence of central party headquarters (letter of 28 March), without the base having been consulted. If you move in the way I have said (which is not simply a pretext), you will manage to learn a great many things. Then: you should go to the popular quarters of the city, to interrogate and listen to the *women* in their places where they live and work, in the markets and so on, wherever they are normally found. Women always know a great many facts about the material conditions of life, and also about children, who represent the future. They are much better situated than men to know this sort of thing, and they generally speak better than men. *You are a woman and you have to utilize this fact 100 per cent in order to establish a new relationship with women.* You are under no obligation to go out and beat people over the head with party propaganda; go instead to listen and learn. Above all, a good electoral campaign means being able to listen, to know what the people have on their minds. The 'mass line' means starting from what the masses already have in their heads. If you are not a candidate like the others, and if in addition to that, you are a woman candidate, you must find new ways to upset and re-define the traditional style of electoral campaigns, so that you can come to know and to establish relationships which do not end when the campaign ends.

All that I am saying about these concrete 'means' of overturning the old method of election campaigns is, perhaps, utopian and impossible. If this turns out to be true, you will have to find *something else*, but you *absolutely* must find something.

Watchwords:

(1) Beware of electoral cretinism and especially beware of the cretinism of an electoral campaign.

(2) What concerns you goes *far beyond* the campaign; it involves means *and ends* of a quite different order.

(3) Find the *means* which are appropriate for this *longer perspective*, which serve these *ends*, and which include the electoral campaign as a simple *opportunity*, as a *provisional* moment.

(4) Politics is a protracted war. Do not be in a hurry. Try to see things far in advance, and know how to wait, today. Don't live in terms of subjective urgency. Know, too, how to put your defeats to use.

(5) The electoral campaign is a simple *episode*, a minute episode. Do your best to learn the lessons it holds, but do not entertain grand illusions.

Louis

Dear Louis, *Naples, 7 April 1968*

I have tried to benefit from your suggestions, and I will tell you how. But first of all I have to spell out the personal-political situation in which I find myself, in connection with two precise questions (a) and (b). (a) What is my particular situation as a woman candidate, sent by the 'Centre' to Naples, i.e. 'parachuted in' in the opinion of part of the rank-and-file and especially of the apparatus; (b) within this frame-work – going by what I have clearly been told by the comrades I have questioned in the sections and by what I have been able to learn – what is the role that they think 'the deputy' ought to play? I will start with this second question.

Many comrades see the Deputy as being, as it were, directly man-dated by the needy and the lumpenproletariat to go to Rome and act for them in such business as they have with the Government: pensions, welfare, social security, housing, etc. Many communal and provincial councillors and deputies end up as a kind of parliamentary-adminis-trative bureaucracy of the party, whose task is to get as much as possible, on the practical level, out of the existing social order. This kind of activity is not seen as any sort of revolutionary practice; instead, the representatives are simply expected to be good, efficient functionaries, whose contact with the state apparatus allows them to obtain what is possible, within the confines of the system. Just as illiterates still use public scribes in Neapolitan market places, so too does the Deputy receive his vote, which is a mandate to open a rep-resentative's 'office' in Rome, from which he can deal with the prob-lems of the alleyways of Montecalvario, Stella or Forcella.

These quarters are all overwhelmingly inhabited by the sub-proletariat. They live by expedients or, when they work, as I saw first-hand, they have no idea whatever of the relationship between work and exploitation; indeed, they are convinced that 'work' is a form of grace bestowed by some unseen benefactor. Their major concerns are pensions, sickness benefits, the search for a job, and many similar mundane matters, including marital disputes. One student of sociological issues explained to me that 'the Neapolitan politician is applauded to the extent that he succeeds in obtaining jobs and housing'. *Clientelism*, or the cultivation of personal followings, has its roots in these social conditions, as do apathy and an absolute indifference to the role and political affiliation of the 'representative', who can be either of the Right or the Left. Nor do abilities seem very important. A noted Socialist Deputy, running again this year, is spoken of ironically as 'the man who in five years has never spoken a wrong word in Parliament . . . *because he has never spoken*'. But it is clearly understood that this is of little importance to the electorate. He could even be the lawyer for what Maupassant called a *Maison Tellier*,[1] but to confront him publicly for such 'activities' would not only not hurt him, it would gain him support, for people would then know that he had *entrée* of an exceptional nature into all sorts of political parlours and antechambers which were closed to others.

'Recommendations' are everything here. Without them is like being 'in Heaven without saints'. And the notable – who of course wants to maintain the myth of his own efficient omnipotence – keeps everyone believing that 'recommendations' are needed for everything . . . even to pay your gas bill. The common people are kept in a continual state of subservience with regard to the public administration, and are compelled to reinforce the chains of their subordination to notables. The notable, for the common man, becomes the perennial, and only, link with the offices of the administrative bureaucracy.

So, for five-year stretches, the elected representative is told to concern himself with pensions, medical certificates, housing allocations, subsidies of all types, aid to invalids, teachers' transfers, the assignment of a new marshal of the *Carabinieri* to a village, or the replacement of a communal secretary. A comrade who is a Deputy told me, just to scare me, that he, with the aid of one assistant, handles 300 such 'dossiers' every month. Others have converted their homes into bureaucratic substations, with their wives learning to type out form letters to various Ministries. The comrade I spoke with is like the Paris telephone directory: he has memorized the telephone numbers and addresses of over a hundred functionaries in the Ministries in Rome,

1. i.e. a brothel. (Trans.)

from ministers themselves to undersecretaries, and all the way down through the ranks.

Deputies, above all, keep extremely busy asking official questions. They question the Ministry of Postal Services if the post office of the Vomero is backlogged with packages, or the Labour Ministry if the Tigullio Hotel in Ischia has no water. Every question, by law, is printed in the official Parliamentary Bulletin, and the Deputy then sends reprints of the relevant pages to his constituents; this of course shows unequivocally how such-and-such a problem has become the Written Word, black on white, in the Annals of the Republic. I wonder, frankly, if the forms themselves really have much effect, if they really resolve any problems. Sometimes you hear that they do, other times that no, they do not. It is clear, though, that the really important thing is the arrival in someone's house of a letter with *Chamber of Deputies* engraved on the envelope:

'One Deputy managed to get the Minister himself to write – that was about a job.'

'But did the person get the job or not?'

'No, but the family says that they will *always* vote for him; even if he isn't "recommended" by the Party in that town, he'll always have 2,000 preference votes[2] on account of those letters he sends. . . .'

On my way to give a speech a Deputy, on the list with me, said that if I wanted some good advice, it would be to tell everyone right from the start that I would not get involved with following up 'dossiers'. I thanked him, saying that if it was really so complicated, I wouldn't do it. But I think I fell into a trap. '. . . is it true that you won't handle any dossiers?' I am asked continuously now. Word has spread.

State, Government, and Parliament are, for the sub-proletariat and the disinherited citizen and labourer, fundamental enemies of the people, completely cut off from their daily existence. So far so good, but the struggle that 'the Deputy' must wage against the power structure is not a political struggle; rather, it is a sort of drawn out hand-to-hand combat, or arm-wrestling, with continual flashes of the most imaginative kind, but endless. Take the unfortunately typical case, in 1968, of the lengths you still have to go to in order to get a veteran's pension for an old man from Vico Zuroli. He is eighty-one years old and the pension is for the First World War! And, still, before he would see a cent of the benefits, you would probably need San Gennaro

2. See note on p. 36. (Trans.)

himself to come down and swear that the man was to this day carrying shrapnel from a wound suffered at Caporetto. I met this man, so I know that the story is true: he has white skin and white hair, like a wax figure, and greeted me from his *basso* in Vico Zuroli (territory of the Party's Borgo section). In long, curved, trembling hands he waved a sheaf of papers at me: certificates, receipts, official request forms, and so on, that he has been working on for twenty years so the Deputy will be able to get him his pension 'in the City of Rome'. Will I really succeed? He looked at me for a long time and I could see his distrust; it was all the worse because I did not want to be dishonest and raise his hopes. Besides, I was half-asphyxiated by the smell of lye – the same whitish liquid they use in barrack toilets – which he had used to wash the place out in the hope of keeping rats and lice away.

The Deputy has, in the popular neighbourhoods and important centres, a purely *personal* 'clientele'. This relationship passes completely over the head of the Deputy's party, for the Deputy–client relationship is not a political one, but more the kind of work relationship of a businessman. The Deputy bases his clientelism on a dominant social group or category: now artisans, now shirt-makers, now communal employees, now construction workers, and so on. The Monarchists – and at Naples there still is a very powerful Monarchist Party led by a shipping magnate named Lauro (who was mayor of the city for six years, spreading corruption like radioactive fallout over all the parties from Left to Right) – have their basic clientele among the pimps, blackmarket cigarette peddlers, prostitutes, etc. And hence any of these characters who happens to fall into the hands of the police knows that he is going to be set free as soon as the Monarchist Deputy intervenes. Except in homicide cases.

This conception of the Deputy, rooted in the very bowels of the popular quarters, is reflected in certain party sections as well, and is the result of an erroneous viewpoint which often is deeply entrenched simply because no one has ever fought it openly: the Deputy as a Dalai Lama, someone born with a sign of distinction on his flesh, whom the Party discovers and then lets rise to the highest possible post and, from what is commonly believed, to economic security as well. Certain sections from the 'belly' of Naples were, in 1952–6, perhaps above all as a result of direct competition with the Monarchists for the vote of the common folk of these areas, swept up in the sub-proletarian tide. This is another way of saying that a number of leaders came to identify more with the craftier elements in the sub-proletariat (called *'cardilli'* – a dialect word for 'goldfinches' – at that time by the Federation, because they could 'sing politics' so well) than with the working class.

In fact what happened was that workers and youth in general were shunted aside, or else they quit of their own accord to form 'Chinese' groups or involve themselves exclusively with political work in the factories. Sub-proletarian leaders of some sections are still hostile and polemical towards the working class, which they consider privileged, with a secure salary. Thus their reaction to a strike is likely to be that it is just one more sly way used by the workers to stuff an already well-filled bag. The 5,000 trolleymen of the ATAN (the municipal tram-workers' association), whose strike is now in its fifth day – they receive a 120,000 lire[3] a month maximum, with 40 per cent suffering from nervous exhaustion – not only have not received any popular support, but are considered, even by comrades in the popular quarters, in the same league with crooks who have pulled off a successful bank raid.

Not all of the PCI's sections are like this. They tend in fact to fall into one of three categories: sections where sub-proletarian leaders are prevalent, sections where the petty-bourgeois intelligentsia assumes 'left' positions but is still very cut off from any real contact with the workers, and sections where the working class plays a leading role. I have been speaking exclusively of the first category or section, because I have been in the midst of them for seven days running – I haven't really seen any other kind of section so far. I have almost literally been swimming this week in a sea of the foulest misery and poverty, only reaching the shores of the normal world – where houses have windows, bathrooms and electricity – late at night.

Now that I have dealt with point (b), let me tell you about (a). My personal situation is a very difficult one. I am in trouble because I offer no 'guarantee' that I will fit that stereotype of a Deputy that I have been describing. And this is what is wanted, especially in those sections where the leadership, which has consolidated its power bureaucratically, wants to choose a Deputy on the basis of a high-level compromise-cum-agreement between the section and the Federation apparatus, and indeed regards this as the index of its own political influence with the Federation leadership.

3. At this time – 1968 – the exchange rate was 630 lire to the dollar, 1,750 to the pound. (Trans.)

This is why I have serious doubts about the whole question of how democratic my candidacy can be. I have learned, without being told in so many words, that my nomination was opposed in the Federal Committee – which many people see as a kind of springboard for people who want to hold public office. So there were challenges, based mainly on the fact that I was an *outsider*, a *foreigner*, who belongs neither to the Neapolitan apparatus nor to those within its immediate orbit who won't 'follow up "dossiers" in Rome'; who won't come to the 'belly' of the city, to talk not only about politics but also of the daily events in the streets; who does not understand the 'reality of Naples'. I do have the official support of the small central nucleus of the Federation leadership, but they are extremely careful not to compromise themselves too much for fear of offending the 'notables' or the sections during an electoral campaign. And as soon as you cross the line from real politics to clientelism, it becomes clear that I cannot really count on anyone.

But at the same time, I am getting some discreet help. Perhaps it is the Federation's desire to show that I do *not* refuse to try to understand 'the reality of Naples' which keeps them sending me, day after day, into the depths of the city, from which I surface only on Sundays when I join the rounds of speech-making in the main squares. My task, above all, is to gain acceptance, alone and as a result of my own efforts. I can see that, politically, no one has ever bothered to explain to anyone just why I ought to be a candidate, and so I must do it myself. An old Senator in the Party, when told by me that I was using my time in the popular neighbourhoods to discuss the political function of a Deputy from Naples, said, fraternally, 'Daughter, if you want those preference votes, you had better be careful not to do that any more!' But I continue on my own path, somewhat stubbornly, in my attempt to transform 'electoral cretinism' into a real political campaign, using this form of contact with the Party to understand and explain things from the following perspective: (a) to understand what the Party is, today, in Naples; (b) to understand who the people are; (c) to explain to the comrades what a revolutionary Leninist party is, with politically revolutionary objectives in Italian society, and how Parliament relates to this perspective.

But it is not easy. Confronted with my candidacy, a lot of comrades have reacted like someone who comes to a banquet and finds that the first course has evaporated just as he was sitting down to eat. They are not in the least interested in having a woman on the list; indeed, the retirement of the woman I am replacing seemed, to many, after twenty years, a golden opportunity for the *stronger sex* to take up its dominant rights again. In fact, in the entire South there are only two female deputies, the one already mentioned in Naples and the other in Apulia, the daughter of the Party's most famous union leader, Giuseppe Di Vittorio, who was put on the lists after her father died. As far as being a 'parachuted' candidate is concerned, the more I become aware of the general lack of honesty between the base of the Party and the leadership, the less vulnerable I realize I am. I hardly think about it any more, and when I do my thoughts move in a *political* direction: my entire history of political activity in the Party is connected with Naples and the South, and I have made a *political choice* by assuming this candidacy, which for me is one more militant's task. Besides, Parliament is only one sector of activity; what is really important is the link with Naples, and I have that, win or lose.

It isn't that I am not respected: it is just that I am not trusted, for I am someone who can never be *one of them.* Or else they must think that I am going to 'teach' them things which have no relation to this world, or else things which, because they are unknown, demand new confrontations, new efforts, and hence generate inferiority complexes. To every proposal or suggestion I make, the response I hear most often is, 'We know, we know. We've tried that already, we've done that already. . . .' When I speak up in Federation meetings, every once in a while I see someone who, with heavy irony, pokes another in the ribs and says, 'Hurry up and take notes, can't you see that *she* is speaking . . . .' I pretend not to notice. At times they seem to be caught up endlessly at old games. My friend Paolo Ricci explains that the diffidence towards someone who comes to Naples from the outside world is the product of a particular complex: the fear of being ignorant of what is *à la mode* somewhere else, the things that generate discussions and inflame passions, which are followed and known *elsewhere*, in other countries or, as they still say here, 'in the City of Rome'. In sum, it is the fear of being cut off from the reality of a world which is fundamentally different, not Neapolitan: the fear of being *out of it.* After Naples was dethroned as capital of a realm which had commercial, diplomatic, and cultural relations with half the world, *neapolitanism* became the motor force which reinvented – through fantasy or isolation – a Naples which was the last word in science, in life style, in taste, in culture, in politics. It is a defence mechanism, an inferiority complex.

I can honestly say that this whole complex simply does not concern me, and this is my strength. But I am also extremely sensitive to every-thing that comes, not from the *apparatus*, but *from the ranks* of the Party. I get enormously depressed at times – especially since I am aware of having been 'cast adrift' among the contending elements of a party divided by electoralistic polemics. At the same time, I try to stretch my intellectual capabilities to the limit in an effort to under-stand the political meaning of what is happening to me. I am fully aware that I am living out an exceptional moment of my political life, in contact with the people, and that I and the comrades in the sections communicate openly and frankly, without any smokescreens, hypocrisy, or false obstacles. I know that I am able to make people relax, that I am not condescending, and that they know that I am only trying to understand what they are thinking.

Once you get over the bureaucratic hurdles which the old leaders at times create, then contact with the real people, with the Party at its *base*, becomes an easy and rewarding thing. It is true that at times I notice a distinct lack of what might be called 'proletarian fraternity' with respect to me, and sometimes I get very disturbed by this; but it is becoming increasingly clear to me that when certain sectors of the party end up giving the 'elected representative' (or the trade-union leader) the task of dealing with (rather than overturning) the social order, then the behaviour and attitudes of the apparatus deteriorate as well. This is not a moral problem, it is a political problem. Marxism is not a 'humanism'. And I am continually telling myself: less moralism and more politics. More truth, and less ambiguity. And yet, it is pre-cisely this Leninist truth, revolutionary in itself, which can appear as the truly unsettling fact to someone who without ulterior motives finds it. For then he must force himself to question the practices he sees around him, and he must force himself to act. The whole process of writing these notes out and furnishing this material forces me to be as honest as I can in drawing up a portrait which is the most political portrait possible – not a moral portrait – of the Party.

Let's take a day like Thursday, 4 April. I return to Naples from Rome feeling terrible, with a temperature and the 'flu. Since all public transport is out on strike, I call the Federation's propaganda office for a car to come and pick me up at the station and take me to Vico

Cavaioli, an obscure street in the Stella quarter. They tell me they don't have any cars, but after I argue with them for a while they finally agree to send someone. After an hour's wait in a bar, I finally see a thickset old man with white hair, who I do not recognize, come up to me with an angry air and, without any greeting, he says, 'It's you, Macciocchi.' Leading me to a Fiat 500, he continues, 'Come on; you knew me once. It looks like we have both grown old.' As we ride along, he fires questions at me: why don't I have a car; why don't I know Vico Cavaioli and its area; why do I arrive now and not five months earlier? The whole theme of 'we have both grown old' keeps recurring in the discussion and I realize that, among themselves, they must tell each other that they are being saddled with a decrepit old woman for a Deputy, who has, to make it worse, come from France to take the place of *one of their own*. He asks me if I know that *they don't want me on the list*; not him, but people in the Federal Committee because the Party sends people from the centre to get elected in Naples, and then they go to Rome and are never seen around Naples any more: Amendola, Napolitano, Chiaromonte and now me. He says they are all *infuriated*.

'But why with *me*?'

'Because it's easier,' he says frankly, 'with you than with the others,' since I completely lack any *political power*. 'If the Party wanted to make a Deputy out of you,' he adds, 'why couldn't they put you in Tuscany or Emilia?' What it amounts to, then, is that once again they feel tricked by the North. I explain my work to him, and that I really do not care so much if I am elected or not. I speak of my feeling of being involved in a general political battle, and add that if they have sent me to Naples it is because this is where I worked as a political organizer for five years. When he says that 'no one in the Party here knows me', he is being unjust and dishonest, since my name has appeared on articles, for fifteen years, throughout the Party press. He doesn't try to deny it – he even adds that he has always been a reader of *my* articles.

But things always come back to the usual objections: will I go into the popular quarters, will I handle 'dossiers'? He says that these doubts, more than being his own, are those of the Federation, of the apparatus, and that 'they have spoken to Party headquarters about it'. I remind him that at Naples I succeeded in organizing the departure of 10,000 children from the popular quarters for Tuscany and Emilia, along with the workers of the Ilva and the OMF factories, and that we were the ones who created the 'Committee to Save the Children of Naples', which was the most successful mass undertaking of the entire postwar period. He concludes, generous Neapolitan that he is, by promising that he and his family will vote for me; it isn't true, he'll change his mind many times, but this at least is a cordial salutation, compared to the way he first greeted me. He drives the 500 right into the narrow alleyway, to the mouth of Vico Cavaiola itself, and then takes off again like a rocket, with no interest in hearing my speech, saying that he has 'other things to do'.

In Vico Cavaioli, I find the Party's sound truck, which is busy playing *Bandiera Rossa* and showing a documentary on NATO while waiting for me to arrive. I look around: this place is the 'Court of Miracles', a Brechtian scenario which appears to have been designed by some ingenious artist for 'The Threepenny Opera'. The steep alleyway is cut off at its highest point by a misshapen, decrepit building, and is flanked by houses which lean in towards the centre of Naples, all in different stages of collapse. It is a dark abyss, seemingly without beginning or end. We are in the highest part, and we have propped the screen against the wall of the house in the middle.

At the microphone, a comrade calls out, 'Would some kind citizen be good enough to give us some light?' A woman comes up and offers to connect the cord to her meter. We give her our propaganda leaflets, called 'Vote for the PCI' or 'You Too, Woman!', but no one is out on the street. The women all stay looking out from their windows. Some of them send down their *paniere*, the little basket tied to a rope which allows them to shop from roving salesmen without having to come downstairs, and we deposit our leaflets in them. Our public is primarily composed of about a hundred kids who are waiting to see what kind of show we can provide. They swarm up for the leaflets like avid, enthusiastic readers, but our comrades, who know them, chase them away with slaps and shoves, defending themselves as if from a swarm of mosquitoes. In order to get their hands on the propaganda, the shrewder ones shout out 'It's for my father, it's for my mother'. But no one believes them.

There are only two women in the crowd, one very old and the other middle-aged, with buttocks like round buoys. They are watching the film on NATO attentively, but the younger one, Filomena, confesses that she really doesn't understand. She has always voted for the

Monarchists, but this time she wants to vote Communist, she says. On the screen you see Marines marching and bombs raining down. Impressed, she draws me aside and asks, 'Ma'am, are they Germans?' I tell her they are Americans, and she is stunned: for her, the Americans are those blond, good-natured young men with alert, wide-open eyes she remembers as walking down these very streets, accompanied by young women of the area, who were very pleased to be in such a situation, loaded down with cigarettes and vitamins. So I tell her, 'The Americans are making war on Vietnam, dropping tons and tons of bombs', etc. 'Is there *really* a war?', she asks me, suddenly very alarmed. She calls out to the other, 'Nanní, the lady here says that there's a war. Where is it? Mamma mia, I didn't know there was a war.' They think the war is here, like in '42–'43. I explain, *not here* – calm down! – but in Vietnam. It is useless, completely useless. 'Vietnam' is a word without any sense to them. The tom-tom that spreads the news in the sub-proletarian forest about deaths, lottery victories, the collapse of houses, and marriages hasn't yet got around to the war in Vietnam. I feel like an explorer who has reached the farthest outposts of the political jungle. It makes me think about the absurdity and *total abstractness* of our electoral propaganda: the documentary on NATO projected in the alleyways and squares of Naples is about as comprehensible to the people who live there as are the hieroglyphics deciphered by Champollion. I ask myself what on earth I can possibly tell those women up there, hidden behind their window-sills.

I look up. Clothes lines extend as far as the eye can see, looking like festive banners, one attached to the other, in a permanent patron saint's holiday. At first you get the feeling that they have hung out their whole wardrobe, or else that maybe the custom here is to hang your clothes out on the line instead of keeping them in dressers or closets. But this 'mystery' is really much simpler than all that: the people possess few clothes and the women must wash continuously to keep a fresh change ready.

My stage fright is almost total since first realizing that they don't know anything about Vietnam. I would prefer to speak – it would certainly be easier – in a hall on the Rue d'Ulm, or at a conference of qualified politicians. Johnson has just announced – it was in the 1 April papers – that he will not be a candidate for the presidency again, an indirect admission of the US defeat in Vietnam. The whole political discussion now hinges on this. But in Vico Cavaioli, the navel in the belly of Naples, no one knows anything. I feel like a TV announcer, standing there with the microphone in my hand. Immensely ridiculous, as well, with all my precise and disinfected language. Then I have a flash of inspiration: I turn towards the fat woman, who is chewing on a piece of fennel which she has divided up with her daughter, and I tell the crowd precisely what she has been telling me: she is a washer-woman, she has five children, her husband, a carpenter, is out of work, and when she doesn't wash clothes, she sells roasted chestnuts at the entrance to the street. If all goes well, she makes 400 lire a day, and she is responsible for all the family's needs. With this 400 lire, she, her unemployed husband, and five children must live. The place they live in alone costs 5,000 lire a month. I tot up these figures, for her and for the others, and from this I go on to the 'Centre-Left' government, and then to a brief analysis of capitalist forces. In this way they start to understand.

I speak in a sea of screaming kids between five and ten years of age, who are playing, climbing all around me and are still determined to get hold of our propaganda leaflets. The comrades defend me, kicking the kids away, and the two women also pitch in, pulling them away by the ears. Slaps ring out during my talk like the clapping of an invisible audience. At the end, the children ask for my autograph, as they have seen done on TV. The mothers have by now disappeared. My interest in them was too direct, and I was too foreign, not to have embarrassed them.

The Stella-San Carlo Arena quarter, of which Vico Cavaioli is part, has 149,797 inhabitants on 966.4 hectares[4] of urban territory. The only information on its social composition I could get was on the basis of the Stella section's voting list, which includes 33,004 electors. Among these, there are 7,271 workers, 14,230 housewives, 3,093 artisans, 2,491 clerks, and other white-collar employees, 747 students, 666 professionals and 886 pensioners. The territorial density of the quarter is like the rest of the centre of Naples – *the highest in Europe*: 3,074 people per hectare, here at Stella. But in the quarter of Vicaria the index is more than twice as high: 6,710 per hectare. And the over-crowding in the *bassi* is unbelievable, with three people for every two square metres in Stella. The houses themselves are like ant hills where rats and people enjoy equal rights and are locked in a perpetual struggle. '*Le zoccole*', '*le zoccole*', the women are forever crying – screaming in impotent rage at the enormous sewer rats which live in

4. A hectare equals 2.47 acres. (Trans.)

the driest parts of the *bassi*, in the ceilings. In Naples, according to official statistics, there are seven million rats! Six for every citizen (if you adopt the statistical method whereby a chicken eaten by one man is averaged out as a half-chicken each for two men). In reality, of course, you have to subtract the rich and the well-to-do, in order to count how many rats there are for every poor Neapolitan.

My head is spinning like a top by the time I leave Cavaioli to go to the 'Stella' section of the PCI. When I get there, with the help of the comrades of the section, I do the calculations I have just mentioned, using the 1964 electoral figures. There is a map of the quarter there in the section, broken down by socio-economic and political differences. As we go over it, it seems to me that the 14,000 housewives represent the most compact social mass, and that we should base our strategy on them. I think that it is from them that we could learn the most, and I say this to the other comrades. Here, too, the workers do not come to the section any more; here, too, there are 'Chinese' next door; here, too, there is the same veiled mistrust, and even though I have known some of them for years and years, whatever dialogue there is proceeds very cautiously.

Everyone looks me over, scrutinizing me carefully. Right next door to the section headquarters, I am shown the house of a Deputy, a comrade, who died of a heart ailment when he was only forty-five; the house is almost some kind of sanctuary. There are still plenty of people in the area who do not know that he died three years ago, and someone even asked 'What number does A. have on this year's list?' You should know that each candidate has a number that corresponds to his place on the (alphabetical) list, and it is with this number that voters indicate their preference for him.[5] In the South, you might transform Oscar Wilde's play into 'The Importance of Having Your Name Begin With an Advantaged Letter of the Alphabet', meaning one which comes very early, like 'A' or 'B'. Apparently, illiterate voters find it easiest to mark the simplest combination, 1-2-3-4, called the *quaterna* in the lottery. Thus after the *capolista*, the next to be elected

5. In the elections for the Chamber of Deputies, a voter may either simply mark an X against the symbol of a party (only symbols figure on the ballot-paper), in which case his vote is taken as also being a vote for the first four names on the official slate of candidates as drawn up by the party; or, alternatively, he may – in addition to his vote for the party in question – also cast four 'preference votes' for individual candidates on the list, by writing either their names or more commonly their numbers on the ballot-paper. (Trans.)

is often somebody whose name begins with 'A'. All that he has to do is spread the word that people are to 'play the *quaterna*', and he can get in. They tell me that a comrade whose name begins with 'A' – the head of a union of 17,000 construction workers – had a picture of himself printed up with the *quaterna* underneath, and then went around promising that he would build a house for everyone who lacked one. Naturally he was elected by a large margin. The Federation asked him to resign, and not only did he refuse, but he ran again in 1963 – the first time was in '58 – and won. But this ingenious comrade, no doubt exhausted from trying to keep up with the thousands of requests with which his electors flooded him, died of a heart attack in 1965. And the one who succeeded him (the person who had received the next highest number of preferences in the 1963 elections) was, of course, the one right behind him on the list, another 'A', Abruzzese. He has something of a following in some of the larger quarters, such as Pendino, Forcella and Borgo, and his electoral base comes from the municipal clerks, he being one of them: with 15,000 of them in the city, you can see that it is a political force to be reckoned with. When his term as a replacement had expired, Abruzzese wanted to be proposed as a candidate in his own right. The Party, by now attuned to the whole business of the letter 'A', refused unconditionally and unequivocally. Abruzzese then formed a list of his own, called the 'Communist-Socialist Renovators', quit the Party, was then expelled, and so on. The comrades in the Communist sections in areas that 'belong to' Abruzzese are confused and do not know whether to vote for him or not. For everybody is arguing about the rights and wrongs of these electoralist manoeuvres: the sections' directives contradict those of the Federation, several federation leaders have clashed with the national leadership, and so on.

In fact, a good four-fifths of the pre-electoral debate is still over which people should be elected, rather than over what strategy the political-electoral struggle ought to have. This kind of distortion and deformation is also the cause of another phenomenon, whereby, at times, certain leading figures of the Party, along with other candidates, seem to be more concerned with their own electorate than with the general direction of the Party and the concrete work that the comrades are doing. When you note their absence from important meetings at headquarters, you always hear something to the effect that they are out holding a 'back-room meeting' in some far-off part of the city or province.

At any rate, this time the Federation got off easily with the letter 'A' that is to come first behind the leaders. One Nello Ajello, a worker in the Navy Shipyards of Castellammare, has been selected, and he is a simple militant with no electoral ambitions. An unthreatening 'A' has been found.

I am still here in this section, called Stella after the quarter in which it is situated. I don't have any idea why this name was chosen because, believe me, *nothing* shines here. I feel feverish and have a sore throat, and I can't tell if this is as a result of speaking or from my awareness of not having known what to say.

Now I am back in my skyscraper of a hotel, where I have a room on the twenty-ninth floor with a 30 per cent journalist's discount. You can see the Bay from here, a dark sheet lit up by the lights strung out over the huge American warships of the Sixth Fleet, stationed here at Naples, whenever they so desire, as a result of the 'Atlantic Pact'. It all reminds me of Nelson's fleet.

I feel as if I were in a balloon, raised high above the poverty of the alleyways. And I see the Bay. Did you know that 'the sea doesn't bathe Naples'? The multitudes who live in the poor neighbourhoods never see it, and they have to come down to the seafront – which is a rich quarter where the only proletarian you see is one who works there – to get a glimpse of it. I, however, with a place looking over the Bay, can see the Maschio Angioino, a virile medieval fortress, and the harmonious dark red edifice of the Royal Palace of Naples, which used to belong to the Bourbons. On the left is Vesuvius, and the gentle Sorrento peninsula spreads out away from the volcano. One Hélène told me, in Paris, 'What you can see from your own window is very important.' And it is. However, it is also true that your choice of panorama is determined – in inverse proportions – by the reality which you feel is crushing or smothering you. The most famous Neapolitan journalist of the late 1800s, Scarfoglio, wrote: 'Naples is the only Eastern city where there is no European residential quarter.' I am only a Communist, aware of my helplessness when faced by the primordial force which makes the exploited either into unintentional supporters or into mere creatures of capitalism.

I put my head outside the window. A light, dry breeze tasting faintly of salt blows around me, massaging my face and eyes. The clamour and bustle of the city, from up here, is very muffled. Everything is dark, quiet, restful. And tomorrow will be different in many ways, mostly because I will be able to cope much more rationally with the cluster of problems which assails me. For tomorrow your letter will begin to play an 'active' role in this candidate's experiences.

Maria Antonietta

Dear Louis, *Naples, 10 April*

Writing forces me to reflect, it is the necessary step which fixes 'facts' on paper, saves them from the vacuum of oblivion, and gathers together that which is 'most positive, precise, and material' in the political reality of Naples. As I write, I am almost in a state of collapse from lack of sleep. But I keep at it, thinking that seeing the facts can have – as you insist – a certain theoretical value, from the perspective Lenin called a 'class point of view'.

This morning I put together the following list of 'categorical imperatives' which I dug out of your letter: propose an *unprecedented method of electoral campaigning*; question the women on the *material conditions of life* because they after all are the ones most familiar with them; profit from my being a *woman* in order to establish a *total contact with other women*; invent *new forms of dialogue* with voters; utilize my imagination and intelligence, etc.

I have this political sextant firmly fixed in my mind, and I have begun to give my electoral activity a new orientation, which lessens the chances that I will succumb to 'cretinism'. Without *rushing*, without *deluding* myself, I can tell myself, just as a philosopher does when he sits down to write a theoretical work of some length, that I must see things in perspective and take a very long-range view of things. The two months of the electoral campaign must serve as a political test for me, one I will continue to study and think about long after this given period has passed. Seen this way, things become more reassuring and even stimulating. What I feel and learn is no longer in relation to me as a *candidate*, but is part of my experience as a *political being*. Hence it loses its random nature and acquires the weight and duration of a *political* process. I discard what is not political, for I am already aware that it is a passing phenomenon, a few days' whim. The process is similar to sifting sand for the few flakes of gold that turn up.

It immediately makes you less personalistic, it pushes you away from subjective knowledge and towards the more objective realm. This method permits you to look back at a day's activity and draw a number of *pure* and *absolute* political reflections from your experience. And you work on them at night, you think about them even while asleep. It is true that a part of me is already asleep, but the other part of me, that I am describing, remains indomitably insomniac.

Know how to put your 'losses' to use. I arrive at Vico Zuroli A1, where a meeting with the voters has been set for 6.30. It is the Pendino quarter: 64,000 inhabitants in yet another miserable, poverty-ridden area of Naples. Vico Zuroli is a huge, ugly square, with the doors from about ten dilapidated buildings facing on to it. There is no one in the street itself. An old watchman, closed into a little cabinet where he stitches together disintegrated shoes, shrugs his shoulders and says, 'They came, showed the film (the standard NATO documentary), and then left'. Schedules are a very relative thing here, but whereas they are often delayed it is hardly ever the case that they are early. But now just that has happened. I feel crushed. But I have decided not to get upset; instead, I must above all try to 'understand'.

So I go straight to the 'Curiel' section of the PCI, the one that called this demonstration and prepared the handwritten leaflet that they gave me in the Federation and that I enclose with this letter. They receive me coldly: who was *first* to arrive, who came *later*? – like arguing about the sex of angels. Right then I decide that I am going to spend the rest of the evening with them, even if they pretend not to notice me, and with that I sit down quite calmly. Everyone seems, almost deliberately, to be involved in something else: they are writing out, on large pieces of cardboard, the votes for every ward. No one looks at me. But then, I just happen to have a red marker in my purse, which is precisely what they need. I loan it to them and this, my first useful act, breaks the ice.

I strike up a conversation with the only comrade who isn't bent over the statistics and deigns to notice me. I ask about the electoral campaign and what he thinks of the televised debate a night earlier, particularly what he thinks of the Communist who spoke. This is not idle chatter for me, but rather my means of beginning some sort of dialogue. The comrade responds: 'The speaker for the PCI sounded like a trade unionist, he never once used the words "revolutionary party" when he spoke of our Party.' The others come forward now: 'Our speaker and the one from the PSU (Unified Socialists)[1] sounded like two peas in a pod: ours didn't attack him, and he didn't attack us.' By this time we are into a discussion of the PCI's position towards the PSU, and everyone seems to be participating.

It turns out that my question has touched a sore spot: in this section there is a very strong, even polemical, attitude towards Party headquarters. The Socialists, who some time ago broke the workers' unity by joining the DC in the government, creating the famous 'Centre-Left', have not, in these comrades' opinion, been attacked and exposed sufficiently. In Pendino quarter, the two sections opened by the PSU are run today by two ex-monarchists – known only by their nicknames, 'o'formaggiaro' (the cheese-peddler) and 'o'spruoccolo' (the sprig). These characters went over to the Socialists because the latter now provide more 'goodies' – money, packages, recommendations, patronage – for them to distribute to their followers in the Naples slums than even the Christian Democrats do. For the comrades, these are huge problems. They are convinced that the only way to reconstruct a common platform with the Socialists is first to denounce their corruption and their integration into the system and smash them electorally.

The comrade who is busy with the red marker joins in the discussion too. Another comrade who is an artisan arrives with a copy of the Italian edition of *Monthly Review*. An economics student comes in: he took part in the occupation of the Faculty of Oriental Languages the day before yesterday. He tells me that six months ago they wanted to throw him out of the Party for being too 'Leftist' in his views. He says that he will go with me to the Faculty tomorrow (but the next day – after a two-hour wait – he doesn't show up). We talk about Che Guevara, Vietnam, China, and the current state of the workers' movement. This section's general orientation is that of giving everyone room; letting any opinion, even those opposed to the PCI's official

1. The Social-Democratic Party (PSDI) split away from the Socialist Party (PSI) in 1947 because it objected to the PSI's close collaboration with the Communists. The PSI's distance from the PCI progressively grew, however, and in 1963 it joined a ruling coalition, the Centre-Left, which included the PSDI. With the major barrier between them apparently overcome, the two parties merged into the PSU in 1966. But in July 1969 they re-divided. The PSI took back its old name, and the new social-democratic rump took the name of 'Unitary Socialists'; its initials, confusing, are also PSU. The 'PSU' referred to above is the PSI-PSDI. (Trans.)

line, be expressed; underlining what is valid in every movement of a working-class character; and repudiating the whole logic of 'excommunications'. They claim that because of this, they are the only section which has not had some sort of 'Chinese secession'.

So you can see from this that I made something out of my initial 'defeat', i.e. the deliberate sabotage of my meeting. Instead of chatting in an empty square, I communicated with and learned a lot about the leadership of a section. They may be uncertain of their direction, but they seriously attempt to analyse things; and their scepticism does not conceal their real concern and knowledge. In this single evening of hard discussion, planned by no one, I gained a bit of faith in myself and, who knows, perhaps I was also accepted a little more. Had I left immediately, offended or even just displeased, I would have left them with the impression that I am a candidate out for personal votes and popularity in the quarter and nothing more.

My invention of a new electoral method began two days ago. After reading your letter I concluded that the accepted practice of electoral propaganda must be completely reversed. Stand it on its head. Instead of it being *we* who always speak, make the *people* speak; create a situation where the denunciations – and the speeches themselves – are not conducted by the official propagandist, but by the public, by the people. I tried this out with the women, who have the least reticence about speaking up.

Here is the general setting: a dirty courtyard in the Borgo section, behind Piazzetta San Fernandino, where the famous Neapolitan Repertory Theatre is located. It is a quarter of cigarette vendors, black-marketeers, street pedlars and *magliari*.[2] The women, unkempt and uncombed, with one baby inside and one just out, at the breast, come to watch from their balconies, which are actually no more than the half-doors of the *bassi* around which the more 'well-off' erect little wooden fences, with pots of basil on top. I go to them and greet them, one by one; I call them out. One onlooker lends us a table, another some chairs. In this way we end up seated in a circle in the courtyard. The first one to speak is Giuseppina Parente, twenty-eight years old, six children and one on the way, with a husband who is a *piattaro*, selling crockery from a barrow. She tells how he earns a thousand lire every now and then, and how *at home there isn't any food*. Another

2. *Magliari* are door-to-door, high-pressure salesmen of inferior goods at inflated prices.

woman, thirty years old with ten children, speaks. I ask her, 'Would you like to have fewer kids, would you like to feel less worn out than you are?' To myself I think: is it possible to raise the issue of 'The Pill'? Are they interested? But the comrade from the section interrupts right then, before I can open my mouth, and he lets me know I have committed a *gaffe*. 'Babies are so beautiful,' he says, all effusive, and the next thing you know, he is kissing all the little kids who are milling around the table. 'I would like ten of them' he goes on, 'and I only have five. Maybe my wife could have some more; after all, she is only forty.' And the women chime in: 'Of course she could!' He goes on, 'You should have ten, twelve, as many children as you want. The real issue is that the working man should be provided with whatever is necessary to raise them properly.' It is clear from this that the comrades have discarded, *a priori*, any question of the Pill. They think that, all things considered, it is a bad idea to talk about it.

I am not so sure. The woman with six children takes me aside at the end and says to me: 'Ma'am, is it really true that there is some kind of medicine which keeps you from having so many children? Could you tell me what it is . . .?' Meanwhile, I certainly cannot do everything at once. I make believe that I don't really understand. But I promise myself to explore again, perhaps more privately, the whole issue of the Pill in this electoral campaign. Birth control, in my opinion, can become a political propaganda theme for these women, who give birth to sickly offspring here in the stench of the back streets. Naples boasts the highest birth-rate in Italy, a hundred a day, which works out to almost twice the national average. At the same time, the infant mortality rate here is seventy-one per 1,000 live births, which is also the highest in Italy. Every year 2,500 babies die.

As the women speak, I find out yet another crucial fact about the social relations of the Neapolitan masses. These women, for the most part, are not housewives at all – which is the way they are officially registered by the Bureau of Statistics – but *underpaid labourers*. They are labourers and they do not even know it, and they also do not know that, working at home, they receive from industry (which hires them on the sly) a salary five times lower than that of a regular female worker. They have no welfare benefits at all, no insurance, no social security, no pension. The women of the back streets sew shoe uppers, gloves, umbrellas, trousers; they are the workforce of the 'shadow factories', against which it is impossible to organize a strike or any kind of struggle for wages since the bosses have no faces. The women are not signed up in the unions even as artisans since, among other reasons, they cannot indicate who it is that hires them – they do not even know his name.

Anna Astuto speaks. She is twenty-five and a glove-maker. She begins by telling us how she is expecting her first baby. Then she explains what it is like to work on gloves. A little boy, who she knows only by sight, brings her a package of cut gloves once a week. It is her job to place them on a form, an 'electric hand', and sew them together. The unknown boss has provided this form, *this machine*, over which she stays bent day and night. She gets ten lire per glove. In a week, by sewing a maximum of 650 gloves, she can earn 6,500 lire. The kid who brings her the gloves later brings an envelope (on which there is no sender's name, of course) containing the amount which corresponds to the exact number of gloves which have been sewn. Now that she is expecting, Anna Astuto has given 3,500 lire – she stresses that this comes to more than half a week's pay – to 'the accountant' in order to get herself insured as a maid employed by a cousin. With this on the official records, she can get maternity benefits when she goes to the hospital. In a voice shrill with emotion and strain, she shouts that there is no maternity leave for her on this job, and not only will she have to sew right up to the last moment, but she will have to work harder than usual these next few months to accumulate something for the child who is coming.

Another woman – this one old – also tells of insuring herself as a maid, working for a cousin, and she hopes that this ruse will provide her with some sort of pension. Such are the sly tricks Neapolitan women have to learn to use against the bosses! I ask a white-haired woman what she thinks the most important issue is to discuss with women in this electoral campaign. 'Pensions,' she says, 'security for our old age.' Everywhere I go, I repeat the question: what is the central problem to point to in accusations against the Government? 'Pensions, old age,' repeat the older women. 'Work, social security,' affirm the younger.

Now, suddenly, a man I haven't seen before comes out of one of the *bassi*. He has been listening to the 'meeting' held by his neighbours, from behind his half-closed window. 'Speak with Maria Paciotta,' he says, 'my wife.' And he calls her, as they do in Naples, by her maiden name, not her married name. His wife, as small as an elf with fingers like dark brown cigarette-butts, is pushed forward.

She says she sews umbrellas. She earns forty lire for sewing twelve ribs to twelve pieces of cloth: forty lire for 144 knots sewn by hand. She, too, does not know the name of her boss. She goes to 'the teacher', which is what they call the agent of the big employer in this area, and the teacher gives her the packages of ribs and the material. She carries home, by herself, dozens of pounds of steel shafts for the umbrellas. Her husband, at this point, brings out a package, still in its factory wrapping, just as it came off some assembly line. Brusquely, he tells me to feel how much it weighs. Taking it, I am amazed at how heavy it is. 'My wife carries home twelve of them at a time,' he tells me, as if throwing down a challenge to the other women. Then Maria Paciotta herself steps in and tells with some pride how the 'teacher' might, after all, prefer to have someone else in the neighbourhood to do the work, but instead has faith in her. She calls herself the favoured 'disciple'. Teacher and disciple. The 'instructress' gives out the umbrellas and the 'pupil' sews them. This is the way 'professorships' are created in the back streets, in this refined school of super-exploitation.

I do no more than draw out the conclusions from what the women themselves have said: I explain to them that, far from being housewives, they constitute a very real part of the Neapolitan economy. Indirectly, the European Common Market reaches all the way down to the twisting, narrow streets of these neighbourhoods in the sense that gloves sewn for ten lire a pair by Anna Astuto sell in Paris or Brussels – with the label, 'Made in Italy' – for 5,000 lire. It is the same story for shoes. So too for the umbrellas of black silk which go, for the most part, to London.

The women look at me with shock, and perhaps disbelief. Now, the problems are these: (a) organize these women in unions as categories of workers, which of course they are; (b) transform their sub-salaries into salaries with all the rights that go along with real salaries; (c) organize the women, at the same time, politically, teaching them the rudimentary elements of how labour-power is exploited, and hence the reasons for the political battle against capitalism.

But the problem of identifying the bosses of these industries is a very difficult one. As soon as someone threatens to go to the unions, the bosses change intermediaries. Moreover, the boss who controls this mass of underpaid workers will only admit, officially, to ten or twelve employees at most. Once in a while the truth comes out, but it usually happens purely by chance. It was in this way that 1 learned that in Miano, a little town on the outskirts of Naples, one of the owners of a clandestine industry had died. He had admitted having only fourteen workers (both to the fiscal authorities and to the unions), but when the time came to divide up what he had left, it suddenly came to light that 400 Neapolitan women were dependent on his business. When the boss died and the business was closed down and sold, 400 women who were convinced they were 'only housewives' found themselves destitute. Revelations of this kind have provided me with a thread which I have decided to follow in this electoral campaign: to what extent is the mass of Neapolitan 'housewives' really a mass of labourers?

Before I left, a woman, seemingly embarrassed, asked me in a very hushed voice, 'But who are the ones who write "Get NATO out of Italy" on the walls? The Christian Democrats? The Monarchists? They tell me it is the PCI, but I don't believe it.' I am dumbfounded. Finally, I answer her: 'Yes, we Communists are the ones who write that.' And she replies, 'But how come? My brother and thousands of poor people work for NATO. If NATO leaves Italy, who will feed them?' She cannot understand how the Communists could put forward a proposal which would 'take the bread out of the mouths of her brother's family'. And this is a damned hard thing to explain. I realize that in the people's heads there are questions that we never ask ourselves. The people often think in very different ways from *politicians*.

The secretary of the PCI's Borgo section recorded the whole talk with the women. He uses the recorder, bought only yesterday with money from the section's electoral fund (35,000 lire), and he never tires of listening to things he has taped. He laughs and is as happy as a baby. I insist that we get down to serious problems and I almost have to force him to shut off the machine, which is going full blast.

There are six old men seated in the only room in the section headquarters. The youngest – who must be *fifty* – introduces himself to me saying, 'I am "Chinese", both in appearance and in my heart.' *In appearance* is easily understood by looking at him, for he has almond-shaped eyes which slant upwards toward his temples. *In his heart*, of course, is obvious.

They tell me that the committee of the Borgo section, which is entirely 'Abruzzese territory' (see above), has decided not to give preferences to anyone. Earlier, things had gone so far that they were ready to take down the 'PCI Section' sign painted up outside. Then they calmed down somewhat, and after a vote, it was decided that on election day they would vote only for the symbol of the PCI.

Then they turned to me. Did I know that 'they' did not want me? Yes, I knew, I answered, by now with no shame and even with a sort of tactful understanding and resignation. Then the usual: 'Will you come and live here? Will you come to the section, to take care of pension dossiers?' They had introduced me to the women at the meeting by saying, 'This comrade journalist you see here will come to the square every week and take care of all your problems.' When we meet back at the section, I explain to them that this is too much, it is impossible, they are exaggerating. How can I possibly solve *all* the problems? They speak again of Abruzzese and hold him up as a symbol, in spite of the fact that he has gone and put together his own list, with his own private 'hammer and sickle'.

The secretary of the section works for the city of Naples while at the same time managing to find time to run things for the Party. In the discussion, he makes clear that he is hostile to workers in general and to those of the section's territory in particular. He says that in the Arenaccia area of Borgo, where the workers live, the section has been closed down. The workers, according to him, have become an aristocracy. They earn too much, and they spit on the common people (*popolino*). The San Lorenzo quarter, of which Borgo is a part, has 99,000 inhabitants. This is 6,000 less than in 1961. The reason for the decline is that both workers and clerks, as soon as they get their placements from the housing authorities, leave *en bloc*, abandoning their old neighbourhoods. I open a drawer and all I find are three old decks of cards. It is clear that the old comrades pass their evenings playing cards among themselves, and even now as we talk it is likely that all they really want is to settle down round the table. Once we have had a cup of coffee together, it is obvious that they want me to leave. As for the secretary of the section, he is by now all a-tremble in anticipation of listening to his recorder once more. In six months, the directing committee of this section has held only three meetings, and all three were called to discuss the composition of the electoral lists. I understand: it is time to 'make tracks'. But at least I can be excited by that direct dialogue with the women, by having reversed the old practice of electoral propaganda. Now I have decided to try this method out in public, in a real meeting, with microphones.

Maria Antonietta

Dear M.A.,   *Gordes, Easter Monday (15 April)*

I received your 'special delivery' safely, and have been reading it with great interest and emotion. Since we are friends and you have enough faith in me to take my suggestions into account, I want you to understand that, at most, I can only provide very general and abstract 'indications' from such a great distance. All I can really say are such things as: you should look this up, you should look for that, you should examine things in terms of their long-term implications, etc. You must know that aside from the general ideas which I draw from the classics, and which I have hardly invented, I too can make mistakes and say stupid things, just like you, and, given that you are 'in the field' and see things as they are, I am likely to do so much more than you. So, with this in mind, we come to your letter.

(1) I think that you are very effectively utilizing your electoral campaign experience. Do not fall into the cretinism of the campaign, but try to benefit as much as possible from the ways the campaign makes it easier for you to see what is going on at the *base*: (a) at the base of the Party and the unions; (b) at the base of the masses, in all their diversity. Your watch-word for a long time must, it seems to me, be *learn, learn* (words of Lenin and Mao), learn from the masses, learn from militants in the class struggle – including learning from the errors that both make (e.g., learn how certain strata of the masses, and certain dedicated militants, are caught up in terrible contradictions, such as that of NATO, or that of the section leader who is against the workers because 'they have become an aristocracy'). For a long time, I think the best thing to do is *learn* as much as possible, in the most profound, ample, and critical way possible, *without being in a hurry to intervene.*

This last point seems to me to be perhaps the most important one to clarify, because you might be tempted for ten different reasons to *intervene too soon.*

Of course, there is 'intervention' and 'intervention'. One can take part in a conversation by making short comments, or by choosing when not to say anything. That is all part of learning. In order to learn, you do not have to let the other person do all the talking. You must, at certain times, ask questions which focus their demands and which help them say things they otherwise (internal blocks, taboos, etc.) cannot say on their own. But I think you have to be alert to certain kinds of interventions which can be premature and dangerous.

An example: Your observation on the incredible number of children produced by the women in these poverty-ridden quarters of Naples. Why so many babies? You think about the Pill and so on. But is it not also true that the number of children ensures a minimum fixed 'income', however small in absolute terms, from state family allowances? Isn't it true that having so many children means reaching the limit beyond which you receive enough in family allowances to have the possibility, at least to have the *impression* of a fixed and assured minimum of material security? What is your opinion? 'Rationally', it is unquestionably a false calculation and absurd behaviour to act in this way, but we cannot project *our* 'rationality' onto the behaviour of these desperate people: their 'means of subsistence' are derisory, they grab whatever they can, most often by mortgaging their own future. I really do not know; perhaps there are also other illusions which are the real key to the problem: for example, that having a huge batch of children means having members of a family who one day will somehow manage to find work and hence bring a few pounds home each week? Everything that I say in this regard – apart from the question of family allowances, which I am pretty sure about – may be incorrect. But there has to be a reason, other than the simple *ignorance* of birth control methods, which explains this abundance of babies.

Ignorance is never a cause. When we use the word 'ignorance', what we really are doing is describing a vacuum, which is primarily that of *our own* ignorance of causes we have been unable to discover. It is hard for us to realize that these causes even exist, for they are so foreign to those to which we are accustomed, i.e. to causes that affect us. This is why I am so sceptical of the notion of the Pill as a 'solution'. Of course it is a 'solution', but only in very well-defined circumstances which are easily verified: when there are no other 'causes' to worry about. But in the specific case under discussion, there are certainly infinitely more profound 'causes' at work, which make the slogan 'take the Pill' laughable. What is needed is to discover these causes in order to figure out how then to deal with them. There is very little chance indeed that they can be dealt with by means of the Pill before a very long period of time has gone by. The Pill is – in the present state of things – something for the bourgeoisie and the petty bourgeoisie.

Another example: the situation of the women who are not 'house-wives' at all but really workers in their own houses, exploited scandalously by factory owners. This is a classic situation. Marx speaks about it at length in *Capital*, and what you describe nearly a hundred years later fits his analysis almost word-for-word. It is clearly a terrible situation, but you should be very, very careful before intervening. If you want to launch the idea of *getting all these women signed up in the unions*, you had better, before you try this, make sure that they are organized so they can defend themselves, for otherwise you will risk provoking something of a catastrophe. I really am very afraid of this, for, as a direct result of such action, they would lose their jobs and their meagre means of subsistence – and, after all, it *is* a means of subsistence – and the bosses would have no trouble at all replacing them. I do not mean by this that you should give up the idea of organizing them some day, but right now this is unquestionably *premature*, and a premature initiative can be very dangerous. Hélène, who is very well-informed on this issue, is of the same opinion. *Be careful.* On the other hand, two actions do suggest themselves:

(a) It should be possible to identify the bosses, and denounce them. The women do not know who they are, but this is because they are in a rotten situation and don't have the means. But they can be helped, by providing the means *from outside*. Certain comrades in the Party surely can help in this task of identification. And once the owners have been identified, they must be denounced. But even more the *general system*, above and beyond any individuals, has to be denounced. You cannot begin by putting these poor women in the front ranks of a mobilization, for this in reality would mean exposing them without any defences. You must begin by supporting them actively *from outside*, doing in effect what they are unable to do by themselves, and *making the facts known to the working class*. Once these sub-proletarian workers have external support, they will perhaps then, but only then, be able to move to the first stages of organization and action.

(b) You have to explain to the women why things are as they are, i.e. you have to begin to create consciousness among them, making them understand that which they cannot understand on their own. Be careful of the following: the 'intermediaries' who distribute work and money to the women are not necessarily so far above them; they are very often persons closer to the sub-proletariat than to the bosses, even if they are in the direct service of the latter. Hence, with regard to all these poor or semi-poor people, you have to act very cautiously, for if you do not, you are likely to find yourself being asked the same kind of questions raised by that woman you mentioned: 'You want to throw NATO out of here, but then how will we all eat?'

I go into all this to insist once more on my primary point: give yourself time to learn; have the patience to learn, even if it requires a lot of time, and know how *not* to interfere where an intervention, without the requisite preparation, will have disastrous results. Once again, however: *to learn* does not only mean *to listen*. You must go where the people are. You have to listen to them. But in order to be able to listen, you also have to make them speak, and you yourself must therefore *also speak*, not, of course, at any random moment or in whatever form strikes your fancy. To make others speak by *letting them speak* (letting them say everything they have in their heads and in their hearts) is the *passive* approach. There is also an *active* approach, making people speak in the sense of knowing how to listen politically (in the most general sense), of having a politico-sociological 'hearing' which helps you discover which are the points on which you ought to push farther, and hence the points you yourself have to discuss. When people speak, they say certain things on their own. But there are also things that they hide or disguise, things they often *consciously*, but most often unconsciously, avoid. The listener must be able to discover these silences, and put questions to the speaker which permit him to express himself in a way which would be impossible without such outside help. The thing that permits you to discover these 'silent areas', and which permits you to overcome them, is your political experience based on Marxist-Leninist theory. In this scheme of things, the militant is somewhat analogous to a psychoanalyst: he 'knows' more than the person he listens to, but what he 'knows' is on a different level than that which the speaker 'knows', which is the specific contradiction. The militant does not 'know', a priori and in specific detail, just what the lives of the persons he listens to are made up of and what the major contradictions are; he learns this by listening to them and discovering a great many things he previously did not know.

Hearing these things, the militant 'understands' them in a certain way, for he 'reorders' them within the framework provided for him by Marxist theory and by the general mechanisms of society, whose laws, ruses, mechanisms of exploitation, and 'tendencies' he knows. This is what permits the militant to 'comprehend' beyond what he is told. It permits him, in particular, to 'diagnose' the sensitive spots, which are generally those 'silent areas'. It is at this stage of the 'analysis' that he can and must raise pertinent questions of his own in order to break down these silences and make the speaker discover things that he knows, *but that he is not aware of knowing* because they are disguised, – clouded over, repressed – covered over by causes that go to the very heart of the conditions in which these people live and to the heart of the pitiful means by which they try, in spite of everything, to get by. In this type of sociological-political 'hearing', a 'non-directed' interview is a trap.

Apart from all this, given what you have written, I think that what follows is also an essential point. You say that the secretary of such-and-such a section shows hostility towards the workers. All right. This expresses, for whatever it is worth, a type of reaction typical of the sub-proletariat when they look at the conditions of life of the workers in the factories. In appearance, and perhaps even in reality, the workers seem to be better off than the sub-proletarians. But it would be more important to know the reaction of these workers and of worker-militants to the conditions of life and the general problems of the *sub-proletarians*. Because, in any event, it is not the sub-proletariat, but the proletariat, which is the 'leading force' in the class struggle, and it alone is capable of assuming this role and this responsibility, *even if it does not do so at the moment.* It is a political and theoretical question of the first order to distinguish between the *leading force* and the *principal force* in a given *conjuncture*. There can be, in one form or another, forces involved in the struggle which are the principal force without being the *leading force*. During the Chinese Revolution, the principal force was the workers (even though they were few in number compared to the peasants). And look what is currently going on with the students in many places, in West Germany for example. They are involved in highly advanced forms of struggle. They may even, in the present moment, give the impression of being the 'vanguard'. With regard to their class of origin (petty-bourgeoisie), they are a vanguard. But it is precisely their class condition which prevents them from ever becoming the 'leading force' – even if for a time they occupy, alone or almost alone, the foreground of the political scene. Only the proletariat (urban and rural) can be the 'leading force', the 'vanguard force'. For this reason, it is important to know what the workers think about the conditions of life of the sub-proletariat. And if they really do not pay much attention to these problems, which is a definite possibility, it becomes politically crucial to:

(1) Inform them of the real conditions of the sub-proletariat, entering into minute detail, telling them everything that goes on, including the question of the number of children, the condition of women, etc. If I understand the situation, the men work, when possible, about one day out of three, but the women *always* work, in addition to doing the housework and caring for their children, and it is really they who keep everyone alive. This is an aspect of the condition of women in Italy which ought to be made known, because it goes a good deal farther than the simple stories of legal inequality, which the petty-bourgeois press (e.g. *L'Express*) likes to use to fatten its circulation.

(2) Ask them to consider the condition of the sub-proletariat, with the end in mind of developing forms of support, solidarity and political action which will, gradually, create *an alliance between the proletariat and this stratum*. The initiative for such an alliance cannot grow spontaneously out of the sub-proletariat, *but only through the mediation of the proletariat*. This corresponds to what I said earlier: organizing effective support, aid, and protection *from outside* (and 'outside' can only mean the proletariat itself) will permit the main elements of the sub-proletariat to go forward, and at the same time these concrete indications of support can be tied to developing the first stages of consciousness of the sub-proletariat. It should always be remembered that the *division* between the workers and the sub-proletariat is one of the most powerful instruments in the hands of the bourgeoisie. It uses this division to maintain its hegemony over the proletariat, for the sub-proletariat is the 'reserve mass' which the bourgeoisie draws upon in order to keep the working class under the most miserable possible conditions of exploitation. It is therefore really a crime to leave this 'division' intact, since it objectively serves the bourgeoisie while objectively hurting the proletariat. For these reasons, every effort should be made to dismantle and destroy the division. Here, too, of course, I am speaking as an outsider, and you are really the only person who can judge, with concrete 'evidence', just how things

actually stand. You can find out if the secretary of a factory workers' section says the same things as your secretary of the sub-proletarian section or not. Or perhaps he *does not say anything about this at all*. Of course, if he says nothing at all, it is a pretty bad sign.

You have to understand that one person can only do so much, and you certainly ought not to expect miracles. But a person can inform himself, and think about what he sees, and he can do this for as long as is necessary. The key is *reflection without taking premature initiatives* – because even though the initiatives which you can take with the working class do not present the same serious risks as with the women, the correct 'method' still has to be found, and this can take time.

Hélène, to whom I have been reading what I am writing here, has made some comments on a few of the most important points that I have made, and I will summarize them below (she will develop what she thinks is most important in a postscript):

(1) I have spoken of 'family allowances', which of course is a French concept. The institution may well not exist in this precise form in Italy: perhaps it is more a question there of 'assistance' to mothers in proportion to the number of children they have. But, in one form or another, something of this type simply has to exist.

(2) There is another 'cause' which needs mentioning in the whole discussion about children, which in part can be seen from the comments of your comrade with the recorder: the whole question of the ideology of 'virility' among Italian men. This must be a 'thorny' problem, and it cannot be easy to find out all the real factors involved. But if one relates this masculine ideology to the fact that it is the women, if I have understood correctly, who provide the bare minimum of survival in the sub-proletarian strata (through the number of children they have and the financial 'assistance' they are thereby entitled to; through their industrial work in the home, etc.), then this all constitutes a terrible problem. The conclusion is certainly not brutally to tell the husbands of these women that they are 'exaggerating' with their cult of virility; this could be disastrous, for, in this ideology of virility, which produces swarms of children, these men unquestionably enjoy one of the rare privileges that their miserable condition has left more or less intact: a sexual life and identity.

The solution ought to be to make the proletariat itself understand more fully the true role of women, of proletarian and sub-proletarian women alike. The role they play is a tremendous one, and what they do grinds them down. This has to be communicated to the proletarian men – not attacking their ideology directly, but indirectly, by defending the women. After all, there are numerous texts among the classics on the *revolutionary role of women* (esp. Bebel and Lenin) which can help get these ideas *across to the proletarian men* without, for the moment, attacking their ideology directly. You can also add to this the whole discussion of the role of women in the countryside, which is different but no less central.

(3) On the issue of how to ask questions, I must insist on two things. First of all, you should show the most profound, attentive respect towards everything the speakers have to say. Then you should question them *taking off from their own statements*. This is the best way of giving them the respect they deserve, and it is also the best way of getting them to *recognize themselves* in the questions they are asked.

Example : You can pick things up by saying, 'If I understand you correctly, the question is that . . . or that. . . . Is this what you mean ? Is this what you meant to say?' In this last question, you introduce your 'pertinent' question, the one that is aimed right at one of those 'silences'.

Take, as an example, the issue of the number of children that the women have. You absolutely must avoid asking, 'But why do you have so many children?' This is, as you yourself have realized, a *gaffe*. You have to make them talk about their children, their vitality, their beauty, etc. Then you have to pick up their statements in such a way that the women are able to recognize themselves in what you say and to see that you take them seriously. And you have to pay attention to the reasons they give, because it is by doing so that you can then expose 'limits' in those reasons, limits which quite naturally lead to 'pertinent' questions: 'Do you mean that you can't live without having lots of children? That it is beautiful to have a lot of children? That babies add something to life? That they help you get by? Do you mean that one day they will be able to work and bring some money home? At what age do children usually start to work around here? What kind of work do they do?' etc. Or else, by following up on other points, you can find ways to ask questions about 'assistance' and related matters. This is just a simple suggestion, very formal and schematic, but it is a concrete *form* of what is called 'a link with the masses'.

Louis

P.S. Dear M.A.,

Louis has dealt with the most essential points and I have little to add save a few 'technical' clarifications which you might find useful.

(1) With 'intermediaries', the important thing to understand is that it is a question of a 'communitary' *system* of expedients (in both the economic and ideological sense). Because of this, you cannot attack the system frontally, as it *appears*; you must above all understand it in terms of its *objective necessity*. For example, it is this system which staves off the complete social disintegration of the sub-proletariat. Bourdieu has demonstrated that the same phenomenon exists among the Algerian sub-proletariat). I personally am inclined to believe that these intermediaries are the unhappy victims of bourgeois exploitation in exactly the same way as are the women to whom they give jobs. You therefore should not exclude anybody: when the time comes, the situation will have to be explained to these people as well. But as Louis rightly notes, this explanation will have to come from the outside, i.e. from the organized working class (at least in the first stages of activity). Then, too, I wonder if you might not be serving your own interests by meeting two or three of these intermediaries and having them speak of themselves and their real material and economic situation.

(2) On children. Here there is *one* particular question that you could ask, staying within the bounds of the method indicated above: repeating the reasoning of your informant, using if possible the same words; in this 'playback', you ought not to edit anything, but remain absolutely faithful to what the other person has said. The question I refer to has to be introduced at the right moment, and is, '*What kind of future do you want for your children?*' Answers to this question are *always* useful in helping understand both the economic *and* the ideological situation in a broad sense. These answers will also be very helpful for orienting yourself on other issues which will come up later in the discussion. Do not be unduly concerned by lots of contradictory comments: at this level there are always these surface contradictions which more or less obscure real contradictions.

Another suggestion I would make, drawing on my own experience, is to beware of the more *spectacular* phenomena in this type of inquiry. These do not play a dominant role. What I mean is that economic data always serve to obscure a legal-political, and especially an ideological situation which is much more complex than it at first appears. A hypothesis: It might well be the case for the sub-proletariat (as well as for small-holding peasants) that their ideology is the (principal) obstacle to a better understanding by them of the real causes of the exploitation they are subjected to. In other words, we have to ask if it is not the ideology to which they are constantly exposed (and which they 'spontaneously' reproduce) which prevents them from achieving a more adequate class consciousness. If this is so, as is highly probable, then you have to keep in mind that the ideology itself is made up of *contradictory elements* – and this is why responses to the question about the kind of future desired (or fantasized) for their children are so interesting. In general – with the proviso that they must then be related to the real social conditions of existence – the answers to this question provide facts which permit you to analyse and interpret with precision the antagonistic elements in their ideology, the place these contradictions occupy, and their origins (to what do they refer, etc.).

All of these methods are not only methods of sociological knowledge (understood in the sense of a 'science' divorced from practice), but principles of *political knowledge* (cf. Marx, Lenin, Mao) which are indispensable for creating and developing a fruitful political activity.

As far as your repetition of what your interlocutor has just said is concerned, it is better not to underline the contradictions when they are there (and they are always there), but instead try to see how *the simple fact of your repetition opens up*, for the other person, an area of reflection – whose results will only emerge later. You must leave him the time to think over the problems you have raised, starting precisely from his own words and own line of argument.

H.

Dear Louis,   *Naples, Sunday, 21 April 1968*

I write on the run between one speech and the other. On Sundays, taking advantage of the day off, we make two speeches. It upsets me to have so little time, and to practically have to gasp for breath; writing is a tremendously exhausting enterprise for me at this point, since the only way I can do it is to give up some sleep. I would like to use much more precise language and imagery, I would like to think things over more completely and, especially, I would like to be able to pull things together, synthesize, more than I am able to do in these circumstances. But my time is so restricted.

In any event, my only intellectual pleasure in the diabolical and often stupid mechanism of this electoral campaign is to take advantage of the campaign in order to learn. All I can do is *try to understand, to study,* and *to think* about what I see and feel. It is like trying to read the whole of Lenin's works in two months, if that helps you understand the kind of feverish tension in which I am caught up. Your analogy is really very much to the point: I really am like a psychoanalyst, my 'politico-sociological hearing' is that of someone who has an additional sense, an unknown capacity of sight or hearing or brain which does not show up in a cursory physical examination. The comrades in the Party are amazed that I ask the electorate so many questions, that so many things interest me, even those things which appear banal or obvious to them, or that I ask for figures on every conceivable subject, and for information on the most minute aspects of existence. But since they see, oddity of oddities, that this inexhaustible curiosity – rather than making people suspicious or distant – opens them up in an intimate fashion and hence draws us closer, the militants think that it is politically efficacious to follow this method, rather than explain from A to Z why one ought to vote for the P C I.

Not only do I question people with respect, I find myself wholly involved in the interchange, and I identify my role as a militant with their exploited condition. The problem is that I am a little too sensitive, or fragile, I don't know which: I would rather be all brain, all cool logic, but sometimes, in this 'belly' of Naples, in the dark bowels of twisting streets, I have tears in my eyes instead. This is what happened to me yesterday in one of the alleyways of Politi, a fetid labyrinth of narrow streets where the garbage is piled up in huge pyramids. I met a 'housewife'-worker who sews trousers entirely by hand, for 500 lire a pair; she showed me the neat, precise stitches all in a row, and then, when she tried to thread the needle, I realized that she was half blind. She told me that for twenty-five years – she is now forty – she has wanted a pair of glasses, but she never has been able to get together enough money for them, not being on any social security register nor receiving any sickness benefits, etc. And her work is 100 per cent 'eye work'. It is like forcing a cripple to run hurdles all her life. I tried to thread the needle for her, but I was unable to do it because of the tears in my eyes. She was astonished and I was furious at myself, because by that point I couldn't even talk to her any more. And these things happen to me every day. In the evening, when I return very late, I tell myself I cannot stand such a shocking spectacle of poverty, day after day. I see-saw between the burning humiliation that the people's tragedy inflicts on me, and the desire to flee, to go back to reading and writing, to do something into which I 'fit' more easily. But the next day I begin again. Why? Not to be elected Deputy.

The 'belly' of Naples is like Harlem, and Naples is not New York. You have to go through all of it, street by street, in the dank network of twisting alleys, in the intestines of disconnected lanes which rise suddenly or plunge downward, inside the tenements where men and rats fight for space. You have to walk around the buttressing scaffolds which were originally set up as emergency measures to hold up the sagging buildings, but have become such permanent fixtures that the roving vendors attach their little 'shops' to them: candies, sweets, melon seeds; you have to penetrate the clouds of stench and kerosene which are as much a part of these neighbourhoods as incense is to churches. And you have not only to enter these depths, but to stay there, discussing life's problems, with people broken down from continuous child-bearing, while throngs of incredibly pale children, all eyes, swarm all over you. This is how you learn that the 'belly' exists.

For twenty days, I have lived inside of this, immersed in it. I have gone through the quarters of Stella, Avvocata, Montecalvario, Borgo, Forcella and Pendino. I have been swept up in all the misery and poverty of sub-proletarian life. The stink that comes out of certain sewers stays with me long after I come home, and above all I keep hearing the screams of the women when they announce the stalking of their children by the 'beasts' of this jungle, shouting, '*Le zoccole, le zoccole. . . .*'

In the speeches I make in the streets, the word *zoccole* just will not come out of my mouth, because *zoccola*, in Roman dialect, means 'whore'. So I say *topi* [the standard Italian for 'rats']. But a rat is a rather pleasant animal compared to these vicious rodents that infest Naples, for they are often as big as cats. I might add that I have never seen a cat in the streets, perhaps because the rats eat them. Nor do you see dogs, for the Neapolitans are continuously killing them for fear of rabies.[1] Then a comrade came up to me and asked, 'Excuse me, comrade, what do they call *zoccole* in Rome? Sewer rats?' He was very kind, and he wanted to make me understand that you have to say *zoccole* around here if you want people to know what you are talking about.

Here you have a good example of *linguistic* revulsion. There are other kinds of revulsion as well: I am convinced, for example, after passing hours and hours in the *bassi*, amid that silent host of seven million waiting rats, that I must have some kind of rash on my scalp, and as a result I scratch my head incessantly. These are not petty-bourgeois sensations, but rather, I think, a physical, or at any rate psychosomatic manifestation of the traumas I go through during the day. Naturally, I cannot talk about this with anyone, for any reference to these issues only accentuates my 'foreignness', and furthermore a lot of people in the Federation seem to have become completely accustomed to the idea that the poverty of the populace is ineluctable. This threatens to become simply defeatism and an inability to see these problems as tied to a strategic line centred on the Neapolitan working class; they are seen instead purely as a matter of relief work and the presentation of piece-meal economic demands.

Several leaders of the Federation, and my fellow-candidates, can almost always be found – at least during this election period – at the Town Hall. There they receive pathetic little groups of eviction victims, or women seeking pensions or housing, etc. If no clear strategy

1. See the *Guardian*, 9 March 1968: '208 More Dogs Killed in Naples'.

is connected to its actions soon, the Party really risks becoming some kind of welfare mission. These distortions and tendencies make it almost impossible to push discussions as far as they have to be pushed. The major problem is that there is no real political action being undertaken, and the very idea of a revolutionary perspective has been shoved into the background. The linking of workers and sub-proletarians, the end of this separation which so well serves the interests of capitalism, the clear identification of the working class as the *leading force*, even if not in all cases the *dominant force*, is *the* political problem in Naples. From what I have already written, you have already singled out, lucidly, this number one political-theoretical issue. It is in terms of this issue that I intend to learn as much as possible, contacting the workers in the near future – in order to understand how to start building up an alliance between the workers and the sub-proletarians.

I think that, as a candidate, my approach leaves a lot to be desired in the eyes of certain people, because it is not 'electoralistic' or spectacular enough. I also am aware that I do not have the support of those groups in the sections who constitute a *small bureaucracy* in themselves and, depending on the relationship of forces, deal with the functionaries of the Federation. They too are clearly 'divided' about me, and this presages some tough battles for me in the future.

I have become aware that at times some pretty paradoxical situations arise: the rank-and-file members are often engaged in polemics with the section leaders; the leaders of the sections with the City Committee and the Federation; and the Federation leadership with the 'Centre' in Rome. With lesser or greater doses of Machiavellianism, there is always a wide-open political contest going on based on a sort of *do ut des*. No matter which level of the Party you look at, it is the same. There are numerous internal squabbles, especially among those who, at every level, fear being *shunted aside*. Hence if the internal 'democratic replacement' of personnel is not possible, it gives rise to great tensions and profound dissension. One of the reasons why the predictions for the PCI in this election are so uniformly bleak is the number of changes in our electoral list – partly as a result of some Federation leaders having recognized the need for a change. But many interpret the disappearance of the old veterans and the arrival of new candidates as an electoral catastrophe. I contribute more than a normal share to these disruptive forces, for I am a profane outsider twice over: as a candidate, and as a woman.

But the idea of becoming a 'leak' in the Party's airtight electoral structure makes me extremely uncomfortable. For this reason I try to do more than I am capable of, preparing my speeches as if I were going to address the whole country, trying to write articles on Naples for *l'Unità* with every ounce of journalistic skill and training that I have acquired, in other words giving what is usually called 'of my best'. Then too, I often have the feeling that all these goings on that the others use to terrorize me are nothing but internal squabbles, and that the masses don't really give a damn about any of them, for the masses are infinitely ahead of us and care about the concrete, the real, and actual possibilities for moving ahead; they examine and judge us in the most political way imaginable: they judge our capabilities and our combative spirit as a Party, not these squabbles.

Thinking back over this first stage of agonizing personal contacts, I have to say that I have been received best by the *older comrades* (but not those who have reached the topmost positions) and by the younger generation – both inside the Party and outside it. This, anyway, is my impression. The older comrades receive me naturally, and the younger ones are inquiring and friendly. For the older working-class comrades – from the OMF and Ilva metalworking factories[2] with whom I was involved in struggles back in 1948 – my 'return' as an adult who has lived within and in contact with other situations is like having a child return home after completing his studies. Comrade Gennaro Rippa, all white and thin and transparent as a wafer, the symbol of a whole era of workers' battles, embraced me – this is rare at Naples – with great tenderness. It was the first sincere human relationship I have encountered since arriving. I asked him if we could work together a bit, but he explained that he has had two operations on his stomach and isn't the man he used to be any more. But he did suggest a lot of things I could do. The others are just like him, and every now and then I run across them working in the sections; for example in the section in Miano I saw Vincenzo Riccio, who used to be a worker in the Ilva plant in Bagnoli. These are all really marvellous people, a

2. The metalworking segment of the Italian working class (*metalmeccanici*) can literally be translated as 'metalworkers', but in fact extends far beyond what an English-speaking public would understand as metalworking. In Italy, this definition extends not only to iron- and steel-workers and skilled tool and die makers, but, for example, to automobile workers as well. This group has been, historically, the most combative part of the Italian proletariat. (Trans.)

mixture of generosity, proletarian morality, objectivity and unshakable attachment to the Party. Their advice is always useful.

Then there are the young Communists, who want to talk to me only about my articles, those on Ben Bella from Algeria and above all those I wrote from France – including the interview with you, which was my last piece from Paris. The youths I meet here in Naples, in the Federation, or in the sections on the periphery of the city, seem to be interested by the 'new politics' which I represent, not only on account of having read what I have written over the years, but also because a woman like me represents in herself the reverse, the opposite of the Catholic-petty-bourgeois-conformist tradition which dominates the South. I also think this interest relates to my writing about great issues of foreign policy and world politics, towards which the young people are really turning for the first time with so much political force and internationalism. And it also relates to my 'being a woman' but 'speaking like a man', which accentuates the breakdown of the old scheme of the subordinated woman; the younger generation does not accept these traditional roles. Finally, I think this interest grows out of their disgust with electoralism, petty arguments over the composition of the lists, and so on. 'The young listen to you,' one comrade said to me. Another comrade, our list's most prominent figure, said rather dryly: 'I hear that at T., after your speech, the Marxist-Leninist Youth decided not to hold their meeting.'[3] Yet another comrade, one getting on in years, told me that I simply *had* to speak to the youth. 'A woman leaves an unforgettable impression,' he said, and went on, 'I will always remember an Egyptian woman whom I used to run off to see when I was young. . . .' This story of the *Egyptian* woman, from what I can make of it, means that she possessed some magic, surrealistic powers and gave the impression of other worlds, other horizons, encouraging fantasy, imagination, and so on. Apparently, our comrade thinks of me as another Egyptian woman.

Thanks in large measure to the reactions of the young comrades, the word has also got around that I *know how to make a speech*. But the Party Establishment – even if they are beginning to learn that they have not had some completely worthless baggage dumped in their laps – are still against my candidacy.

3. Most Italian Maoist groups call themselves 'Marxist-Leninist'. The 'prominent figure' referred to is Giorgio Amendola. (Trans.)

But even if, as a 'candidate', my campaign is not going so well, as a militant I am very conscious of being here, in this objective historical situation, in a sort of enormous political laboratory which allows me to perform every type of experiment, every serious exercise of my political knowledge in relation to reality. And I am becoming aware, first of all, that a good part of the people's *reality* is different from what we politicians imagine it to be: there are those 'silences' to interpret – of which you spoke – and the 'reservations', and it is necessary to discover the 'secrets' that dominate the life of the people, that determine their attitudes.

And it is true that it is neither ignorance nor irrationality which determines events which seem so upsetting to us. Since your letter, I have again taken up my investigation in a new way, on the question of child-bearing and the Pill, a question which, in such a superficial way, I thought I had found the answer to. I began, delicately, to question the women regarding the reasons for having such a flood of off-spring. These are the basic motives: family allowances and other subsidies of various types which go to larger families; child labour which, from the age of eight or nine on, becomes one of the pillars of support for the family; and, finally, the myth of the man's 'virility', which makes his power and potency known to the entire neighbourhood through the number of children he sires.

In the streets of Politi, I find a woman named Antonietta Di Mauro sitting on the steps of the doorway to her building like a brooding-hen, with six children swarming around her, one at her breast, one between her feet, one on her back, and so on, all of them small, from a few months to ten years old. She tells me that she is thirty-five and has nine children. I ask her where the other three are. She answers readily, 'They go to school in the mornings and they work in the afternoon.' Where, I ask, do they work? 'The oldest,' she says, 'is ten and works as a shoemaker. He makes 1,500 lire a week. The second is nine and works as a shoemaker's helper: he gets another 1,500 a week. The third, eight years old, works for a wine shop and gets 500 lire a week.' So the mother manages to have an extra 15,000 lire a month coming in from these three children. Her husband, who is a cobbler, earns another 60,000. What with the family allowances and their work, the kids actually 'bring home' more money than their father (I will go into the whole business of the allowances later). So it is clear why, as soon as they 'grow up', i.e. reach the age of eight or nine, the kids become so important.

With the mother's permission, I go to see little Luigino, who works for the shoemaker a few dozen yards away from the *basso* where he lives. Luigino looks more like a six-year-old than a ten-year-old. He is very short and quite frail. He puts shoes into boxes, with a very serious expression on his face, and like a 'little old man' he doesn't lift his eyes from his work. When he has filled ten boxes, he takes a flashlight and, balancing everything on his spindly arms, he carries the shoes up into an attic. Antonietta Di Mauro looks on with the fierce pride of a lioness, but she says nothing. She does not even greet him, for, after all, *work is work*. Luigino is a *worker* who brings home 1,500 lire a week. The boss is a comrade, a member of the P C I – and here Hélène is really right when she says that the 'intermediaries' are also victims of exploitation – and he tells me, denouncing Luigino's mother, that 'what she does wrong is to send the kids to work instead of to school'. I answer that she told me they go to school in the mornings. 'That isn't true,' the comrade responds, 'she lies. In order to get by around here, mothers take their kids out of school when they are eight or nine, and send them to work.' Antonietta is there all the while we are discussing this, and she doesn't say anything. Her eyes are all afraid and evasive. Is this a criticism? But she loves her children! What do they want from her? She would like to snap back that these are the family laws which govern the lives of the sub-proletariat. Instead, she says nothing, all the more because she is right in front of the 'employer' of her son. The family as a patriarchal, consumer-oriented cell is brutal, for there is increasingly a completely commercialized relationship between its members, and especially between mothers and their children.

I follow along with Antonietta, and we arrive at her house. Now that we are confidantes, and I have been with her to see *her children on their jobs*, I ask her 'if she doesn't feel the burden of having put so many children into the world'. I cannot tell whether she is sincere or not when she answers. 'I didn't want to, I don't like the idea. But it is my husband who wanted it like this. "What dost thou want, O husband of mine?" . . .' and she gives a mysterious smile as if indicating some amorous Hercules that she, alone, possesses in this quarter.

The comrades who accompany me around their home territory of Vico Politi – one is called Assuntina Pochet (a French name), another 'Pupetta', and the third Bianca Rosa (nicknamed 'la rossa', 'the Red') – explain to me in greater detail about masculine 'virility'. What they say, more or less, is this: the proletariat has nothing, it is dirt-poor. No one drinks (because at Naples hardly anyone ever drinks alcohol, only coffee or lemonade), or gambles (except for a few hundred lire in the lottery): the only really happy pastime is the conjugal bed. 'We don't have anything' – that is what the father of twelve children told G., from the Federal Secretariat, 'the only thing I can do is *go to bed with my wife*'. Around here, what they say of someone with ten children is 'poor guy', but in an affectionate, almost envious way, the way you would talk about an unrepentant womanizer in Paris.

A study which appeared in June 1967, in the magazine *The Home* (put out by certain Catholic groups), records – and this is the only treatment of the problem I have been able to find, by the way – the following dialogue between an unemployed bricklayer and his wife, expecting their sixth child. They live in one of the huts of the ARAR Camp,[4] and the years of their children's births are 1959–60–63–65–66. While he was going on and on about their poverty, his wife interrupted. 'It is because you have too many children.' She argued that it wasn't right to have so many children, it did not leave her with a minute of time to herself. He didn't take issue with that complaint at all, but said that having so many children was a direct consequence of being poor: 'Why don't all the big shots have so many children? I'll tell you why – it's because they have mistresses; thanks to that, when they come home they aren't in the mood so much. . . .'

So in other words, it is a question not only of proving your virility, but it also is a question of regaining your freedom, through Eros, in bed. The only trouble with this reconquest of one's freedom is that the woman is the first victim, obviously. And from this arises the necessity for the other myth; namely that a woman loved or desired by her husband has to be one who reproduces like a rabbit. On account of this, I learned that you can never ask a woman, unless you want a suspicious or hostile answer, 'But why do you have so many children?' It would be like saying, 'But why do you make yourself so loved?' or 'Why does your husband find you so attractive?', or something to that effect. The whole subject is an extremely delicate one not only for the men – who, subjecting their wives to these assembly-line pregnancies, assert their *inalienable rights as Latin men* – but for the women, too, who, in this highly visible way, maintain their hold on their men. An

4. *Azienda Rilievo e Alienazione Residuati*, the distribution and sales outlet for army surplus in Italy. (Trans.)

old woman, Assuntina Pochet's mother, said to me, noting my pre-occupation, 'Today, the younger generation has changed everything. They want three or four children and that's it. They have a completely different attitude. . . .' And I realized that she said this with an atavistic disapproval of this *amorous decline*, in terms of the secular canon that regulates relations between men and women.

The connection between these two elements – economic and erotic – is incredibly complex. But one thing is certain, and that is that it is not due to ignorance that these children keep coming along. The people here know exactly what they're doing, and what they want to do. And for me, *this is the lesson*. And to think that I saw it all in terms of the Pill!

I continue speaking on the same subject with my three comrades as we move on through the back streets of Politi, where they have lived all their lives. (If they ever put together a Poor People's International, its headquarters should be here.) They are warm, open, intelligent women. They have come along to 'protect me', and to take me into *bassi* where I can meet comrades or sympathizers. We move along together through the steep Montecalvario quarter, stopping at various places. They *really want* me to get elected, and they want it in a much more political way than the men do. They speak to me about woman's condition, her inferior position, and the battles which have to be fought to correct these injustices.

They also had an electoral brainwave. As I have written, every candidate has a designated number on the list. In all, there are thirty-five or thirty-eight of us, I can't remember which, in alphabetical order. Those in the list who get the most personal preference votes – i.e. that the electorate has indicated on its ballots, either by name *or* by number, after voting for the Party's symbol – get elected. And the number, for someone at Naples who doesn't know how to write, is everything. Down here, numbers all have meanings, and they often are assigned magical, cabalistic, or interpretive powers by the people. One's dreams play a big role in this, as can be seen with the lottery; when people see certain images or receive certain impressions in their dreams, they try, on waking, to find the appropriate number which will reproduce or best approximate the dream-impression. Well, my number on the list is 25. Assuntina Pochet screamed it like 'Eureka!' when she found out: 'Christmas Day! The comrade is Christmas, remember everyone: twenty-five, Holy Christmas, Antonietta Macci-occhi.' Later on she said to me, 'A beautiful number to have. It is so easy to remember!' So now, when they go with me round the *bassi* on my daily pilgrimage, they always say at the end, 'Twenty-five, remember everyone, that the comrade is twenty-five. *Christmas!* Write "25" on the ballot', etc. I start feeling like a Christmas tree, complete with lights, tinsel, and silvered garlands.

But let's come back to the prolific child-bearing. My companions explain to me, in private tones, that a mother receives a family allowance of 6,000 lire a month. They are very self-conscious and somewhat embarrassed, these comrades, to be giving me the crude economic terms of the whole business. But finally they do speak sincerely. When a woman has her sixth child, she goes to the Town Hall and registers her family as a 'large family'. This provides certain modest public benefits, which are: exemption from the sanitation tax (10,000 lire a year); payments from the ECA;[5] free nurseries (although these hardly exist) and primary school, including textbooks; and, finally, the husband is put on a priority list for new jobs and new housing (but who doesn't have six children?). The people try to resolve the family's financial problems by creating, in spite of the number of mouths already at the table, a fixed income based on sheer numbers, made up of the allowances and welfare benefits accruing to a large family. These are of course laughable sums, but among the disinherited poor, they suffice to provide a 'minimum wage'. Clearly, these abundant offspring provide the basic salary.

Then I ask, 'What about more than six children?' Here, things get even more complicated. There is on the one hand the whole thing about male potency, and there is also the income scale of sorts which the mother, through calculation and experience, puts together. According to this, the first child, when he is ten, is destined to become a 'worker' who, besides giving her the right to 6,000 lire a month from the family allowance (this continues until the child is eighteen, unless he moves away from home), is also someone who, with the extra 1,500 lire a week that he brings home, helps her to support the smaller children. In fact, it is the mother herself who goes to the child's employer to pick up his daily or weekly 'money' and who figures out what he has earned, because he is 'too small', Of course, the smaller the children are, the less productive they are.

But this is not all. If, in this genealogical tree, the father should happen to die, it is the collapse of the whole elaborate castle of family

5. *Ente Comunale Assistenza*, the municipal welfare department.

finance that the mother has constructed. In Politi, I met Giuseppina Romano, a woman wasting away like a fast-burning candle: she is thirty-four and the mother of ten children, and her husband, who worked off and on for the city as a street-sweeper, had just died of cancer at thirty-six. When the man, the socio-moral fulcrum of the family, disappears, then the pyramid of familial economic relations and obligations simply caves in. This occurs because the woman no longer has the primary justification for doing all this: the man, the 'head of the family', the charismatic representative of the family in the neighbourhood. I speak for a while with this poor woman, and then all of a sudden she asks me, 'Ma'am, could I give you two or three *small* babies?' As if she were asking me to take the smallest arrivals from a pet's latest litter. She explains that her oldest child is sixteen and her youngest is four months old. She has already given the youngest one away – something she would never do if her husband were alive – to a childless couple. 'They put such a nice bonnet on his head,' she says tenderly, 'he looks like a little rose.' But she wants to 'give me' the two-, three- and four-year-olds. She persists: could you take them from me? Or could you *get them put in some institution for me?* The older women who crowd around her provide a supporting chorus, nodding, making understanding noises: if the man dies, the mother, without any shame or embarrassment, can give up her children. For when the man dies, the Neapolitan Family, with all its secret laws and taboos, no longer exists. With the disappearance of the man, the family itself disappears as a collective social organism.

Children are a workforce, plain and simple. In Vico III, Politi, I come upon a strange family firm which operates primarily on the labour of kids of eight, ten, and twelve years of age. It is a shoe shop. The children are beautiful, with bright, sad eyes. The older cobblers hammer away, nailing the uppers to the soles, and the little ones put the shoes into boxes. In this case they are all either the children or the nephews of the 'boss'. So you can see that the fathers and cousins have a 'home-made' labour force, all these miniature workers conceived, raised and trained in the job in order to replace grown-up workers. None of these children goes to school any more, and they usually have only attended for one or at most three years in all. The father, Vincenzo Blelé, who is a Communist – and has a big portrait of Kennedy on the wall – tells me: 'I'm a poor devil, but at least I have taken care of my kids and found them work. Years ago I found myself faced with a simple choice: I could starve to death, or else I could get them work which would enable *all of us* to survive, *them and us.* And, also, *it is not true* that school doesn't cost anything. My cousin figured it out: to send a child to secondary school costs 200,000 lire a year. Where could we find 200,000 lire a year?'

Maria Antonietta

Dear Louis,   *Naples, Monday, 22 April 1968*

The whole intricate web of the family economy was still in my mind yesterday when I stopped writing long enough to go and give a speech in the outer 'banlieu' of Naples, at a small place called Licignano. It is a dormitory town: the workers come to work in Naples, and it is only now that a few small artisan enterprises are beginning to appear.

The women are all sitting outside in the street, among constellations of children. I ask permission and then sit down among them on a wooden bench. They welcome me warmly and we begin to talk. Their first question is whether I am married, and I say yes. They respond that they all thought I was single, and then ask me if I have any children. 'Yes, a twenty-one-year-old daughter,' I reply. There is a great commotion and surprise, and they repeat that I 'look like a girl, so young and all'. One of them mentions, as if recalling some forgotten truth, that 'to have all this worry of children really wears women out'. They then turn to me and ask whether I didn't want any more children, or is it that *they just didn't come*? I don't know what to say, but they take my evident embarrassment for an answer. And they look at me a bit inquisitively, also a bit sympathetically, for they think that perhaps in my life there has not been a real lover, a real man. But they are very delicate about the whole affair and do not ask any more questions along these lines. . . .

Among these women I find one who seems to me to summarize, symbolically, all the questions I am trying to understand. Her name is Jole, she is thirty-four years old, and has nine children, the youngest of which is only five months old. The baby is there in her mother's arms, dressed in a few strips of rags, but they are white, as if for a celebration. Her husband is, in her words, an *ammazzapolli* – he kills chickens and brings them to the butcher – and this 'trade' earns him 12,800 lire a week. 51,200 lire a month. I calculate rapidly: with nine children she gets 54,000 lire a month in family assistance. So the net income from the family allowances is equal to the husband's weekly take-home pay in the finances of this particular household. And now, *he* is unemployed. So the only fixed income is the one she has provided by having put nine children into the world. This has been her 'assembly-line' work. And this is still her work, now, as she raises the children.

I now realize that the maintenance for a poor child must cost less than 200 lire a day, and that the parents live on whatever is left over. Still, the women, even when questioned in the most gentle and indirect way possible, continue to say that they have so many children 'because they keep coming', or 'because God wills it', or 'because this is what my husband wants', and so on. So, whether for reasons of sheer self-delusion or out of respect for a *morality* from which they don't want to deviate, they never speak of family allowances or the work done by the older children, etc. And I have managed, for the first time, I think, to enter into the tremendous labyrinth of the economy and the psychology of the Neapolitan woman, which is at the root of this whole situation.

I, too, am now convinced that the Pill is basically a petty-bourgeois problem. Here, the problem is work, work, work – real, regular, and predictable – and this is what would change the sub-proletariat into a proletariat.

I returned to the hotel very late, one or two in the morning. In the elevator, which only takes three minutes to climb to the twenty-ninth floor, there was a little lift-boy, with his cap on backward, at most thirteen years old. We were alone in the elevator and he, getting up his courage, said, 'Ma'am, you gave a great speech at Casoria.' I was stupefied. 'How do you know about it?' I asked. 'You mean you didn't see me?' he replied. 'I was right up there behind you on the stage. And everyone liked what you had to say.' He went on asking me how I could possibly have missed him. There in the elevator, we were both adults. He is thirteen and makes 20,000 lire a month. He knows thirty-five French and thirty-five English words in order to cope with foreign tourists. He is a Communist, who stands on the platform at Party meetings. But, above all, he is an *adult* because, with a real salary, he represents the economic base and the hope of his whole family in Casoria.

This, too, is another of the images which stay locked inside me, which move me, hurt me, and keep me from sleeping. As I left the elevator, I shook his hand, as if he were a man, and at the same time I couldn't help noticing that little cap, worn backwards, accentuating his child's face. And those eyes of his which dream some unknown child's reverie, of games or sports or, even, of school. Whatever there is in me that is human – and maternal – suddenly came charging to the surface so quickly that I practically had to run away to avoid embracing him. That would only have upset him. Because he is *a man*, a worker with a fixed salary in one of Naples' most luxurious hotels, and he already has found a place in the political struggle: he goes to listen to speeches when he is off from work.

Maria Antonietta

Dear Louis,   *Naples, 22 April 1968*

Meetings don't amount to much. People go to them for a thousand reasons, including that they simply cannot think of anything else to do with themselves at that moment. I have plumbed my imagination, trying to be inventive and come up with a new form of electoral propaganda, a type of speech which reverses the traditional flow of verbiage, having 'the people, inside and outside the Party' speak before we do so it is *they*, for a change, who raise the questions to be discussed. And I have now done this in the main squares, not just in little back-street courtyards like the one near the Borgo section.

My itinerary yesterday was like the stops on the slowest local train you can imagine, one after the other in the quarter of Montecalvario, which is just behind the Via Roma – which to Naples is what the *grands boulevards* are to Paris: Sant' Antonio ai Monti, Piazzetta San Sepolcro, Gradoni di Santa Maria Apparenti, Via Cariati, Via Spreanzella. Montecalvario's socio-economic profile is the following, drawn from official statistics: 107,600 inhabitants, of whom 11,845 are officially listed as housewives, 1,912 as artisans, and 772 as students.

The population density is 563.06 people per hectare. An indication of the poverty of the area is that 1,607 families are down on the poverty register.

The quarter disintegrates a little more each day, from old age or never-repaired war wounds, and the buildings which are officially designated as unsafe number 990, which means that there are just over twenty-two crumbling structures per hectare. There is only one hospital in the entire area. Even with the overcrowded standards considered 'average', there is officially a shortage of sixteen nursery schoolrooms, eighty-five primary schoolrooms and 184 secondary schoolrooms.

With three comrades from the 'Centre' section, I left to explore this self-contained universe. One of the comrades, Anna Bocchetto, is the section secretary and, given her sex, this fact is not merely rare: it is unique. We set off in a van rigged out with loud-speakers, and a hand-microphone with a long lead which allows you to take advantage of any place suitable for an impromptu speech – a rise in the ground, a step, an open space, etc. So, with 'Bandiera Rossa' blaring out of the speakers, we wove our way through the twisting, clogged streets, passing through the midst of which is almost as trying a test of driving skill as are the twenty-four hours of Le Mans.

Sant' Antonio ai Monti is high up, with flight after symmetrical flight of steps pursuing each other down the slope in front of it. Right at the top there is a fine open space where we parked the van. We found ourselves immediately surrounded by hundreds of ecstatic children, who promptly sat down, legs crossed Indian-style, all around the vehicle, as they waited for the show to begin. Aside from them, however, there was no one else around. Their mothers, as usual, looked out from their windows, weighing the situation carefully before deciding whether it merited a trip downstairs.

At this moment I go back inside and take out the microphone and begin to invite them to the meeting – all the while trying as hard as I can not to seem like a circus barker. 'We have come here to let you speak up. So come on down and give us your point of view, tell us about your problems.' Even as I pronounce it, I realize that the word 'problems' – constantly on my lips – is meaningless here in Naples. You have to say 'your situation' or 'your affairs' and so I belatedly switch terminology. I ask, I insist, I invite, trying every kind of cajolery my fantasy can bring up. Finally, as the three comrades steal looks at me, thinking, 'Now who can say what will come of this?' some people begin to walk towards us: a woman, a girl, then an old man, and finally a small group has formed over on the left, where they are isolated somewhat by a slight rise which maintains a certain distance between us. Now a lot of heads are peering out over balconies to see what is going on.

I get out of the van clutching the microphone in my fist like a holy-water sprinkler and, advancing towards a woman, I ask her if she wants to speak. I ask her name. It is the simplest possible question you can ask anyone. 'Filomena Niola,' she answers. Her voice, her first and last names, spread out like a sonorous wave first over her, then over the entire street. This is the new fact: 'You, Filomena Niola . . .,' as they say in solemn declarations. She is speechless at this magic, at her familiar name which now echoes around her as if she were a celebrity. I keep it up, though I am positive that I am more panicky than she and, having decided to push things farther, I ask her what she does. 'I'm a domestic. I get 40,000 lire a month, I have seven children, and I have to lay out 8,000 lire for our place. . . .' I suddenly see that the simplest, most direct questions are the ones which find an instinctive response, an echo; they work, while the more complex questions just float out into the air. 'What about your husband?' I ask. 'He is out of work,' she says, already in a flowing tone as if she were speaking to herself, 'he is looking for a job, anything. I have to look after our seven children, and they are in the streets the whole time I am gone, from morning to night. . . . No, I have no insurance stamps, nor a pension, nor any sickness benefits . . . they treat us like dogs.' *Like dogs!* her voice echoes from step to step in the street, it reverberates off the walls and plunges out into the heart of Naples. Now everyone is starting to come out into the street, wanting to know what is going on. What is happening is that, 'Filomena, she's giving the speech!' In terms of time, it is not a long experience, for her; yet it is highly effective, because it represents a new form of struggle, her against society, and she is aligned against society as a single individual more deeply than she ever could have realized before now. Her courage, or her strength, comes to her from 'contesting' life in the quarter, from the painful burden of all her children. In fact, what she says is, 'I am like the Madonna of the Seven Pains'. I tell her to go on, asking whether it has always been like this, or whether she has ever been happy. *'No, it has always been like this; we are all in the same boat.'* With this, she wheels on the others, as if enraged, and says, 'Hey, come on, speak up for yourselves, or maybe you are better off, eh? Maybe you're all princesses . . . what's the matter with you?'

Only the silence of the street greets this challenge. Even the children stop their yelling, pinching, and poking and stare open-mouthed at Filomena, as if she were some strange creature, and all this because she had 'said her piece'.

Now, on my right, I see a young man with a very intent look on his face, inching forward. 'Do you want to say something, comrade?' I ask, and I give him the microphone. He doesn't seem at all nervous, and it turns out that I was right in calling him 'comrade'. But for him, too, this is a new experience, here in the street: he is speaking as a worker to the sub-proletariat, now that Filomena has broken the ice and has brought the 'problems' out into the open. 'I'm a construction worker,' he begins, 'and my name is Salvatore Vampone. I bring home 12,500 lire a week, and I'm the only one who is working now because the ceramic factory where my wife works fired her as soon as she was expecting our first baby. . . . They said that women with children don't produce anything. . . . I pay 20,000 lire a month for our flat,' and he indicates a few floors up where a sheet is hanging from a pole. It really *is* a flat, not one of those one-room, windowless *bassi*, but it eats up one-third of his salary. 'I vote for the Communists,' the worker continues, and as he says this it is as if he were freeing himself from his loneliness, or from his *exclusion* from the sub-proletarian world that surrounds him. He ends up by calling for a PCI victory, because it is the only party that can 'change things'.

In a window covered with what at first seems like dust but which, looking more closely, turns out to be thousands of fly droppings, some stockings are hanging, 'for sale'. When the women aren't artisans or domestics, they 'sell' a little of everything, whatever they have been able to get for fifteen or twenty lire less than usual and can sell to the others. Hence, in the tangled streets of the quarters there are thousands of little unauthorized shops and resale businesses run by the women, and thousands of 'door-to-door saleswomen', who live off the others, off the proletariat of the neighbourhood, in a curious blend of house and 'business'. A woman's head pokes out of an opening which is half door and half window; above the stockings the picture of a typical 'notable' is stuck up: the son of the ex-'King' of Naples, Gioacchino Lauro.

The electoral campaign is confirming for me that the women of Naples always work and are the keystone of the family economic structure. The 11,845 'housewives' of Montecalvario are really 11,845 workers without any rights. No one has ever really studied the problem, either in the past or today. In all the travel diaries of the great foreigners who visited Southern Italy, from Goethe to Dumas, it is hard to find even a passing reference to women's work. There is a whole literature from the mid-1700's which discusses the *lazzari*, and no traveller's book ignores this topic, which is usually dealt with in a light or amused tone. It is almost like the review of a theatre critic who is pleased to find such a vast *population of actors*, a gigantic, living, human theatre.

Stendhal, in his *Diary* (1811), is somewhat more sensitive and understanding with regard to the tragedy of these common people, and he even takes issue with the great Montesquieu over what meaning to give to the existence of the *lazzari*.

'The lowest class of people at Naples is well known in all Europe by the name *lazzaroni*. The word is derived from Lazarus in the Bible, and was applied to them because of their nakedness. They live in the streets and on the edge of the Bay. They can particularly be found near the marketplace, where they carry out the lowest kinds of tasks for everyone else. Everything they own amounts to a shirt and a pair of cloth trousers, and when they have neither house nor bed, they sleep beneath the benches on the edge of the streets. They eat macaroni, fish or vegetables in the streets, and they have nothing and do not wish to acquire anything. Their tasks provide them with the barest necessities, and in this way they calmly live out their lives. They once gave Montesquieu the opportunity to say a truly stupid thing. . . .' Stendhal alludes here to Montesquieu's comment about 'the *lazzari* who quake with fear when Vesuvius erupts. Wretches that they are, what have they to lose?' Montesquieu asked. 'Their lives,' responded Stendhal.

Benedetto Croce – who is the (philosophical) patron saint of the South's intellectuals, and who beams his grace down on the entire Italian intelligentsia – made a brief, scholarly reference to the Neapolitan *lazzaro* in *Aneddoti di varia letteratura* (Volume II, pp. 428–39). It is only thanks to Marx that the *lazzari* of Naples have become, at least for Marxists, the Neapolitan sub-proletariat; i.e. they have acquired a scientific classification, in the larger perspective of a society divided into classes, in the same way that their wives or daughters have also become sub-proletarian women.

If you do not actually live among the people, in the depths of the back streets, it is extremely difficult to become aware of the fact that the women work. This is because feminine labour is so little mentioned that a sort of general *omertà* covers it, or else everyone simply pretends that it is a natural part of the family's economic situation. The man, from early in the morning, goes out *looking for work*, but the woman, from early in the morning, is effectively at work. Even when you read the work of the most famous 'Southern specialists' of Italy, from Giustino Fortunato to Dorso, they never even hint at the problems of women. 'Out of 650 pages that Fortunato devotes to the Southern question, you have to read right to the last page,' comments Dominique Fernandez, in *Mère Mediterannée*, 'to find this timid, hesitant proposal: "it would suffice if the women had fewer children"!' I think of all this as the women follow each other up to the microphone, and from everything they say, one overwhelming fact emerges: they are simply underpaid workers.

In this reverse speech, letting the simple folk speak for themselves, you realize three things: (1) that the women are by far the most courageous speakers; (2) that they denounce working conditions that the men do not even mention, and they are actually the ones who discuss their husbands' work; (3) that while what they are doing as they speak is a fleeting experience, it is one which already contains within it, *in kernel form*, a break with existing society.

Near the improvised display-window with the stockings, there is a very young girl who obviously wants to speak but hesitates, afraid. I probe gently and finally her personal history emerges there in the alleyway; 'My name is Rosa De Simone, I'm a part-time domestic, three hours a day, and I make 10,000 lire a month. My husband is a glazier, but the factory at Portici fired him last year, he's been out of work since then and we have to get by on what I bring home, and now I'm pregnant. . . . I don't know how we'll manage. . . . My father died last year', and then she adds, 'he was a Communist.' She starts to cry silently, but the microphone makes the sobs reverberate like pistol shots. The women, for their part, know that all this is true. But, having taken it for granted previously, they also know that they have never really thought about it before: Rosa has been a domestic since she was twelve, she married this worker, then he lost his job, etc.

Unhappiness has been a part of her, like a second skin, since childhood, but it is clear that this Communist father of hers must have helped her face life – which is something that her husband, apparently, has not done.

As time passes more women come out of their houses, and by now there is quite a crowd around the car with the loudspeakers. I have the political task of publicly drawing out secret pains: I am the silence-breaker. For the people, the act of speaking about themselves is already a revolutionary break with their conditions, like lighting a long fuse which leads to the explosion of rebellion. The women say everyday things, at times less precisely than we, perhaps, might be able to, but what is important is that they no longer feel themselves to be *objects*, but rather *subjects*. Speaking, a *question* remains, and it takes shape inside them and outside them as well: 'And then?' This leads to yet another question: 'What can we do?' They get more and more aggressive and set their hands on their hips, in a position of readiness for a brawl with the unknown enemy.

My roving microphone picks up Valentina Parlato: '. . . My husband's an invalid and doesn't work. . . . I live in a *basso* in Via Sant'Antonio ai Monti, number 41, with my seven kids. I pay 7,000 lire a month for that cave – you know,' she says to the others, 'you've seen it. . . . I had to put up a wall to keep the rats out of the place, to keep them from biting my children. But that wall can't keep out anything, and I keep worrying that the rats will get in.'

I take the microphone towards an old man. He is completely white – skin, hair, eyebrows, shirt, everything. He is at his window on the street, looking at all this confusion, and he has heard the women speak. He starts to talk immediately, because by now everyone is waiting for me to come up to them. He speaks rapidly. 'I'm a retired blacksmith. After forty years on the job I get a pension of 20,000 lire . . . and who can live on that? My name is Antonio Tuole, Salita Cacciottoli, number 22. The Government did us pensioners a big favour before the elections, they gave us sixty or seventy more lire a day. They really emptied their pockets! . . . What do I do? I stay home all the time. I have to take care of two spinster sisters, and I pay 7,000 lire a month for the *basso*.' Behind him I see two heaps of rags, one on each side of the room. That something is alive in the rags becomes clear from hand movements and a whisper now and then. The sisters must be very old by now: spinsters for half a century waiting for a husband (the blacksmith probably cursed this fact throughout his whole life), and now the old man had to provide for them, too.

Only after the others who wish to have said their piece, do I take up the microphone, to summarize and conclude. I pick up the main points of everyone who has spoken before me, and I use these as a take-off point to speak of a concrete electoral programme: housing, jobs, social security, pensions, and education, all as seen through the eyes of the citizens, the women of Montecalvario. But I am not happy just to repeat things: I tell them that both men and women can rebel, destroy the existing state of things, and create a socialist society; that the revolutionary path is a long one, but its victory takes shape as one goes farther along the road of radical changes. I realize that this is the only way you can really play a propagandistic role that goes beyond abstractions and platitudes, and that goes beyond the vote-getting phrases of elections.

Now it is over and I am drenched with sweat and barely able to even start to relax after what I have put myself through. But I think, overall, that my shyness and timidity have helped me gain acceptance. 'She's sincere', the women probably felt. This is the right road to follow in the electoral campaign. If we can get the people to make denunciations, in every neighbourhood, then we can get beyond the scepticism and suspicion that propagandists have to face, when the people claim, with justice: 'You have always said good things, but what have you done. . . . You want our vote, but then we never see anything after that' – and we can turn the citizens into political protagonists. I ask myself whether you really can revolutionize electoral propaganda; the answer may well be that you cannot, but this, at least, is *a new way of organizing propaganda*.

I think I have been able to put some of the suggestions in your letter of 2 April to concrete use. If everyone began to denounce the existing state of affairs, if they all began to make themselves, in the first person, into protagonists, it would amount to a first act of refusal to accept this society; from being 'integrated', they would become protestors. If the questions, 'What can be done? and then?' multiply and spread from one back street to the next, then this will mean that new possibilities have opened up, even if they remain far off in the future, and even if it is hard to see exactly what they might be. What is really important is that the feeling of rebellion will have made progress, from the inside, and that the questions will have been asked from below, not posed facilely by leaders of one type or another. In this fashion, people will no longer be objects of propaganda, but subjects of action. The general scepticism towards 'politics', which includes us Communists at times as well, will give way to new forms of political participation, and above all one can begin to glimpse the emergence of a not-yet-clearly-defined characteristic, which is the sub-proletariat's class antagonism to society.

But things do not always go so smoothly. It is damned hard to *get beyond the silences*. The back streets of Naples are thronged, filled, peopled only by those who actually live in them. Hence all you need is to arrive dressed in a certain way, and you immediately become the object of curiosity. They ask you: 'Are you from up North? Are you a foreigner?' But at least the blaring of a loudspeaker and leaflets with a hammer and sickle on them remove enough of the mystery to get some interest generated, for, hearing and seeing this, the people know immediately what you want.

For the common people, 'politics', in the last twenty years, has come to be a derogatory term; it usually means wheeling and dealing, corruption, individual success stories, ambition, and so on. At Vico Cariati, on the corner of Caricatori, I try to approach the women who have come out of the *bassi*, but the political atmosphere is broken by an old, bony woman, not only clearly disenchanted but openly cynical, who asks me, 'What have you brought us? Do you have *pasta* coupons?...' 'No,' I answer, 'this is the PCI's electoral programme, etc.' She steps away and then wheels and turns her back on me in a clear demonstration of profound disinterest. And, at her window, I once again see the chubby face of the head of the Monarchist Party. Every portrait that is glued up and kept up throughout the campaign, with 'Vote Monarchist' printed on it, is good for 2,000 lire and two kilos of pasta.

My speech, in the street, takes on the form of a rebuttal to the old woman's questions; its theme is something like 'what purpose does it serve for the people to sell their votes to the bosses?' At the end, I find someone willing to speak, Giovanni Stuzino's wife, Vera Fanello, and what is so striking and important is that it is *she* who feels moved to say something, more against the old woman than in my defence. 'They buy and sell us as if we were wretches,' she spits out, 'like beggars, they give us a little charity and then we stay hungry for five more years.' In front of her house, she describes the conditions in which she lives: 'My bed is held up by paving stones. And rats come in through the ceiling; Salvatore the bricklayer plugged the hole with lime, but the rats chewed right through again. . . . I pay 7,000 lire a month. . . .'

I continue at a fast pace, with all the equipment, towards the Piazzetta San Sepolcro, but there is only a church and sacristy here. The people's houses are behind and so high up that no one can even hear me. There is only a young man seated against the bottom half of the closed door of the solitary *basso* in the square. I stop and talk with him, and he seems to know everything, he speaks very articulately and sensitively, reads the papers, and knows the electoral programmes. Then he tells me that he has had polio: he is totally paralysed from the waist down, and his sister-in-law and sister drag him from his bed to the doorway, where he stays until dark, every day. He has never had a wheelchair. But he has a friend who is a welder, twenty-four years old, who works in the garage next door, and he bellows out his name. Out comes this friend, filthy and greasy, and he takes a big pile of leaflets. . . . 'Youth is rebelling,' the welder says, 'and all parties, including the Communists, have outlived their usefulness. But it is better to vote for you than not to vote and hence help the Christian Democrats and Socialists.' The other agrees, and he too takes a whole selection of propaganda, saying: 'I stay here like this every day, doing nothing, and when people pass, especially those I know. . . .'

Day after day, in this fashion, in the slums of Naples, I have learned to let the men and women speak for themselves, whether on the street, or in their houses, or in Party sections. We also organize little meetings in the houses of women who have a room where a bed or table can be moved out of the way, or a 'living room' where we can project a film, but this inevitably turns out to be a problem, because the 'technicians' are so clumsy that we always end up sitting in the dark, with all the fuses blown. The 'better off' people offer us coffee, and then we chat. For those present it is like an extraordinary celebration. I learn an enormous quantity of things, and I find myself involved every day in the incredible substance of daily life; for the women, as they tell their stories, mix these in with the more directly political issues. You have to listen to these things, as well, if you want to be concrete, and not abstract.

Take for example the discussion in the apartment of Clementina Inserra, at 21 Vico Lungo Trinità degli Spagnuoli, where a mother – who had been a Christian Democrat activist – tells of having broken definitively with Father Molino of the parish after her son's electric guitar was stolen in the church. The moral seems to be: 'Don't leave your guitar in church'. The mother had bought a guitar for her fifteen-year-old son to play in church, spending 150,000 lire – which seems an immense sum to me. He played quite well, and she no doubt dreamed of a career for him as a pop singer, when the guitar suddenly disappeared. One is led to understand that relations between the mother and priest were violently and suddenly interrupted . . . now the woman has decided to work actively for the PCI. But could we do something to help her retrieve the guitar, to see justice done vis-à-vis the priest? In these meetings, generally, I let others do the speaking, intervening only when it is necessary to re-animate the discussion, and after a bit it is as if they are not even aware of me as an outside presence. They go on and on, talking about everything: illnesses, all kinds of problems, everything.

In the streets, when you hear shouting, when two groups of women square off against one another, one group on the high side, one on the low side as if it were all stage-cast, when they hurl scathing insults at one another which include both present and numerous past generations, the reason for this little 'war' can almost always be traced directly to children. The people begin with the idea that their 'dear little creatures' are sacred, and thus anything that 'a little child' does is an act of innocence and therefore tolerable. This is not, however, an attitude shared by the injured or offended party, who is ready to go into battle against every abuse committed by these innocent 'creatures'. Both Greeks and Trojans agree on at least one thing, and that is that war is for adults. You can stay in the streets, literally for hours, watching mothers screaming at one another, using the most terrifying linguistic constructions, and only at the end, and not always even then, do things actually come to exchanging of blows, a true show of force. In a meeting in someone's parlour, a woman tells me that her child is in the Pausillipon Hospital: a friend severely damaged his optic nerve with a rock. . . . 'He turned his head, and if he hadn't, according to the doctor, he would have lost his eye right there. Now they have to operate.' But then there is another mother – not a victim, but a 'butcher', at least by proxy – who describes how her son walloped another young schoolboy over the head with his briefcase. But there was a bottle of water in the briefcase, for the teacher never lets you get up to get a drink, and when this bottle broke, the boy ended up in the hospital with concussion. Now, like Montagues and Capulets, the two families have narrowed into rival factions, harbouring intense hatred for each other. As you can see, then, when we have these meetings, long before we can get to other issues, we first hear about the typical dominant concerns: *children, husband* and *work*.

There are basically two lists which compete for the women's votes in the poor quarters. These are the Monarchists, with their 'Stars and Crown' list, and of course the Christian Democrats, also known as the 'Priest's List'. The Lauro on the Monarchist list is not the head of the dynasty, Achille, but 'Achille's heel', his son Gioacchino.[1] They say that Gioacchino is as stupid as King Ferdinand IV, who was dubbed 'King Big Nose' by the people. According to Dumas (*Il Corricolo*, p. 113), Ferdinand 'never opened a book in his life, nor did he ever read a memoir, and he forbade in Councils of State – which he had to attend – any inkwells, for fear that he might be asked to write something. . . . There of course was his signature, which he had to write, once a day, at least . . . but King Big Nose invented the stamp to get around this.' Gioacchino's speeches, like performances by Barrault at the Odéon, are unique. He never speaks in the first person, but instead affirms, 'Daddy says . . .' or 'Daddy told me to tell you to vote for me as if you were voting for him. . . .' One day when the microphone failed as he was speaking, he said, with great assurance, 'Call the technocrat'. He meant, of course, the technician.

These Lauros, who took over the Naples sub-proletariat completely from 1952 until around 1960, have always based their fortune on the distribution of money, food, packages of all kinds. A comrade from the Petraio quarter, which is the extremely poor area that links two of Naples' main avenues, the Vomero and Corso Vittorio Emmanuele, told me of a time he found one of the comrades from his section in one of the houses in the area. When the comrade in the house saw all of the others who had come to look for him approach, he was terribly embarrassed and wanted to hide. But his person – amidst the piles of 'Lauro packages' filled with pasta, cheese and tinned food – was doubly incriminating. Finally he asked the others to step outside for a moment, and he then confessed, easing his conscience. 'What could I do? What can I do? Yes, I give out the packages, but I tell everyone to vote for the PCI.' Then he turns to one of the very poor comrades

---

1. Gioacchino Lauro had an economic disaster at the beginning of 1969 (a figure as high as seven thousand million lire is mentioned), and his father had him suspended.

who is part of the group and says, 'You'll see, this time I'll make sure that you get a package.' At the end of this strange encounter, an *ad hoc* agreement was reached: in exceptional circumstances, a Communist can distribute Monarchist packages, but he must do so with the intention of spreading propaganda for our list.

The electoral campaign is to win over the sub-proletariat. Knowing this, and always out to make a little something for themselves, the onset of the campaign must, to them, be like the arrival of ten ships in the Bay of Naples, each crammed full of foreign tourists. They put up the electoral banners, or else they take them down. They letter posters or placards, or else they deface those that others have made; they sew the symbols and writing on to the large banners that go across the streets, or else they cut up the same kind of banners when directed to. In other words, the political season is one when everyone works, feverishly.

For the Party, everything is done for free, almost always. . . . But if you go into a *basso* to ask three or four people if they would help you put up some posters, they will say, without batting an eye or taking a hand from their pockets, 'ten thousand lire'. Then they realize that you are a comrade, and they get up and change their tune: 'Excuse us, we didn't recognize you; for you, of course, it's another story. . . .'

The first time I began to realize just how many ways a chronically unemployed but imaginative person can exploit a campaign was in a square near the station, immediately after my arrival in Naples, when I attended the first important speech in the ward, one of those affairs with a stage constructed for the occasion, lighting brought in, and of course the red flags. I had gone to learn how one gives a speech in the popular areas, for Giorgio Napolitano from the Political Bureau of the PCI and other very well-known people from the Federation were to speak. I listened very carefully, even taking notes on comments which seemed to get applause, thinking all the while of what I would say the very next day. When the speeches were over, as we were stepping down off the platform, a middle-aged man came half-flying up the stairway, and came towards Napolitano with his arms outspread. 'Comrade,' he said, 'you're tremendous. Everything you said is right. . . . I have five kids, a wife, and fifteen brothers and cousins, now all of us are going to vote Communist! . . . We always voted for the DC before! But now it's all over for them. I swear it on the eyes of my children. . . .' And, going on like this, he embraces Napolitano, shakes and squeezes his hand for a long time, shakes hands with the other comrades, all the while in the most indescribably enthusiastic and emotional way. Seeing such a warm response, I begin to re-believe that speeches really can reach people, if they are good, and as it were illuminate their minds, etc.

It turned out, however, that I was the most interested of our group in this scene, for the others seemed to receive and dismiss the man with a kind of rushed distraction. For this reason, I was the only one who bothered to speak with this person who had been *inspired by the word of the speech*, and only I bothered to ask him questions. But he didn't waste much time – having already done what he had to; he sized me up quickly when he heard my 'foreign' accent and asked me for 5,000 lire to get his expired driver's licence renewed. He whipped out the licence, 'It's two years since I have been able to renew it, and without it, I can't work. I really need the 5,000 lire.' I gave him 3,000 lire, all that I had on me, and he asked me to ask some of the others, who were walking several steps ahead of us. I hurried over to them and asked them, after having explained about the licence and the 2,000 lire more which were needed. . . . But they just grabbed me and pulled me away, telling me that I shouldn't give that character any money, for he pulled the same trick on many other speakers, of all parties, with the same driver's licence, always two years old, etc. In other words, he is a 'professional enthusiast'.

It is so important to penetrate the lives of hundreds and hundreds of individuals in this way, to understand how the people really live. I have already said a number of times how, among the people, it is really the women who work most in Naples. What they make is incredibly small, but they manage to drag themselves along on it, making ends meet, somehow. Questioning them one by one, I have learned how they are active in just about every kind of trade imaginable. If anyone ever did a socio-economic breakdown on the work performed by Neapolitan women – and someone should – the results would really be shocking. At Secondigliano, an enormous outlying part of Naples with about 100,000 inhabitants, I made friends with two women, one old and the other young. Here is a description of their work. Stella Esposito is sixty-six years old and goes into the city every day at 6.00 a.m., carrying – don't ask me how – fifty cartons of milk from the Brunelti dairy. She gets ten lire for every carton she sells, by the time you figure in her transportation costs. So she makes

500 lire a day, when she sells her entire load. And for this she is grateful to the people who run the dairy! 'They are doing me such a favour.' It is always the same thing: *work as a favour*. She asks me not to write anything, for the name of the boss-intermediary is a 'secret'.

The younger one, Anna M., works for a firm that makes wedding gowns, and she too gets 500 lire a day, with neither contract nor insurance. Her work is to iron, from morning to night. She doesn't know that ironing is a trade, and says apologetically that 'it is all I know how to do'. The 'firm is really doing me a big favour' only because 'we are friends of the family'.

The same relationship exists between the women who work at home and the intermediaries, and every day I have re-confirmed for me the accuracy of the thesis that both the workers and the intermediaries are exploited. Three girls, in a little street in Politi in Montecalvario, are sewing beige-coloured uppers for women's shoes. They do all sorts of fancy work and the most intricate stitches. Their mother, who watches over them, explains from the doorway that they get 600 lire for every pair of uppers that they complete. This comes out to about eighty lire an hour, for it takes nearly a whole day to do one pair. The sewing machine – *which belongs to them* – cost, 'when we bought it a little while back', 135,000 lire! I ask the mother to whom they give the finished uppers; suspiciously, she answers, 'to relatives'.

Among the people, the women work at all ages, including the very oldest. In Via Vecchia Santa Maria in Vicoli, I see a skeletal woman behind a small counter filled with decomposing sweetmeats and covered with a glass top with every kind of filth imaginable smeared on it. She is a widow, and near her is a little altar complete with lit candle and photo of her late husband. 'I don't believe in anything any more . . .', she says, mumbling. 'But I'll vote for him,' and she nods in the direction of the faded portrait of her husband. In the whole place, there is only one bright, colourful spot, and that is an all-red hen, pecking away at a plate, tied to the woman's chair by a string. She explains that the hen is for her grand-daughter who is about to have a baby. The belief here is that real chicken broth helps women who have just delivered regain their strength more rapidly.

An old spinster glove-sewer with a sister who is married but abandoned by her husband, 'who ran off with his lover', supports her old father, the sister, and some nephews and nieces. The glove-workers are the largest category of those who work in their homes for subsistence wages. Five thousand women and girls work on gloves in Naples.

We calculated, in the Federation, that every year seven million pairs of gloves are exported from Naples, and ten thousand million lire go into the pockets of capitalists who work on an international level, their markets being Paris, Berlin, London and New York, among others.

There is a law, passed in 1958, which defends women who work at home, but it can't really be applied unless the women are first organized in unions. But we have already talked about this: what first has to be confronted, and will always remain a *wall*, is the problem of the small intermediaries, who amount to several thousand more people, whose rights should also be associated with the rights of the home workers, since they too are victims of the capitalist system.

If on the one hand the *neighbourhood economy* is no longer characterized by the objective necessity of the pre-capitalist epoch which prevented total social disintegration, on the other hand the attitude of a lot of comrades who think one should no longer speak of a *subproletariat* is over-hasty and somewhat suspect. They propose instead the ludicrous formula: 'the monopolies have entered the slums', by way of the whole chain of intermediaries which goes all the way up to delivery on the world market of the goods produced by 'housewives' working at home. This is a mistake, if only because the whole network of middlemen – themselves semi-destitute – is conveniently forgotten. Moreover, and this is decisive, if you take at face value the official position that there are only *employed* and *unemployed* workers in Naples, then you have to be silent about the enormous mass of the population, above all about the tens of thousands of women who either work for sub-standard wages or carry out petty services.

It is clear that the political consequences of this mistaken conceptualization are very serious indeed: if you erase all these forces from the socio-economic and political map of Naples, you of course also eliminate, on a 'strategic' level, the fundamental ally of the Neapolitan working class – the sub-proletariat. And then, as is happening already, alliances are increasingly sought among leaders, between parties, or with the 'intellectual strata'. This is, however, a dangerous way to view the class struggle. For if the proletariat needs allies, it must be able to choose them on a class basis, not by means of 'deals' made between leaders.

Maria Antonietta

Dear Louis,   *Naples, 25 April 1968*

If, by chance, you were to come to Naples one day, I have three pieces of advice for you:

(a) Do not bring a car, because at a certain point you would just want to set it on fire to be rid of it: in Naples, there are 500,000 cars registered and, since the traffic moves at an average speed of four miles per hour, people pour 82 million lire a day into the coffers of the monopolies, just for petrol. By some sort of obscure magic, all these cars seem to be together in the streets at the same time, from ten in the morning until ten at night (the certified figure for traffic is, in fact, an average of 290,000 vehicles).

It is just about impossible to estimate how many hours before an office opens or a meeting is scheduled you should leave in order to arrive on time. In fact, the notorious lateness of Neapolitan appointments has roughly doubled since small cars came on to the market . . . by comparison with the performance of horse-drawn trams! The fastest – and indeed, for Naples, a near-supersonic – mode of transportation is the ancient Vomero funicular, and those of Chiaia and of Montesanto. If you walk, and you are thin enough, you can probably squeeze yourself through what is left of pavements which have become mile-long parking lots. And, if you are fairly tall, you can still see, from Via Caracciolo, the Bay of Naples over the roofs of the cars. Another fact: the tens of thousands of cars that fill Naples all blow their horns continuously, in unison, just as church bells all ring out in unison at Easter, and the effect is like being under a dentist's drill. Any attempt to sleep is definitely a losing proposition. If Ulysees' sailors were kept from insanity by putting wax in their ears to block out the Sirens' song – I'm afraid the same remedy here is much less successful.

Public transport is in total crisis, and things are steadily getting worse. About half the population, according to official statistics, no longer take buses or trams because they have bought cars, and those who do dare to board public transport vehicles remain virtual prisoners for hours, because buses in traffic are completely immobilized, surrounded and attacked by the little cars, like rhinoceri by clouds of insects.

Forty per cent of the 5,000 transport workers in Naples – who called a five-day general strike from 4 to 8 April over contract renewals – suffer from 'nervous exhaustion' or 'extreme fatigue' (for they regularly work double shifts). In the single year 1967, they drew sickness benefits for 153,000 workdays lost.

The ways in which the car monopolies have been able to foist cars on even the wretchedly poor Neapolitans – extorting from them their 'earnings' as shoe-shine men, water carriers, *magliari*, street vendors – ought to move people to more profound reflections on the distortions produced by this capitalist-dominated 'consumer society'. It has managed to force its fetishes and idols into the most poverty-stricken *basso*. In the show-window of the largest Fiat dealer in Naples, there is a gigantic portrait of Senator Gava, *capolista* of the D C, the christian Attila of Public Affairs, conqueror on points of the Monarchist ship-owner, Lauro, in the ring of clientelistic production. The *clientela* now plays a mediating role between the centralized power of the monopolies and the interventions of the state bureaucracy for the benefit of Naples' business strata, which are a part of the 'Gavian' system. This bloc of personal power, bloc of party power, and reactionary bloc between northern monopolies and Naples' entrepreneurial ruling class, is magnificently 'concretized' by the great, bovine head of Senator Gava, which, in this election period, grins from the windows of the Fiat showrooms.

Here is another example of the monopolistic implantation of the car industry. Two days ago, on Sunday, I went with Matta the artist (who had come to Naples to hold an exhibition at Federation headquarters), to Pozzuoli, which is just a few kilometres from Naples. It took two hours. Right ahead of us there was a huge bus, and there was only *one* person on it for the entire trip: think of it, this enormous vehicle, with a driver and conductor, was running for this one person, for *fifty lire*. In every '*Cinquecento*',[1] on the other hand, there were five or six people stuffed inside, often on one another's laps. Finally the single passenger got off, and his place was taken by a woman, who paid another fifty lire for her ticket. So the bus between Naples and Pozzuoli collected for its whole trip 100 lire. Matta and I were fascinated by this, for while it clearly was reality, it bordered on the surreal. And, in our car, we faithfully followed the scorned, luckless, abandoned public transport vehicle, isolated ahead of us in the diabolic swarm of thousands of small private cars.

(b) My second bit of advice to you on your hypothetical trip to Naples would be to get hold of the famous report of Matilde Serao, *Il*

1.   Fiat 500. (Trans.)

Ventre di Napoli (The Belly of Naples), which is divided into two parts, the first written after the great outbreak of plague in 1885, when the 'Rehabilitation Law' was passed to combat the devastation of the cholera epidemic; and the second, written in 1904, called *The Screen* (referring to the 'Rehabilitation'). You then will have in your hands the best political Baedeker imaginable – save of course Karl Marx's *Capital*, which is even more indispensable – for understanding the perennial fraud which the ruling class of Naples perpetrates on the proletarians who live in the 'Belly' of the city.

I would like to try to describe to you the trauma that a traveller faces when he moves through the 'Belly' of Naples. I challenge six journalists from the six Common Market countries – just so we have a political entity the European bourgeoisie can recognize as valid – to pass just one week in the viscera of the city. They would end up re-writing, as I am, Serao's *Ventre di Napoli*, which, in 1968, still remains the only reportage which can really state things as they are. With the possible exception of Malaparte's *The Skin*. All you have to do is go behind the *screen*, wrote Matilde Serao, to see the kind of swindle that the 'Rehabilitation' really was, attracting half the construction trusts of Europe in a voracious competition to secure the building contracts. 'Inside these *bassi*, inside these shops, in the depths of these cellars, everything that was there previously remains, but in much worse condition. . . . Old crumbled houses, old dead ends, piles of every kind of filth, everything, everything is just as it was, so dirty as to make you sick. . . . The people have been pushed and shoved behind the 'screen', and they are now jammed together even more than before: where there used to be eight people, now there are twelve; space has diminished and the population has grown. It is a fragile and insulting screen which cannot hide anything from anyone who wants to know what is going on behind it; it is made of a unique substance which lets one see behind the scenes into darkness and filth, where everything is rancid, foul and nauseating.'

You ask me to explain what the *bassi* are: there is a whole body of literature on this topic, given that Naples has never changed its basic structure, which is that of a 'pile of houses', as a German 19th-century poet described it. The *bassi* are a tangle of structures made up each of a single room, or cave. They open on to the ground floor, or, more precisely, the street, with divided wooden doors like stables. Since there are no windows, the doors also serve for ventilation, and for this reason they are almost always partially opened. In the *bassi* – which are house, workroom and shop all in one – space is so restricted that people are born and die there side by side; the toilet, with a flowered curtain around it, is right next to the stove and pans, and the floor is made of paving stones, exactly the same ones you find in the streets. There is only any light in them at night, when the electricity is switched on or, in the case of the poorest people, when a candle is lit.

In order to make living conditions hygienic, the women of the popular quarters work incessantly, transforming the *bassi* with sweat and strain. In these miserable hovels, where daylight is a constant shadow, they continuously wash the paving stones and never stop laundering. This, in fact, is the mysterious explanation for all those mysterious lines of washing strung out across the alleys: it is to guarantee a continuous change of sheets and clothes, given the limited amount that they own. On the basis of statistics calculated in 1967 by some Catholic sociologists, 200,000 people live in some 50,000 *bassi*.

A woman from Barra named Veneruso, who lives on Corso Sirena (!), used these images to express the horror of the *basso*. 'All my life I have wanted to have a window, to open a window with shutters, to look out of a window. . . . At night sometimes I even dream of a window.' Paolo Ricci writes (in *Paternalismo e speculazione nello sventramento di Napoli*) that Garibaldi, upon his arrival in Naples, with his Decree of 18 October 1860, 'provided for a vast construction programme for workers' housing, and for the construction of new streets. . . . But, from Turin, Garibaldi's policies were seen as dangerous and revolutionary, and hence the general's programmes were pushed aside. At the same time, the Lieutenancy was increasingly taking on the characteristics of an oppressive power, almost of a colonial nature, and the whole undertaking of the liberation of the Mezzogiorno became, in fact, in the eyes of its people, an imperial conquest. . . .'

The most relevant answer to the question, 'What are the *bassi*?' is still that of Marino Turchi, a member of the Naples City Council in 1861, when in a Council meeting, he raised the issue of *popular housing*: '. . . they are the abominable habitations of the unfortunate classes of our city. I looked before I wrote, and then I wrote down what I saw. I walked through the most obscure and obscene streets, I visited the dwellings of the poor and of the labourers, and I only wish I had a vocabulary ample and rich enough to describe the horror and the disgust which that view provided. I went into cellars which it would be more precise to call pits of Hell. They were everywhere, but in a narrow area near the port I was able to count twenty-nine of them, where the 1837 cholera epidemic ran unchecked. . . .'

I return to Naples after twenty years. These readings have a big impact on me because the city is as decrepit, noisome and filthy as ever and the 'solutions' are only those of land and building specu-lators, who fatten their profits. This is the super-exploitation of the 'hunger for houses' that Engels talked about over 100 years ago. In the past, everyone relied on help from institutions, philanthropic associations and the 'charitable' intervention of the state. In those days, people spoke of 'rehabilitation'; today they speak of capitalist 'rationalization' for Naples, of state participation and of housing plans.

If the 'screen' of Serao's time was the Rettifilo – hacked out of the area cleared of slums, and today little more than a dirty avenue – the new screen is the curtain of concrete blocks of flats which are going up on the Vomero, Posillipo, the Colli Aminei, and whose bold, prison-like outlines you can see from the train from as far away as Mergellina. The screen is also made up of the rows and rows of re-inforced concrete boxes in areas like Rione, Traiano, Marianella, Barra, and Piscinola, which resemble unmistakably the hovels of the sub-proletariat in the back-streets; for they too bear the mark of social underdevelopment, with the concomitant lack of jobs, infrastructural vacuum, and shortage of streets, means of communication, schools, hospitals, and parks. You get the impression that the steady flow of thousands of millions of lire pumped into the quarters by the specu-lators only serve to continuously resurrect Old Naples in the new quarters. By some monstrous form of reproduction, Naples continues to give birth to quarters which in time will be like those of the 'Belly', since they lack anything which makes it possible for a human com-munity to breathe. The new has the same cankers and boils as the old. And the new ends up being absorbed by the old. The workers – it is no accident that Naples has no workers' quarter such as one finds in Turin or Milan – continue to live in Traiano and Marianella. They are caught up in the dreadful interweaving of factory life with the con-stant sub-proletarian siege they undergo in the quarters where they live, which conditions them both morally and socially. The worker responds to this state of affairs by isolating himself, and his answer is his *silence*. Neapolitans who are out of work try to move their petty hand-to-mouth businesses into the new quarters along with the first household furnishings that arrive; once again they become street vendors, peddlers of black-market cigarettes, shoemakers and water carriers, and the women sell vegetables, candies, seeds, sew trousers or gloves, etc. The backward economic system of the old quarters takes root and spreads, in this fashion, as soon as there are enough inhabitants of the new quarters to provide a likely market.

Yesterday I went to Miano, a new quarter on the periphery of the city, with Nobécourt, the *Le Monde* correspondent. There you find a perfect example of the coexistence of the old and new city. The *old* part of Miano is as rotten as the innermost parts of Naples. But the *new* is, in certain ways, perhaps even more prone to decomposition. The brand-new, box-like apartment buildings are all *closed off entirely at street level*, to prevent the birth of new *bassi*, to 'rationalize' in this way the life and commerce of the quarter. This is the great innovative genius of capitalism. The buildings stand in rows, with ditches and dirt and rock trenches between them. They built the houses, but somehow they forgot to build *streets*, or schools, or hospitals, or anything else. We see a large area under construction, the *only one* being worked on, and the comrade who is driving leans over to tell us that this is where they are building the church. Our car proceeds like a jeep, and we bounce from one part of it to another as if we were on a battlefield. The new Miano, like the old Miano, has no garbage collections; no market; no chemist's shop; no first-aid station.

Here in Naples building speculation has managed to sack the city. Do you remember Rosi's film, 'Hands Across the City'? Well, the situation is exactly like that. Only the speculators' choices have changed. Rather than rebuild in the old city centre, they find it more profitable to let the old city *collapse*, while they feverishly build up the area around it, making use of all the public institutions, with their thousands of millions of lire, which were established, according to the slogan, 'to give the Neapolitans a roof over their heads'.

The question which comes to mind constantly as I face this situation is: isn't it necessary to link closely the struggle for jobs with the struggle for housing? And, in any event, to have a general strategy which ties the workers and the sub-proletariat together in the struggle against capitalism? A Neapolitan without work, even if he has a *new* flat, will still be part of the *sub-proletariat*. And his 'morality' will infect the workers. Either it will 'suck them down' or it will simply see them as *aristocrats*. The political problem of the Party at Naples is to create an alliance between the industrial proletariat and the sub-proletariat. But no one seems to bother with this classic Marxist problem any more. The word 'sub-proletariat' has effectively been banned from the political lexicon, which has in general been dis-infected and bureaucratized under the semantic influence of social democracy and radical 'third forces', which only speak of 'projects' and 'planning'.

Furthermore, as a result of the continuous mouthing of phrases like 'the unity of the Left' and 'the new unity of the South', and all the other obsolete frontist 'alliance' formulas, the Party has moved steadily away from a Marxist-Leninist analysis of the motor forces of the revolution, the working class and its fundamental allies. The result is that it is almost impossible to speak of theoretical education in the P C I today.

Three days ago, a comrade who scrapes a living as a part-time taxi driver, Gennaro Todisco, pointed to another comrade and said, 'He's a property-owner, that one.' So I found out about him. The 'capitalist', in Vicolo Politi, was a municipal employee with a fixed salary of 68,000 lire a month! And it goes on and on like that. In a section in Pignasecca, during a meeting, an unemployed youth, son of sub-proletarian parents, suddenly jumps up and gives vent to all the prob-lems that have been gnawing away at him: 'I say that these busmen are ruining us. They want a rise, and rises make prices go up, and we are the ones who have to pay! They think they're so high and mighty. They get married and rent apartments for 30,000 lire a month. It's because of people like them that there is so much unemployment. . . . I'd like to kill them. They go on strike and the cost of meat, vegetables and everything else goes up. The Party should keep them from striking. . . .' He must have heard these ideas in the streets and at home for some time, where the busmen represent the only part of the proletariat with which there is any direct contact. He confuses the busmen with capitalism.

Another comrade explains to him that 'the busmen have a long tradition of struggle in Naples, going all the way back to when the police used to charge on horseback and they used to block them, holding them off. . . .' But this makes no impression at all on the youth, who merely shrugs his shoulders. Then someone explains to him that capitalism is really what lies behind his complaints. But it is very clear that a lot of long, intense discussions will be necessary to dispel the suspicious and hostile attitude, typical in the slums, towards the working class, represented here by 'the busmen'.

The same relationship – distrust and suspicion – exists in the new quarters as well as between the sub-proletariat, which 'invents' its source of labour every day, and the proletariat. In these new quarters, the sub-proletariat rapidly becomes the *dominant force*, but the workers never succeed in becoming the *directing*, leading force.

To return to the topic of housing, on which I have been able to find a great deal of documentation. A summary is necessary to see how really bad the situation is, to see what a famine exists. Condemned houses, between those damaged in the War and those which are simply collapsing from old age, condemned buildings whose inhabitants have been ordered to move out by the police, number 462, housing some 69,000 people. In the Vico Lepre in Montecalvario alone, eighty families live where experts have diagnosed a collapse as imminent. In compensation for this, they get a payment of 10,000 lire a month from the city as being officially homeless, and this becomes their only regular income. There are a further 451 'homeless' families like them – but the right to receive the payments is only valid if the total income of the family does not exceed 55,000 lire a month. Every three months, the police investigate to ensure that income remains under the quota of 55,000, and I have personally witnessed at the Town Hall scenes of biblical despair when the police have reported that the family has some unreported income. In one case, the installation of a telephone was cited as proof of more money than was being reported, but it then turned out that the police had seen a child's toy.

Those with no real roof over their heads, or those who live in shanties, number 10,000, or roughly 600 families. In addition to these people, there are also those who have been put in 'hotels' (i.e. boarding houses of the lowest grade) and who, in some cases, have been living in the same 'hotel room' for sixteen years, eight or ten to a room. To round out the picture, there are another 3,673 families at Naples – roughly 18,000 people – who have not been evicted, but whose houses are so decrepit that the city has issued injunctions to the landlords to repair them.

Buildings which have been abandoned – I saw one in Vico Noce which collapsed in 1963 – stand like precious archaeological ruins, with scaffolding on all sides to hold them up, right in the middle of inhabited areas, but by now with grass growing out of cracks in the walls. In Vico III Politi, on the foundation of the old Cilento building, which collapsed in 1958, I see that the children on the block have built a playground of sorts in the ruins. New, gaping holes keep opening up all the time, and it is frightening to think of what might happen. The whole old centre of the city is destined to disintegrate, it is all eventually going to decompose, since no one does anything to reinforce either the buildings or the ground on which they stand. The day I arrived in Naples, I wrote to you that I had learned that for the forty-second time this year a huge, gaping hole had opened up somewhere in the city – on that occasion at Fuorigrotta. A few days later, it happened for the forty-third time. You get used to everything, apparently: even in *l'Unità*, this only merited a one-column headline. On the other hand, the disaster that befell one *basso* rated a three-column headline. There, the electricity had been shut off for non-payment of the bill, and hence they were forced to use candles. The result was a fire and two babies were horribly burned. But I am becoming aware that it is I myself who am most 'traumatized' by all this, and that the statistics I learn make a much deeper impression on me than on anyone else. I get the feeling that the workers in the 'belly' of Naples must nourish the secret impression that things are like this everywhere, that people live exactly like this in Milan, Bologna, or Turin, that, in other words, as Maupassant wrote, 'this is life'.

As soon as possible, families who have a small income or who have been assigned a flat by the Housing Authority leave the belly of the city to go and live in the stone 'screen' which has been thrown up all around it by the construction speculators. But the rents or mortgage payments are so high in relation to the incomes of the more exploited work force of Naples that what happens is that the poor worker or sub-proletarian who manages to get a flat from the Housing Authority (paying 32,000 lire a month in mortgage payments on it) cannot afford to keep it. He usually turns it over to someone else, *making a little bit for himself out of the deal*, and returns to the *basso* or shanty from which he had originally departed.

In Vico Politi I found one of these buyers and sellers of new flats, who had already had one at Miano and one at Pianura, and was now back in his *basso* in Olivella. I asked him why in the world he had moved three times. His answer: 'for professional reasons', meaning his job. But his job is selling birds. Now he is in a new 'competition' to be assigned another flat. He has more points than anyone else (you get a flat on the basis of a point-system, and once you get more than fourteen you are almost certain to get one): twenty-four points in all, because of his enormous family, his semi-unemployment, etc. I asked him if he will have the money to pay the rent. Cut to the quick, he swears falsely that the money isn't the important thing, it's the clean air, better sanitary conditions, and so on.

(c) If you ever come to Naples – and here is my third piece of advice – remember to steer clear of the 'Southocrats', our southern sub-species of the 'Eurocrats'. These characters send shivers of joy up the spine of *La Stampa* of Turin, the *Corriere della Sera* of Milan, and even *Le Monde*, because they write, in their little house journal *Nord-Sud*, that 'The Southern Question' has been solved, that agrarian reform is very much a *démodé* phenomenon, and that the real future of Naples and the South lies with industrialization, exemplified by Alfa-Sud, which will employ 15,000 people.[2]

Meanwhile, between January and October 1967, the number of workers in the industrial sector declined by 15,700. There has also been a net loss of 16,000 other jobs on the general labour market. Only in the service (tertiary) sector has there been a rise, of 14,000 new jobs. But if you consider that in Naples the total number of employees in the public administration is 77,000, you will see that Naples is well placed to beat New York in terms of the number of public employees! The city continues to take on more and more the qualities of a 'tertiary' economy, since there is already a stupendous disproportion: total employment in the service sector is 382,500, against 298,000 in *all* industrial enterprises (leaving out those officially unemployed). In both the city and province, according to the official 1967 statistics, the total employment picture is as follows: 104,000 (13.3 per cent) in agriculture, 298,600 (38 per cent) in manufacturing industries, 305,400 (38.9 per cent) in 'tertiary' activities, and 77,100 (9.8 per cent) in public administration. The last two figures combine to give you 382,000 or 48.7 per cent of the employed work force (this last figure, drawn from the Regional Plan for Campania, is 15,000 higher than the original projection of the Chamber of Commerce).

The only purpose Alfa-Sud seems to serve at the moment is to give all the Christian Democrat, Socialist and Republican bosses the

2. 'Alfa-Sud' is the plan for Alfa Romeo to establish a plant in the South which will produce an Alfa Romeo 'at popular prices'. (Trans.)

opportunity to provide jobs on paper, in order to win votes, for their throngs of clients. In a longer-term perspective, it will create a new market for the monopoly in the South, and will furnish tens of thousands of additional family cars. The entire policy of the Centre-Left Government in Italy, without the slightest inconsistency, is in favour of the interests of monopoly capital. So the government continues to build beautiful American-style superhighways, our famous *autostrade*, at the same time that there are drastic shortages in schools and hospitals. Just think that the single region of Lombardy has as many hospital beds as does all of Southern Italy.[3] And in the case of Alfa-Sud, the great monopoly is in practice simply setting up an assembly plant for its cars in the South, since it is claimed that Naples has neither qualified workers nor the schools to train them (these are all in Milan or Turin). The traditional tendency of capitalism in Naples, which first emerged in 1897, is to set up a modern industry but to be sure that small and medium industrial enterprises are never permitted to grow up around it. The latter, of course, are necessary for the creation of a general industrial environment and a normal social structure. So the 'great' modern industries of Naples, paradoxically, are really just so many oases destined never to expand in terms of a structure of small or medium industry, and hence destined never to spread in such forms though the city, 'irrigating' it socially. As a result, following this long-established pattern, Naples will never have a new 'factory' which simply *unloads* the northern monopoly's product (in this case cars) in the South. The bosses will also make a second killing on this squalid affair, since the parts and accessories for the cars will be built in Turin and Milan. Original projections had it that these parts, if manufactured in the South, would have provided jobs for 50,000 more Neapolitans. With the decision to build in the North, which is now definite, these new jobs will never materialize. Last Sunday, 18 April, the Prime Minister – a dreary clericalist who mouths vague, evasive formulae loaded with 'technological eschatology' – came to lay the cornerstone for Alfa-Sud. He was surrounded by all the big names of the South, and of course the bishop. There were also a number of young workers at the ceremony, though the older ones were nowhere to be seen.

3. The 1961 census figures show that the population of Southern Italy was 18.6 million (12.4 million excluding the islands), while that of Lombardy was 5.1 million. (Trans.)

A few days earlier, the PCI's poster addressed to the workers of Pomigliano d'Arco had not met with any success at all. In fact, the workers had torn down all the posters! I don't know what was written on them, but it is more than likely that it was merely a *moral* protest. Now, I might be wrong, but I see the problems of Naples and the South in terms of the fundamental contradiction between capital and labour, between exploiters and exploited face to face in the productive process. The equilibrium of the system is made possible today thanks to an organic relationship between development and backwardness, since the very mechanism of capitalist accumulation has a growing need – similar to what happens in the case of imperialism for entire continents – for great underdeveloped areas, for great social masses pushed to the margins of society, where their misery, poverty, alienation and humiliation are increased, where capitalism is able to buy human muscle and sinew for next to nothing, and where, furthermore, it has the new markets which are necessary for the further intensification of exploitation.

Now the identification of the socially 'marginal' strata in the South – youth, sub-proletariat, women, the extremely poor urban and popular masses – as *anticapitalist* is essential if we want to shatter the equilibrium of the system and really get to the heart of its exploitative and accumulative mechanisms. When Alfa-Sud is seen in these terms, it acquires real meaning as both the symbol and the reality of a new thrust by the (capitalist) car market into the disinherited Mezzogiorno, and has nothing to do with the industrialization of the South, as the devious third-force 'technocrats' would have us believe.

This whole business of Alfa-Sud has become one of the main focal points of the election. The ruling class and the parties in the Centre-Left coalition, even if they haven't completely given up trying to buy votes 'with a little spaghetti', are now trying to present themselves as more modern and sophisticated. So, to create an alibi for collaborating with the bourgeoisie, the 'leftist' members of the Centre-Left in particular are forced to tell fairy tales about the forests of factory smoke-stacks which will soon be seen on the Neapolitan skyline. Also, instead of paying out subsidies of 2,000 lire in exchange for votes, they now sign papers with 'promises' of employment in some future industry. The Socialists have replaced Marx with the technocrat-baron Compagna, the editor of *Nord-Sud*, a millionaire Radical with enormous property holdings. And the PSI now rejoices to know that one can 'theoretically' justify the split in the workers' movement, its integration into the bourgeois system of power, the end of the 'Southern Question', the 'industrialization of the South', and the Centre-Left as 'the new answer to the problems of our times' (Nenni's slogan!).[4] When Compagna himself speaks, it is a slightly different, if equally ludicrous, discourse one hears: Naples as the California of the Mezzogiorno (!), with highly technologically advanced industries, such as electronics, *producing very small products with very high returns.* This reconfirms the traditional tendencies of capitalist development; ignoring the backward misery of millions of people, one thinks of cultivating 'gardens of prosperity' for restricted élites, in order to thrust Naples into an 'advanced' role.

On the other hand, this whole ideological masquerade is hardly ever challenged by anyone, for in twenty years – this is at least the span of time that I have had personal exposure to Naples – the city has undergone a profound cultural decline in the broadest sense, which explains a lot of things. The crudeness and narrowness of the non-Communist politicians, who ape the 'technocrats' while at the same time basing their fortunes on the old 'transformism',[5] is a phenomenon which moves as fast as the plague. Hence there is good reason to fear contagion, and therefore intellectual and even political indoctrination. Seen in this context, the general crisis of southern writers and intellectuals is best understood in terms of their having become *integrated*, thinking all the while that they were putting themselves in the avant-garde of new and original developments.

I really believe that Naples is an ideological and cultural void because of the ideological corruption sown by these Radical-Socialist grouplets, under the hegemony of the Gavas, the tainted heritage of the Lauros, and the 'young lions' of Nenni and La Malfa (*capolista* of the P R I, the Republicans, in Naples) who roar in the southern jungle of the *clientele.* The only thing to do – and this too requires a change of line by the Communists – is to launch an all-out attack on this 'ideological power centre' created by intellectuals integrated into the bour-

4. The Centre-Left experiment, as noted earlier, brought the Socialists into the Government in 1963. The PSI majority led by Pietro Nenni – a staunch advocate of close collaboration with the PCI until the late fifties – justified its entry into the government by affirming that it would be able to pressure the other parties into carrying out necessary reforms.

5. 'Transformism' in Italian politics means the process whereby 'opposition' politicians are co-opted and absorbed into the governing élite.

geois system. And this means being completely intransigent on a theoretical level. What else is there to do, given Naples' poverty, with people like the technocrat writers and journalists who compute statistics on the number of TV antennae over the *bassi*, which they then inform us is evidence that we are moving into a newer, more modern world? Aside from the fact that the women I have spoken with often do not even have a TV set, they have told me that, when they do watch, 'if politics comes on, or that guy with the white streak in his hair [Moro] makes an appearance',[6] the people usually just switch off their sets. This also helps explain why they sometimes do not even know that there is a war going on in Vietnam.

The ideological poverty of the integrated intellectuals is extreme: a character named Rea, an ex-Communist and 'committed', realist writer from the fifties, wrote an essay for *Nord-Sud* called 'Cummeo Goes Bowling'. His theme is that old Cummeo, a poor devil without any job, *no longer exists, because these days he has the money to go bowling.* In other words, there is no longer any need for rebellion, to say nothing of socialist revolution, in the South, because the Technological Revolution has, magnificently, reared its head and now Naples is a miniature American Society, or at least is on the way to becoming Americanized: every doorman has three cars, the new rich sub-proletariat has luxury accommodation and smokes Havana cigars, etc. I heard these strange descriptions in Paris from Rea himself – in a meeting he gave at the Institute of Italian Culture – as he presented Naples to the French as another Washington, D.C., in this way trying to justify his own loss of commitment in his writing, and indeed the general crisis of all 'committed' literature.

In Paris I could only make judgements on the cultural and intellectual level of the man himself. But since arriving here, my intellectual contempt for the fraudulence of his account has really exploded.

Ideological corruption is only part of the general corruption that marks the election's atmosphere. *Material* corruption is everywhere. I'll give you some more examples: In Via Stella Polare, an old, skinny man whispers in my ear, 'What does this leaflet you have just handed me entitle me to receive?' He is clearly thinking of Lauro's 'coupons' for Easter 'doves' (cakes) or spaghetti, or of the hand-outs the DC

6. Aldo Moro, a top leader in the DC, former Prime Minister and holder of numerous portfolios in various governments. He was the principal architect of the Centre-Left.

and PSI are lavishing on the slum areas, according to the time-honoured and established 'ideological' formula that says that the people must think of electoral campaigns as the occasion for a suplementary Piedigrotta Festival, at the parties' expense. For the Bourbonic ruling class that governs Naples, you don't run an election by presenting platform, but, always, by buying votes. Naples has not changed: petty corruption is rampant everywhere and one of the most hotly contested issues is whether you should 'trick' the Centre-Left and Lauro by accepting their packages and then voting against them, or if instead you should simply drive the vote-buyers out of your street. At the ARAR settlement – a shanty concentration camp – the inhabitants bodily threw out the men who had come around to give out 'Easter doves'. This victory of a new political consciousness caused more fuss than the victory of 'Napoli', the revered local football team.

Still more on *corruption*. I insist on its importance, even if it is not the primary factor. It is always with me as I move through this campaign, and I just cannot avoid talking about it. We had a women's meeting at 23 Via San Cristoforo all'Olivella – the house of Assuntina Pochet. The tally for that street was as follows: the DC gives two litres of olive oil to whomever will vote for them, the Socialists give a coupon worth 2,000 lire, Lauro (the Monarchist) gives spaghetti, Easter 'doves' (giving these cakes is a great innovation) and money to come to his speeches. All of the comrades have their tales to tell. One old comrade, Ernestina, who is wearing a red blouse for the occasion and seems to be straight out of Brecht with white hair standing like a halo round her head, tells of her *personal electoral experience* in the field of corruption.

She got 2,000 lire to go to Lauro's speech and yell 'Viva Lauro' and applaud; the rally was held at the Metropolitan. She took the 2,000 lire and went, but she found a way to 'trick' them. Instead of shouting 'Viva Lauro' she yelled 'Viva Gioacchino Muratti' (Murat). One of the Monarchist organizers, hearing her words, asked her why she was shouting Murat instead of Lauro. Ernestina, telling her story, says, 'I answered: "Muratti was a king too, and his name was Gioacchino just like Lauro's son. For me, Lauro is the king and his son is prince."' Then, going on with her dramatic account, she adds, 'When the time came to applaud, I raised my clenched left fist. They asked me why I did that, and I said because my other arm is bad, and anyway I noticed at other rallies that this is the way a lot of people salute.'

Old Ernestina's story met with general disapproval. She had been so proud of herself, and now all at once she was overcome by humiliation. Comrade Viviani, daughter of the famous actor and writer Raffaello Viviani, tells her, 'You have to stop that kind of stuff. Everyone has always said that they take the 2,000 lire and then they don't vote for Lauro or the DC. But tell me, where do all those votes that the Christian Democrats and Rightists get keep coming from? Naples has to acquire her dignity, just like the other cities. You don't find elections like these any more in the other cities. If Lauro starts in again with packages and shoes – (the idea is that you get the left shoe right away and the right one after the election) – it means that these methods are still paying off for him. We have to take this system apart. We have to get people to turn down money, cakes, oil, promises of jobs, and all those other things. Neapolitans are good people but they don't use their wits, and it is about time that they began to do so.'

Ernestina lowers her eyes, stricken. She thought she had precisely used her wits with Lauro. She had even told us about the fine meal she had made 'in his honour' with the 2,000 lire: a nice pizza and a beer 'in his face'. But the others all agree with the speaker and come down hard on Ernestina, repeating how bad it is to take these packages. Finally, Ernestina has had enough: 'Don't act like little Madonnas around me,' she says, pointing them out one by one, 'all of you have taken cakes, too – you and you and you. And as for your son, I saw him take two. . . .' No one replies. To cut a long story short, out of the twelve women at the meeting, those who haven't accepted anything are definitely a very small minority. The only ones I am absolutely sure of, in fact, are myself and Viviani.

To conclude, let me tell you that I myself saw a Socialist Deputy, a 'brilliant young intellectual' and technocrat, go into the Town Hall to get stacks of free tickets for the merry-go-rounds and shooting galleries that are set up on Municipal ground. 'They are tickets for the voters' children; you give something to the parents and something to the kids even if they don't vote. The mothers always like it.' He was calm, smiling, and perfectly cynical. These fairground tickets were *the new Socialist answer to new problems*. It is enough to make you want to hide under a rock. But who even notices these things any more? I keep thinking more and more about this humble truth: I find myself surrounded by people who have *always been tricked*, people that no one, in a serious and systematic way, has ever tried to *enlighten*.

It has been a long time since I have had any word from you, and I wonder what it is that has gone wrong. Is it the mail, or are you just tired out by all this?

Maria Antonietta

Dear Louis, *Naples, 30 April 1968*

Who are the enemies? I keep trying to understand just who we are, and what are 'the forces and resources we can count on'; I am trying to go as deeply as I can into the people's consciousness, but in order to understand the people, you must also simultaneously be able to use methods of research and questioning which are capable of hurting the enemy. This has to be done not simply to oppose the enemy, but to defeat him. It is not a question of overestimating him, or 'spending all one's time worrying about the adversary's strategy', but rather of 'taking account of the enemy's strength and his policies', knowing full well that 'you can see clearly into his plans and schemes' only by knowing fully the forces which make up the people.

The oppressive power system here in Naples is personified by one family, the Gavas. They hold in their hands the reins of the Christian Democrat Party, of banking and finance capital, and of the whole world of shady business and speculation in the South.

A literary allusion is called for. The Gavas are *not* Thomas Mann's 'Buddenbrooks'. The decline of this dynasty – whose beginning I believe these elections will mark – will be that of a family power free from the slightest bit of idealistic or soul-searching torment. Vulgarly intent on its single purpose – plunder – it is utterly and organically incapable of resolving any of the city's problems. Naples alone of the larger Italian cities does not even have a development plan, and Campania is the only region without a regional plan. The Government put aside 100,000 million lire for Naples in 1962, but it has taken until now to get even a few million spent. Not, of course, that these 'plans' mean the end of all problems, but their absence indicates the total dominance of the Gavas, without so much as a fiction of formal control from outside, even of a purely 'paternalistic' kind. The only limits are those imposed by the internecine struggles between the various 'clans' of the family.

Silvio Gava, the chieftain of the tribe, has put together his modern operations on three levels. *First*, draining the Monarchist cadres off into the DC, in this way using the Monarchists' 'camorristic' dynamism to reinvigorate the DC; in exchange for this, he gives them a slice of power. *Second*, he entrusts to members of his own family, or trusted lieutenants, all the levers of power at his disposal, from the Provincial Administration to the *Isveimer* (an Institute of the Bank of Naples which finances industrial loans), to Fiat, to the *Cassa del Mezzogiorno*,[1] to the Consortium for the Naples area, to the daily *Il Mattino*, and a whole myriad of banking and financing companies. All are bound together in a highly articulated network of power. *Third*, he has managed to identify the interests of the major industrial and business groups in Naples (whom Lauro had very successfully mobilized in complete opposition to public economic intervention) with the various state agencies and with centralized monopolistic power. In this way, he has neatly played the DC's basic trump card, which is that of revealing to the southern notables and clients the existence of State Capitalism and the State agencies for the development of the South, the possibilities of utilizing the central public apparatus as a feeding-trough and the advantages of an intimate connection with monopoly capital.

'Gavian' power has been woven like a spider's web by the various members of the dynasty. The father, Silvio, now the DC *capolista*, is the brains of the team. His son, Antonio, is President of the Provincial Administration, though his father has him destined for far higher political honours when the moment is ripe; he is the disinterested 'planner' *ad usum delphini*.[2] Another son, Roberto, is a city official at Castellamare and the general director of the Stabian Baths (a thermal spa which he has already managed to put in the red); he is also the administrator of the vast, recently-acquired family fortune from an old office at 55 Via Cervantes. Acanfora, the old man's son-in-law, has the Fiat distributorship and is entrusted with the riskiest

1. National Fund for the South. (Trans.)
2. Lit. 'for the use of the prince'. Originally referred to books expurgated and annotated for perusal by a royal heir. Here this means that provincial 'planning' serves the interests of Antonio himself. (Trans.)

financial and banking operations . . . and this doesn't even cover the other in-laws, clients of high standing or 'friends'.

The key to Gava's rise to power can be dated quite clearly from his successful siege of the 'red fortress' of Castellammare in 1954. Silvio, by forming an alliance with the extreme Right, beat the coalition of the Left by just over 100 votes. Then, amid popular uproar, he put together a coalition which included Monarchists and Fascists (now, with his sights adjusted somewhat, Gava has replaced them with Socialists, just as occurred at Naples). In the biography which is distributed in profusion to the voters, Gava neatly forgets this 'detail' and has the gall to call himself 'antifascist'.

Minister of Industry under De Gasperi,[3] Gava, according to his biography, left the post in 1956, 'resigning dramatically in protest over a policy which threatened fiscal stability'. But other sources see it somewhat differently, and according to them Fanfani, De Gasperi's successor, personally forced Gava to resign when it became known that this Minister of Industry was, at the same time, president of a company called FIMI Machines. It seems that the firms which dealt with FIMI also found themselves in the sudden good graces of the Minister. Not only that, but Gava was simultaneously president of ENAP (the National Agency for Professional Training and Preparation), which used state money to put new lathes (from FIMI of course) in all the state vocational schools. (FIMI Machines has now been 'bequeathed' to the son, Roberto Gava.) Because Fanfani threw him out, Gava became an anti-*fanfaniano* and a rabid *doroteo*.[4] He also quickly understood that the most secure route to power was to get rid of any big personality who might stand in his way inside the DC at Naples. Thus he soon managed to compulsorily retire Naples' most famous political personality – Giovanni Leone, who now, for the first time, he replaces as *capolista* – by having him 'kicked upstairs' and named Senator for Life. Emilio Colombo, the Minister of the

3. Alcide De Gasperi, leader of the DC and Prime Minister almost uninterruptedly from the Liberation to 1953. (Trans.)

4. Fanfani dominated the DC as Secretary-General from 1954 to 1959, but his power slipped in the last year of his leadership, when his faction, officially known as 'Iniziativa Democratica' but commonly called the *fanfaniani*, lost its majority within the party. The group that deposed him was led by Aldo Moro, and was named after the place of its formation, the Convent of Santa Dorotea, hence '*dorotei*'. It was this faction which led the DC into the Centre-Left and dominated every government in the 1960s. (Trans.)

Treasury, highly thought of in European financial circles and no 'child' in political intrigue, was also knocked out cold. Gava has not yet been able to get rid of Cardinal Ursi of Naples, who in an attempt to keep his hands clean has refused open support for Gava in the elections with a letter to the Neapolitan clergy instructing them not to get mixed up in politics. But Ursi remains only because the Vatican is in Rome not Naples, and because Gava is not actually a Borgia.[5]

To reconstruct the entire, intricate financial system in which the Gavas are involved would take the genius of Inspector Maigret. But I have attempted to find out a few essential points. In 1965, the collapse of the Banca Popolare di Napoli (eight thousand million lire in savings and six thousand million in investments) catches thousands of small investors. And the Gavas are up to their necks in it. It is learned that the Acafio Company, one of the Bank's major investors and whose head is Acanfora, Gava's son-in-law, is one of the largest debtors. At the same time, Roberto, one of the Bank's main partners, 'had undertaken', as *Espresso* wrote, 'extremely unorthodox operations which can only technically be distinguished from writing bad cheques'. The Treasury Minister, Colombo, faced with a noisy scandal, was forced to name an investigating commission. Incredibly, he chose *one of Gava's men* as its chairman.

This is Professor Gaetano Liccardo, whose 'credentials' to look into the Gavas' misdeeds are the following: member of the General Council of the Consortium for the Naples area, representing the Provincial Administration which is run by Antonio Gava; member of the Administrative Council of Kerasav, where Roberto Gava is president of the Auditory Committee; auditor of accounts for the Fiat Company, whose vice-president is Antonio; president of the Auditory Board of the Banca Fabbrocino, whose chairman is Antonio; partner in the Stabia, S.p.A. (the Fiat distributor) along with Mario Acanfora. The latter is widely known at Castellammare as '*o formaggiaro*' (the cheese peddler) to underline the professional origins of those members of the 'Great DC Families' that Fiat promotes as representatives of its monopoly in the South. Anyway, even an idiot could see how the

5. Silvio Gava was named Minister of Justice in the present Rumor cabinet [Mariano Rumor succeeded Moro as head of the *dorotei*] at the end of '68! In January 1969, at the ceremony marking the start of the court calendar year in Castel Capuano, Gava had to leave by the service entrance to avoid the protest demonstration against him by magistrates and lawyers.

Gavas succeeded in emerging untarnished from an investigation run by such a home-grown commission. Not only that, but the functions previously covered by the Banco Popolare before the failure (loans at usurious rates during the construction boom) have now been assumed by the Banco Fabbrocino, whose auditor, remember, is Professor Liccardo – the investigator! – and whose real head is Antonio Gava.

Liccardo, given a field promotion for having so successfully got the Gavas out of a tight spot, sees his authority increase in the Banco di Napoli, which is one of the strategic points Gava needs to control to complete his hegemony. This is at least partly due to the fact that the Banco owns the daily *Il Mattino* (a political scandal sheet with a real flair for misinforming its readers). This the Senator intends to make into his personal organ in the same way that Lauro owns the *Roma*, taking it away from any possible public control. The operation is a success, and the chief of the Gava tribe now writes articles on 'the law' and 'social behaviour' for *Il Mattino*, which the Banco di Napoli has practically hired out to him. In a series of articles, he has reflected profoundly on eroticism and virility under the heading 'Nature's Order and the Correct Marital Relationship'. One comes away with the impression that this old clericalist is more zealously concerned with 'marital relations' than a young cleric. From these articles – which I read with great enjoyment, for they are filled with the most genuine, if unintentional, humour – the Senator emerges as a rare Freudian case. I'll only cite one passage for you: 'A casual carnal relationship without long-lasting spiritual compenetration between the lovers will be a bitter gratification of the senses – never love. Nature has given real men more than organs of generation. . . . Everyone who loves feels that he will love forever, and incessant love is the reciprocal promise that lovers make to each other.' The Senator is sixty-nine years old.

At the side of our septuagenarian Senator emerges the chosen son, the *Dauphin*, Antonio, who blends political power and private business without the slightest scruple.[6] Antonio's clan brings Chicago during Prohibition to mind. In 1964 his personal secretary, Professor Enzo Franco, was elected to the City Council (fourth in preference), but he was never able to so much as set foot in the Chamber, since there was an arrest warrant out for him, for having bounced 120 million lires' worth of cheques drawn on the Banco Popolare. Seventy million of the total was paid on the piazza at Ischia in October-November 1964,

6. Antonio Gava became Provincial Secretary of the Naples DC in March 1969.

which coincided with the period when Antonio Gava was on the island conducting his own campaign for the Provincial Assembly.

Perhaps the most fitting example of the powers of imagination displayed in his ventures by Gava, Jr. is his attempt to have the province, of which he is secretary, sell at a ridiculously low price the woodlands of the former Royal Palace at Portici – where the Faculty of Agriculture has been for the past ninety years. The prospective purchaser was the firm Poligrafica Carte e Valori, which claimed it needed the land to build a factory which would employ 200 people. But it then emerged that the company's 'headquarters' was at the notorious address 55 Via Cervantes – the same, that is, as the law firm of Silvio, Antonio and Roberto Gava – and that Roberto was president of Poligrafica Carte e Valori. The Neapolitan Communists exposed this scandal in the City Council, in a series of speeches by councillor Del Rio. The scandal could not be contained. Finally the Prefect revoked the permit which authorized President Gava of the province to sell part of the Portici Woods to a company headed by his brother.

Antonio Gava's clan has ramifications in the 'academic' circles of Naples as well. The chairman of the Faculty of Engineering, Luigi Tocchetti (who is also president of the 'Rehabilitation' Society, founded in 1888), and Signor Beguinot – who holds the Urban Studies chair in the same Faculty – are the real planners of the dynasty. They drew up the development Plan for Naples (which was rejected), the project for the huge Combined Hospitals Polyclinic on the Aminei Hills, and another for a whole new central axis of the city. Finally, they also did the co-ordinating plan for the coastal strip; this allows for a road fit for King Croesus to be built from Castellammare to Massalubrense and Sant'Agata, and then doubling back via Positano, Amalfi and Vietri to Salerno. A real crock of gold. And while Antonio is by now drawing up his regional plan, his little brother Roberto is plotting the chart of all the hotels which will rise along the new highway and is buying and selling land frantically around Vietri-on-Sea, Agropoli and Paestum.[7]

7. The Twelfth Congress of the National Urban Planning Institute, which was to take place on 14 November 1968 in Naples, was closed an hour after it convened because of the disruptive tactics of student demonstrators.

On the platform at the congress there sat Antonio Gava, his brother Roberto and Prof. Beguinot, together with national figures in urban studies, like Zevi and Piccinato. The students succeeded in getting on to the stage, where they hung

The Gavas have the 'Open Sesame' to the *Cassa del Mezzogiorno*, and the Minister in charge of the Fund, Pastore – who claims to be on the left in the DC – *ordered* the millionaires' highway to get immediate financing, in spite of all the protests by Neapolitan architects, engineers and urban specialists. After a sham 'debate' in the Council in March, in which the Socialists also got involved, Antonio Gava can now present himself, his father (who is running again as Senator from Castellammare) and Achille Lauro with this *Diamond as Big as the Ritz*, the Sorrento Highway. The Massalubrense land in fact belongs to Lauro, and Gava hopes, by handing him such a plum, to get what is left of Lauro's old political organization (the DC is already one-third ex-Monarchists). As far as the other land holdings go, there are enough options and manoeuvres open to Antonio to guarantee his possession of the parts the road will cut through.

The road itself sounds as if it were designed by paranoids. The Provincial Council has approved a first stretch from Castellammare to Vico Equense, a distance of 4,714 metres. In this single stretch, there will be fourteen bridges; six of them will be 120 metres long, and one 325 metres in length. These bridges will be supported by immense reinforced concrete structures which will blight the beauty of the Sorrentine landscape as surely and as effectively as vitriol thrown in someone's face. And then of course there is the incredible waste of money and building material, here in the South, where schools and hospitals are a luxury; all you have to do is think of that and you understand the mechanism of monopolistic profit which links the interests of Gava and the DC so tightly to those of the car monopoly Fiat and the *Cassa del Mezzogiorno*.

Gava may have begun as a humble provincial lawyer, but the dynasty's fortune certainly was not earned in courtroom fees. The money can now be counted in thousands of millions of lire, and it finds more hospitable surroundings outside the country, so they say. You could guess this by noting an interesting fact: the Kerasav Company, which had its headquarters in the well-known Via Cervantes offices, is now linked to unknown owners based in Lugano and Vaduz; the Poligrafica Carte e Valori, which wanted to get its hands on the Portici Woods, is also linked to unknown partners in Munich.

---

banners made of toilet paper, inscribed with the word made famous by General Cambronne. The congress and the protests brought the corruption and barbarianism of urban development back into the news.

Roberto Gava, following who knows what instinct, resigned as chairman of the board of Kerasav in 1966, and all the other honoured members of the family have also arranged to have themselves replaced by 'friends' in the intrigues of their joint-stock corporations. The Gavas are the brazen face of the D C in the South, while Petrucci – ex-mayor of Rome who was caught stealing from a State charity for mothers and infants four months ago and is now in jail – is its scoundrel's face: the Roman pickpocket.

Silvio Gava will be judged in the forthcoming elections partly on the basis of this dossier which I have been putting together, tediously, through three weeks of inquiries and discussions with those who know – in this fashion breaking a lot of the *omertà*[8] surrounding his doings. This list of accusations, as I am sure you understand, represents an act of pure honesty and courage. The workers of Castellammare were the first ones to put me on this track, and they are the ones who insisted that everything I have been saying should come out in *l'Unità* as well. The issue with my article in it sold like hot cakes. The workers even organized a special distribution, and in the Castellammare area, in front of the factories alone (Castellammare is, as I noted before, Gava's senatorial seat), 600 copies were sold above and beyond the usual number. There were very curious developments: D C voters, and even priests, came to P CI headquarters looking for copies of the paper, which by then were sold out on all the newsstands. The workers are convinced that politically an all-out attack on Gava is the decisive link in the chain, for our attack on capitalism in this campaign. I have taken their advice, and I know they will defend me.

Maria Antonietta

8. *Omertà* is the Sicilian 'law of silence' surrounding the Mafia's activities. (Trans.)

Dear M.A., *Paris, 1 May 1968*

I have not been able to answer any of your letters you have sent to Paris since my letters from Gordes because I am quite seriously ill. One of the effects of the illness is that I will not be able to read or write for several weeks. I wanted to inform you in advance of this silence, and I know you understand how involuntary it is. But I also want to insist that you continue to write, even if I will only be able to answer you later on. I think of you a lot, and of all the problems you have to struggle with. Your second and third letters from Naples provide an extraordinary account of the incredible conditions the poor people live in, and of their various reactions. Everything you wrote was extremely moving, not only because of the subject matter, but because of your involvement in it.

I think of your courage and of your patience. Especially of your courage: perhaps it is easy for some people to do certain things, but to try to do what you are attempting requires more than sheer will-power: you need courage, intelligence, and humanity.

Your letter on housing: it cost me a great effort to read it (because of incredible fatigue) and it was very difficult for me to understand certain expressions and words from the Neapolitan dialect, of which I have no knowledge whatever. But a pathetic picture emerges of the life these poor people must lead. You are really getting down to details – and I think this is most important for you and for what might result from what you are doing.

I would like to have a long discussion with you on these questions of the 'new' housing, but in general I think my observations would coincide with yours. If my memory serves me, there are several pages on this subject in *Capital*, on the means of capitalist exploitation through intermediaries:

(1) on building-land speculations;

(2) on conditions of rent-indebtedness among the exploited masses; in other words, 'new' housing – if my memory is not playing tricks on me – is a form of super-exploitation already described by Marx.

You should keep writing so that your experience is recorded and communicated. It is too exceptional for you not to do this.

I send my love, and I wish you more of the same great courage, dear Maria Antonietta. I will take up our correspondence again one day, perhaps even sooner than expected.

Louis

Dear Louis,   *Naples, 3 May 1968*

Your letter, which arrived today, has made me incredibly sad. I had already been upset not to hear from you, and I suspected that there was something lurking behind this silence. I sent you that telegram to tell you that without your letters, everything was much more complicated for me. It was to prod you into revealing what was going on. This letter today has thrown me into the deepest kind of depression: for you, it's the *affreux noir* that Stendhal talks about. And it is the same for me as well, in a certain sense, for your letters helped me so much to face this difficult test. Moreover, they helped me to see beyond the 'immediate' and put problems in a more general perspective, pushing me continuously *to act in order to understand*. Giving me so many hours of your time, thinking about the questions I asked, is as if you 'took me by the hand', trying to offer me the weapons which would help me understand and fight better. I remember the quotation from the letter of Marx you use as a preface to *Reading Capital*: 'only those who do not dread the fatiguing climb of its [science's] steep paths have a chance of gaining its luminous summits'. I also think of this last gesture of yours, made up of generosity and true political friendship: even though you are in no condition to work, you send me this letter anyhow, to insist that I continue to write from Naples in order to 'record' this experience of mine. What can I possibly say? Only that I promise that I will continue to write, even if our thread of contact is broken for now, and even though I will not have my interlocutor before me for a certain period of time. It is hard, but it is the only way to keep up my part of the agreement, in the continuing effort to *work*, and to avoid *bureaucratic routine*, to think more profoundly, both in terms of details and more general questions, and to be able to draw lessons from this experience which are both concrete and not completely transitory.

Writing has become almost a catch-as-catch-can affair by now, and I should warn you of this. I have so little time on my hands that I have begun to use a tape-recorder, precisely in order to record the various moments of the campaign, since I often am no longer able to write out my thoughts and experiences by the end of a day. So now I just jot down notes as I go along, constructing a sort of skeleton which I then flesh in verbally with the microphone.

I don't know whether anything useful or politically intelligible will come out of this 'magma'. I wonder about this mainly because I feel like someone swimming in a wild, uncoordinated way, thrashing my arms furiously out of fear of being caught in a storm, which I am trying desperately to put behind me. Furthermore, I am simply exhausted physically from this work, and my nerves are at breaking point as a result of the breathless rush I am continuously in.

Here I shall put a full stop and open a new page, one taken from the 'book of life', written in the past. What I want to do is provide you (and myself) not with what we Italians call an attempt at 'historicization' (untranslatable word!) but rather with an attempt to find a 'takeoff point' for our experience as Italian Communists, born in the antifascist struggle – an experience summed up in Togliatti's great phrase of the period, 'We have come from far away'. I am trying what might be called, in cinematic terms, a flashback.

The idea of a flashback came to me, to tell the truth, as soon as I got to Naples, when I went to the Town Hall to see a Socialist I knew from the old days, Lelio Porzio, who is now deputy mayor in the Centre-Left majority on the council. I was with a group of women who were being evicted from the condemned buildings of Vicolo Lepre ai Ventaglieri in the Avvocata quarter: eighty families to whom the tiny compensatory payment of 10,000 lire a month had been generously granted, and who had been waiting eight years to be rehoused. Now, instead of being rehoused, they had got orders to vacate the premises. The women were like a whole horde of Ibárurris, formidably eloquent in their accusations and great orators against the Commune's mistreatment of them. One particularly beautiful woman, with blazing eyes, looked exactly like a famous local actress, Pupella Maggio, according to everyone there. And similarity did not end with her looks, for driven by her inner contempt she unleashed a string of denunciations with such fluency that they sounded as if they must have been learned by heart. It was right then that I underwent my first 'crisis' as a 'propagandist-candidate'; how could anyone ever speak like these people, to say nothing of speaking better than them, I thought. For they were so splendid and colourful in their fury, shaking their fists in the face of the little Socialist deputy mayor, who stiffened more and more with every passing moment, retreating progressively behind his massive walnut table as if it were some trench he could leap into.

Now, I knew this same Socialist deputy mayor in 1946, when he was co-editor of *La Voce*, a really fine daily founded in Naples after the Liberation by Communists, Socialist and other groups on the Left. I just could not avoid comparing the man-symbol of the united and popular Front of those days and this grey, wizened gentleman. It was like looking at Dorian Gray's portrait. As is customary whenever the masses come to the Town Hall to protest, the Christian Democrat mayor and all the other municipal dignitaries had disappeared; either they had slipped out by the service entrances or else they had used the old trick of sneaking out of the Town Hall in a Red Cross ambulance which leaves the building with such a shrieking of sirens that you are sure there is at least a patient under intensive care inside. They had just left the Socialist there, to stem the tide of popular fury.

This is what the Centre-Left amounts to: the DC, having tricked and manoeuvred the Socialists into the corridors of bourgeois power, now puts them into the front line whenever popular protests spring up. The Socialists are up to their necks in the mire. But the other side of it is that the Socialists – for a slice of 'power' – accept this humiliation, and the trembling, living example at that moment was poor little Signor Porzio, dismayed by his own complicity. As soon as he saw me there he turned and asked me, exposing his own doubts for a second, 'But you, Macciocchi, weren't you better off in Paris than you are here? What can you do here?' And I: 'The *relevant* question right now is, what has happened to *you* that you let yourself be put in this disgusting situation?' And he, shrugging his shoulders, with a stubborn expression, 'Well, I couldn't stay in opposition forever . . .', clarifying for me, in brief, his ineluctable promotion to the position of an 'official authority', his definitive selling out for power. 'But you are still in opposition,' I answered, 'only now it is against the Neapolitan people, who assault you like an enemy, and against us Communists....'

I didn't feel any personal bitterness, only an awareness of the profound laceration and disintegration of the unitary democratic fabric that

Togliatti had created after the Liberation, and whose centre was the *party of a new type*, the *mass party*, as Togliatti had defined it, pulling it up out of illegality and reinforcing it with a new purpose in 1944 when he returned to Italy.

When I go back in time, the image which keeps coming to me is not a political one, but one of those which recur in dreams.

The beach at Vietri extended as far as the eye could see. We were running barefoot in the sand along a path which now seems endless and as if it were hung in empty space. None of us was older than twenty or at most twenty-two, with enormous energies and hopes. We were part of a tremendous generation, those who beat Fascism and finished the war against the Germans. We arrived at Naples, at Salerno, some from Rome, liberated 4 June 1944, some from Emilia, crossing the front lines to do so, some from scattered towns in Campania (where the Fascists had created numerous places of exile), some from Apulia and Basilicata: none of us was important then, but the historical moment was extremely important, and, through it, so were we.

Salerno was an ugly city, a heap of rotting war ruins, the sea-front avenues full of fallen plaster and the streets all broken to pieces. PCI headquarters was in an old musty building whose doors did not close and whose toilet did not work. The doorman was called Matteo, and he was a cripple who walked with a gigantic stump of a crutch, which thudded loudly on the broken floor as he hobbled along. We had more or less captured the place, by throwing out – through a political struggle – the Ciriello-Manucci group, anarcho-*bordighiani*[1] who opposed the organization of the Party on the basis of cells. Things had reached the point where one night a character named Furno threatened Pietro Amendola with a pistol, Pietro who had come to Salerno from the Resistance in Rome and had spent four years in Fascist prisons.

The Manzos: a Communist family who served up meals for all of us in their own house. The unvarying menu was salt cod with chick peas, pasta and broccoli. They also had a large room which, before we found a more permanent place, served as a temporary shelter for us – and innumerable, happy, red and black beetles. In Naples, on the other hand, we ate in the Federation, in Via San Potito, or else in the dining-room of a home for deaf mutes in Pignasecca, with which

1. Amadeo Bordiga was the first Secretary-General of the PCI, expelled from the party in 1930. (Trans.)

the *Voce* had worked out some sort of 'arrangement': seated at long tables, facing the wall, we were served up, along with the patients, a plate of bean soup with pasta. We were practically penniless. I had sold my diamond ring, which was a wedding present from my mother, along with some other things, and that had brought me in a few thousand lire. Those who had nothing to sell were given provisions by comrades from the countryside, who brought wine, cheese, eggs, dry biscuits and fruit into the Federation. But our material situation, for us, was irrelevant. We were undertaking that enthusiastic work of building the Party, bringing it back from illegality, in dozens, hundreds of towns. We opened up PCI headquarters with hammer and sickle over the door, elected leaders, etc. We made what I believe were the first legal speeches of the PCI in that period, and the crude microphones gave off such shocks that even today, when my mouth gets too close to the microphone, I jump back with an old, instinctive reaction. For us, this was the beginning of our 'Long March'.

Togliatti had just left Salerno, after Rome was liberated, but he still lived in Naples. He lived in an apartment in Via Broggia, an immense, filthy place, some sort of warehouse, where he, like the others, had a single room. He wore a grey turtleneck sweater, and over it a crumpled, misshapen suit – the only one he had, I think – and wore his hair quite long. He wrote on a wobbly little table, stacked high with papers. When I went to see him, he looked at me for a long time from behind his glasses with that penetrating stare of his, which was at once all thought and full of irony. It is the same look which survives, over all these years, in the portrait of him done by Paolo Ricci, which I have. I know that, for him, I came out of the haze of a distant past. I had on a red skirt with white stripes, and a necklace of red wooden beads; complete with ribbon in my hair, I had the face of a nice, respectable girl who had completed her petty-bourgeois life of studies in Rome, in Fascist schools of course, but who also had been in the Resistance and who had been a partisan. I must have represented, to him, one of the many images of a world he was preparing himself to re-enter. I looked at him avidly, and I saw the wisdom and charm that emanated from him. I think this impression resulted, above all, from the fact that he truly thought about every word he said, he didn't just toss words around, and his language, without a bit of pomposity in it, seemed almost scientific, in the sense that he was so precise and able to say exactly what he wanted to with a minimum expenditure of words. After all the Fascist rhetoric, this was like 'gaining the luminous summits of science'. When, in Nazi-occupied Rome, we heard of him for the first time as leader of the Party, it was a disappointment to us. He sounded so anonymous, with all those sharp consonants in his name, and we really had never heard of him before. Then came that proclamation signed at Salerno; the 'turn' and the order to continue the War at the side of the Monarchists and Badoglio in order to defeat Nazism and Fascism; then the 'pacification' and our acceptance in Rome of turning over our partisan arms to the Allied troops, who sent the *Carabinieri* to search our section headquarters. Many of us didn't understand.

In Togliatti's room there were suitcases scattered all over the floor, half-opened, apparently serving as drawers, from which there emerged a profusion of socks, books and shirts. Next to the wall was a hammock. I continued to stare at him avidly. His socks were all bunched up around his ankles, he wore a pair of cheap sandals. He had not shaved for some time. It was he who had voiced that phrase I have already quoted to you – 'We have come from far away' – and that is just how he looked to me, as if at the end of an interminable journey; his twenty-year wanderings from one end of Europe to another, Spain, France, the Comintern, and the long years spent at Moscow. He appeared as inscrutable and untouchable as the exciting history of the revolution and the USSR from which he had just returned. 'How is everything going in Salerno?' he asked. It was a banal question, but it was exactly what he wanted to know, which is why I would have been so pleased to be able to respond with a precise evaluation, rich in all sorts of detail. I told him about our work there, the demonstrations, our trips through the province among the peasants of the Cilento, or the new Party sections opened up in remote country districts. He said we should *work*, keeping on with the things we were already doing, but he also insisted that I concern myself with the problems of women as well. He told me to go to Naples and talk with Comrade Maddalena Secco, who had also just returned from exile. He spoke to me about *Noi Donne*, at that time just a mimeographed bulletin edited by another recently repatriated leader, Nadia Spano.[2] Finally he said that a tremendous effort was needed to build the Party in the Mezzogiorno as a 'mass party'.

2. The author would herself become editor of *Noi Donne* in 1950. (Trans.)

His wife Rita, whom I saw for a moment, was at that time, if I am not mistaken, the head of the PCI women's movement. She was a large, happy woman who laughed frequently; a profoundly good and simple woman, but also one who clearly did not just look after her husband's clothes. (Togliatti's second companion, Nilde Jotti, in the years to come, also became the head of the women's movement, and hence a member of the PCI leadership, just as Jeannette Thorez Wermeersch did in France.)

It is only now that I am able, perhaps, to understand how Togliatti thought the enthusiastic girl who stood there in front of him should fit into the movement – not because it was me, but because I indirectly represented an entire generation, the one emerging from the schools and universities in the antifascist struggle. Also, it is only now that I begin to understand what he meant when he told this girl to *work*, to discipline herself, to meet people more mature and experienced than herself, to seek a link with women, and to help people – all of them and each of them – find a way to enter the *new party*. It was as if he were already aware of exactly what events, in what sequence, were to follow and, seeing them, he also was calculating just what the Party would need to meet them. The new generation was, on the one hand, going to need a strict, hard, and sometimes severely disciplined education at the hands of the people who had been through 'the storms'. But on the other side of the coin, this younger generation was the fertile topsoil which was indispensable if the seeds of a *new mass party* were to be sown, a force capable of carrying Italy's bourgeois-democratic revolution through to the end, after Fascism.

It is clear that he trusted the old group that now surrounded him and that had supported him, followed him into exile and emerged faithful to him in the debilitating internal struggles of the PCI. Although at times they appeared to him to be lacking in political experience and culture, they were tough, forged in 'Stalinist steel', had survived blows and insults, and had seen comrades or relatives fall before firing squads or suffer torture without flinching at the hands of the Stalinist police. But it is equally clear that he wanted *another kind of party* than the old one. And for this he knew that he needed the young, the new forces, the masses, in great numbers.

None of us, at that time, was aware of the fact that there had been a 'division' of the world into spheres of influence between the USSR, the USA and Great Britain. So of course we did not know that our part of the West, all codified and packaged in the treaties and protocols of Teheran and Yalta to remain under the aegis of capitalism, had been excluded from any prospect of a socialist revolution. In this perspective – of which Togliatti was perfectly aware – his task was that of trying to construct what he called a *progressive democracy* here in Italy, which would put the country out of the danger of a reactionary – American or internal – coup, and this was to be done by constantly enlarging the democratic area. In order to do this, he needed the largest possible Communist 'army', the broadest possible alliances, the widest possible trade-union unity, and, first and foremost, the *mass party*.

The talk with Togliatti seemed so exciting to me not because I then understood what I am now writing with the aid of twenty years' hindsight, but because I had *seen* the head of the Party, and he had seemed to me to generate a limpid and penetrating intelligence. That day we all ate together around the table in Via Broggia, sharing a common meal on the spotted tablecloth. Even the plates and glasses were spotted, decorated with fingerprints which seemed to have been carefully applied by two women, an old mother and her daughter, inside the cave-like kitchen. They brought us pyramids of pasta, covered by mountains of tomato. All of us had an insatiable hunger after the long months of the Occupation. This, then, was the field-canteen of Italy's revolutionaries – aside from Togliatti, there were also Spano, Sereni, Reale, Cacciapuoti (a worker), and others – and the grease and disorder must have been similar to those of the front lines, which extended beyond Rome all the way to the Alps. It was July 1944; Togliatti would leave in a few days and I would only see him again many months later, in Rome.

Naples was such a circus in those days that I was afraid to cross the streets, which were flooded with people who milled about in crowds, shouting at the top of their voices, and through which jeeps and military transports opened a path by adding to the din with their horns. The city seemed like one gigantic fry-shop, with '*zeppole*', '*pizze*' and '*calzoni*' sizzling on every street-corner. All the American oil and flour seemed to be kneaded, fried and eaten there in the street. Men with trays full of doughnuts would get on to the trams, hawking their wares, and the people would buy and eat them on the spot, with the grease dripping on their clothes. It was an endless carnival, continuous eating of a Pantagruelesque nature, day and night.

By that time, 'prostitution' had long since ceased to be a term with negative or recriminatory connotations, and had become an objective means of entering into a businesslike relationship of buying and selling with the soldiers of the Allied armies. These men appeared like King Midas, able to turn anything into gold with their *Am-lire*, 'American lire', with which, along with cigarettes and canned goods of every type, they were always loaded down. An American soldier would first be made sufficiently drunk and then passed from hand to hand on the piazza, sold and re-sold, until the last to have him would clean him out entirely, leaving him in the gutter with only his underwear. There were basic *list prices* for G.I.s, depending on such things as their rank and the colour of their skin. The American and other soldiers, on the other hand, got human goods in exchange, old and young women, girls or boys, depending on how the bargaining went, i.e. depending on whether or not one could trick the foreigner or, if he were too crafty, whether one had to deliver quality goods.

These phenomena are all well-known, though it is still necessary to add that Naples was neither Sodom nor Gomorrah. After centuries of slavery and starvation, the Occupation was like a breath of hope which swelled and purified the city because, all other considerations aside, this was the first time in history that people had enough to eat, and enough money and sufficient opportunity to demonstrate their inherent ingenuity. And there were no longer any bombs to rain down in their midst, and even mighty Vesuvius had fallen silent. People were happy, and that it was transitory didn't lessen the intensity of the happy feeling itself, given that poverty and misery – in these people who are incapable of hating deeply – had always been an accepted fact.

The first battle to align the sub-proletariat and people of the city against us Communists was the struggle between Republic and Monarchy in the referendum of June 1946.

The explanation of the visceral pro-monarchism of Naples in those days is to be found in the city's history and social structure. Over the course of centuries, a genuine 'plebs' grew up around the Court, the nobles, lords and high-ranking administrators. It lived off the crumbs that fell from the King's table, off the great noble houses and off the innumerable religious and charitable organizations. This plebs was completely *marginal* to productive society, and yet it was an integral element of that society's general well-being, for the entire society was based on a network of clienteles and private interests, on bankers and tax-farmers who made the city the centre of exploitation for the entire realm and the populace into a vast and extraordinary servants' pool. Goethe noted in 1787, during his trip to Italy, that 'the Neapolitan mask is that of Punch . . . and Punch is a patient, tranquil and lazy servant, even indifferent: but still, he is witty'.

We have spoken on other occasions about the Parthenopean Revolution, on which an immense literature exists and which had, to use Coletta's particularly appropriate phrase, 'only an unhappy and solitary virtue'. I only note this to underline a basic fact of the revolution of 1799, which is that those who wanted to establish the Parthenopean Republic[3] found the plebs to be their principal enemy, and the Republic was destroyed with the enthusiastic help of the common people. They fought very courageously against the French Republican Army, and they gave their full support to the reactionary-peasant-papal army headed by Cardinal Ruffo. At the same time, the cannon of the English fleet commanded by Nelson – the Americans of those days – protected the King, his flight and his re-entry into Naples; and, finally, the illustrious patriots of the Directorate of the Republic were hanged on the yardarms of those same ships (they had incidentally been promised full military honours after surrendering). In payment for this massacre, the King gave Nelson the 'Duchy of Bronte'. The young French general, Championnet, who led the army which had come to defend the Republic, found himself – as you yourself wrote to me when you dedicated my copy of Feuerbach's *The Essence of Christianity* (published in your 'Theory' series) – faced with the 'religious fanaticism' of the plebs. However, as you wrote, he settled the problem by utilizing the liquefying of the blood of San Gennaro, Naples' patron saint. This miraculous act, this 'heavenly sign' which must be accepted by every occupant of the city, still occurs regularly every year during the month of May. Championnet deftly countered the aims of the reactionary clergy, who wanted to keep the miracle from happening as a demonstration of divine wrath against the revolutionaries – in the hope that this would incite the crowd to lynch them. He found the one way out: putting a sword to a high-ranking prelate's throat, he ordered him to liquefy the blood in five minutes, or else pass on to a better life. The blood liquefied immediately, as Dumas recounts very entertainingly in his book on Naples. 'San Gennaro

3. The title was derived from Naples' name at the time it was first settled by the Greeks.

would not have existed without Naples, nor could Naples exist without San Gennaro,' Dumas wrote during his stay in Naples. 'It is true that there is no city on earth which has been conquered more times by foreigners, but, thanks to the active and vigilant intervention of her protector, Naples has remained. The Normans reigned over Naples, but San Gennaro drove them out. The Angevins ruled Naples, but San Gennaro drove them out. The Aragonese, in turn, usurped the throne, but San Gennaro punished them. The Spaniards tyrannized Naples, and San Gennaro defeated them. Finally the French occupied Naples, and San Gennaro drove them from her doors.' So even Championnet's 'miracle on command' did not fool the Neapolitans, who knew the trick and knew how to use their supreme *protector* to the best advantage, interpreting him in correct political fashion as the occasion required.

As I said, the revolution was mercilessly suppressed: the Parthenopean Republic, proclaimed in January 1799, had fallen by June. The crowds picnicked around the bodies hanged in the Piazza Mercato, singing verses in dialect. When the hangman, having already executed seven other Jacobin leaders, put the noose around the neck of Eleanora Fonseca Pimentel, one of the heads of the Republican government (she was the most powerful example of an Italian female revolutionary and thinker, but in Italy, while the praises of all the woman saints are sung endlessly, almost nothing is ever heard of her, not even in school). Maybe this is because her virile intellect and revolutionary activity conflict too strongly with the 'bourgeois model' of the Italian woman and when her body dropped to death on the end of the rope, the people sang the following sinister lines.

> 'a signora donna Lionora
> Che cantava 'ncoppa ò Triato
> Mò abballa 'nmiezz' ò Mercato.
> Viva, viva ú Papa Santo
> Ch'a mannato i cannuncine
> Pé sparà li Giacubine.
> Viv'a forca 'e Mastro Dunat
> Sant'Antonio sia p-riato . . .

> (My lady Donna Eleonora,
> who harangued from atop the Theatre
> Now dances (on a rope) in
> the middle of the market-place.

Long live the Holy Father, who
sent guns to fire on the Jacobins.
Long live Master Donato's gallows,
and let Saint Anthony be praised.)

Vincenzo Cuoco writes that Pimentel faced death with courageous indifference. Before going to the gallows, she asked for a coffee, and her last words were spoken in Latin: 'Forsan haec olim meminisse juvabit' ('Perhaps it will be useful to remember all this one day'). *Were the plebs obliged to know Latin?* Maybe she spoke in this way to underline how the people *felt* that this revolution had nothing to do with them. . . . Or, as Diderot wrote – and he, as a bourgeois intellectual, however progressive, had in mind not just what, since Marx, we have termed the sub-proletariat but *the people* – 'the progress ideas can make is very limited and cannot penetrate the outer extreme of the city, for the people are too bestial'. King Ferdinand, on the other hand, described as being 'as vulgar physically as spiritually', saw matters more clearly and wrote to Cardinal Ruffo when Pimentel's body was taken down, 'All the congregations in the Realm should sing Te Deums to render thanks to the Almighty'.

This Parthenopean Revolution, hated to its very core by the people ('Long Live the King, Death to Jacob! [the Jacobins]' was their cry), nevertheless represented the detonator for the breaking of feudal relations and signalled the first steps of the transition to a bourgeois state with a few trappings of constitutionality, and this would in turn evolve further in the next decade under Murat. The French Revolution had a long-distance effect, ten years after the fact, on the intellectuals of the Neapolitan Enlightenment (who were the heirs to the philosophical tradition of Vico). These are the ones Queen Caroline, Marie Antoinette's sister, defined as 'hotheads, enlightened spirits, philosophers and, above all, ambitious'. But this earlier 'Spartan' republic, created by pure and hard intellectuals who spoke to the people – for them an undefinable and threatening body – in their noble political language of equality which nobody understood, was smashed to pieces by the people themselves. The plebs were Monarchist, Bourbonic.

In 1811 Stendhal wrote in his Diary from Naples that 'The common people love King Ferdinand very much; he speaks their language and he is full of vivacity, humour and indecent gestures'. Another noted chronicler of the epoch, the learned lawyer De Nicola, wrote, 'The truth is that our Solons know everything except the art of governing, which is an extremely difficult art, particularly in the first moments of revolution involving five million souls who, after 800 years, cannot understand any language which does not speak of King and Realm, and who believe that it is impossible to live without a king.'

In 1946 as well, the people of Naples believed that it was *impossible to live without a king*. Pre-capitalism, fascism and capitalism had and have made the existence of the Neapolitan sub-proletariat, living by expedients around the centres of power, rent and speculation, increasingly functional for their own development and for the specific forms this takes in Naples. The first modern proletarian nuclei were implanted in a populace already reduced to desperation and decadence, since from 1860 on even the few paltry elements of clientelism previously grouped around the Bourbon Court were no more. Naples was cut off from large-scale commerce with foreign countries; from diplomacy; from international contacts of all types; and finally she was even cut off from the countryside and cities of the South and from her own hinterland (see the excellent essay of Emilio Sereni, 'Naples', published in 1938 in the journal *Stato Operaio*).

Following the unity of Italy, exploitation passed into the hands of the country's new capitalist élite, and Naples fell under the control of the agrarian-industrial bloc, dominated effectively by the northern ruling class. The date of the beginnings of a real industrial proletariat can be set quite clearly in 1867, for it was in that year that the Armstrong Company of London – in order to circumvent a strike in its English arms factories – decided, in a telegram, to join the Consortium of Southern Italian Industry 'for the Pozzuoli cannon factory, as well as for the construction of the new Naval Yards in Pozzuoli itself'. And the capitalist development of Naples in the future would also obey this tendency: to avoid the creation of a modern, productive proletariat, instead creating circumscribed industrial zones in the midst of a basically consuming population which seeks its living in expedients, and which therefore conglomerates around centres of existing wealth and power in order to scrounge enough to live. This tendency also means, naturally, that petty corruption must become an integral part of social intercourse. It was with this conception of 'the infallible instinct of *what is immediately useful to one's own survival*' (as Croce defined the attitude of the plebs in 1799), that the people of Naples launched themselves unselfishly in defence of the Monarchy.

In 1946, then, who *wasn't* a monarchist? Old men, old women, adults, young people, children, newborn babies, even the unborn were all pro-monarchy. And the most monarchist of all were the sub-proletarians. Croce was a monarchist, and used to say of himself: 'old monarchist that I am'. And so were the lawyers, dentists, washer-women, hairdressers, teachers and Latin professors. The back streets of Naples, in those days, were not only 'off limits' to us Communists, but to *republicans* in general. No one who called himself a republican could go there without running the risk of being mobbed, given the famous idiosyncrasy of the poor masses with respect to the Republic which has existed just below the surface since 1799. Some 'heroic' propagandists, whose names I now cannot recall, would now and then try a brief harangue from a convenient balcony, on the spur of the moment, but they inevitably ended up beating a hasty retreat under a shower of rocks and other undesirable objects (e.g. chamberpots, including their contents), which would be thrown at them by the inhabitants of the neighbourhood they had been foolish enough to invade. At Salerno, the only time I was stupid enough to speak publicly on this issue, I ended up caught in a hail of tomatoes so ample that I am sure there were enough there to make at least two kilos of tomato sauce. I remember this: they hunted us ceaselessly and mercilessly. The monarchists showed themselves to be full of dramatic imagination. The women would march at the head of their demonstrations all draped in the Italian tricolour with the Savoy coat of arms in the middle (the old flag under the Monarchy). Just like ancient Roman women in their *pepla*, they would slowly, arrogantly and bravely advance. The children, for lack of flags, would put together hats and clothes out of Monarchist posters, held on with pins like stage clothes. The Knot of Savoy, the symbol of the royal family, was everywhere: on the foreheads and cheeks of the children, in the buttonholes of respectable businessmen, on receptacles for holy water, on women's breasts, in house windows, on walls, in restaurants, in cinemas, in hospitals, in jails; there was no place – including the most intimate – where these knots did not appear. And this was not merely a question of *ignorance*, or of sentimentalism about royalty.

People continued to believe – for reasons tied to the specific forms of capitalist development in Naples which I have already described – that the King, the Monarchy, the great estates and the nobility were their only 'providers of work', in the sense that these were the people who 'generously' extended benefits, charity, subsidies, assistance. They believed that without these benefactors, everyone would end up controlled by miserable wretches just like themselves, the communists and their friends. *If you put 'beggars' in the place of the rich*, what kind of advantages can be drawn from *that*? These beggars would only try to enrich themselves – thought the people – by taking everything they hadn't already got, and in this way, the common folk would be robbed twice over: first, because the King and his rich entourage would be driven away, and then a second time because the *parvenus* would soon have tried to fatten themselves at the expense of the poor. In the same way that a worker defends himself against the dismantling of a factory, the common people of Naples defended themselves against the dismantling of the Monarchy. 'And who will give us something to eat?' was the furious cry they raised in response to republican arguments, while at the same time their feelings towards the royal family became increasingly tender: that nice King and Queen, and those sweet little princes and princesses.

On 2 June 1946, Naples and its province gave 87,220 votes to the Republic, and 347,433 (80 per cent) to the Monarchy; in the city of Naples, just 31,000 people voted for the Republic. Now at the same time, the Socialists and Communists obtained 128,367 votes for Deputies to the Constituent Assembly (74,559 for the PCI and 53,808 for the Socialists). This means of course that not even all our own comrades voted for the Republic. In Palermo, the number of people who voted for the Republic was less than the number of Communist Party members. So the Republic was therefore able to get on its feet only because of the North and Centre of the country, where there had been the struggle for Liberation, and where class conflict and mass politicization had been determining factors.[4] As Togliatti wrote, there was a danger of a total cleavage of Italian society, the isolation of the Party from the working masses, and civil war.

At Naples on 15 June, after the official proclamation of the Republic, the Neapolitan masses tried to storm the PCI Federation, which was, in those days, in Via Medina, right where the Ambassador Hotel now stands. My most vivid memory is of women wrapped in Monarchist flags, marching at the head of this crowd which fully intended to break into the Federation and massacre the Communists. It was a

4. In the nation as a whole, 12,717,923 (54 per cent) votes were cast for the Republic, as against 10,719,284 (46 per cent) for the Monarchy. (Trans.)

full pitched battle. The comrades managed to repel the assault, and then the troops stepped in. Seven people died, seventy were injured and 200 were arrested out of that crowd. These are well-known facts, but I remind you of them here to provide a general political picture of the times. In a letter sent to all the Party's organizational units on 8 June, Togliatti defined 'the struggle for the referendum as the greatest battle fought to date by the PCI on the terrain of democratic legality', and 'the victory of the Republic [as], for the Italian people, the necessary culmination of a twenty-year struggle against Fascism and unequivocal affirmation of their own will to survive'.

In the city of Naples, from 31,020 votes in 1946, the PCI went to 98,011 votes in '48, to 112,579 in '53, 147,571 in '58, and 155,850 in '63. This rise – especially between 1946 and 1958 – hinged largely on the Party being what Togliatti had defined as a *mass party*, or *party of a new type*, born in the objective historical situation I have outlined here. Togliatti based himself on the tactic of the 'United Front', spelled out in the report of the Seventh Congress of the International in 1935, which in turn was a reflection of the first prospect of a 'Popular Front' in France. He also drew on the lessons of what, in *Stato Operaio*, he termed the 'specificity' of the Spanish Revolution. In other words, his starting-point was the antifascist struggle in Europe launched by the '*Appeal for Unity*'. And right after his arrival in Naples on 11 April 1944, just off the boat from North Africa like a clandestine immigrant, he formulated the structure and tasks of the 'mass party'.

The 'new party' had to 'participate enthusiastically in the constitution of this new Italy', and it had to be a party with 'a national policy, and with a policy of unity'. It was a question of leaving the narrow confines of the concept of an illegal party, and creating a link between the veteran cadres and the broad movement which involved thousands of new political combatants. It was these people that the Party needed, and it had to put itself at the head of this movement; in this way it would exercise hegemony over the clamorous, powerful advance of the masses: peasants, workers and others. It had to do this without losing its essential reference point, which was the class consciousness of the working-class nuclei, among whom there was a simultaneous struggle to be waged against *sectarian*, i.e. Bordigan residues. This new type of party would not be restrictive in an ideological or political sense, and it had nothing to do with the *Leninist vanguard party of the proletariat.* It was to aim to prove itself in terms of reality, reality in movement, linking itself to everyone, whatever their origins. It was to act on concrete issues, whenever necessary and possible, in order to defeat poverty; give direct succour to the masses; at the same time, raise up an impregnable wall against any future reactionary wave; provide a barrier against the 'Cold War', which was to split the West into two opposed camps; guarantee the development of democracy in Italy with the struggle to put the Constitution into effect; and carry through to the end, at the head of a vast system of alliances, the bourgeois-democratic revolution, before going any farther. The object was to avoid ending up like Spain or Greece, and to guard against a Gaullist *coup d'état.*

The relationship between the Party and intellectuals, which you have often noted as typical of the PCI, is a characteristic element of the 'mass party'. This *notable presence of intellectuals in leading positions within the Party*, and within the unions, and at all levels of the Party organization, is something you do not find in any other Communist Party. It is hard to say exactly what role Togliatti assigned to intellectuals in his conception of the *new party*, or why he should have wanted to promote them at every level of the Party, as he in fact did on his return to Italy. But two good reasons certainly did exist: the one political and the other ideological.

The first: to counter the ferocious campaign conducted by Fascism and capitalism against the shaggy Communists with knives in their teeth, Togliatti wanted to demonstrate conclusively that we were, in fact, a civilized, educated, advanced party. He even went so far as to recommend to the older comrades that they pay attention to their manner of dress and appearance. Instead of his sweater, he himself took to wearing a very proper double-breasted blue suit, which almost concealed the red tie he often wore. And Togliatti used to spend much of his time doing the rounds of the antique booksellers in Rome, searching for 18th-century French books, which he collected. He loved to argue with intellectuals of every type. In the evenings, he often used to go out to eat among the people, in the *trattorie* of Trastevere, which excited Sartre so much that he mentioned this in his essay on Togliatti's death in 1964. Moreover, although Togliatti maintained the old internal hierarchy as a solid bedrock, he also did introduce new people into the highest reaches of the party structure and into the most highly qualified positions. Many of these new leaders were noted intellectuals, or people already known politically, or the children of prominent politicians of the pre-Fascist era. He made, in short, a direct attempt to organize the Party in such a way that the presence of intellectuals throughout the Party, the unions and the local administrations was a significant one, in a continual effort to produce an amalgam with cadres of other social origins.

But you can't really understand Togliatti – and here is the second and even more profound reason – without going back to Gramsci, who interpreted the conception of 'intellectual' very broadly, and who attributed to what he called *organic intellectuals* an organizing and connective function, as the 'agents' of the dominant group, carrying out the subordinate functions of social hegemony and political government.

In *The Intellectuals and the Organization of Culture*, Gramsci assigns the primary task to the Party: to make the organic intellectuals into organizers of the consent of great masses towards the party of the working class – just as the State (and, in my opinion, the Church) did for its own class ends. 'The political party,' he wrote, 'is nothing other than [the working class's] specific way of elaborating (its) own category of organic intellectuals . . . [it] is precisely the mechanism which carries out synthetically and over a larger scale, in political society. In other words, it is responsible for welding together the *organic intellectuals* of a given group – the dominant one – and the traditional intellectuals.'

I have looked out Togliatti's speech in Florence on 3 October 1944, which is absolutely essential for understanding what, at that time, the tasks of the *new* party were to be. I'll quote a few of the most relevant passages: 'The popular, mass character of the Party: the Party gathers about itself all the productive forces of the country; it directs them towards the reconstruction and rebirth of the country, resolves the concrete problems of the masses, faces the great problems of national life and the small problems of provincial and local existence. For, if it did not do all this, the mass of the people would turn their backs on us, since what they want is for these problems to be resolved, today. . . . The Party will be unable to perform these tasks if it remains a more or less numerous association of propagandists for our general and ideological objectives. . . . We must know how to provide answers to all of the questions which arise for the nation and for the labouring masses, and we have to know how to work in order to resolve these

questions. . . . This means that we have to establish links with everyone, this is why we must become a great mass party. . . . We say to
our old comrades who have the tendency to remain a small group of
purists, faithful to ideals and theory: "You are wrong; you will only
be a real nucleus of leaders to the extent that you succeed in making
our party a great *mass party*." '

In Togliatti's *new party*, the most pressing, tangible, concrete task,
in Naples, was to go to the aid of the children of the sub-proletariat,
who, after the ephemeral comforts of the Occupation, were thrown
back into the most grinding poverty. We put together a great committee, headed by Giorgio Amendola, which included liberals and democrats of all kinds. Even Croce's daughter, Lidia, a timid, quiet girl,
was on the committee. I was the secretary. We managed to transfer
10,000 children – who had neither TB nor other infectious diseases –
from the South to the North. In order to get them, we had to examine
twice that number. Trains full of '*scugnizzi*' (urchins) shuttled up and
down Italy all through 1946 and 1947, and the various services which
were needed – to keep order, keep them safe, and keep them supplied
with food – were all organized by the workers from the great metalworking factories in Naples. In this way that bond of solidarity, so
lacking today, was created for the first time between workers and sub-
proletarians, in the form of concrete aid.

The 'Hotel for the Poor' was created by Carlo III as an immense
hospice (originally suggested by a famous priest, Father Rocco) in
which to gather up 'thousands of chronically disinherited plebeans';
it was eventually abandoned and, by the late 'forties, was full of
cobwebs. It was here that we installed our 'hygiene headquarters' for
the children of Naples. We repaired and cleaned the 'baths' in the
basement, and then in teams – workers in the lead – we washed, dis-
infected, and clothed hundreds of little Neapolitans before the departure of every train. We would put a number around the neck of
every child, but the littlest ones would often tear the numbers off, and
we would then all go crazy trying to reconstruct their identity through
police-style interrogations. In the end, we would arrive with the
children in the snow-covered cities of the North, and there we left
them, in the arms of comrades and citizens who instantly showered
them with food, toys, etc. Their letters home were full of lavish
gastronomic descriptions, as well as the news that they were going to
school.

Their mothers, for the most part, were the ex-leaders of the Monarchist bands, the very same ones who had assaulted the Federation. There were, in that period, famous political conversions, such as that of a formidable woman known as La Pachiochia, as prolific as Hecuba, wife of Priam, who commanded, through the various branches of her genealogical tree, an entire quarter of the 'belly' of Naples. La Pachiochia, vast and regal, dressed in heavy overlapping black skirts which came all the way down to her shoes, paid us a visit after her nephews had been sent to Emilia. Her arrival at the headquarters of the Children's Committee in Piazzetta Augusteo was like the meeting of Garibaldi and Victor Emmanuel at Teano, the sign of peace being made.

But relationships between the Communists and the sub-proletariat suffered a terrible reversal in 1952, when a majority of votes in the city went to the Monarchist boss, Lauro. He teamed up with the Fascists and, amid great popular acclaim, became mayor. He was reconfirmed as mayor in 1956 even more triumphantly, getting 280,000 votes on his own, with no Fascist help. But then, in the next elections, he was defeated by the people themselves, thanks to the tenacious work of Communist militants and leaders, who by that time had succeeded in constructing a Party capable of raising the consciousness of the masses, in this way enabling them to forever demystify Lauro and all forms of 'Laurism'.

If Gramsci's emphasis on the relationship between North and South is one great theme still actual today, the other essential theme – always weak and at times non-existent – is that of the connection between Naples, her working class, and the peasant populations of the South of Italy. In order to reinforce these themes, we organized a 'Congress of Peasants of the South' at Bagnoli, in which workers' delegations from the North took part as well. At that time, two trends came into sharp contrast with each other. On one hand, you had the break-up of trade-union unity, the expulsion of the Communists and Socialists from the Government 'on American orders', and the split in the Socialist Party which gave birth to the P S I (Socialists) and the P S D I (Social-Democrats). On the other hand, once we were definitively out of the *coalition government*, enormous workers' struggles developed for the first time in the South, most notably in the big factories (OMF and Ilva) in Naples. These battles were great high spots, for they resulted in the prevention of the dismantling of the plants (which the main capitalist forces had ordered). At the same time, this period marked the historic phase of the 'breaking' of the Southern latifundia, the process which eventually smashed agrarian feudalism. This victory certainly was not won by any *structural reform* decreed by Parliament, but was the result of an extensive popular struggle, with the occupation of large estates by entire village populations, marching in closed ranks with the PCI's banner at their head. There were dozens of deaths, hundreds of wounded and thousands of arrests. There were interminable trials which threw all the peasants of a village into the same cells. All this occurred in the 'fifties.

I will stop at this point, not so much because I moved from Naples to Rome – for I returned to the South regularly for political work until 1961 – but because the fundamental objective of these letters is to talk about *today*.

I have drawn, from my *own* experience, only the images and facts which seem relevant to the political thinking which characterizes the kind of party we are today. This is why I have tried, in the reflections you have just read, to tell you what the Party has been and why and how it came to take a certain form as Togliatti's 'mass party'. Twenty-four years have passed since then, and the Party of Togliatti is *no longer new*. Indeed, several times during the campaign it has appeared *old* to me, infected by its external environment by means of some sort of involuntary symbiosis, exposed to bourgeois ideological attack whenever it has failed to make Marxism-Leninism the driving element in its policies. Because the Party has *acted politically* less and less. This is because so much of its nervous and muscular system has rigidified from bureaucratization.

To sum up: we built a great Communist Party in Italy after the Liberation, one defined by French left intellectuals as a jewel of a party among all the communist parties of West Europe. We founded the Republic, drafted some of its best laws and saw to it that they were respected, saved democracy from any *coup d'état*, beat back – with vast mass struggles and hundreds of casualties – capitalism's frontal assaults, safeguarded the parliamentary-democratic structure of the country, to the point of winning the fame of having developed a 'model' for the West.

During the same time-span, capitalism has extended its modern power, changing Italy from a predominantly agricultural country into one whose industry puts it among the ten most developed countries in the world. (We usually forget that just as the 'German Miracle' had

American capitalism behind it, so too does the 'Italian Miracle' relate to our own docility with regard to the USA, to our 'inoffensive' foreign policy and to our going along with American priorities. In Italy, there is only one anti-American party, and that is ours, aside from the tiny PSIUP.) But at the same time that the social and political structure of the country has changed, so has the working class greatly increased its influence and its central role in the general struggle for liberation and for power. It is now powerfully backed up by the younger generations, which even further increases its ability to pressure the system and break free of its strait-jacket.

At the end of these twenty-four years of uninterrupted tensions, both internal and international, we can today see in a fairly integral fashion the various phases of what has been called our *war of position* or *defensive* war. In this arc of time, which spans the reconstruction of capitalism in Italy, the political power of monopoly capitalism has stabilized itself. And we, in spite of everything, have not been able to block the successful consolidation of a type of monopolistic development which, measuring these years by the yardstick of its own expanding influence, defines them as years of *well-being* or *opulence*. Even in the kind of battles we have fought, there have been periods of notable political setbacks, like the years between 1956 and 1962, when we had to cope with a very difficult period of transition which ended in the consolidation of a new bourgeois power bloc. This bloc was made possible politically by the rapprochement of Nenni's Socialists (who used the contorted XX Congress of the CPSU as their alibi) with social-democracy. The result was the social-democratization of the PSI and its entry into the *Atlantic-capitalist* ideological area, culminating in its open collaboration with the DC in the famous Centre-Left, which in fact offered a new organized mass base for capitalist domination.

The characteristics of our *defensive battle*, in phases like this or like that of 1960,[5] have almost always seen the Party giving precedence to

5. The reference is to the Tambroni Affair, when the DC Prime Minister of that name, no longer able to form a majority with the 'Centrist' coalition, announced that he would accept the support of the Neo-Fascist MSI. When the MSI attempted to hold its party congress in Genoa shortly afterward, rioting broke out all over Italy, with ten fatalities. Tambroni was forced to resign and any 'opening to the Right' was clearly perceived as impossible. But the PCI did not try to take the mobilization of the masses further, once this objective had been achieved. The Tambroni Affair was the background to the Centre-Left strategy of the DC in the 'sixties. (Trans.)

a *defensive alliance policy* rather than an *offensive class initiative*. The former, as I have said, has its roots in the International's antifascist unity policy and in the Resistance, and has been considered since that time as a strategy which is *still valid* for a country like Italy, in order to raise up a barrier against the enemy, who at times launches frontal assaults, and at times tries to encircle and isolate us. We have always declared that we want to avoid the so-called *politique du pire* [i.e. the worse things are, the better it is for the revolution]. And our political impact certainly has grown. But our influence, which has grown politically in Parliament, in Italy's democratic institutions, and in the political superstructures in general, has not been accompanied by any real successes in opening up breaches in the general configuration of capitalist power. Even our acceptance of the trend towards the expansion of the public sector of the economy (through planning and government participation in industry) does not appear to have borne fruit, given the forms that state monopoly capitalism has taken, which are those of integrating itself with private monopoly capitalism. In the same way, the distinction we make between *private* and *public* capital risks obscuring awareness of the class nature of the state, and makes it impossible to expose the error of the social-democratic claim that the state is neutral and *efficient*. This can already be seen to a large degree in the PCI's programmes or slogans, as for example in our requests to the Government that it 'solve the problems of the South'. Our alliance strategy, which is always aimed at existing groups of leaders, and our call for antifascist unity, which are more than thirty years old as 'theories', may well be able to boast a good number of achievements; but they also clearly indicate how a revolutionary party like ours can pay dearly for them when powerful popular forces emerge in the country – forces which want socialism and, in that sense, could and should be educated and mobilized by the party of the working class. Popular movements show – even when they are outside the parties and unions – that the masses have grown politically and can no longer be assumed to be integrated into the old capitalist society.

Meanwhile, even today we still risk getting bogged down in this sterile dialogue for *a new majority*, not only with the oppositional fringes of the PSI and the DC, and the ridiculous Radical 'Party', but even with their ephemeral provincial prophets, and with every kind of highly-placed dissident. Twenty-four years after its birth, this aspect too of the *new party* must be re-examined in order to open the way to a new communist militancy. There is a whole custom of 'dialogue' which should be re-thought as well. When we used to see, in years past, Party leaders playing up to bourgeois journalists with ingratiating smiles and gestures, and at the same time practically ignoring the editorial staff of *l'Unità* (regarded as third-rate employees and, anyway, already won over to our side), as revolutionaries we felt humiliated. After my polemic against '*La Malfa napoletano*' in *l'Unità* (La Malfa, of whom you have certainly never heard, is the leader of a lilliputian republican party, with whom some of our leaders have been talking for a quarter of a century in the hope of softening his anti-communism or under the illusion that he is a worthwhile person with whom to discuss), I received this message: M.A.M. is apparently unaware that there is a gentleman's agreement between Neapolitan Communists and Radical-Republicans, whereby for twenty years we have not had any attacks on one another. I complained about this 'message' to my comrades here, but they all deny knowing anything about it.

Another way that seeking alliances at the topmost leadership level of the parties hacks away at our political morality can be seen in the great rush which occurs towards any modest, even if respectable, person of the Left who stands to the right of us, as if he were a decisive ally. We have a particular preference for 'intellectuals'. We offer them positions in Parliament, in the Senate, etc. The comrades in Rome, for example, are very upset that we weren't able to find room for at least one of these Independents on the whole PCI list for Naples. But here in Naples, the comrades tell of having gone knocking more than once at the door of a likely candidate, a physicist I believe, to offer him a seat in Montecitorio [the Parliament building]. But the person in question always firmly refused, and finally he entered the Republican list. A great 'loss'! I met a journalist from one of the North's largest papers, and he too told me that they had wanted to put him on the list, but he had said *no thanks*. 'Look,' I told him, 'the extraordinary thing is not what happened to you, but to me: to be a *Communist* journalist and have made it on to the PCI list.'

Now that it is twenty-four years since our Party returned to legal existence, we cannot fail to put it – in all respects – under the kind of scrutiny required by the new times, times as new as those in which Togliatti found himself in 1944, and even richer, with fuller theoretical and practical implications. It just will not do to say, like Candide, that since we have had so many successes, everything has gone *for the best in the best of possible worlds*. We also have to reflect on our failures, which are as rich in theoretical and political lessons as are the successes. And above all, we have to re-examine our way of looking at the new social and political reality of Italy, which has its points of original creation, of new cultural life and of expansion all originating from the masses, *from below*, in the factories and in the fields, in the schools and universities, in certain Catholic circles and labour organizations. And its principal actors are not the rhetoricians of culture and politics, but young forces who have entered the terrain of revolutionary class struggle.

'It is by means of the criticism of capitalist civilization,' Gramsci wrote in his *Prison Notebooks*, 'that the unitary consciousness of the proletariat has been formed, or is being formed; and criticism means culture. . . .' Everything that Togliatti thought in the past about a *mass party*, in a given political and historical situation, if one accepts the Leninist principle of 'undertaking a concrete analysis of a concrete situation', today needs serious scrutiny, and a *Leninist revision*. It is not a question of oiling the joints of our traditional structures, but of modifying them according to a politically revolutionary line.

The mechanical and bureaucratic application of certain rules for political alliances, based on a cherished *timid frontism* towards parties and personalities and traditional intellectuals of every type, conditions the political activities of the Party to such an extent that finding the *real* allies who exist in the reality of Italy today is often an extremely tortuous undertaking. Or else it happens that the new revolutionary forces are mistaken by some of us, indiscriminately, for 'enemies of the Party line'. We see-saw between the desire to absorb these new forces painlessly and mechanically, and the wish to put an end to 'splits' in the Party – even at the cost of eventual wounds and mutilations.

In this general picture, our political initiative runs the risk of ending up in the refrigerator, as does our link with the masses (understood as the primary protagonists of history). The problem which urgently needs examination is: To what degree does our Party reflect in itself the crises and contradictions of Italian society? In today's struggles solutions are emerging which show bourgeois democracy to be obsolete. Perspectives and solutions of a socialist nature are maturing. The working class and poor peasants strengthen their vanguard role every day, and the degree of political consciousness and the desire to participate in the sharing of effective power is steadily rising, above all in the new generations of the petty bourgeoisie (secondary school and university students, intellectual workers of all kinds, intermediate cadres, etc.). At the same time, however, there is a proportional drop in the capacity of the parties and traditional institutions to represent these masses.

This means that the interdependence of the struggle for more democracy, the struggle for political power, and the struggle for socialist solutions to society's problems has been tremendously reinforced, and that the *potential* terrain for political and social confrontation has, *in reality*, moved to a very advanced level. But to what extent is the Party capable of grasping what is *new* – in terms of its *structure*, the present state of its *internal democracy* and *its link with the real movement of the masses*? Our party was born and grew not just to build a democratic society, but to destroy capitalism and construct a socialist society. This is the central point, which daily makes clearer how inadequate and 'tired' the Party is, in a moment which appears more and more to be one of those when 'history takes a leap'.

Maria Antonietta

Dear Louis,   *Naples, 3 May 1968*

One evening, while I was speaking at Casoria, I met a girl near the stage. She had the hard, closed face of an adult which, at the same time, was as round as a child's. She had smooth, shining hair combed straight down. Her black eyes were alert and vivid, and in them I discerned a political thought or interrogation. The reason that she immediately aroused so much curiosity in me is that I know that usually, if you want to find women, you have to go to their homes. They almost never come to speeches. So you can understand my reaction when I saw her come right up to the speakers' platform. I went over to her and began to ask her about herself.

Her name is Nunzia Galante, and her job, until last November, was that of a highly specialized tester of electronic equipment. Her employer, the famous firm Geloso (a big supplier of TVs, radios, and aircraft equipment for the Common Market), fired her after she had successfully organized a strike of all the women in the plant. This strike and the active intercession of the unions won a decent labour contract for the workers.

The strike and her summary dismissal occurred in November 1967: the head of the plant had told the women workers that anyone who joined the union would be thrown out of the factory. And Nunzia led the struggle! Since then, she has been looking for different ways to carry on a struggle against the boss, and against all bosses.

Casoria, a small town fifteen km. from Naples, is called 'the Milan of the South' by the 'Sudocrats', because a few large northern firms (Rhodiatoce, with 1,800 employees, and the electronic firm of Valenzuela-Geloso) have located factories there in order to make use of an underpaid *feminine labour force*, without any labour contracts. Nunzia tells me that in the place where she used to work, the women are all sixteen to eighteen years old, are hired without any written agreement on working conditions, are forbidden to join the unions, and are paid between *sixty and eighty lire an hour*! The skilled workers get 130 lire an hour! There really ought to be a study of the forms which super-exploitation has taken in the new plants which have sprung up around Naples. These factories draw their workers from the countryside, and the people who have to convert themselves in record time into an industrial work-force are almost always very young female peasants or day labourers. Some of the factories, like Pirelli in Giugliano,[1] make candidates for jobs take psycho-technical tests to determine optimal productive capacities, and then fill positions on that basis. The girls are taken on at the age of 16–17 and eliminated at 20–25, 'when they are old'. Wages are roughly identical to those earned in the fields, the big difference being essentially that they are regular.

As I spoke with Nunzia, she told me she had begun to write about her struggle and her 'defeat' in a notebook, really a diary of sorts, but that she hadn't yet completed it. I begged her to do so, and I read over what she had done. We talked a lot about her writing, and finally she gave me what she had written. It is an extremely rational testimony

1. In January 1969, eight young female workers occupied the Castagliola Distillery in Giugliano, which has seventy workers (all of them women), for four days. Finally the police arrived and threw them out. All eight were fired, but they provided a real example of what a true workers' struggle can be like to the others.

on women's working conditions, especially because it is so precise and free from rhetoric.

It is also a very rare text, since so few examples of workers' literature exist. It is all the more rare since there are no examples at all of writing from women in the South. It is almost impossible to find a woman like Nunzia who spontaneously sets about writing down her human experiences and her involvement with capitalism, the one connected so closely with the other. In the South, which undergoes such violent pressures seeking to condemn it to have *no* class consciousness, there exist, in reality, exceptional feminine revolutionary energies.[2] Now Nunzia Galante has gone to work in the electoral campaign, a little with me and a little with others in Casoria and Ponticelli (another workers' centre). She has organized a number of meetings between me and her working comrades, outside the factory at 6.00 a.m., as they enter for the first shift. I am sending along what she wrote. She really is like a rare plant, pushing her way upward between cracks in a brutal landscape. I haven't 'edited' anything she wrote.

Maria Antonietta

I went to work for Geloso on 2 April 1954. I was assigned to the Variable Condensers Department. To be precise, my first job was the construction of these condensers. In three years, my bosses never had anything to complain about with my work. We worked from 8.00 until 6.30, and since it was precision work (involving the alignment of fins which were one millimetre apart), few of us could manage such hours; those of us who did do the work were the ones with a clinical eye (that is what the supervisors called us). In addition, I was also a tester.

One morning, I was stopped by the director, Signor Gagliardi, in the month of March 1957. It was only a few months until my wedding, and I had plans to quit my job. But, as I said, the director spoke to me, in the name of Signor Valenzuela and the foreman, and he said they were unhappy that I was leaving, that they were very pleased with my work,

2. The seasonal workers of the Cirio plant in Castellammare—here too it was an avante-garde of thirty who led the way for the other 270—held their ground successfully against police aggression in November 1968, at the cost of three injured. The women won the battle, which concerned, as well as the question of wages, their general working conditions. The local unions in Castellammare called a day-long strike in solidarity with the Cirio workers.

and that if I wanted to, I could stay on after I got married. Because of this, I accepted and agreed to stay on. But then things changed. I have nothing on my own conscience, because I always did my duty, even though I always got a starvation wage. When I had my first pregnancy, I took work home with me. I returned after my maternity leave elapsed. But things had changed notably, mainly that there were continual clashes between workers and managers, but, I repeat, I had never done anything wrong. First I was demoted, passing down from testing to simply 'alignment'. Then I caught bronchitis and I was called in by the director. I pointed out that for three or four years, aside from maternity leave, I had never presented any problems, and he answered that production was what counted and workers shouldn't get sick. From that time on, if I was ever absent I ended up getting called into his office and getting told off. Then the head of the factory relocated the plant, that is, we moved from the Arenaccia to Casoria where the boss had bought some land and put up a shed. During the transfer period we were all laid off, but I was the very first person to get sent home.

My foreman told me these exact words: 'Galante, since you are the head of a family, since you have a daughter, we thought you should be sent home first.' With this I asked permission to bring my tools home with me so they wouldn't get lost in the move; but he told me that this wasn't necessary since in the new plant we would have all new tools.

After a three- or four-month layoff, during which time they paid us for a grand total of forty hours' work, I was told that I could go back to work (but I have to add that I was the first sent home and just about the last one to be called back to work). The group I worked with before was all split up and two were not rehired. One day one of my co-workers asked the foreman why these two girls had not been recalled, and he said that they had sacked all the troublemakers, and, turning towards me, he said, 'You should have been fired too, but Signor Valenzuela didn't want to let you go.' So I said, 'I'm sorry you only tell me this now, because it is too late to thank the boss'; so he added, 'I was kidding, how could you fall for that?' 'I didn't fall for anything; it is the boss who should thank us if his business is growing.' As for the details on our rise, our group got eighty-five lire an hour, and it was said that we would get a ten-lire rise. When I got my next wage packet, I realized that this wasn't so, at least not for me. So on Monday, when I returned, I asked my colleagues and they told me that they had got this rise all right. So then I went looking for some explanations from my immediate superior, but he told me that he wasn't responsible for any of this and the person to see was the director. I went to the director and he told me, 'Do you want to know why? Because you don't pay attention to your work, you don't produce as much as you are supposed to, you are forever asking for special favours, and then, too, you are absent a lot.' I responded, 'Ingegnere, I didn't know that in this place things were based on whether you like or dislike someone, because I can easily disprove every single thing that you have just said.' At this point, he called me ill-mannered and walked away. But a little later he sent for me and I had to report to his office where he showed me the attendance record of someone who wasn't even in my department, called Luisa Solemme, and I pointed that out to him and let him know that I wanted explanations that had to do with my group and not those from other parts of the factory and that everything he had said as a reason for my not getting a rise were accusations with no foundation, since the fore-man signed the production reports every day, and next to each figure we all initialled the report. In this way, I could always see how my production compared to that of the others. For this reason I knew I had been treated unjustly and then the director told me that if I didn't take any holidays for the next month he would give me the rise. To this I answered, 'I am sorry, I cannot promise anything, because I have a baby and if she gets sick I have to stay at home, and I think that your wife, if she were in my situation, would do the same thing.' To keep this job, I have run the risk of dying a lot of times, because in order not to get into trouble with the bosses, I kept avoiding having children and one time when I had to go to the hospital on account of this, Ingegnere Valenzuela (Senior) himself came to tell me that I was absent too often. So, once again, I had to go through another appeal procedure, and even though I told him just how things stood, he threatened to fire me.

One day De Feo sent an invitation to all the girls from Casoria who worked at Geloso, and so I went to Casoria to this assembly. With me were a few co-workers who come from Naples. After I spoke for all of us and explained our working conditions, De Feo promised us that he would go and have a talk with the Ingegnere, saying that he would see about getting us into a union. But after De Feo's talk and after all the foremen and some of the workers went to the union, the boss had us all meet in the plant and he began to go into the usual sermon, that is how we could com-plain all we wanted, however we wanted, but he wouldn't give us a lira more. We could even go on strike and nothing would change. However, there were people who could decide to improve themselves, and they would get promotions and more money. At this point I asked some questions, namely that I didn't have anything to improve since I already had a higher qualification recognized by him on paper: in other words, I was down as a tester. But to this the boss said that I would have done better to stay at home. So then I said, 'Ingegnere, many years ago when I got married I wanted to leave, but the director told me then that all of you were sorry to hear that; then it was convenient to you to keep me on, and now it is convenient to me to stay here.'

I had another run-in with Ingegnere Aldo (the boss's son). Our group had been dropped from our earlier form of work, the construction of radios, and we were put in a little area off to the side and directed by the boss himself, the senior engineer. We made the instrument panels for a certain kind of radio, and I was chosen to wind the coils for the oscillators and aerials. Not even half a day after the boss had first shown me how, I began producing them regularly, but a day later, as I have said, his son came along while I was at work and asked me how many of these coils I had turned out, and I said a few of one kind and a few of another. The production rate was eighty panels a day, and in less than a day and a half I was working at a rate of 160 coils a day. When I gave him my answer, he said that I was sleeping on the job, and he walked away before I had a chance to answer. However, after two or three days, I called him over and I made him see what was going on, and from that time on, things went differently with the boss's son; then, from the alignment of variable condensers we were to move on to the construction of receivers. I was put in the preparatory section, that is, everything that had to do with the preparation and construction of receiver-sets. Unfortunately, just then my husband got very ill and had a stomach operation. Naturally, I had to miss several days' work, and when I got back the trouble really began. The director sent for me in his office and told me that he had already taxed his patience with me and I answered back that I was sick and tired of all these warnings and he could do whatever he wanted, for all I cared. It then happened that I got sick and it wasn't anything that I invented. I had the heart specialist of the Mutual Fund write up his diagnosis and I brought it to the boss. In spite of this, when I came back, he said to me in a sarcastic tone: 'Galante, are you really always sick?' I said that he already had my answer, and that if he expected me to quit, he had another thought coming. He always gave me the most complicated jobs to do, and that is how one day I ended up putting together the medium-band radios; every evening I had the habit of cleaning up my workbench and leaving my tools all lined up in a row. It was, unfortunately, a Friday and there was no work the next day. I cleaned my bench, but there was a blob of tin that I couldn't remove with a rag, so I pulled at it with my thumbnail, and the point went into my thumb. At the time, I didn't pay any more attention to this, but that night it hurt so much that in the morning I could see that there was already some pus under the nail. On Monday I went to the family doctor to get a shot of penicillin, and Dr Masi asked me how I had hurt myself. Naturally I told him what had happened to me on Friday while cleaning the bench and then the doctor told me that I should go to my place of employment, report the affair, and hence have it covered by sickness benefits. So I followed his advice and went into the office to get the application form. But the accountant went to the director and the director came to me and said that the foreman didn't remember my being injured and so if I thought I could pull a fast one I was mistaken. I said that I was sure I knew what I was doing. I told how the incident had occurred and said that my conscience was in order.

Another time, I had been absent a few days and my punch-card got all mixed up, and instead of punching one side, the other side came out marked. When I got my pay-check I noticed that I was credited with a good number of days less than I had actually worked, and the only thing I could figure out was that I had been credited with too few work days. So I went to the accountant to get things straightened out, but we had an argument, so he went away with my pay-check and said that he would have to straighten things out with the director. The next morning, the supervisor made a big speech right in the middle of the shed, telling all of us that before we opened our mouths we should make sure we added things up right, and I said that mathematics was not a matter of opinion, and hence it didn't make any sense to waste so much breath because the fact was that I really was several days short on my pay. Then the supervisor went into his office and had my cards put in order, and he found that they really had been added correctly, but that the wrong side of the cards had been marked in some cases.

Then there is the case of the twins. After seventeen years on the job, they just left because they didn't have any more strength to put up with more injustice. Because neither one of them is married, they didn't have a family the way I have one, and so they dedicated themselves to their work. But Previteria, their supervisor, had never liked them and so, after all those years, they were forced to quit. Another co-worker of mine who still works there and who also had a stomach operation is also not liked very well by any of the bosses and she too has to put up with continual harassment. Her name is Emilia and she is a good person and does everything she is asked, but still she is not appreciated by anyone. I could give a lot of other examples but it is enough to say briefly that to resist in that factory you have to be apathetic or else you risk ending up in an asylum.

Only a few days after I was taken on I was shifted from the group I had originally been assigned to (alignment of variable condensers) and I immediately got to see the way the boss thought. In fact, he, in the presence of the department supervisor, promised the girls something extra for all those who exceeded the production norms. The working day was ten hours for a maximum pay of 3,300 lire. 2,200 was more or less normal pay, and the beginners got around 1,500. In other words, the basic pay was about 200 lire an hour, and you had to work ten hours, so the girls did the best they could to increase production. The obligatory quota was to align about sixty variables a day, and I leave it to the imagination to understand the kind of effort these poor girls had to put in. But a month went by and they did not see any more money, so they decided to go to the boss and discuss the promise that he had failed to keep. The bravest one, her name is Lidia De Francesco, spoke up, and this is what she said to the Ingegnere : 'We have decided to ask for that raise.' And he answered : 'You may have decided on this, but I haven't decided anything.' Hearing this made me feel terrible, because I was so recently hired and had to keep to myself what I would have liked to say. And my dislike for these fancy bosses began that day and lasted all the way to the day of the show-down, the day I managed to organize a strike and bring the boss's name out before public opinion. And it is still not finished, because I am completely dedicated to organizing another strike. But this time nobody must lose their job, but the boss must bow his head before his employees who are fighting for their just cause.

Whoever reads these lines should know that in this brief diary that I have written, this last conclusion is the bitterest one of my life. You have to know how to fight if you are going to win. And, dear readers, I know that you are all workers, but being fired has cost me a lot; I grew up in that plant, and all my co-workers, male and female, liked and respected me in spite of the constant fights I had with my boss. I had to struggle a long time in order to face up to all the injustices I suffered for years and I, especially, had to provide an example for all the men and women who, like me, are exploited to the maximum. It is for this that I decided to *initiate the struggle, saying to myself: whatever the cost, this state of affairs has to end once and for all. 102 of us agreed to join a union and form a shop-floor committee [commissione interna]. A group of us went to the CGIL union and we told them about everything we had to put up with in our plant. The pay is laughable, the fines were increasing, the girls would pass out continuously and no one tried to understand or remedy anything. And when a girl was put on the line they immediately expected her to work like crazy without allowing any time to get used to the work pace, and then if she couldn't keep up she was shunted aside like a worn-out machine. Everyone who listened to us was outraged, and they gave us even more encouragement to start this struggle; but they warned us that it would be a hard struggle because they knew we were up against people beyond every bound of humanity; but none of us backed down except for a small group of four or five girls. We went to the union every day for a week, and the people there helped out a lot, but oh my! when the day came that we got our petition signed and sent it to the boss by express delivery, the evening of 27 November 1967, the supervisor came around with a list of names and invited nine of us to come to the office because the boss had something to tell us. We went, keeping up our courage, and the boss gave us the fatal blow, that is he calmly told us that we were being fired because of cutbacks in personnel. I, having been there the longest, spoke for all of us and I pointed out to the boss that nothing he said was true, and we were being fired in retaliation, since we all just happened to be the ones who were supposed to be on the committee and that was how he had our names. I concluded by saying that matters would not end there. That very evening we went to the union and they told us to start the strike. So we were on strike for twenty-one days; we went to the Prefect, to the Inspectorate of Labour, in other words, the union took all the steps it could to make that slave-driver come to terms, but we didn't get anything because the boss had a head start on us and this head start, we realized, was due to the leaders in power, because it is they who help the capitalists turn their workers into animals. And who knows what they think the little bit of pay they provide gives us, for, after all, the workers are at the bottom of the social ladder so they must suppose they don't need anything anyway. And if the bosses should learn that their workers have some electrical appliance, they say they have too much, they are getting too many vices. They just do not know the kind of sacrifices a worker has to make to buy a refrigerator or a washing-machine or even a television set. If the Christian Democrats say that the workers have achieved parity of salaries with the rest of society, well, then, I say that the people who are in power are beings who ought not to live in the midst of decent society.*

Nunzia Galante[3]

Dear Louis,   *Naples, 7 May 1968*

These words are being recorded, to get things down before they are dispersed; time is increasingly scarce. Work is a chaos that completely surrounds us, and our energies simply are not sufficient for the kind of effort that is needed to 'round off' a campaign.

I want to tell you about a new development in my relationship with the Party in Naples: this turn in events is marked by my meeting with the Neapolitan working class. 25 April signalled a notable change, whose political significance is very clear to me. At that moment, I was, in a sense, adopted; I was taken under the wing of the workers' leaders, whom up to that point I had never met in the city, where so often the life of the sub-proletariat takes precedence. On 25 April I was sent to Castellammare, a centre with a population of 70,000 where there are, as well as several very large factories in the metalworking sector, also the famous Navalmeccanica Shipyards with 2,000 workers, most of them highly skilled, as well as a few others also numbered among Italy's most important shipyards.

I spoke in front of 1,000 people, maybe more. As you know, the twenty-fifth is the anniversary of the Liberation. I didn't use any tricks: I discussed the historical importance of that epoch and why, today, it could be something less valid and decisive for the younger generation – not out of any fault of ours, but because Italy's capitalist society, her 'consumer society', had also tried to take this important date and 'market' it, trying, in an attempt to integrate it, to make the Liberation a kind of national holiday. It had made it into the tinsel, the emblazoning on a rule that is hated by the young people, and makes them sick. I kept speaking of a 'New Resistance', insistently, addressing myself to the younger people in the crowd. And I tried to

3. Nunzia's husband, without employment either, left Italy at the beginning of 1969 and went to work in West Germany. In April, Nunzia also became an emigrant worker in West Germany.

re-create a link between adults and youth in a political perspective that would be one of a party carrying on a revolutionary struggle. No paternalism toward the students, but a continuous reference to a struggle which would in turn open up a space for them to carry out revolutionary activity.

It was a long speech: it lasted an hour and fifteen minutes, I think, and a lot of it was dedicated to Vietnam and the Tet Offensive, which is a revolutionary 'model' for the youth, and to an analysis of what this was, and what imperialism represents on a world scale, with its burden of crime, misdeeds and wars, and its present total lack of ability to control events. For this reason, it is a *paper tiger*, or better, I said, a giant with clay feet. Such a long talk of this type will seem strange to you, but it really came out of me with little effort before this workers' gathering, for they follow everything and read the papers and know what is going on; in fact, they see things with more acuteness than we do, and with a more critical, less conformist spirit. In such a situation, a speech becomes an extraordinary means of communication; I think that for a political leader there is rarely such a high moment of tension as when he puts himself into such direct contact with an alive and conscious electorate. One topic triggers another, and facts generate other facts until you arrive at a total global picture – that of the reality which you are trying to capture and develop like a photograph in public. It is a *rational*, I mean even an *illuministic* attempt to gather together everything salient in political reality and transfer it into a public gathering, among thousands of people, as you are bathed and blinded by the lights.

I was aware of being in another world. 'Plebeianism' had not only disappeared, but so had every form of rhetorical bravado: everything became ordered, efficient and went as it should; from the microphone that finally worked, to the introduction of the speakers, to the dry concision of the speakers who preceded me.

After my speech, in a nearby piazza in the same city of Castellammare, the infamous De Lorenzo, head of SIFAR,[1] was scheduled to

1. In 1967 there were widespread allegations in Italy that a military coup was being plotted by elements in the Army, and that the centre of the conspiracy was in the army intelligence agency, SIFAR. Its commander at that time was Giovanni De Lorenzo, a general and career officer who promptly retired and became a Monarchist Deputy, which entitled him to immunity. Not much light has been shed on the affair since then, and the Government has been particularly lax in initiating investigations or proceedings. When such investigations do take place, the most

speak. De Lorenzo is a meddling opportunist, which is evident simply by looking at him, with his monocle wedged into his left eye, and in spite of this he managed somehow to become a lieutenant-general, the head of SIFAR, the commander of the Carabinieri. *How are certain careers made? These at least aren't military secrets,* I said. And to these questions De Lorenzo could and should give some answers tonight; 'De Lorenzo's Secret' was completely hidden behind 'State Secrets'. The centralized state makes use of its security claims to avoid any scrutiny by the people and by the masses. I reminded the crowd that last year the Constitutional Court had finally struck down a 1909 law which talked about *railway secrets.* Thanks to the filthy manipulation of 'security' that the bourgeoisie carries out in Italy, anything can become, if you want it to, a 'breach of security'. I recalled the wartime episode of the general who decreed that there had to be one hour per day of a cork exercise, during which time soldiers had to stand at attention with corks in their mouths to impress on them the importance of silence. I concluded that this is the same thing that happened with SIFAR: the Government put a cork in the mouths of millions of Italians. No one could say anything, and yet SIFAR had compiled 147,000 dossiers on Communists, Democrats and all other types of citizens, including even 4,000 priests, gathering tons of the most detailed information, including personal habits as private as marital 'indiscretions', heterodox sexual behaviour, petty vices and so on. This gigantic police-blackmail machine was based on thousands of spies, police, carabinieri and informers, whose 'discoveries' were recorded and transcribed by thousands of typewriters, whose constant noise must have sounded like a feverishly buzzing beehive, and whose echo penetrated everywhere, from the Government, to Ministers, to Parliament, etc. And then, when the scandal finally exploded, everyone claimed not to know anything, not to have ever heard anything about it. From the Minister of Defence, to the chairman of the DC, to the Government: everyone responded unperturbed: We didn't know anything, we were never aware of any of this. And they knew even less of the fact that right there in our ministerial offices, someone was plotting to overthrow the state.

So I then invited the citizens and youth of Castellammare to go and question De Lorenzo in person. The young people didn't have to be

crucial information is inevitably withheld on the grounds that it is a military secret. It is to this practice that Macciocchi alludes in the passages that follow. (Trans.)

asked twice, and they went to the piazza to find this ridiculous character, only a puppet in the hands of key people who hide behind his *belle-époque* monocle. The piazza was the same one where, shortly before, we had left a wreath for the fallen partisans in honour of the Liberation. And, to cut a long story short, De Lorenzo was unable to speak. The young people whistled him down, they noisily and happily danced in the midst of the scattered crowd that had come to listen to the general's speech. Finally he hurriedly ran down the stairway of the platform as absurdly as he had pranced up it. It was a first victory.

But the politically decisive event, the one behind the new turn of events, was neither my commemoration of the Resistance nor the denunciation of the attempted *coup d'état* via my accusations of De Lorenzo. It was, rather, this: my implacable, documented accusation, breaking every undercurrent of *omertà*, every conspiracy of silence, against Gava, the very face of monopoly capitalism at Naples. I saw, in the dark, that the crowd got larger and larger as I went on reconstructing the whole network of oppressive power controlled by the Gava family, providing first and last names, as I unwound the skein of scandals and corruption there in public, ending, finally, with a call to all citizens to get rid of their fear, to drop the camorristic persecution complexes and help Italy get rid of the exploitation represented here by the potentate Gava, whose particulars I have sent to you in an earlier letter.

Let's do something now, I said to the people – who peered out fearfully from behind café doors, as if he were right there – so that you and your children will no longer have to go through the well-established, humiliating routine: if you want a job, go to Gava; if you need some money, go to Gava; if you want to keep your job, prostrate yourself at Gava's feet; only Gava commands; keep quiet, submit, and take your hat off when Gava passes. Especially the professionals, the urban middle class, in great part subordinate to and slaves of the D C hierarchy, seemed to stop holding their breath and let out a deep sigh there in the dark.

Later we got together in a section, with happy and proud faces all around. On one side were the comrades, young and workers alike, and on the other there I was, in a deeply emotional state. I finally felt that I had found, in the span of this particular day's political work, the Party in the way that I understand and imagine it to be, with the working class there at its head. In the days that followed, I returned

several times, at six in the morning, to be at the gates of Navalmeccanica and other shipyards in Castellammare. I went to distribute
l'Unità and take leaflets with Party propaganda, and I handed all these
things out to the workers who hurriedly passed through the gates with
their lunches under their arms. They would snatch the sheets out of
my hand and rush into the factory with barely a greeting or a smile.
But these too are extraordinary moments: I would grip their hands,
with not even enough time to exchange words, but their honest,
strong faces remain burned in my memory, real proletarian faces; and
even if I only had the time to glance at them, this was a moment which
gave me a boost which got me through the rest of the day. I thought
of this reservoir of political strength, this patrimony of uncontaminated and combative energies that we have at our disposal.

So for me, in spite of the great fatigue of this electoral campaign,
in spite of the many times that I have come home to my hotel at one
in the morning, I still set the alarm for five to return to mingle with the
workers of Navalmeccanica and the other plants.

Among the many people I met at Navalmeccanica, a true comrade
and friend is Saul Consenza, the worker from Navalmeccanica I mentioned earlier. He is a strong, honest man of about forty-five whose
twenty-year-old son, Matteo, works for the Party in the Youth Federation. He was really the first person there to put his trust in me. He
never says anything about it, but I think he understood that I found
myself in a very difficult situation. And, at least in that area, it was he,
as secretary of the section, and the other comrades of the section
(whose leadership radiates out among the villages along the Sorrentine
coast), who took it upon themselves to 'run' my campaign.

They called a women's assembly in town, in a cinema, where we
first showed 'The Battle of Algiers'. I realized, again, how women like
nothing better than to hear their problems discussed, their grief, the
petty events of their lives, those little slices of daily reality that are
made up of their suffering and their exhaustion. This is the point from
which you must begin in order to arrive at larger questions. There is
no doubt at all in my mind about this. If you go about it from the
other end, you make a serious mistake. The women, at least, simply
won't understand you. And this is just what happened to me in my
talk to the women of Castellammare: I had prepared a 'learned' introduction, in a manner of speaking, with references to the 'Feminine
Question in the South', to Southern literature and to what people like

Eleonora Fonseca Pimentel had meant to Italian and European history at the end of the eighteenth century. Then I brought the discussion up to more recent times, to the revolutionary message of certain categories of women, such as the field workers of the South who had broken feudalism and opened the way to agrarian reform. With the exception of this last reference, to two peasant women killed by the police when the Fragalà Latifundia was occupied in Calabria, I might as well have directed the rest of the discussion to the wall. I had the feeling that my words were bouncing in a vacuum of embarrassed silence.

It all changed as soon as I began to speak of their lives, of what a worker's, or a mother's day was like. When I spoke of the crushing, unspeakable exhaustion that is the lot of the women of the people, and presented it to them in political terms. When I spoke of the shanties of the San Marco area, where viral hepatitis is rampant because of the rats which infest the place. When I spoke of the abominable conditions that families are reduced to, living with ten people jammed into a space perhaps ten metres square. All I am trying to say is that you keep learning that you cannot come to the masses with abstract ideas, especially when the masses you have before you are simple women, whose daily existence and reality is made up of purely material questions and problems.

My meetings with the working class have not been restricted to Castellammare. In Gragnano, a little town stuck on to the coast like a seashell, I found workers of the 'white art', millers and pasta-makers, who have recently been turned out of their jobs in droves. It is a town with a mixed workforce, half workers, half peasants. At the rally, I and a young comrade spoke: an excellent, relentless orator, as for that matter are almost all the youths who are 'allowed' to speak by their elders. Gragnano has a piazza like a theatre, with a perfect *settecento* fountain in the middle of it, rising up like a floral trophy and which, on this occasion, had a few dozen youths who had climbed all over it with red flags. And then there is Torre del Greco, with 90,000 inhabitants, many of whom are in the merchant marine; poor people who get on boats, go to foreign countries and return to their families after three, four or even ten months at sea. Torre del Greco is like a permanently docked ship. And here too it was easy to contact comrades. The seamen's union leader in the city, Aniello Cuciniello, a man with such a reverberating voice that he sounds as if he had a microphone hooked up permanently to his throat, was a bit suspicious at first, and he too greeted me with what by now had become familiar words: 'Well! So we see each other again after twenty years! *Look how old we have grown.*' But then my speech convinced him. He is the one who, later on, in a meeting of Federation activists, gave me what is perhaps the best encouragement I have received, telling me that at meetings I had been able to take almost any topic – e.g. that of the 'dollar crisis', which had blown up in that period – and really 'embroider' it.

I often feel so separated from the others that the slightest bit of flattery is enough to give me encouragement. Then I don't feel alone any more, and I think that I am *understood*, and that I have been correctly *interpreted*. Moreover, news of my *political acceptance* at Castellammare – apparently a decisive political test – has spread. 'We hear that things went well for you at Castellammare . . .', etc. The comrade who gives out speaking engagements has loosened the purse-strings, which is to say that he now manages to 'save' for me, from the daily 'bag' of important rallies for candidates, a few which are not secondary.

It looks as if the rumour about having been 'tricked' by Rome now has fewer supporters.

Maria Antonietta

Dear Louis, *Naples, 8 May 1968*

The sinister presence of Naples' jail, Poggioreale Prison, has entered my electoral campaign. Physically, it is one of the largest in Europe, with its immense pavilions occupying 67,000 square metres: eight cell-blocks are lined up like the teeth of a comb, while three more form its spine. This massive structure – a carry-over from the Bourbon king's conception of punishment as inseparable from physical torment and spiritual desperation – was originally built (1919) to hold 7,500 inmates, but since the building has long been in a state of disintegration and collapse, it now holds only 3,500.[1] The overbearing size of the

1. Halfway through July 1968, this jail was the scene of a great prisoners' uprising, after two days with no water during a heatwave which featured temperatures of over 100°F. The juvenile detainees began it all with a hunger strike. Fifteen of them were put into punishment cells by the Director, and in addition were mer-

place is such that it demonstrates pretty clearly how the bourgeois ruling class at the turn of the century wanted to guard its flanks with a gigantic 'cudgel', in the form of a penal institution large enough for a whole city, Naples, the old capital of the Mezzogiorno, which had to be kept in line under the bosses of the North – and hence of the South as well, since the unification of capitalism had occurred long before. From its beginnings, it was never conceived as a place for redemption, but rather of humiliation and *submission*.

Creating jails is a lot easier than creating structures which guarantee work. This is typical of the policies of a plundering ruling class that has sacked the South since the unification of the country, keeping it in a subordinate state. For this is what is required by the system to maintain its equilibrium; these are the demands of 'advanced capitalism'. I have come to see, though I can only make rough estimates, that a very high percentage of Neapolitans pass through this jail, or at least pass through the trials that keep them from going to jail, or that give them freedom on parole before the entire sentence is served.

The 'first circle' of this hell is therefore represented by the Hall of Justice situated in the Castel Capuano. The building literally drips history: it was begun in the twelfth century; was enlarged by Frederick II of Swabia; was restored and fortified by Charles D'Anjou; in 1535, Emperor Charles V stayed there and then gave the castle to a faithful knight of his, the Seigneur de Lermoy; and so on all the way up to the most recent restorations, which deface it terribly. Here is where all the 'Tribunals' of Naples are brought together, and the main entrance is still guarded by the eagle of Charles V. Even after walking my feet off in the confusion of modern Naples, coming here leaves me with the impression of stepping back several centuries. You get this same feeling of living in the past from everything around you: the crowd that is found on the pavement in front of the Court from morning to night; the whole system of 'services' (stalls with food, ice cream, fruit, fried snacks, candies, seeds and sweets) which are provided for the people who wait, endlessly, wandering about, for their lawyer, their hearing, the arrival of a witness, the disappearance of a witness, for absolution, for the imposition of a penalty. . . .

---

cilessly beaten. At that point all of the prisoners went on strike: three cell-blocks were destroyed, two were partially destroyed, and all the others were severely damaged. Squads of blue-helmeted riot troops arrived with sub-machine guns and they finally succeeded in restoring *penitential order*.

I have the impression that I am in Buñuel's film, 'The Exterminating Angel'; that because of some inexplicable spell cast on us, we have all been rendered prisoners within this perimeter awash with congealed humanity; we return to the most basic state of nature, where the most brutal explosions of selfishness take place, and to the truth of life – in this case that of the people rather than, as in Buñuel, that of the bourgeoisie.

Furthermore, time only exists here as a general point of reference. You can camp here for a whole day, in the presence of *Justice*, or even longer, until the *Exterminating Angel* arrives. Usually, in Naples, 9 o'clock means 10, but here it can even mean noon or later. Hence I started using the telephone to see whether the lawyer who was supposed to accompany us was coming or not. . . . A Parisian frenzy, if you like. But those I am with are absolutely calm. Everything possible will be done. I have to keep reminding myself that the rhythm of life is very different here. So I try another course, just as a river does when it is blocked. But I am hopeless – still being at the stage where I miss all my appointments, not because I arrive late, but because I come at the agreed hour. Now I must acquire a natural, internal compass, with the most sensitive of needles, so that I will understand that the agreed hour, let's say ten, means a quarter to eleven or 10.30, depending on a whole number of factors, including the importance of the person, the traffic and the weather. It can also mean *never*. In the end, everyone understands, marvellously, using some strange code other than the one most humans are provided with. If in Naples there is a traffic jam bad enough to stop traffic altogether – hardly an uncommon phenomenon – some sort of underground telegraph goes into operation and somehow it communicates to people with appointments that the appointment has been broken, and hence no one gets angry – including, in this campaign, the comrades who have been standing around waiting to hear a speech.

So, out there in front of the courtrooms, where my watch seems frozen and the sun fixed in a single spot in the sky, I am thinking about these facts when the lawyer arrives, only half an hour late, which is a sign of extreme courtesy and consideration. We enter the Palazzo di Porta Capuana together. The harmony which flows out of its old, noble construction makes it dizzyingly beautiful inside, and at the same time it is infinitely decadent under the dust, the crumbling stucco, the ceilings all mouldy and bloated by the humidity, the enormous libraries of judicial acts and records – seemingly millions of dossiers with the entire history of Naples and its people – which weigh like a battleship on the foundations of the building.

In the outer waiting halls (the gigantic Salon of the Court of Appeals is as large as a city piazza) one can see portraits on the walls of famous Neapolitan lawyers who have passed on to a 'better life', and I recognize two men I knew when they were alive: De Nicola (the first President of the Republic after the Referendum) and Porzio. I feel a terrible sense of age for myself, for them and for the Palazzo. Naturally, Naples has had vigorous and famous speakers for centuries and is the most illustrious forum of judicial oratory and forensic elegance in all of Italy. The line of portraits stops halfway around the wall, and it is apparent that there is still plenty of space left. My lawyer-guide tells me how the highest ambition of every great lawyer is to have his own portrait added to the line of severe 'Princes of the Bar' inside Porta Capuana. The challenge and goal of life is to occupy a little rectangle of wall in the glowing perpetual motion of the Palazzo: to send your unchanging face across the unchanging centuries. I examine the lawyer closely to see if he, too, has *problems* of this sort. But he appears to be calm, still young. Running back and forth in these corridors and labyrinths I try to achieve, in the briefest possible time, my objective, which is to get a permit to visit two incarcerated Neapolitan women, arrested almost a year ago for having 'resisted the forces of public order' which had come to evict them from their house. They have been practically forgotten, even by us. It is like the whole business of the cave-ins in the city, which are lucky to get four lines in the papers by now: '42nd cave-in at Fuorigrotta', etc. And now I would like to use these women as a symbol, in this campaign, of the conditions in which the people have to live: *they are in prison because they were defending their right to have a place to live. On 19 May they won't be able to vote; Women of Naples, vote for them, vote as they would have voted.* I have been going around for two days, mulling this over as an electoral slogan. But first I have to see them, talk to them, listen to them, reconstruct the facts, all for reasons of intellectual honesty that I can't get rid of, and that will not let me speak or write that 'I have heard of. . . .'

Ever since Comrade Geremicca from the Federation told me about this, two days ago, I have been searching desperately, talking with Deputies and lawyers, to find a way to get the President of the Assize

Court to give me a 'visitor's permit' which will allow me to meet Filomena Cancello and Immacolata La Porta, inmates in the Women's Section of Poggioreale Prison. I finally manage to meet this high-ranking jurist, whom everyone calls 'Excellency', and who is seated in a magnificently restored office, with a beautiful eighteenth-century painting over his desk. He grants me my permit with great magnanimity, as would be done for a foreigner from the Red Cross visiting Naples who had asked permission to bring relief packages to two 'unfortunates'.

With the way cleared for me, yesterday morning I arrived at Poggioreale with another communist woman Deputy. In the blazing sunlight, the heat and the dust, we walked around a good portion of the looming outside wall, since, by mistake, we went to the *regular* jail first, through the central doorway, only then to be sent all the way to the other side of the prison where the women's cell-block is located. In this way, we ended up 'circumnavigating' the jail. The building's main characteristic is that of Gloom – as perfect as the Platonic idea of it. Around the outer wall there is nothing but a wilderness, with the asphalt of the broken paving softening and bubbling in the sunlight, and only a few stores where people can buy snacks for the prisoners – in the same way that you find stores which sell coffins, headstones and flowers near cemeteries.

Sixty per cent of the prisoners in Poggioreale are between eighteen and twenty-five, arrested for the following crimes: pickpocketing, petty theft, car theft, dealing in black-market cigarettes, pimping, etc. From their family and school (never completed) they go directly to prison before being sent to reformatory or sometimes to an asylum. This is the 'education' or *apprenticeship of the young sons of the people.* Just as a cell reflects the characteristics of its organism, so too does this enormous prison reflect the life of Naples. Law has never enjoyed the slightest respect among Neapolitans, and rightly so: it is considered the law of a class who are the enemies of these people. They have in fact countered every law ever written with *permanent disobedience*, finding other, unwritten rules for themselves and for the conduct of their own lives, rules fundamentally opposed to those of their masters. When the Italian bourgeoisie talks about the supposed civil inferiority of the Neapolitans, it is because they really see, on the contrary, their civil superiority. Naples is really a very honest city, where people with no work invent, with great imagination, a way of finding work, by means of humble tricks, poor stratagems and modest thefts. What the Neapolitan really gets from all this is in effect nothing: it corresponds to a day's work, at times only to a kilo or two of pasta, to the few lire necessary to play the Lottery, and so on. The treasure of energy and intelligence that goes into this *daily* petty theft would be sufficient for a week of work or of the creative energy needed for a regular job, if there only was one. In addition, there is never any violence involved: there is instead a continual skirmish between the intelligence of one Neapolitan and that of another – or better still that of a foreigner (an American in particular), or an *outsider* (that is, an Italian from Rome and points North) – always with the demonstration of his own *intellectual superiority* as the ultimate goal.

The first 'international' example of this craftiness goes all the way back to 1722. In the chronicle reconstructed by Daniel Defoe of the London Plague of 1665, the London saddlemaker tells how, among the announcements made by charlatans passing themselves off as healers, under the heading 'Infallible Pills against the Plague – Universal Remedy for the Plague', there appeared this text: 'Italian gentlewoman, just arrived from Naples, knows a secret method to ward off contagion, discovered by her with the help of her profound experience, and advantageously applied on the occasion of the Great Plague of Naples, which caused 20,000 people a day to perish.' From this ancient example to the present, 'swindling' has been a game of cunning and 'desecration' of rules in force which, in my opinion, actually amuses the person who is doing it. In the end, Naples, despite what people say, is a more upright city than many others in the world, including Rome and Milan, where theft is a 'hit', studied in all its details so as not to leave the slightest trace.

The kind of things that happen to you, in person, are typified by the taxi driver who does not lower the flag on the meter, and charges you for your ride plus that of the previous passenger. He takes advantage of your great hurry to catch a train in order to double the price, or else he will tell you, as you frantically try to pay and run, that he doesn't have the correct change; it is *either-or*, and he knows it – if you want to catch the train, you have to leave the change. If you get angry, if you insist – and miss the train – then you get involved in one of those extraordinary duels between the Neapolitan and the outsider or foreigner in which it is demonstrated to you that you are wrong and he is right, and that for a mere thousand lire you really could have taken the train (and you, inside, have to agree!). A Neapolitan in action, and this applies to the law, to politics, and to oral conflict of all types, manoeuvres his tongue in the way a Parisian – to give you a familiar example – handles and dominates French. (This made Stendhal positively enthusiastic. 'The language of the people,' he writes in his Neapolitan *Diary*, 'seems at first to be shrill and coarse: it is energetic and expressive like all dialects, but it has particular graces. It seems to have been created to make people laugh. There are many operas which have been written in this tongue. Different areas have different dialects, as would only be expected from a people full of life, for whom religion is not a brake but a passion, and which is never bothered by any law, and is full of natural simplicity.') At the end of a long argument, you end up on the side of the person who is wrong, backed into a corner by inexorable logic. The porter takes my luggage: 'Are you an American?' I answered, furious, *'No!'* but still he wanted 400 lire from me instead of the 150 due to him.

Hence the Neapolitan really gains very little from his victory, in a material sense: at most, perhaps a few hundred lire. But what matters more to him is that he has asserted his superiority over you. The only way to put an end to this little game is to say that you will call a policeman. But this is not in keeping with the 'rules of the game'. The kind of look you will get should you resort to this threat will be one of scorn and hate, as if you stuck your leg out to trip someone as he ran by. The other, atavistic, look that you will get is that of the famous Poggioreale Prison towards which I am walking, whose sinister presence explains so many things to me about the most secret psychology of men.

Poggioreale is kept in disgraceful condition for an institution of a civilized country. The lawyer told me that there are no proper lavatories in the prison, only wooden buckets in the cells, which people have to wait their turn for – and which are like the Apple of Paris for spreading discord among the prisoners. Every once in a while there is no water at all, and the inmates go crazy from thirst and the filth. Out of 2,000 prisoners, only 400 have any kind of work 'for educational and recreational purposes', as the rules would have it; the rest tattoo one another or knit to pass the time. The Prison Code dates from the Fascist period, and has never been revised. Requests for prison reform, first presented in 1947, have been tabled in every legislature for more than twenty years. This is the way things proceed. The projected law for prison reform is presented and then the legislature always comes to an end without ever having discussed the issue, and the project expires. It is like Sisyphus rolling his boulder up the mountain.

At the main entrance to the prison, as soon as you pass through the walls, there is a kind of immense, grim courtyard, where families with visitors' permits wait to see their relatives. It looks like a square in some Arab country, children and women squatting over their bundles, together with a number of pedlars. All this takes place in the most indescribable filth. But we ran out of there before we had a chance to take a really good look for, as I have said, we realized our mistake and had to travel more than a kilometre around the desolate wall, until we finally found ourselves in front of the other door, with a guard peering out at us from a peephole before he finally opened the door and iron gate for us and let us pass. The chief jailer now checks our passes, and then directs us toward the visiting area, where two guardian nuns with shocked faces say that the 'detainees' will come in immediately. And sure enough, just a few minutes later the *prisoners* appear in front of us. They are quite bewildered, and they await some sign of understanding or recognition from us – their eyes meanwhile as watchful as those of caged animals – which will tell them how they are supposed to behave in front of us and what we want.

They sit down before us on two seats, hands in their laps, and one of the guardian Sisters sits down right between them. I am really moved to see these two faces, so eager to ask us who we are. And for just that reason I try to drop all formality. I tell them immediately that we are two Communist women, unknown to them, but moved by friendship – one a Deputy and one a candidate in the elections – and interested in their case. We explain that even though we do not know them personally, our aim is to help get them released since, for us, they have not committed any crime but have only acted in defence of the most elementary right of men and women: the right to a home.

The women take some courage at this clear declaration of principle and political affiliation. Even though the guardian is still there, they sense that she is now a little intimidated. The youngest, who is thirty-seven years old, has blue eyes and a quick, precise way of speaking. The other is quite shapeless, and has a hard face, marked by experience; alert eyes peer out from under a heavy black helmet of hair which is all burned by perming and dyeing. 'Don't worry about anything, you can say whatever you like,' I tell them. 'Tell us why you got thrown in here in the first place.' The nun by now, as the women could see, had the kind of resignation on her face generally reserved for superior powers. (She was no doubt asking herself how we ever managed to get a permit, and if this meant that Italy was now in the hands of the Communists.) Recognizing this, the two proletarian women took heart and, interrupting each other in turn, they launched into their incredible story, enumerating the 'charges' which led to their receiving the following sentences: Filomena Cancello, twenty months and fifteen days; Immacolata La Porta, sixteen months.

This is what happened: when the building at 110 Via Santi Giovanni e Paolo partially collapsed, and the order to vacate the premises arrived, they carried all their household goods out into the street. They wanted to carry out a great public protest, to attract the people's attention and to obtain from the Centre-Left city council of Naples another place to live. Their protest was defined as 'obstructing traffic and blocking a public thoroughfare', to which 'resisting the forces of order' was then added. So, on 3 November 1967, nine women, including one who was pregnant, were arrested. They were dealt with very swiftly and quickly received varying terms of confinement. They have by now already been in prison for eight months, and even if the Court of Appeals acquits them (their case is now due to come up there), one of them will have already served more than a third of her sentence and the other will have served half. *Is what we did really a crime?*, they ask us, for by now they are completely frank and open, and their voices shake with rage. 'They even kept us in here for Christmas and Easter!' – holidays which are sacred to everyone, thus making their segregation all the more horrendous. Then they calm down a little. They ask us, insistently, to get them released on parole, to help them at least with this specific detail. They boast of their 'good conduct' in jail in front of the Sister, who gives a moderate nod of the head as if to say, 'Yes, it isn't bad.' What *good conduct* means in a place like this is not terribly hard to figure out. It means servility, or even turning informer. Looking at the nun, they also mention that every once in a while there are even films in jail, and they saw a film of 'Ciccio and Ingrassia', who are two popular comedians, completely innocuous, poor, shabby actors. In the women's cell-block, there is a social worker (*one*) and, from what we can understand, four chaplains. The women sew, and illiterates have to learn how to read and write. This is how it happens in the South: if they are acquitted, they will think of prison as a place where you are lodged, fed, educated, and even get to see a Ciccio and Ingrassia film. But I just cannot believe that they go to school. . . . .

They say all these things in a calm way in front of the Sister, who approves. But then they forget their servility and the uncontainable fury which is a product of their desperation simply explodes from inside them. This frustration is due mainly to the terrible plight of their family and children, outside. They tell their pathetic personal stories, declaimed in loud voices as in a Greek tragedy, and all that is missing is the chorus. Now they no longer fear anything, and they unsheathe their claws, speaking of their abandoned homes and children. The nun withdraws, and even moves quite a distance away from us, it is not clear precisely why. Does she already know about these familial disasters, or is it simply that there is nothing further for her to check with regard to us? Immacolata speaks in this fashion of her house and her 'little creatures': 'My husband is out of work, I have five "little creatures", the smallest, a girl, was two years four months old when I was arrested, and now she is already three. The oldest, thirteen, is half blind. A seventy-year-old aunt looks after them, but she says she is too old and tired to keep taking care of them. I have those abandoned "little creatures" before my eyes day and night. I see them in the middle of the street, in traffic, and a car can run them over. My husband lost his job when they threw him out of the Capodichino Glassworks, and he can't stand on his own two feet any more. When he comes to visit, all he can do is cry.' The other woman, Filomena, has two children by someone who now lives in America. She is the head of the family, and the family just about disintegrated when she was arrested. It atomized: 'One of my sons went to do his National Service,' the mother says, 'and the youngest, Giuglielmo, left without anyone to give him even a piece of bread, has also been arrested, in a fight. Now he is here too, in the other part of Poggioreale. I asked why he never came to visit, and I was told that he was sick with a fever. Then, when the older son came home on leave some time later, he told me what had really happened. Giuglielmo would never have been arrested if I, his mother, had been at home.' It turns out that Filomena's son is not there for fighting at all, but for petty theft, like 60 per cent of all the young inmates of Poggioreale. 'How could he eat without me?' she says, and she justifies what he did, she justifies it with all her heart.

The nun returns with muffled steps, just in time to hear Immacolata turn to us Communists with the tones of a comrade to say, 'Before the elections, you have to do something for us, at least get us paroled. We have already done more than a third of our sentences and no one can give us back that time. We are innocent, because shouting your protest when you don't have a roof over your head isn't like going out and robbing. . . .'

'I give you my word of honour,' I say hastily, because with the emotion I feel, the more I want to be forceful and energetic, the bigger the lump in my throat grows. I breathe deeply, draw my breath better, and repeat, 'I give you my word of honour, both of you, that everywhere I speak in this campaign, I will speak of you two, Immacolata and Filomena, to all the women of Naples. . . . I promise that I will ask for your freedom publicly, to honour that simplest of aspirations, to want a home, as your right. You two aren't guilty of anything, and you are really a lot better and braver than us in a lot of ways. . . .' I added the last few phrases hurriedly because once again the women looked bewildered at my promise and they looked, again, at our clean suits, our shoes, our handbags, etc. At this point I embraced them, one at a time. To embrace, in the South of Italy, is not, as in France, an affectionate greeting, it is a gesture of profound intimacy, such as passes between sisters or brothers, between father and daughter or mother and son, and at times it does not even happen between them because one is not supposed to express one's feelings with gestures, for there is still often a lot of outward prudishness in this regard. The nun, who has certainly seen all kinds of things in jail, is somewhat startled and then for the first time a kindly expression crosses her face. With respect and great consideration, she turns to the two prisoners to lead them back to their cells, while I rapidly head for the exit, where a jailer returns my personal documents, which were held hostage during the entire visit, as prescribed by the law.

Maria Antonietta

Dear Louis,   *Naples, 8 May 1968*

Last night, in the Stella quarter, I spoke about the two imprisoned women. I sketched in the faces of Immacolata and Filomena for the crowd. Stella is the quarter where I went on my first electoral excursion, to Vico Cavaiolo. This time I saw that in the time that has elapsed since then, I have begun to understand people better, and I have also begun to acquire some nerve, force, and simplicity in my style of communication. I am not so afraid now of speaking and not being understood. I entered this situation with fear, and with pain, but now I am starting to 'get into it'. At the same time, I have the advantage of not having been absorbed by the situation, and I still manage to see, with the eyes of a newcomer, without tired or reflex reactions, all of the distortions of this society.

Amendola spoke as well. This is the first time that I have been on the platform with a really important politician. After I spoke, he said, 'Well done. I see that you have really got into the swing of things. . . .' The crowd was huge and extremely friendly, with red flags everywhere, unending applause, hundreds of women and thousands of children. The enthusiasm of the crowd caught you up like an ocean, wave after wave, finally carrying you along with it. This is the way it happens after a speech that goes over well in the 'belly' of the city: the crowd carries you away, almost literally, towards the P C I section, precisely the one I had found so close-mouthed and wary when I first arrived.

My visit to Poggioreale and the meeting with the two inmates opened the sub-proletarians' hearts to me in that quarter, and, without having intended this to happen, it acted as a passport of sorts which enabled me to enter the maze of back-streets where every family has had either direct or indirect experience with the 'fortress prison' of Naples, Poggioreale. The Neapolitan edition of *l'Unità* had an article, with photos, on the family of Immacolata La Porta. In these pictures you see five children, including the semi-blind girl with her very thick glasses, who represents a classical martyr figure, only with a little straw hat instead of a halo. And I wrote an article on both women for the national page of *l'Unità* as well. Many Communist speakers, even those a long way from Naples, now speak about these two imprisoned women, as symbols of the police-state repression which is unleashed in the South against the labouring masses when they act to defend their rights.[1] I have also been speaking with lawyers. I think we can

1. In January-February 1969, 6,000 citizens, 900 families in all, occupied about 900 empty Gescal flats in Naples. A spontaneous people's struggle. The 'occupiers', however, quickly found themselves opposed by the 'assignees'. The Prefect,

get parole for the two women, but I do not know if we can do it before 19 May. For the disinherited, Justice is a very slow mechanism indeed.

Maria Antonietta

Dear Louis,   *Naples, 9 May 1968*

An electoral campaign increasingly takes on the character of an oratorical contest as it draws to a close. The speech is a spectacle: it is a football game and each orator has his own fans, his own devoted following, as if he were a famous sportsman or singer. The candidate, the speech-maker, is dead tired or voiceless, his head stuffed full of words, noises and handclapping, when he arrives at the already-crowded piazza which awaits him. At times, and this has happened to me, you do not even have time to pull your thoughts together before you are thrown into this confusion and have to face a public which awaits your 'pearls of wisdom', which in turn will trigger the requisite amount of applause.

From an oratorical point of view, there are two kinds of speakers: those who try as hard as they can to respect the audience, to explain, teach and dialogue with them, and then there are the others, those who plunge into oratorical battle with slogans, with words which vary from the mellifluous to the cruel in an attempt to galvanize their listeners. These people, in my opinion, are miseducators in an electoral campaign. And here in the South, I have learned, the presence of a candidate in the main square of town is still an event somewhat tinged with awe and magic. I have had many opportunities to observe, in the last few days, numerous comrades coming into the Federation to beg someone to spend 'a minute, just a minute, on the speakers' platform in our town'. Make yourself seen, then leave, just like a saint's statue in a religious procession. If the role and supposed initiative of the masses is not discarded entirely, it is pushed far into the background,

---

Government and political parties then found a so-called 'compromise solution', offering the occupiers 30,000 lire a month until the end of 1969. Two months' payment would be given immediately to anyone who abandoned his flat at once. Many of the occupiers did not have to be asked twice, and they quickly returned to their shanties and makeshift lodgings with their little hoards, abandoning the new flats.

and pure propagandistic speaking ability is what achieves this. Perhaps it is for this reason that large-scale struggles and mass participation in such struggles almost disappear whenever there is an election.

I think speeches are an old, obsolete form of communication when compared with modern propaganda techniques, especially TV. Imagine the use you could make of TV if it were not in bourgeois hands. My experience in this campaign is that direct dialogue counts more than anything else, if you have that ability to (as you once put it in a letter) 'break silences'. You penetrate to the depths of an individual's personal reality, which is always different from what we imagine when we make general comments, from a platform in the middle of a piazza. This is why I came up with the idea of interview-speeches, which raised quite a fuss. Unfortunately, you cannot do this sort of thing in major population centres.

It is impossible to make real contact with the public from high up on a stage. You might as well be in a balloon. How can you understand what their life is about, and exchange points of view or guide them towards new ideas, new visions of the world, in this kind of situation? That is long-term work. Then, too, the crowd you see at a speech, in general, is already *yours*, in the sense that it is convinced *a priori* that your politics and your opinions are correct; the speech only serves as a supplementary stimulant, which tells already-convinced people that they ought to support the PCI, and which shows off your oratorical abilities. I think we would do better to speak to this impassioned mass we find in the piazza in a whole number of diverse meetings, made up of small groups, which at present could, say, fulfil the simple (but, in the South, decisive) function of teaching the people how to vote. But, instead, with all the permanent ideological and organizational lacunae which exist in the South, here we are adding yet another element of confusion – the oratorical passion that overwhelms all others.

To give you a better idea of the way speechmaking has come to be seen as a definitive act in itself – almost like an operation – and how, in my opinion, it is high time someone began to fight to change this form of propaganda, let me tell you about a conversation in Piscinola with a comrade who works for the Sanitation Department. His name is R.: a large man, massive in fact, with a reverberating voice. We start to talk, and, with me speaking in normal tones, he almost instantly breaks in with, 'But comrade, you have no voice.' I tell him that it is true that my voice is not very high-pitched, and that it has got even lower during this campaign. Then I add, 'Listen, there is also the problem of *what* you say, isn't there? I mean, there is also the problem of brains.' I prod him a bit maliciously: 'Which do you prefer, Giovanni, brains or voice?' Shrewdly, he answers, 'I'd like to have both!' 'All right,' I go on, 'but what if you had to choose between one and the other?' Once again, he intelligently dodges the question: 'Well, comrade, that would depend on where you had to speak.' I persist: 'And in this area, where I have to talk this evening?' With no hesitation at all, R. answers, 'Voice, voice!' I tell him, in all sincerity, 'Well then, Comrade R., I just don't have that kind of voice.' R. is suddenly very quiet, as if he had just received tragic news. The comrade from the Federation, who was standing there all the while, now comes to the rescue, remarking in an amused way, 'Don't worry, R., and cheer up. I have the voice and our comrade here has the brains.' And, because of this, everything ends on a cheerful note. But this episode is very representative of what I have been saying, which is that it all boils down to your main qualification being a powerful voice, not your arguments. And this is especially true if you have a tenor or soprano voice, one that carries well. In this way you mesmerize the comrades and convince them that since we can shout louder than our adversaries, we must be right.

As the campaign draws to a close, I keep catching myself saying things which are not very well thought out, for by now I am really worn down by fatigue. This is what is called 'electoral cretinism', an infernal machine that grinds on, crushing you in spite of your best efforts at resistance. By evening, I arrive, with almost all my powers of speech gone, at town after town where they still want to hear speeches. I feel like a boxer awaiting the bell for the last round. By the time I get up on the platform, the only thing that has a stimulating effect on me is to hear 'Bandiera Rossa' or the 'Internationale' being sung. When that happens, these hymns of struggle and the barricades echo inside my head until they unleash a strange cerebral process. Somewhere in me lies this deeply-rooted trigger of ideas and convictions, which are intimately and mysteriously identified with the most glorious moments of the workers' struggle or drawn from the classics of Marxism-Leninism. All I have to do is hear these songs – I can't really explain this *Freudian* phenomenon very well at all – and I regain some of my strength. At times it is enthusiasm, at times a fighting spirit, and other times it is simply physical energy which enables me to speak once more before a large crowd. But then, ironically, inevitably I see myself as one of those circus horses which starts to prance in a certain way as soon as it hears the notes it has been trained to respond to.

What I notice most frequently is word association. This, I think, is also basically a Freudian phenomenon; it at least deserves to be studied from that perspective. For example, one day when I was speaking in a city of 50,000 in the Province of Naples, a candidate I will call 'L'. said that the DC 'had closed ranks (*fatto quadrato*) on the pension issue'. To that point, it was fine, but after a brief pause he immediately added, 'just like the Quadrilateral (*quadrato*) of Villafranca'. *Villafranca* is one of those patriotic episodes that you learn about in elementary school when you study the history of the Risorgimento: it has nothing whatsoever to do with the DC or with pensions. With the person in question, then, it is clear that the first usage of *quadrato* automatically touched off another *quadrato* in a totally different context, drawing out something memorized, or incessantly repeated to a teacher, when the speaker was a small child.

Words irresistibly trigger other words. And the chain reaction is not between one concept and another, or one argument and another, but above all between one word and another. Here is another candidate: a happy, Pickwickian type, whom I was with on another platform. We were both to speak at Piano di Sorrento, right in the middle of the Sorrento Peninsula, on 5 May. Imagine this scene: the sun is blazing down on the piazza, which has the platform raised so high that it seems like an altar. The crowd stays in the shade, knowing how merciless the sun can be, and hence it is distributed in two long winding lines down two sides of the square piazza. We, on the other hand, are fully exposed to the sunlight on this blazingly hot summer day, out there on our 'altar' like the Holy Sacrament. My fellow-candidate is supposed to speak first, but just as he is about to begin, he pauses for a moment, then tells us, 'Just a minute; please give me a few moments to collect my thoughts.' He puts a hand to his forehead, and stares at his shoes with profound concentration. Then he looks out at the crowd, back to his shoes, and so on, as the minutes pass. Sweat is pouring down our faces, and finally his preparatory concentration appears to be at an end, for he goes up to the microphone and begins to speak. The first thing to come out – and here we go back to the Freudian phenomenon I mentioned as common in the speeches I have heard – is 'On this historic 5 May. . . .' Now 5 May is just a normal Sunday, but he insists on defining it as an historic, unforgettable 5 May. I ask myself why he should have called such a day 'historic', and later 'unforgettable', and tell myself that some strange mechanism must have been set off in his head which identified this 5 May – a banal day in every respect – with that of the death of Napoleon described in Manzoni's famous poem which all of us learned when we were schoolchildren. The confusion of dates – and this comrade happens to get everything, days and years, confused – can always be traced back to some mnemonic notion from school, or to some political shock, or perhaps to a significant date in one's private life.

A candidate who believes in speeches as the ultimate charismatic form of electoral success will, if he throws himself completely into a campaign mentality, end up giving eight or nine speeches in a day. In fact, my fellow-candidate abandons me as soon as he has finished the speech with all the dates mixed up and tells me that I can rejoin him in a nearby village, Seiano. I am hence obliged to get there on my own, since we only have one car, which is to take us back to Naples. When my speech is over, I get into the 'Cinquecento' of a busman friend, and together we rush to Seiano, where they tell us that our comrade has gone on to Vico Equense. I get to Vico Equense, still accompanied by the comrade who owns the car, and from there we are sent to Castellammare, where, I am told, the candidate is to give his last speech. But I can't find him there, either; he has lost me along the route of his desperate race to deliver the optimal speech.

Here in the Mezzogiorno, a mass party like ours leaves a lot of room for personalism and the cultivation on occasion of *clientele*; this is most evident during electoral campaigns. They aren't terribly serious phenomena, these personalistic tendencies, but they have nothing whatsoever in common with the moral attitude and customs of a Leninist party.

Remember that the electoral system that we use to choose Deputies has nothing at all to do with the French 'majoritarian' system. There aren't single-member constituencies, with candidates stepping aside for those who have done better on the first round and who hence stand a better chance of getting elected on the second ballot. We vote on the basis of proportional representation, which is not like the Gaullist swindle. All of the votes a party wins counts for that party in the proportional distribution of seats in Parliament. (For the Senate, there are single-member 'constituencies', but surplus votes are counted in proportionally at the regional level.) So a list receives so many votes, and these votes give the right to so many deputies, but then comes the vital point: the Deputies who are finally chosen are those with the largest number of preference votes, as I have already mentioned in another letter. What this means is that the Party has to organize not only the electoral campaign in general, but also the subdivision of preferences.

For example, the other day I received a sheet on which were indicated twenty sections which were supposed to vote for me. There is a comrade at the Federation – an 'expert' – who is in charge of cutting up the preferential 'pie'. So many for you, so many for you. But at this point, from what I have seen and heard, all the private negotiations begin. The candidates – including those who will surely be elected no matter what happens – start going to the secretary of the Federation to try to enlarge their preferential area. They will say, for example, 'come on, give me Castellammare too . . .' or 'can't I have Acerra?' and so on. The pressures can also come from below, as when a section has a miniature crisis because it doesn't see 'its man' assigned to it.

Then the section representatives come to the Federation, asking 'Why didn't you assign X to us for our preference list? If you give him to us, we'd be willing to vote for Y as well.' And it goes on and on like this, resulting in new, extremely complicated calculations, which really need a computer. If promoting X will also mean votes for Y, then maybe Z will be helped too. . . . Looking over my list of 'preferential districts' – and I think I was one of the few candidates who accepted his list without any grumbling – I pointed out the following strange phenomenon to a comrade: I have never set foot even in the majority of the districts where my name has been 'recommended'. 'Maybe I ought to go there,' I said, 'because that way at least it would be more honest. . . .' To this, one of the 'brains' of this kind of calculation responded, 'Oh, don't do that. It will be a lot better for you if you go elsewhere, where you have the chance of getting votes that you might not pick up otherwise, while in the districts which have been assigned to you, they ought to vote for you whether they see you or not.'

As I have pointed out before, the composition of the lists is discussed for an unbelievably long time, at least three or four months and maybe even more. Given this, it is not hard to guess that for this entire period the Party will be practically paralysed politically, while everyone argues over who ought to be entered on the list and who left off – a discussion which does not spare even comrades who are among the most highly qualified leaders in the country. I somehow have my doubts, whatever the claims of its practitioners, that this is really *democracy* in action. I would call it something like 'delegated democracy', in the sense that the leaders from the Federal apparatus and the largest sections determine *among themselves* which candidates the base 'wants'. In my own case, I could see this mechanism at work in the marked contrast between the diffidence and even hostility of some members of the apparatus, and the genuinely warm acceptance of me by the rank-and-file or just plain people, inside the Party and outside it. In any event, by now, after all the discussion and criticism, things should have calmed down. But this is not at all the case inside the Party where, in fact, the waters remain pretty choppy.

Aside from the occasional unpleasant personal episodes in which one may find oneself involved, another general problem that plagues the Party is *campanilismo*.[1] Practically every section, 'standing up for its own', wants at least one local luminary on the list – if not guaranteed election outright. Where there is not a local favourite, you will be told, 'We don't have a parliamentary candidate,' in tones that suggest a major calamity. There are 97 communes in the province of Naples alone, and thirty-eight candidates; to make everyone happy, you would have to more than double the list of the PCI. And yet, if you try to make this eminently reasonable argument to any local figures, none of them will say, 'That's true.' For deep down, they are often convinced that the candidate from *their* town is really a lot better, and worth much more, than the one from somewhere else.

Hence there are clientelistic considerations with respect to individuals, and there are localistic considerations which relate to *campanilismo*. And as far as the thirty-eight candidates nominated here are concerned, it is absolutely clear that a number of them have decided that they will be elected at all costs. And this is where examples – or at least some episodes – of highly questionable behaviour crop up. Some of the stories are really quite amusing, for in them you can see all the ancient ingenuity of the Neapolitan at work as he figures out how to be a success in a given trade. In this case, the new trade just happens to be that of a Deputy. A few days ago, for example, it became

1. Parochialism, local chauvinism, from *campanile* = bell-tower. (Trans.)

known that a PCI election office had been opened up in 'F' quarter, but it soon became evident that this headquarters was only interested in promoting one candidate, whom I will call 'Y'. The candidate in question was called to the Federation and told: an office has been opened in your name in F, and you must know what lies behind all this and who is involved. You must ensure that this place will be closed down immediately. On hearing this 'Y' feigns the most profound surprise, and says, 'Are you serious? Is it really true? What a miracle that an election office should be opened up for our Party in a place where previously there wasn't even a party section. You say that they are pushing my name: this may be true, but it may also be that the comrades there are just a little confused; perhaps they are really campaigning for the entire party.' But the comrades from the Federation press their argument, saying, 'No. We went into the section and asked them in whose name they were working, and they not only told us that they were working for you, but they added that if we kept bothering them they would throw us out.' Here the miracle became even more striking for 'Y': he is all the more appalled to hear this new information, and still insists that he knows nothing at all about it. Only when confronted with an ultimatum, namely, that he shut down the office immediately or – by another 'miracle' – lose every other preference vote assigned to him in all of Naples, did he suddenly succeed, no doubt through 'divine intervention', in shutting down the headquarters in F. I really do not know if the place stayed closed. This is one of those half-laughable, half-pathetic examples of how seriously some people take their own election.

If promoting yourself is one way to gain votes, the other is to eliminate the preference votes of others – since just four preference votes can be ticked on the list – and to see that only your own number appears on the ballot. Remember my story about Montecalvario, one of the areas to which I have been 'assigned', where the women ran around promoting me with the half-mystical use of '25, Holy Christmas'? Now, let's say that there is someone who wants to get ahead of the others on the list. He will go around telling the voters, 'Listen, it doesn't make any sense to vote for, say, Macciocchi, since she will get in for sure. She is getting preferences from all over the province. It's better just to put my name down.' That such manoeuvres in fact go on is demonstrated by the continuous arrival at the Federation of seized packets of ballot facsimiles (used to help explain the voting mechanism) with only *one* number printed on to the P C I space, and this is the number of one of the 'ambitious' candidates. You find these things everywhere, including outside factories, and it always boils down to a candidate trying to promote his own cause, in 'someone else's territory'.

Aside from acting on your own to promote yourself, another favoured tactic is the formation of an 'electoral troika': three candidates who promote each other, always together, wherever they go. But all the candidates, with the exception of a few *ingénues* (there are even a few of these), are hundred-eyed, and they all keep each other under such mistrustful surveillance that when all is said and done this incredible network of reciprocal control becomes an even more effective means of party discipline than democratic centralism. In fact, when the votes are all in, the usual result is almost precisely the one that the Party wanted in the first place, with only an occasional slip-up. We will have to wait a little longer to see if this time, too, party discipline – or spontaneous reciprocal surveillance – has worked.

A day in the campaign begins early in the morning, when everyone goes to Comrade P. – chosen, I think, because of his physical power – to have their speeches 'assigned'. Comrade P., his face inevitably all puffy from a combination of too much work and not enough sleep, sits there with a large chart of speeches to be given in certain places, and names of those who are to give the speeches. This chart is so criss-crossed with symbols and cross-references that it looks like a map of the solar system. By the time all the complaints have been registered, bargains struck and changes made, P. himself no longer has the faintest idea of what is going on. A section representative will shout, 'I want X for tomorrow. This is the third time I have asked for him.' Or else the candidate himself will say, 'I don't want to go to R. They are asking for me at V.' Comrade P. is like a dam, he resists firmly. On other occasions, he gives in, and then he has to pick up that planetary-navigational chart of his and make some infinitesimal change on it for the thousandth time that day. Finally, not even he can find his way any more. And every morning you find the same market, not of man-power but of voices, there in that little room in the Federation. The confusion and the shouts are like stock exchange transactions. And those with the strongest, most stentorian voices overwhelm all the others.

There are also the 'top level' candidates, but they hardly ever show up in this market-place. You know who they are by the fact that they either organize things on their own by direct communication with the sections, or else they are the really important people who come directly from Federation headquarters to only the most important speeches. I, on the other hand, know I will take what P. offers, and so I wait for lunch-time to get my 'singing' itinerary from him. (Anyhow, I am much too timid to press forward in this crush.) We eat together now and then at his desk in the Federation, usually minestrone and Neapolitan pizza which is brought to us if we call up and order by the little kid who works for the trattoria next door. I try to make Comrade P. talk so that I can understand him better, but he is too tired to talk after that experience, and he goes through it every day. P., like the comrade who does the calculations for the preference votes, and like many, many others, is an example of personal sacrifice for and devotion to the Party. Even if these people are not 'brilliant' or 'creative', it is very clear that many of them are profoundly kind and good people. I am thinking as well of the comrade, an ex-worker, who drives me from town to town where I make my speeches. He knows how tense this whole time is for me, and he continually offers me encouragement, cheers me up, assures me that I am *'bravissima'*, that I know so many things others don't. He also always stands in the very first row of spectators and is the first to applaud, or else he gets furious with comrades from the sections when he thinks they are giving me a hard time, and not only does he watch over me when I am exhausted, making sure I have eaten, etc., but he also invited me to join him and his family on May Day for the traditional outing. By now, he and I speak with complete openness. This too, you see, is 'the apparatus', when there is not too much bureaucratization.

My own personal situation continues to be extremely difficult, as I have already written on numerous occasions. No one, not even those who arrive fresh from Rome, bothers to talk about it with me any more; they seem to prefer to talk about the weather. They behave like Pontius Pilate. Or else they will ask me things like: 'But have they had you give a speech in the centre of town, as is usually done when introducing new candidates?' I am forced to answer, 'No'. And then they change the subject. I tell myself that maybe they are helping me in some other ways, or maybe they are finally getting ready to explain to me how this whole business was a mistake right from the beginning, given that I have been 'parachuted' in here anyhow.

The other enemy that must be defeated is *napoletanismo*, the 'defence' of the city against all outside intrusions, as if Naples were besieged by foreign commandos attempting to take the place over. The tendency to succumb to this frame of mind is widespread. A comrade who is a section secretary explained to me how the kind of annoyance felt towards me by many comrades could be summarized in these few words, 'Here she comes now to lecture us.' It makes me feel as if I were a Greek or Norman invader. One day, one of my old friends, in an ironic mood, said to me: 'You, who are French. . . .' But among the rank-and-file, everything is quite different, and we communicate openly and clearly.

The articles I have written on Naples, which strongly denounce the city's situation without resorting to any demagogic tricks, have not received unanimous praise. In fact, a whole series of criticisms has come from the official political-intellectual apparatus, which sees nothing but flaws in my analysis. On the other hand, I have received, care of *l'Unità* in Rome, all sorts of telephoned or written messages which enthusiastically praise what I have written. Some come from professors from university centres (like Portici), and others from the young so-called *'gauchistes'*. The people who walk around, shaking their heads, saying, 'She's completely wrong; she has ignored the capitalist transformation in the centre of Naples; it is clear she doesn't understand anything', etc. I now conclude they really do not want anything other than the old routine of self-congratulation, and have completely closed their eyes and minds to the incredible social drama – and exasperation – which surrounds them.

But I am basing my electoral campaign on the political role of the working class, and on the struggle for a new human condition here at Naples. I am focusing on the question of who are the appropriate allies who can join forces with the working class, both traditional allies and new ones (e.g. students); and I am also concentrating on a denunciation of the desperate conditions in which the people have to live. Doing this, I have tossed into the dustbin of bourgeois ideology – and this hurts a lot of people – things like 'the economic resurrection' of the South, the 'industrialization' of the South, the 'advent of technological civilization', Naples as the 'California of the Mezzogiorno', and 'the new face of neo-capitalism' in the South.

For years it has been *demodé* to speak of poverty in the South, even in certain parts of the Party. This is a result of the subtle but persistent influence of capitalist ideology; it seems that if you shout 'economic miracle' long enough, even Communists will start to believe you. And all this noise is made because a few 'new industrial poles' have been set up by the capitalists. The theories of the 'new working class' (Mallet) have been applied to these industrial nuclei, and this has merely served to obscure a comprehension of the real problems of the Mezzogiorno, where the general mechanism of capitalism is in fact making the whole area more subservient – and functional – to its own needs, as I have mentioned on other occasions.

I am increasingly of the opinion that without even realizing it these technocrats have been influenced in a reformist direction by the society that surrounds them. In essence, the society uses them and gives them in return a comfortable and generally tranquil existence. The most notable, and painful, gap is the one between their original political choice and the reality to which they have become accustomed, if not inured. Entirely missing is any ability to crystallize the general, continuous tension that exists in the masses into general political slogans or great mass struggles. I also feel that the widespread *fear* of these elections can be traced to this failure to appreciate the combativity of the people and the proletariat. To judge from general reactions, the elections are a Sword of Damocles dangling over our heads. Few people seem to understand that extreme poverty can serve as a catalyst for political struggle, and that denouncing existing conditions is one way to call people to the battle. Instead, the belief is that if you write about these things in an article, it means you are 'lowering' the level of consciousness of the masses. It was along these lines that I was arguing with an old friend, when he told me, 'Remember when you write about Naples in *l'Unità* that you are writing in the organ of the PCI. ...' Another said: 'You write about Naples as if it were Sweden', underlining how he thought that I look at things with indifferent eyes, like a foreigner (one of my articles on Sweden had just appeared).

In any event, this electoral campaign has hardly been a vague, imprecise experience for me. It has been, on the contrary, very incisive. I have been able, I think, to use the exceptional period that the Party goes through during a campaign very much to my benefit. I feel that it has helped me break away from habitual schemas, and I have tried to utilize to the best of my ability the gigantic maelstrom of facts and impressions that swirl all around me. Night and day, I analyse, probe and interrogate all sorts of people. I tell myself at times that I have become a one-woman Doxa agency[2] – gathering data and evaluating them in terms of one's own political education and experience. Whatever else happens, I know that I will carry away with me from Naples a tremendous patrimony, and this will be all the greater if you, when you are able, have the time to think about the facts that I have been jotting down in such a rush all these weeks, and to send me a contribution which situates them properly.

Maria Antonietta

Dear Louis, *Naples, 10 May 1968*

It is 6.30 in the morning. Castellammare is already completely awake in the grey-blue light. In the harbour, you can see the outlines of the ships, lined up in rows. The streets are full of people rushing to work in the factories and of buses loaded with workers. The comrades from the PCI section at Castellammare and I, loaded down with copies of *l'Unità* and bundles of the Party's open letter to the workers on the struggle for pension reform, take our customary road to the Navalmeccanica Shipyards and its 2,100 workers. I call it the 'customary' road because it is one I have gone down so many times during this campaign; and yet while everything one does is so predictable, at the same time the people one meets and the things one hears are entirely unexpected.

I stop at the Stabian Baths to have a free drink of mineral water with some workers. They loan me a glass ('Here, drink, comrade'): there is an ancient municipal ruling that permits anyone to drink at the springs from 7 to 8 in the morning. Now, with the sulphuric water in their empty stomachs, the workers rush through the factory gates, telling you rapidly what they think about politics, their own struggles, pensions, and the last televised debate. Between 7 and 7.30, at most 7.45, just three-quarters of an hour in this frenetic rush to the factories, if you are politically and psychologically perceptive, the thing you will learn almost at once from the workers' swift questions and answers is that rage is the most tangible thing here, a rage which signifies a will to change things. The workers rush by, with little packets

2. Doxa is the leading Italian public opinion polling agency. (Trans.)

wrapped in newspaper under one arm (bread and something to eat with it), the other arm extended to grab a copy of *l'Unità* ('and if you don't have the change for 100 lire, comrade, keep it and give it to the Party for the campaign'). You can synthesize the whole worker's condition, on this tenth of May, in this image of the race into the factory. All the workers, in clusters but not saying anything to each other, almost as if they did not know one another, rush to make it inside on time. They will be in there for ten hours, but, at the moment, their only goal is to get there.

I am standing on the steps to the entrance of Navalmeccanica. Those who arrive earlier stand around talking for a while, but, as time goes on, conversations get more and more brief until finally you are lucky if they greet you or shake your hand. Then they are gone, on the run, into the whirlpool, where they will stay until after dark. Everything is rushed, even the petty details of political work. One of the section leaders goes by and, in passing, reminds another, 'Have you asked our comrade here if she can get us a train ticket for Mao Tse Tung?' 'What on earth are you talking about? Is he coming here by train?' 'No,' they laugh, 'Mao Tse Tung is the comrade who sets up the platforms and public address systems for meetings.' (Everyone has a nickname here, reflecting either his political ideas or else some physical characteristic.)

The secretary of the section, Saul Cosenza, about whom I have already spoken, is always among the first to arrive at the Baths in the morning. His job is that of an iron caulker, which is brutal, exhausting work. Today, like every day, he walks along with a black satchel containing his lunch under one arm and a bundle of *l'Unità* under the other. With him are Salvatore (Nello) Ajello, the worker who is a candidate for the Party, Eustacchio Massa, the head of the Chamber of Labour, Scognamiglio, president of the Assistance Fund, Michele Abbagnano of the Factory Commission of the Party, and other leaders, all of whose roots are sunk deeply into the factories. It is to the factories that they always return, like Antaeus regaining his strength by touching the ground, and it is here that they want to remain, *so as not to lose contact with the masses*, they say; *in order not to get bureaucratized.*

Let's take the case of Saul. He is in the factory for ten hours, and then every evening he goes to the section. Now, with the campaign going on, he has taken a special leave of absence, but he still shows up in front of the factory every morning at six on the dot. Then, in an hour and a half, he organizes the tasks for the Party for the entire day. *This* is what a real delegation of political power is like, as opposed to the notion of a 'delegate' who is an elected official and stays in an office most of the time. Saul talks with all the workers who are section leaders along the Sorrentine coast, and they work out the speeches and the distribution of various types of electoral material. Saul's blue eye gleams pride, will and gentleness: he has only had one eye since he lost the other to a flying metal particle while hammering sheet metal. I only learned by chance that he lost his eye in a work accident in 1959: he never speaks of himself.

I also learned that his father was a socialist even before 1921, and was one of those who took part here in the famous 'red carnation strike' (which got its name from the fact that the last twenty-eight workers at Navalmeccanica who held out against the bosses came back into the factory with red carnations in their buttonholes). As a punishment, his father was transferred to Taranto, where he became fatally ill. Then he was fired. Until he died, in 1925 (he was thirty-eight), the Naval-meccanica workers took a collection every week to make up his pay, which they then brought to the family. They did this so that he would never know that he had been left without any pay. These workers are communists from generation to generation; now their children are FGCI militants. This is what Navalmeccanica is: a patrimony of revolutionary purity and dedication to socialism, and it has been this way for more than half a century.

These workers really have no idea at all of what bourgeois liberty or bourgeois democracy – the kind that the DC is for ever prating on about – is supposed to mean for them. Is it freedom of the press for a worker to be able to read *Il Mattino* or the *Roma* (clerical and mon-archist, respectively) instead of *l'Unità*? 'Do our enemies know that we can barely afford a newspaper, and we certainly aren't going to buy one of *theirs*? Do they know that democracy cannot be found in the factories and that unions barely have the right to function? Do they know that the eight-hour day no longer exists, and that we have to stay in the factory for ten hours and more with no power over any of the things that affect us? Do they know that when we leave every day our backs are broken and our heads dizzy, and that tired out as we are, we risk being maimed or killed every single day?' These are the things that the workers say as they rush past into the factories.

Antonio De Luca, who is thirty and has spent twelve years in the factory, shows us his September pay-packet: 90,000 lire for 281 hours, of which 191 are normal time and 90 overtime. We all bend over the pay-packet as if it were some cabalistic text, and the workers argue as they try to decipher the figures. The bosses have really made an art out of this, they joke, so that you need an electronic brain to understand it. Hearing them talk this way reminds me that two young friends I have in the student movement, Piperno and Roberto Bandiera, have been *studying* the pay breakdown of Roman construction workers *for two months*. From Antonio De Luca's 90,000 lire, 6,500 are withheld for tax and another 8,719 for the pension fund ('they have been taking that from me for twelve years, and who even knows if I will last long enough to collect!').

So you can see what he is left with. 'Ask Saul, too,' the workers say. 'In March,' Saul begins, 'I worked the whole month: 106,000 lire for 250 hours of work.' We calculate: 180 hours on the basis of the contract of 44 hours a week, and then *seventy hours of overtime in a month*. People ask whether we have gone back to the last century, and where the 'conquest' of the forty-hour work week has gone.

And that is not all, they add. 'The South is full of low-wage zones, and our designation is three plus. The standard gap between North and South is 20 per cent, but we are a lot better off, since between us and the workers of Genoa there is a salary differential of only 6.5 per cent. But even so, do you realize what this means if you calculate that the last rise for our sector, won only after a long hard struggle, was 8 per cent?' These divisions into 'salary zones' are officially called 'cages' by the PCI, for salaries are marked off as neatly as if people were in cells. Ajello adds, 'Per-capita income in the South is today just a little more than one third of that of the developed regions of the North, and the gap is growing.'

So these are the main points of the battle that is being fought in Naples and its province: (1) against the low-wage zones and for workers' power in the factories; (2) to improve the workers' conditions both inside and outside the factories; (3) for full employment. Someone who caught the enumeration of these demands as he was passing chimed in, 'And why don't you add another: pensions?' A younger worker answers him, ironically: 'What would we get out of that? Without a struggle, all we have is a lot of idle chatter. What we need is *revolution*. To get to work I have to get up at 5.00 a.m. and I don't get home until 10.00 p.m. Instead of protests, I prefer the revolution.' And he runs off, in a great rush, leaving this word palpitating in the air. 'What I want to see straightened out is the question of military service', says Raffaele Esposito. 'Yesterday I was fifty-nine, and I have worked at Navalmeccanica for forty-two years, since 2 January 1926. But they deducted my six years in the army; they don't count towards the pension. Anyone who is my age is in the same boat. Anyone who went to work at eighteen and then had to go into the services and to war should have those six or seven years counted in his favour. Do they think we went off to have a good time?' Luigi D'Auria, of the Castellammare Chamber of Labour, who is known for his accurate memory, says, 'What you have to do is change Article 13 of Law 903 from 1965, where the term used is "according to the *effective* contribution made". The problem is with that *effective*.' He then goes on to cite the CGIL document for the reform of the whole pension system.

Much of our electoral propaganda is centred on pensions and we Communists, as soon as Parliament opens, are going to present a proposal for a new pension law, whose broad outlines we are already spelling out in our speeches. In fact, among the most violent expressions of rage against the Centre-Left, the fury over the pension issue either heads the list or else comes very close. 'The Government claims that it doesn't have money for the old folk, for the pensioners; it claims it is too *poor*,' the people say with a sneer. I have come to understand that among the greatest fears of a proletarian – often even greater than the fear of death – is that of being left old and penniless, a useless cipher, a man who is a burden on his children and grandchildren, who must be fed and taken care of and for these very reasons therefore is stripped of his human dignity and only feels himself to be a millstone around someone else's neck. 'For me,' says a young worker, 'the most important issue is that of the democratic control of the various social security agencies. And that is not a conservative objective; on the contrary, it is a *true reform* that by its very nature could undermine the entire economic plan of the government.' Even though it is already 8.00 by now – fifteen minutes after clock-in time (and an official from the factory comes over to protest) – the workers continue to complain and criticize. The phrases, thrown out almost like political slogans as the workers rush off to their jobs, are the following: 'The pensions are a joke. The bosses have done their homework, they know. The youth pay for the pensions, and the old people go underground before they can benefit from them. A human body, with the last spark of energy squeezed out of it, in the polluted air of the factory, just isn't going to make it through to thirty-five years on the job. You can count the people who leave the factory with pensions on the fingers of one hand. So-and-so finally retires – and they provide names – and a few months later we are at his funeral. If we put our monthly pension contributions into the bank, then at least we'd have that money at the end of our lives.' Other people add further complications: 'There's another problem. They rob you of all your energy when you are young, and then, as you get older, they pay you less and less because you have no more strength left and have to reduce your output. Then they set your pension at 65 per cent of your last three years' work, but they are calculating from a time when you barely have the strength left to lug your body around. We know that the Communists' proposed pension law is supposed to change all this, but will it ever be passed?' So, once again, one hears this widespread sense of distrust and scepticism.

And then, all at once, everything is empty and quiet. The last worker has been swallowed up by the factory after crossing this Dantesque threshold, which has the stink of a capitalist hell. All of us then leave and go to sit in a café right on the edge of the turquoise sea, which provides a dizzying contrast with the closed, grey world of the factory. We speak of everything, and at times I take advantage of the openness of the discussion to raise questions about the role of the working class in Naples and the province, and how to go about creating an alliance between the workers and the sub-proletariat in the struggle for socialism. The Golden Age for the working class, both in theory and in practice, was way back in 1947–50, when it waged massive struggles to maintain its 'worker condition' and to save Neapolitan industry. It was at this time that you really got a clear idea of a working-class activity aimed at winning the sub-proletariat as an ally, and at getting it to recognize the proletariat as the leading force in the struggle, as I have already explained in my retrospective-historical letter.

But, today, a *heavy silence* reigns over any discussion of the working class as the guiding force of other social groups (especially the sub-proletariat) which question the existing order. These in fact are very delicate issues, and it is hard even to ask the right questions. I try to express myself in the most reserved way possible, saying that, when in Naples, one has the *impression* that the worker is a very sad individual. The strong pride that is evident in the North or in the great factories of Europe seems to give way here to sadness, to 'complexes'; the workers do not seem able to relate to other citizens, the Neapolitans who do not work: they seem isolated and closed off almost as if they were living in another world. I am not speaking so much of the great industrial centres, Castellammare, Bagnoli, Pozzuoli, for they have their own social cohesion; nor of centres elsewhere in the province. I am referring mainly to the worker who lives in the city, either in the newer areas on the outskirts of Naples, or else in the 'belly' itself.

What I have been able, with great difficulty, to discover, whenever the situation permitted it, in my conversations with the workers, is roughly as follows. A sub-proletarian, who 'invents' his work every day, has a precarious existence, but he does 'enjoy' a form of freedom and independence from all bosses. And in that sense he does feel himself to be as free as a bird. This is why he looks down on the worker, for – as a comrade told me – he thinks: 'That bloke shuts himself up in a jail all day long, he turns himself into a slave, he agrees to obey a boss. . . .' And when he sees the worker go off at a certain hour and return at a certain hour he reconfirms for himself that the worker's life is one of forced labour, made all the worse by the fact that the handcuffs and chains worn by the worker were put there voluntarily. His, the sub-proletarian's, life, on the other hand, is an *independent* one. And therefore he has no respect for the worker. If they meet on the street or elsewhere, they usually say nothing at all to one another. The sub-proletarian feels himself superior in intellect, inventiveness and, in general, in the art of living. . . . This is among the major reasons why the Neapolitan worker is so psychologically isolated. Any pride that may exist in having a steady job, a trade, is greatly diluted by the realization which is constantly present before his eyes, that he has given up 'another way of life', which his neighbours lead, and which is a life full of great opportunities for adventure and the exercise of imagination.

Moreover, unlike the sub-proletarian, he lives in constant fear of losing his job. Hence even his prospects are severely limited, because the worker, without the factory, is finished. His existence without his job would be that of a cripple, given that he has never learned the petty trades of the street or, rather, that he has never learned to invent a 'business' or a way of making a living. In other words, he has no *resources*. Or else, even if he succeeds, his very success means his complete degradation as a worker. Thus we see that this sadness of the workers has another source: it stems from their renunciation of their entire external environment, where everyone lives all the year round in the open air, in the streets, walks there, works there, carries on his interminable disputes and fights his fights there, and so on. The worker, sealed up in his factory, is like a cloistered monk who has cut himself off from the world of others and renounced that life. In doing this, he is aware above all of having renounced the air, the environment, the rules and the means of *the secular life*, the philosophers of which are the *lazzari*, as the sub-proletariat is called.

At Barra, several days ago, I met a good-looking dark youth, the son-in-law of a sub-proletarian. He lives in a vile courtyard off Vico Sirena, a place so poverty-stricken that I spoke about it at one of my meetings. 'What do you do?' I asked him. He shrugged his shoulders and said, 'I had to go to work in the factory, to work for Ignis.' 'Well, then, you're a worker?' I asked with great interest. 'Yes, by necessity. I got married when I was sixteen and the girl was only thirteen and a half. We got into trouble. We already have a baby. . . .' He told me that he works eleven hours a day, since he does two hours of overtime each day, plus one more hour to make up for having Saturday off. It is clear that he feels like a prisoner, and this detention of eleven hours weighs on him in contrast with the life of the quarter, which is always in motion, extrovert and ready to reach out to the outside world.

The severing of the umbilical cord that ties you to the streets is, in short, painful. After a time the worker gets used to it, and he acquires his own rhythm of life, gaining that particular dignity which goes along with the life of a worker. But he also gets used to a life withdrawn from that of the quarter, and a lack of social ties with his *other* environment. His wife doesn't have friends among the other women, so she is alone. . . . On Sundays, the worker stays at home, because he is tired, or because this is the only day he has any time for his family, or because he has nowhere to go, or because a *Sunday walk* with the family would require him to dress decently in front of the quarter. 'They stay at home out of a sense of modesty and sensitivity to the way others will react,' I was told by a youth. 'At least it was this way for my father: he had only the suit he got married in, but he was ashamed to go out in that on Sundays because it would seem too smart. The only other clothes he had were those he wore to work, but they were too shabby. The same was true for my mother, and so they stayed at home. . . .' In her study on 'the workers' condition', Simone Weil writes: 'Sunday is the day on which everyone wants to forget that there is any need to work. To do this, everyone spends. And they try to dress as if they were not forced to work for a living. Clothes in this context both satisfy people's vanity and give them illusions of power.' The sub-proletarian, however, like the bohemian, has no such problems. His dignity is inscribed in his very choice of life style, and wearing patches on his clothes therefore creates no more complexes for him on Sunday than it does on any other day.

On the other hand, in the peasant villages where I have been, the worker is respected almost as a nobleman, and workers are in fact called 'artists' because they possess the 'art' of making something with their hands. It is pretty clear, then, that in Naples the bourgeoisie and the ruling class have undertaken an extremely successful campaign of psychological denigration. All over Italy, the saying goes that if someone does not have a job at Naples it is because people there do not like to work. Even Dumas, trying to explain what work meant for the common people of Naples, wrote, 'Other peoples rest when they are tired of working; the Neapolitan works when he is tired of resting.' These elements of irony about the people's attitude towards work down here are used by the ruling class as justifications. It is a good way for capitalism to avoid its most serious responsibilities, or simply to cover them up. Once you become somewhat less of an outsider here in Naples, you begin to realize that this attitude has an influence even among us Communists, and there is a tendency to laugh about it and find it amusing.

When I first came to Naples, a Neapolitan comrade, a woman, told me the following parable – stressing to me that I should take care not to try to be a great *activist* and that instead I should try to penetrate the *philosophy* of the 'common people'. A very rich and powerful man, a boss or a 'technocrat', let us say, is walking along the Santa Lucia Lungomare when he sees a young man lying in the sun on the grass. He walks over to him and says, 'What are you doing lying there, young man, without any job or future? Wouldn't you prefer to have a nice, secure job?' The Neapolitan responds rather laconically, '*And then what?*' '*Then* you would take pride in yourself, you could get married, have a nice place to live.' '*And then?*' '*Then* your experience would permit you to get involved in larger undertakings, either in commerce or industry, and you soon could double your money and have a nice chunk of capital at your disposal.' '*And then?*' '*Then* you could provide a leisurely life for your family, you could buy a great big house, a villa by the sea, servants, and you could travel all over the world.' '*And then?*' '*Then,* you could get so rich that you would get to the point where you did not have to work at all; you could simply enjoy life, stay in complete comfort, and never have to worry about anything. . . .' To this the young Neapolitan answers, 'But I already have that.'

These are eighteenth-century bourgeois myths which still hang on, and which act as covers for the specific forms that capitalism has taken at Naples. They also have a strong effect on the masses' will to rebel, and I feel this influence more concretely, like the weight of a big stone, with every passing day of this electoral campaign.

Maria Antonietta

Dear Louis,   *Naples, 11 May 1968*

To really cover the topic of child labour in Naples would take a whole new study, and it would no doubt turn out as horrifyingly impressive as Engels's treatment of the Manchester working class, or Volume I of *Capital* by Marx.

Child labour is one of the pillars of the family economy, and this is as true for the rest of the South as it is for Naples. Relationships inside the nuclear family are entirely commercialized, in the sense that the parents put their household labour-force – i.e. their children – to work from the age of six or seven. The sub-proletarian children often have steadier jobs than their fathers, working near home as assistants in food shops, in bars and cafés, in trattorias, and in small artisans' workshops.

At every speech I give, I see, in the first row of the audience, these little workers, dressed in blacksmiths' overalls, in butchers' aprons, in the white, grease-spotted smocks that indicate that they work in bars

188

or trattorias. Whatever they earn is taken by their parents. In a white paper published by the ACLI[1] there are figures which show that a million Italian children between the ages of eight and fourteen work in factories, and more than 40 per cent of these work more than eight hours a day. 32 per cent do not even get a day off. This means the 'legalized' exploitation of a million children.

The most tragic situation is that of the South, where the children are employed to handle the heaviest tasks; it has even reached the point where some enterprising individuals use girls between eight and fourteen for road construction. In the province of Naples, the use of child labour is heaviest in the harvesting season, when they pick and process fruit and vegetables to be canned or preserved. 'I process tomatoes,' ten-year-old Immacolata O. (from Sant'Antonio Abate) tells me, 'and I make 1,000 lire a day.' Immacolata is in the factory ten hours a day, with no breaks, so she makes a grand total of 100 lire an hour. The numerous small seasonal factories act as offshoots of the large food industries, which take their processed product. They, too, are 'shadow factories' in a certain sense, because they open and close, they exist for a few months on the basis of a contract that the small or medium entrepreneur has signed with some large firm.

The question that automatically comes to mind is how can they be so overt in their use of child labour? Well, I soon found out that the mothers themselves are the ones who aid and abet the bosses, in the sense that, by tacit agreement, the mothers pretend that they are taking the children along with them to work, as if they did not want to leave them unattended at home, or as if they were bringing them to the nursery. Once they are inside the factory, the child takes its place at its mother's side, which amounts to *four arms* altogether for the ten hours. The boss, of course, says that he knows nothing at all about any of this. The mothers themselves, when questioned, say either that they brought their kids along 'to help me out' or else simply so they could 'keep an eye on them'.

Labour inspectors – if there has been a complaint and they find first-hand evidence of the exploitation of minors – impose enormous fines on the bosses, on the owners of the shops or businesses. The

1. The Italian Christian Workers' Society (*Associazione Cristiana dei Lavoratori Italiani*). Originally very closely tied to the Christian Democrats, the ACLI progressively moved to the left, away from any official affiliation, in the late 1960s. By their 1969 Congress, this separation was declared as a matter of policy. (Trans.)

result is that everyone is plunged into fury and despair. I am told that in a few centres (Torre del Greco for one) complaints levelled by Communists resulted in the police finding blatant cases of this sort of exploitation. Enormous fines were rained down on the shopkeepers and small businessmen, and all the children were sent home. The result was that both the families and the exploiters found themselves allied against the Communists, who were said to have been the cause of this common tragedy. This is clearly one case where *being too quick to intervene* caused a catastrophe, just as you wrote on 15 April.

Children. Mountains of them. Batches of them. Heaps of them. How do the mothers manage to 'watch' them if the mothers work? When the mothers go off to work, they pay their neighbours a 'rental' of 50 lire a child to have them looked after. Naturally, this is only for the very smallest children – whom the 'guardians' keep all together in one place like little rabbits in a hutch – because if the woman had to pay out 50 lire for *every child*, goodbye salary!

I was told all this last night at Scanzano, which is a quarter of Castellammare characterized by seasonal female labour in the canning factories. Underneath the stage was an incredible number of little children, a screaming sea which attacked the wobbly stage, jumping all over it in regular assault waves. Their mothers stood behind them, forming a circle, since as long as the children remained within the circle, whatever else they might do, it was at least certain that they would not get run over by the traffic. This scene was a typical one. But there seemed to me to be even more children than usual this time. Later, in the section, I began my usual interrogation of the comrades on *'why so many children'*, etc. At that point one of the comrades took me aside and gave me the following explanation.

The seasonal female labour force of Cirio and other processing plants of the area try to make sure that they are in their sixth month of pregnancy sometime during the course of those forty-five days that they are officially employed. This gives them the right to claim *maternity benefits*, which are paid three months before birth and then again two months after. All told, these benefits only add up to *200,000– 250,000 lire, but with this sum, the woman manages to feed herself and her family for the rest of the year*. In order to 'earn' her annual subsistence, in other words, the woman takes advantage of the only function that capitalist society allows her to perform, that of procreation. But even these desperate calculations, these fiscal acrobatics, often fail because INAM[2] looks into the matter, establishes that the sixth month of pregnancy did not occur during employment, and therefore takes back the benefits and issues summonses to the doctors who signed the certificates. Numerous obstetricians of the area which encompasses Torre Annunziata, Torre del Greco, Castellammare – who are absolutely innocent since no doctor can check out a woman's declaration with complete accuracy – are charged by INAM with issuing *false documents*.

And as far as the woman worker is concerned, given that her poor ruse against the bosses' government did not work, she now finds herself with one child more and that many lire less.

Many of the children I saw swarming around under that platform represent these *annual children*, who are always born under the same sign of the zodiac, along with all the other kids in this part of the province, which just happens to have canning factories as its basic feminine industry. Who knows how many, among these children, came into the world on the wrong day, thus depriving their mother of 200,000 lire and adding new grief to their lives.

The comrades of Castellammare got me a copy of one of the subpoenas – issued by the Court against a doctor, Giacomo Ciampa, and against fourteen women, charged with 'criminal fraud' for having attested to and declared a presumed date of birth different from that which was diagnostically ascertainable. This *judicial act* incriminates fourteen workers of Castellammare. Nothing serves better than this condemnation to show the desperate depths of the condition of women in the South. When I got back to Naples I talked with a doctor, Claudio Calveri, who was involved in eight of these trials between 1963 and 1964, each time charged with 'attesting to a date of birth different from the real and diagnostically ascertainable one', and therefore 'guilty of a criminal design in the issuance of false medical certificates', etc., etc.

Calveri confirms for me that, aside from the fact that it is extremely difficult for a doctor to determine diagnostically the exact month of pregnancy, the women workers go to every length that an intelligence sharpened by need can imagine to find ways to 'put one over' on the doctor. Some women, having failed to get themselves pregnant, try to pull off substitutions right under the doctor's nose. I was told that

2. National Health Insurance Service (*Istituto Nazionale per l'Assicurazione contro le Malattie*). (Trans.)

two women will show up in the office, one of them pregnant and the other not. The seasonal worker will claim to want a friend's presence during the examination, but then, once their identity cards have been shown, the pregnant woman, when the doctor turns his back, will take the place of the worker and vice versa. There are other women who get together with the obstetricians and only declare the birth of their child two months after the fact (which means that these women have to work at this incredibly exhausting seasonal labour in their eighth month of pregnancy).

The conditions in which most of the women of the South have to give birth recall the Gospel according to Luke, in which he says, '. . . while they were in Bethlehem, the days were accomplished that Mary should be delivered. And she brought forth her first-born son and wrapped him in swaddling clothes and laid him in a manger.' If you leap twenty centuries in time and space and land in southern Italy in 1968, the Gospel seems to be describing current events. Here are the figures from the University of Naples Hygiene Institute: 86.2 per cent of women in the South give birth in their own homes, and very few of those who have just delivered ever arrive in clinics for post-natal treatment of any kind. Births take place in primitive surroundings, often without electricity; the newborn child is often helped into the world by the light of candles (as happens frequently in the villages which surround Casoria, the 'Milan of the South'). They come into the world in the presence of their family, other children and at times even animals. Out of every 100 women, 46 do not know even the most rudimentary rules of personal hygiene, 24 never see a doctor throughout their entire pregnancy, 26 show clear signs of malnutrition, and the result of all this is the high death rate both of delivering mothers and their newborn children, which I mentioned in one of my first letters.

So the women go along on this see-saw of 'earnings', from children to work and back to children again. But while the children may be increasing in numbers all the time, work is not. For in the last six years, management has been consistently 'expelling' women from the productive process in what is quite clearly a concerted offensive. All elements of Italian capitalism, but particularly the southern bosses, have been openly fighting the presence of women in the workforce during this period. In the last ten years, more than a million women have been driven out of the factories and out of productive activity in general. In the South, in the last five years alone (or at least from 1961 to 1966), the number of women in the workforce dropped by 350,000, and 120,000 of these were fired just in the region of Campania. When they are lucky enough to have a job, the women are cynically exploited and ground down. If the condition of the workers in general is bad, that of women in the factories is even more terrible: labour contracts are ignored, the required output is such that to keep up is almost impossible, the skilled workers earn 130 lire an hour (the others get sixty), and the bosses state at the outset that the women may work only on condition that they promise not to join a union.

For example, there was no contract at all, and no guarantees, for the very young female workers in a fireworks factory at Secondigliano. The factory exploded, and the girls who died there were almost literally burned by capitalism as sacrificial lambs on the altar of the 'consumer society'.

The other aspect of the general condition of the children of the South concerns the obscure fate of public education. The core of the issue is simply stated: In order to maintain the economic system in equilibrium, the monopolies keep the South in a perpetual state of underdevelopment; hence capitalism does not even bother to build schools; and, because it refuses to provide jobs for the men of the society, capitalism takes for granted that the children must themselves become the supporters of their families, *and hence they will be forced to leave school as early as the elementary years.* And it makes no sense at all to speak of any aid for children, for in all of the province of Naples there are only ONMI[3] institutions, and there are only twenty-five in the entire region of Campania.

Here are the statistics on elementary education, in all their starkness: out of 6,923,570 Italian children below the age of fourteen (and therefore legally obliged to attend school) the number of children who were not in attendance (on 31 December 1965) was 609,090. And out of this total number of 'defaulters', 531,000 were from the South! In the South, only 65 per cent of the children who register for the first year make it to the fifth. And in 1966–67, those who went on to the three intermediate years numbered 160,000 out of 443,000 in that age group (36 per cent). And things are even worse if we look only at Naples and its province: only 90,000 of the 287,000 elementary pupils

3. National Board for Maternity and Child Welfare (*Opera Nazionale per la Protezione della Maternità e dell'Infanzia*). (Trans.)

went on to the intermediate years. And intermediate education is supposed to be compulsory. Moreover, within this pathetically un-representative school population, the girls are even further under-represented. They rarely make up a third of the school population, even though in absolute numbers they comprise a majority of the age group. In the first five years, the proportions are more or less what they are in reality, but discrimination begins as early as the sixth year of school, and in the intermediate years the proportion of girls has already dropped to 40 per cent. These girls are discriminated against two times over by the classist Italian school system: the first time as southerners, the second time because they are female. In the secondary schools, the female population is only 35 per cent of the total. In the universities, it goes right down to 25 per cent. And things are worst of all in the technical institutes, where out of 298,232 pupils, only 66,543 are female.

The total indifference of the Government in the educational field testifies to the logic of capitalist profit whereby the South becomes a vast pool of 'primitive and ignorant' labour. The semi-colonial fate to which this monopolistic society has condemned the Mezzogiorno severs the cultural aspirations of southerners at the roots, 'creaming off' only that narrow stratum which the monopolies have need of. Both the universities and the secondary schools are *terra incognita* as far as the labouring classes are concerned. Taking the capital of the South and its entire province together, there are only 34,635 students in the grammar and teachers' training schools, only 10,214 in vocational institutes! This is simply more evidence of the *non-instruction* that goes on. It is absolutely clear that the entire educational system deliberately obstructs the creation of new élites, which the system does not know what to do with in any event, and instead acts to make even more profound the cultural gap between North and South.

Twenty years ago, when the Neapolitan Communists organized the 'Committee to Save the Children' that I mentioned in an earlier letter, we already had our first indications of a ruling-class willingness to leave a potential 'crop' of minds unharvested and withered on the vine. For, even then, we had to take ten thousand Neapolitan children out of starvation conditions and off the streets and send them to live with workers' families in the North.

Those children, whose tracks can still be uncovered on occasion, are today doctors, teachers, professionals of all kinds: one that I know of is even a nuclear physicist, another the principal of a *liceo* [grammar school]. This, to me, is evidence that these unlucky, intelligent children of the South could become – within the framework of a socialist society – the backbone of a new ruling class. Instead, they are at present forced to go off like a band of mercenaries and sell their labour to the monopolies of Europe. (Of Italy's three million emigrant workers, 85 per cent were twenty-five years old or younger when they left.)

Twenty years later, the children of the women of the South present a traumatizing spectacle. And nowhere more so than at Naples. Uncountable swarms of babies and children play in the garbage, are bitten by rats, only see the inside of a school for two or three years, and are forced to sell their fragile labour before they are ten years old.

The D C, which has always governed in the interests of the monopolies – and which now does so with the willing support of the Socialists – has indelibly stained itself because it has denied the rights of the children of the South to culture and education. The student movement – for reasons that I cannot understand – has never focused its attention on this element of the class structure of the schools in Italy. Had they done so, it could have helped them ally with the proletariat.

Maria Antonietta

Dear Louis,   *Naples, 12 May 1968*

Today the entire staff of the Grand Hotel Ambassador, where I live, went out on strike. The hotel itself is Naples' famous 'skyscraper' that rises up like a mushroom on the edge of the Bay to a height of thirty storeys. The Ambassador was in fact built on the ruins of the old PCI Federation, which was razed to the ground and the site sold off. It is the largest, most modern, most functional and most rational hotel in the city. I stay here because, with the 'special journalist's discount' of 30 per cent, I end up paying less than it would cost to stay at the Oriente, which is the place where the Federation always puts you . . . and the blankets there feel like army issue, to say nothing of the long corridors with peeling walls. . . . But absolutely no one will believe that I only pay 2,800 lire a day here, against the 3,100 I would have to pay at the 'Oriente'. Ever since I used a little common sense and broke with Federation custom, everyone seems to think that I must be terribly rich. They all say things like, 'How does Macciocchi manage to live in the Ambassador?' I explain, I explain again, I have even brought the driver inside to find out first-hand about the price-list, but still no one will really believe me. . . .

I feel personally involved in the strike that is going on. This is because I have spent a lot of time in the last few days discussing the possibilities of success or failure of the strike with the waiters, porters, and other employees of this beehive of a hotel. The comrades were pretty uncertain as to the eventual outcome. My hotel room became, for a time, a sort of general headquarters for the union struggle. I talked a lot with the ones who were holding out against the strike, explaining why they needed complete unity if they wished to win, and I also tried to answer the anguished question, 'But if we strike today won't we lose our jobs tomorrow?' All I could do was try to convince them of one modest fact: that if every single one of them stood firm and joined the strike, then not only would the strike certainly be a success, but repression would be impossible. This fear of repression should also be attenuated to a degree by the fact that, from what I have been told, the owners of the hotel live up in the North anyway, in Milan, I think.

In any event, this morning I suddenly realized that the strike was on. There is no one in the corridors, the elevators aren't running and the switchboards are empty and no calls can come in or out. The hotel has lowered its grilles in the front, as if in mourning, and the only thing that remains open is a little door in the metal gate through which the clients come and go. Those who have just arrived are forced to carry their own baggage to their rooms. And when I returned at 2.00 p.m., I was excited to see that my bedroom had not been tidied in the normal way. This little fact was a confirmation for me of the unity that has brought together all of the workers of this gigantic building.

Let me explain the situation here a little better, for the conditions in which the staff of the hotel have to work constitute an informative example of how the process of capital accumulation allows the monopolies that exploit the South to get exceedingly high profits out of their ventures. One of the keys to the process is the by-now notorious starvation level of the wages that the monopolies can get away with paying in the poor cities of the South. A maid told me that she cannot earn more than 42,000 lire a month; the waiters and porters do a bit better, making it up to 55,000–60,000 lire. These figures are just over half the level established by the national labour contract for hotel workers. A porter – I think he is a Communist – explained to the others the *great hoax* perpetrated by the bosses: these starvation wages are supposed to be supplemented out of the fixed 18 per cent service charge added to all bills; i.e. a certain proportion should, by right, go to the staff as their 'quota'. But the comrade explains that the 'quota' is calculated by the administrators of the hotel, the bosses' representatives, and of course in the process it is reduced to derisory proportions. No one can even check on this process of 'calculation'. And there is no Staff Committee [*Commissione Interna*] inside the hotel, for, as soon as someone tries to form one, he is sacked by the proprietors.

I have already mentioned how the national labour contract is completely ignored; let me give you some details. Not even the length of the work week is respected. And there is a vicious extension of tasks: according to the contract, no cleaner should have more than twenty rooms assigned to him; here, they have at least twice that many to do. I am told that after cleaning up forty rooms in a single day, you go home dead, with your back breaking. They also informed me that there are neither polishing machines nor vacuum cleaners: everything is done by hand, and the shine on the floors comes from pure elbow-grease. It really is incredible. From afar, the hotel seems to be the very paragon of perfect functionality – and the impression remains if you live inside. And yet, it is all due to exhaustive effort, to the arms and backs of the mass of men and women who work inside this 'modern skyscraper'. And, for all this, we can thank a proprietor who has no intention of setting aside even a tiny slice of his profits for machines which ease the task of cleaning. Underpaid labour is a lot cheaper than appliances – even for the maintenance of a thirty-storey building.

For the workers to present demands – things which are already taken for granted in the North and Centre of Italy – is just about unheard of down here. For a job is seen as a gift, a present, and hence a strike is a threat, almost like blackmail, for it challenges the very idea of this gift of a steady job. Of course, the strike is also a two-edged threat when you find only 30.9 per cent of the entire population in the work-force (1968 figures).

In my talks with the personnel of the hotel, I think I did a pretty good job. I was helped out by some comrades from *l'Humanité*, who have come here to report on the elections and who, needless to say, I was thrilled to see, given that we worked together for five years (especially Carrel and Acquaviva). Acquaviva speaks Italian and he, too, had a long series of discussions with the maid for his floor. The woman asked him – as if, right at the end, she was revealing a deep anguish – if it was true that by striking and perhaps voting Communist 'the Russians would soon arrive to occupy Naples'. Acquaviva, in telling this story, admits how the question caught him completely by surprise, but he answered that the Russians would no doubt come to a socialist Italy in greater numbers than they now do, but they would do so as tourists.

This is something to remember. All of the facts we know about socialism in power still do not persuade the people, even the poor. This woman, overcoming her timidity, asked the question which gnaws at her, inside: 'But what, exactly, is socialism?' Acquaviva told her that it means the end of the private ownership of the means of production, a guaranteed job, a pension, school for all the children of the people; it represents the collapse of the system, capitalism, that lets a handful of men exploit many, many people. The things which seem to have most strongly persuaded the woman in favour of 'socialism' concern schooling and jobs. This was pretty clear from the way she asked her next questions: well then, under socialism would my husband have a job? Under socialism would my children be able to go to school? And Acquaviva responded that, yes, under socialism all of man's fundamental rights – to work, to eat, to get an education – have been guaranteed. The problem (but this question is for me, not the woman, whose comprehension doesn't run to such matters), though, is how, after having socialized the means of production in the USSR, one can also socialize power, in the sense of making the masses participants in the running of the country. But this raises an entirely different issue: the evident crisis in which the parties of the Third International find themselves as regards their relations with reality and with the masses in the socialist countries.

When I left the hotel, I met the hotel workers out on the pavement. The youngest among them, those without 'families to support', those who are the most political, were not only carrying placards calling for respect for the labour contract, they were also shouting the name 'Ho

Chi Minh' in rhythm, over and over again. And so, right in front of the Ambassador, as American, French and English tourists come in their droves to 'see Naples and die', one also hears cries of 'Long live labour' and 'Respect the labour contract'. The police were eventually unleashed against the hotel workers, and they arrested a few of them and took them to central headquarters. The great mass of the other workers, at this, all went down to headquarters and, standing together outside, they began to shout, 'Out, out, let them out!' I went in, a number of other communist Deputies arrived shortly afterwards, and after a few hours we managed to have them freed.

While I was finishing my tape-recording of the lines you have just been reading, there came a violent knocking at my door. I opened up and found a group of unknown people standing there; no one was wearing a hotel uniform or even a crest, but they asked me if I needed anything. I looked at them as coldly as I could, and then I just asked them one thing: 'Are you the strike-breakers?' The young man who seemed to be their leader answered with great assurance, 'Yes, we are the strike-breakers.' To which I responded, 'Well, then, I don't need anything from you people. I am in complete solidarity with the workers of this hotel who are out on strike, and for two days I will accept whatever inconveniences may arise in the hotel as a result of the strike.' Then I added, 'You yourselves are workers; the fact that you are now acting as strike-breakers shows that you are out of a job. It shows that you have taken the work because normally, during the rest of the year, you don't have an income.' The young man lost all aggressiveness and lowered his head and said this was true. It is obvious that he and the women with him have been enrolled out of the great mass of unemployed at Naples. I tried once more to explain to them that the only way to guarantee a job for yourself is to stand behind those who struggle or strike. The only way to get jobs is to force society to change drastically. You can't solve your own unemployment by going out and stealing, even for two days, the job of someone who is engaged in a struggle. It works just the other way around: a successful struggle means the hope and chance of weakening the ruling class, and therefore the chance of creating new jobs for Naples. When they left, they thanked me. 'I thank you in the name of my entire group,' said the youth. He spoke of 'his' group, as if he were 'the head of the blacklegs' for this twenty-seventh floor with its innumerable doors.

But the strike-breakers are incapable of managing anything. Just as they did in my case, they knock, loudly and indiscriminately, on door after door. They enter, perhaps while someone is half-asleep, and they shout in his ear to ask if he would like anything. It adds up to the most complete and chaotic disorder, made worse by the presence of these would-be saboteurs of the strike effort. Far from solving any of the problems of how to run the hotel without the regular staff, they only aggravate them. The conclusion, then, is this: if the strike-breakers turn out to be incompetent, they end up by objectively emphasizing the value of the strikers' work.

When I was speaking before about the lack of any machinery for cleaning the hotel, I forgot to add yet another fact which shows how incredibly low the cost of labour is in southern Italy. It concerns pensions. The maids tell me that after thirty years of work, they get a pension of 12,000 lire a month. 12,000 lire is just about enough to pay for a *basso*; for the rest, starvation. I can't predict how this strike is going to end. As I work here, the hotel is silent; the staff have gone away, or else they are all down where the demonstration is taking place. Will they end up victorious? I just do not know. But one important victory in itself is that the strike came off; that it has been accepted and utilized effectively as a weapon.

Maria Antonietta

Dear Louis,   *Naples, 12 May 1968*

The 'mass party', in the twenty-five years since its creation, has become an extremely complex phenomenon, and hence it is very difficult for me to formulate a definitive interpretation of it. For now, all I can do is gather together, from a variety of sources, those concrete elements which I think are necessary for the more thorough political analysis which must come later.

Last night I tried to think about the things I was seeing in precisely this light: with the aim of clarifying my analysis of the PCI as a mass party.

I arrive at Piscinola, a small town – or, better a huge suburb in the poverty-stricken outskirts of Naples – and, as soon as I walk into this primarily sub-proletarian section, I realize that I am breathing hostile air. The comrades are very old, and they are all seated around the same table, where they always pass their long and empty afternoons; they have almost nothing at all to say to me. They look me over and remain silent. I ask them where the meeting will be, if it has been announced, etc. I get a negative response, but they tell me not to worry, for *whatever must be done will be done*. I insist on asking where it is that I will speak, and so I discover that they have not yet set up the platform, nor have they set up the loudspeakers. I ask where D., the secretary of the section is, and they tell me that he has been there until seven, but then went home – to get ready to leave for Turin tomorrow.

It dawns on me that D., whose speech was advertised for the same programme as mine in *l'Unità*, has decided to make a *public gesture* concerning me. Since he was originally against my inclusion on the PCI list, this gesture will show that he still maintains a negative attitude towards the whole business. Democratic centralism when it becomes bureaucratic – and is helped along by political sloth and the encrusted presence of unremovable old leaders – allows, indeed guarantees the emergence of 'notables' and of personal squabbles; 'There are plenty of section secretaries,' I was told by a worker, 'who couldn't be more pleased than when they are greeted by the local chief of carabinieri in town.'

In conditions like those of Piscinola, it is objectively more difficult to organize a speech. But with patience, kindness and the help of another woman comrade from the Federation, we manage to cut through the thickest wall of distrust. We get a small stage set up on the back of a three-wheeler, we rig the microphone up on this, and then I undertake that most horrible of jobs – which I would never ask a friend to do – that is, beginning to shout in an empty square in the hope of attracting people and drawing them closer to the platform, to create some sort of audience. But those comrades from the section who are present are sceptical: they are convinced that without the magical presence of D., the whole thing will fail. There cannot possibly be a speech.

And yet, little by little, people start coming forward and the numbers by the platform increase steadily. The women in the houses closest to our group look out of their windows and then gradually begin to come out into the street. The crowd is 'made'. Just at that moment, a van from the Unified Socialist Party comes by with its loudspeakers at top volume. They announce that people should not gather here, but rather, they should go off to another piazza to hear the PSU speech. At this, my audience reacts violently: fists hammer the hood of the social-democrats' vehicle, the police step in to break it up, this is followed by five minutes filled with incidents. . . . But this 'political clash' has created tension and spirit, and suddenly you feel that the Party has been liberated from its internal bureaucratic structure, that it can now respond easily to a comrade who is speaking about what is true and valid for her listeners, and doing so in terms of what has just been witnessed by all, this petty provocation on the part of the Unified Socialists.

Immediately following this episode, I go to another section in the same area. This is still a part of the great sub-proletarian 'belly', and here I am exposed to yet another slice of the 'mass party'. Here I see that even though it has a mass character, the Party is not at all free from sectarian or authoritarian tendencies. In this section, there is a generational conflict between old and young.

When I arrive at the site of the speech, I find that a young comrade is already speaking. His name is A.S.: he can't even be twenty-one, and therefore he isn't even old enough to vote. He is the son of that transport worker who was so unpleasant to me when I first arrived in Naples. And A.S. is giving a long speech: I can see that he has written out about twenty-five cards from which he is now systematically reading. The old leaders of the section are sitting on the stage all around him, and when I arrive they make room for me as well. I find this whole business of sitting down on stage in front of a crowd pretty strange, as if some high-ranking notables had been called to a conference. Notwithstanding my reservations, I sit down as well. The young comrade speaks on and on – too long, in the older leaders' opinions, and they start to poke him in the calves, shielded by the podium. One man leans over with his cane and gives him two or three blows on the leg, but A.S. continues unruffled. He obviously has decided to go on, and he plans to carry through right to the end. I find him likeable, and my feelings are reinforced when he has the courage to accuse the local priest of not having respected the pastoral letter of the Bishop of Naples, which explicitly said that priests should refrain from getting involved in the election. Instead, this priest had called a meeting of women and given electoral counsel which favoured the DC.

At this point in his speech, I realize that the old leaders have all abandoned the platform; I am unaware of just when or how it happened, but suddenly I notice that only myself and the young speaker are up there. He ends his own speech and then, turning and seeing that the comrade who was supposed to introduce me has fled, he simply mentions into the microphone, 'And now, Comrade Macciocchi has a few things she would like to say to you.' So, like A.S. just before me, I am all alone on the stage. I finish my talk and as soon as I walk down the steps, the older men all swarm around me, congratulate me, and we go off to the section.

In the section I rebel for the first time: pent-up political anger finally explodes out of me in my attempt to make these people understand what is politically correct behaviour and what is improper. I try to stress that the Party is not supposed to be a battleground between old and young, between new and veteran candidates for Parliament, between local favourites and strangers. A Communist Party is something other than this: a revolutionary party has another moral code and another kind of discipline. It is unjust, I tell them, to leave a visiting comrade alone on the stage, in front of a crowd, because of some protest they want to lodge against a young speaker. And then I add that I think A.S. spoke well. But they insist that he committed a number of errors, and, in particular, that the part about the Catholics was a mistake. I instead insist that this is untrue: we have to be both sincere and ideologically rigorous, and this includes saying unpleasant things – things that the whole country knows anyway.

The evening ended on this extremely cold note. Only old S., the speaker's father, still looked at me as if he knew me. I may have shaken everyone's hand, but I am sure that I didn't leave anyone with the impression that I had an 'electoralist' attitude. On the contrary, last night I tried deliberately to show these comrades that there are things that one can and must do, even where a modest issue like a speech is involved. In a moment as sensitive as that of an electoral campaign, and in a section where the Party has 'indicated' me for preference votes, I still had to make the comrades understand that I won't shrink from a political battle on important issues.

There is really a 'generation gap' in the Party today. (The problem manifests itself much more clearly as you move out from the centre to the periphery.) Some older comrades – and I am not speaking here in chronological terms as much as referring to those who have had power 'in their hands' for years and years – look on the youth as *arrivistes* who want to upset the petty but secure positions they have obtained and consolidated after many years of effort and sacrifice. They suspect their juniors as if they were dangerous extremists, since they seem to want to call into question the 'unitary line' on which these older men have staked their very existence: dialogue with the socialists, dialogue with the Catholics, dialogue with the enemy, etc., etc. 'Listen, are you *for* or *against* the line of the Party?' they ask. And the youth, to this rather dogmatic question, respond, 'Just what is the Party line?'

Those who have come to form a kind of stratum of intermediate chieftains in the Party simply do not know how to give a political answer to this question; all they can do is to make professions of faith. In this context, the youth represent a pleasant departure from and break with bureaucratization, and also with 'antidemocratic methods' and the Party's 'internal liturgy'. Hence, at times the Party closes its doors in the face of this youth – sometimes from fear, sometimes out of sheer indifference. One evening at Porta Piccola, another popular area on the fringe of Naples, I met two young *liceo* students who told me that they had been hanging around the section for days on end, trying to speak with the old comrades inside, who play cards in the afternoon and pinball at night. They wouldn't have got a worse reception if they had been gypsies. Faced with this reaction, they were coming to the conclusion that any dialogue was impossible. On the issues that concern them (political, theoretical and ideological issues), there is just no communication possible with the older comrades. About all that the students succeeded in doing, and even this was difficult, was getting the comrades to give them some propaganda booklets.

The meeting arranged that evening by the old section of Porta Piccola was a complete failure. Neither I nor the other speaker ever really got into our addresses, for absolutely no one showed up to listen to us. The young students told me that they had asked if there was anything they could do, but no one had paid any attention to them. In fact, they had been chased away as if they were bothersome insects buzzing around otherwise tranquil people. And things are like this in a number of sections. The head of the Communist Youth Federation is an intelligent youth named d'Alò, with an emaciated face and an air of being on the point of surrendering to the inevitable – i.e. to the existing relationship of forces. He too appears to be under an enormous amount of pressure. He is a candidate too: he is the token 'young person' just as I am the token 'woman'.

When I see things like this, I feel that we have not yet learned from the explosion of the student movement, nor from the fact that it caught us completely unawares. All we were able to do was stand by with our mouths open as the students experimented with original and autonomous forms of struggle and political democracy, like popular assemblies. We stand by while they seek ways to develop a new political consciousness. But the question goes deeper: are we capable of understanding these experiences for what they are, and that these experiences represent new forms of linkage to the masses that our type of 'mass party' is completely ignoring? Do we realize that instead of turning our backs on these experiences, we should ourselves become the standard-bearers and promoters of them? Instead of asking ourselves these questions, it seems to me that, even when we are interested in what the young are doing, we remain fundamentally suspicious of them, and we consider the new forces in the struggle as some heterogeneous element that is beyond all control. The Party is so unprepared to deal with them that, instead of considering the activism of youth as a sign of political movement and growth, they are confused with and portrayed as a factor of political confusion. As a result, we end up saying things like 'They are not mature', or they 'have to gain some political experience' – which amounts to shunting them aside without even realizing that in so doing we are taking a step backward.

The group currently in power, in order to safeguard its own position, defines itself as synonymous with fidelity to the line of the Party. It is, therefore, counterposed to those (never very well defined) who are *unfaithful*. On this basis, just about anything is possible in terms of salvaging (*from above*) the entrenched leadership of a section – or even of a federation.

And this is the situation, clear and bitter as it is, in which I find myself. This also helps explain the 'mystery' by which young Communist leaders who had played leading roles in the students' struggles often found that they faced expulsion from the Party as a 'reward' for their activities.

All it would take to open the door to young students and workers in Naples would be to accept the fact that the decisive question for the PCI here concerns the elaboration of a line which would put the working class at the head of the struggle and at the head of the Party. This recognition alone would represent a break with the intellectual laziness of accepting a never-defined 'Party Line' – a term that you find on everyone's tongue wherever you turn. This break in itself would be a way of telling the young that there is a natural space for them within the Party, and that the political and ideal role that they have every right to play inside the PCI is, in fact, open to them.

As far as the intellectuals are concerned, it would be more proper to describe their role inside the Party (a 'mass party', at that) as that of little potentates. Here there is the editor, there the established book dealer, there the well-known personality from the cultural or professional world. Each of these people, if he so desires (and even this occurs with increasing rarity), lends himself to Party initiatives – and finds it completely appropriate that the Party should turn to him to call a conference of intellectuals, to call a professional group together, or to approach certain highly qualified specialists. Communist federations, like the one at Naples, establish a relationship with their intellectuals by conceding a mysterious 'autonomous terrain' where initiatives are concerned. The intellectuals are presumed to hold the secret key to these activities, and the Party goes to them, hat in hand, to make sure that a particular 'Party action' succeeds. This to me betrays not only a petty-bourgeois presumption on the part of the intellectuals, who see themselves as privileged creatures in a popular, working-class world, but it also betrays a manipulative attitude on the part of the Party, which has become accustomed to treat intellectuals as 'Peers of the Realm' (English aristocrats).

When I meet intellectuals who have remained in the PCI, rather than going over to the 'Southocrats', I find the depressing air of ex-combatants about them. It is like being with people who enjoy the benefits of a special statute or pension. In the bookstore of a dear old friend of mine, for example, I saw, displayed in the most prominent spot on the wall of the office, a photo of Saragat, the social-democratic President of the Republic. Saragat smiles down on the face of my comrade as if he were Ho, Che or Giap. And that picture of him, complete with endearing words and autograph, hangs there in a perfectly tranquil and natural way, in the same way that our grandparents used to display on their walls royal citations that bestowed upon them the title of '*Commendatore*'.

I have also had some specific, and not very happy, contact, with the intellectual community. I organized an exhibition of some of Matta's[1] paintings in the main hall of the Neapolitan Federation: these are works that Matta had never exhibited before anywhere in Europe, including Paris. And Matta himself came, in a gesture of solidarity and friendship. He managed to find the time, amidst his continent-hopping from Cuba to Paris, to come down here to Naples; by telephoning New York and London, he also managed somehow to arrange to have some works never seen before in public sent down here.

Thus, for the first time, this artist was opening a show not in a gallery, but inside the Communist Federation, and in so doing he cast an objective challenge in the faces of the 'official' merchants and critics of the art world. I think this was an important political and cultural act, significant in terms of the break it represents with 'official culture', and also because it reveals the kind of imagination which is totally consistent with Matta's surrealistic orientation. In spite of all this, the exhibition was practically boycotted by the Party's official intellectuals who, with the exception of a number of painters, snubbed both the inauguration of the show and the discussion which followed it. Those intellectuals who think they deserve little fiefdoms independent of the Party; all those who are puffed up with cultural arrogance (even if this is often purely defensive in nature); those who think that on their elect heads rest the laurels of 'Southern Intellectuals' (the fact that the area is half illiterate does not seem to bother them) and who therefore feel they have nothing whatsoever to learn – all of these shining lights felt constrained to demonstrate, by their absence, their disdain for a cultural initiative which had not been blessed with their personal benediction.

Then there were the 'intellectuals' who are candidates for office. They were all so busy scurrying to and fro from one electoral meeting to the next that they never dropped in to so much as glance at the paintings. But this is not, after all, so surprising, given that paintings cannot deliver votes. On the other hand, top-flight critics like Micacchi and Rago came from the *Unità* office in Rome.

In spite of all this pettiness, the show was a great success, for, in addition to the Neapolitan painters, there were also many, many students and young workers who not only came to see the paintings, but who stayed on afterwards to talk with Matta. I will send you a trans-

1. See Matta's letter to *Rinascita* in the Appendix to this volume. (Trans.)

cription of a tape I made of Matta's talk with the public during and
after the show. I would like you to read it because, in my opinion, the
dialogue that Matta began in this city should be seen in the same light
as one of his paintings (on Cuba), which he calls 'Fruit-Bomb'; 'Fruit'
because in it is the suggestion of the bloom of a new life, and 'bomb'
because it represents a violent break with all of the old schemas inside
and outside the Party.

Just as happens in other sectors, the Party's cultural activities and
relationships at times seem to undergo an incredible refractory process. Culturally, the P C I atomizes into innumerable little groups, each
one of which then tries to deal with the Federation from positions of
greater or lesser strength. It brings to mind the way you used to
repeat time and again in Paris what Lenin said about intellectuals.
Individually, some of them (on a political level) can become open and
courageous revolutionaries. But collectively, they are and always will
remain petty-bourgeois, unable to free themselves from a petty-
bourgeois ideology. You used to recall that Lenin even viewed
Gorky – whose talent he admired – as a petty-bourgeois revolutionary.
You would always add: 'In order to become ideologues of the working
class, in Lenin's terms, or organic intellectuals of the proletariat, in
Gramsci's terms, intellectuals will have to carry out a radical revolution
in their own ideas; it will be a long, painful and difficult re-education,
a battle without either internal or external limits.'

In the course of this campaign, I have realized again and again that
what you said in Paris corresponds to reality here: I mean this not only
in terms of what happens when you meet the 'great' intellectuals (who
are non-existent anyway), but even in terms of the most modest of
intellectuals. You know that the South is full of titles, and one of the
most common is *dottore*. Whoever has a not-too-shabby appearance
and wears a tie and a nice shirt is instinctively called, by waiters, taxi-
drivers and everyone else, *dottore*. Down here, the title of 'Doctor' is
extremely important; if you forget to bestow it on someone who
deserves it, he will be deeply offended. It is a class attitude. Several
days ago, I went to the Prefecture and asked if I could speak with a
certain Signor V. 'Signore? But his title is "*Dottore*"! You should say
"Dottore V.". . . .' To which I responded, 'No, I mean *Signor* V.' He
then replied, with the kind of officiousness you come to expect of
Italian petty bureaucrats (playing on the dual significance of *Signore*:
'Mr' and 'Lord'): 'Our *Signore* is in Heaven; down here, everyone is a

Doctor or Professor. . . .' All I could say to this was that I thought that one title was as good as the other, and that they all were essentially the same. Hearing this, the listener simply stopped talking altogether, looked me up and down, and asked, 'Are you from Milan?'

There is yet another thing that should be said about the intellectuals. As I have had ample occasion to witness, the presumption of intellectuals can become a source of humiliation for workers, even when the intellectual is 'cordial' towards the workers – i.e. when he is paternalistic, tapping someone on the cheek, throwing an arm across someone's shoulders or even suggesting: 'Let's go and have a coffee together.' At times, without even knowing it, intellectuals inside the Party carry around this pride (inherited from Croce) in being members of a 'superior' class – with its special meeting places, in which it can mingle and 'discourse' among equals. Perhaps all this strikes me with special force because I remember your own modesty where such issues are concerned, and I remember the way you go, without calling attention to yourself, to the cell meeting in your quarter. I also have in mind your most pressing question after the publication of your interview in *l'Unità*: 'Do you think this will be read by workers? Could you tell me what their reaction to the interview is?'

By the way: when I asked you, back in Paris, why you were so withdrawn in your work as a philosopher, you answered by spelling out all the bourgeois traps an intellectual was prey to: 'Ever since I have become a bit "known" I have, out of principle, refused to talk about myself. I am a communist philosopher, and my place is in the struggle of the proletariat. I am simply one militant among tens of millions: no more and no less. We live in a society which "constructs personalities" in order to sell them at a higher price, both commercially and ideologically. A communist must defend himself ferociously, for "personalities" and "intellectuals" do not make history; the masses make history, through the class struggle.'

Of course, it is hard to keep the bourgeois press – which has its own aims in mind – from 'speaking of' someone. For the capitalist bourgeoisie is quite intelligent. It 'peddles' Marxism by the truck-load, in books, in the press, on radio, on television, in films: Marx, Lenin, October 1917, Soviets, Mao, not to mention Che or Debray. The bourgeois have understood. You can render a revolutionary theory inoffensive or even useless if you absorb it by according it verbal recognition.

The easiest thing in the world for the bourgeois press is to 'capture' an intellectual, even a 'Marxist'. All that is necessary is to guarantee him his 'freedom of expression'. Do you know how they shoot thrushes in Provence? They take one thrush and put it in a cage. Then, in the winter, they attach the cage to the highest branch of a tree. The thrush, seeing nothing but clear sky overhead, sings 'freely'. The result is that all the thrushes passing by alight in the tree near the caged bird. And the hunter shoots them. He does not kill the bird that sings; he kills only the others. Here in Italy, there are many singing thrushes who make believe they are free.

The carryings-on of intellectuals outside the PCI often border on the absurd in a southern electoral campaign. One of the more ridiculous cases of this campaign concerns a certain Radical intellectual who dressed up like Carlo Pisacane for his electoral posters, since he was running, on the Socialist list, in the electoral district of Sala Consilina in the Cilento region. It was here that Carlo Pisacane disembarked during the Risorgimento, only to terminate his ill-fated campaign – and his life – under the peasants' pitchforks at Sapri. Now, under the title, 'Pisacane Has Returned!' we find the face of the historic personage off in a corner of the poster, while in the centre foreground are instead the professorial glasses of the editor of the weekly *l'Espresso*. From his weekly vantage-point he can usually be found flailing out at the vices and low standards he finds all around himself, and he usually does this in deeply moralistic tones. This whole business of dressing up like Pisacane is an episode typical not only of the South, but of the North or Rome as well. It also shows the way in which intellectuals who come from those areas somehow feel authorized to consider the entire South as their colony as soon as they break through the 'sound barrier' – i.e. pass Lake Trasimeno.

This 'intelligentsia' of Naples is forever playing war-games with industrialization, defining itself as *a modern political class*, drawing up hypothetical lists of a future *efficient* government, and gossiping about how many cabinet posts will be given to this group and how many to that group, how many votes will go to this person and how many to that one. My definition of them, *sudocrats* (Mediterranean affiliate of the Eurocrats), appears to have been picked up by a number of people. And meanwhile, the electoral campaign carried on by the various *dottori*, *professori* and *ingegneri* (technical consultants) is truly staggering. The thing that is most visible on their electoral posters is the professional title next to their names, followed by a gigantic number which is, of course, their position on the electoral list, and which they want to make sure no one misses. At times it seems as if the whole electoral campaign is nothing more than a great elimination tournament for professional and academic titles.

The walls of Naples are plastered with thousands of posters from which peer down the most anonymous, banal and dull faces imaginable. The overall impression I get is similar to the feeling I have when I pass a photo studio and find hundreds of portraits on display, or when I glance at one of those coin-operated photo machines (one franc for six pictures) which has strip after strip of sample photos stuck up outside. When one is confronted with this myriad of absurd faces all over the city, the cumulative impression is one of vast anonymity – which, incidentally, is close to the truth, for behind these empty faces lies not any personality of character, but the bourgeois ruling class.

At the same time, our Party is prey to a contradiction which it does not even see, for it persists in maintaining a purely mechanical and manipulative relationship with its *own* traditional intellectuals (who are a pretty haggard lot). While the PCI carries on in this fashion, it misses the fact that in Naples and throughout the South new cultural centres are springing up. They are rising up almost spontaneously, and no longer within corporative limits. They are growing in the country-side as well as in the cities, and they are developing above all in the universities. This new development on the cultural scene represents the potential for communist cultural militants of a new kind, coming neither from *above* nor from *outside*. Sectors of society which traditionally have been all but impossible to politicize are, today, mobilized in political conflicts. This even includes professional centres like the courts, and even the hospitals. If I am not mistaken, the major implication of all this is the following: the Party, as a collective intellectual capable of connecting everyday struggles to a broader vision of the entire revolutionary process, must find out how to create a system of alliances with the intellectuals that is not manipulative and fleeting, but contains within itself the characteristics of the new socialist society for which it struggles. It therefore must also contain within itself a vision of a new socialist culture, at least in germinal form, around which people can unite in the course of the struggle for the conquest of socialist power. And it must do this as quickly as possible.

In the last few days, I have re-read Gramsci's book on 'Intellectuals and the Organization of Culture'. I think it is really important to re-study certain aspects of the work with great care. Gramsci's is an original theoretical conception which could serve very well as an approach to the problems which face all communist parties, not only those of the West. The question he raises is that of the hegemony of the Party over society, and intellectuals play an important role in establishing this hegemony. For Gramsci, all men are intellectuals, but not all of them serve an intellectual function in society. There is no human activity from which all intellectual intervention can be excluded, for the simple reason that it is impossible to separate *homo faber* from *homo sapiens*. The most widespread methodological error, according to Gramsci, has been to see the distinguishing criterion of intellectual activity, which marks it off sharply from the activities of all other social groupings, as being intrinsic to intellectual activity itself, whereas in fact it should be sought in the entire complex of social relations. The worker, for example, is not characterized specifically by the fact that he does manual labour, but by the fact that he labours under specific conditions or within the framework of a determined set of social relationships. (No work, no matter what kind, is purely physical. This is true of the most mechanical tasks, for even they require a minimum technical qualification, i.e. some degree of creative intellectual activity.)

This approach to the problem, as Gramsci noted, results in an extremely broad extension of the concept of intellectuals. But it is only in this fashion, he went on, that it is possible for us to arrive at some concrete approximation of reality. He also wrote, in the same work, that 'the most interesting problem for the contemporary period is that of *the intellectuals and the modern political party*, its real origins, its developments and the forms which it takes'. The party succeeds in creating its own intellectuals 'in proportion to its ability to carry out its fundamental function. That function is to work on and prepare its own members – elements of a social group which has sprung up and developed in "economic" terms – until they become qualified political intellectuals: organizers and leaders of all the activities and functions which are inherent in the organic development of an integral society, a society both civil and political. . . . To say that all members of a political party should be regarded as intellectuals,' Gramsci concludes, 'is an assertion which appears to leave one open to ridicule and

212

caricature. But if one thinks about it, nothing could be more exact. . . . What matters is the function, which is directive and organizational, i.e. the educational, i.e. intellectual . . ., which must be assumed by those who actively adhere to the political party.'

Some of these quotations would make no sense if one did not at the same time keep in mind the evolution of the P C I as a *mass party* in the quarter-century since it was first established as such. In the same way that a cell reflects the characteristics of its organism, it seems to me that the mass party reflects the characteristics of an entire society, including its limits, its religious superstitions, its superstructures, its deformations, its periods of political laxity, its continual risk of social-democratization. This is true also for the enormous amounts of energy that a party of this type is capable of generating (as if it had thousands of antennae which could pick up the mood of the people), especially in a society like southern Italy: a land full of contradictions and rebellion, where passion almost always wins out over more rational forms of thought, and where invention overthrows accepted schemas and in the end destroys and scourges all bureaucratic forms.

The basic question is this: How can a 'mass party' consistently follow a *mass line*, linked directly to the masses, and carry out its struggles *inside* democratic institutions without risking reformism? How can it safeguard its revolutionary characteristics?

The Party seems to have abandoned all ideologically educational activity; it does not even propagate its own doctrine, Marxism-Leninism. And this makes things even more complicated than they already are. There are specific episodes which seem important to me to get down on paper so that you will be able to think about them. These things provide, I think, very good evidence of just how 'socially specific' a mass party is. Let's take a particular aspect of this specificity: ours is a party where, as Amendola has pointed out recently, Catholics outnumber atheists. This is a general point, but it leads us to a specific one. For example, I recently met a female worker, employed by the *Manifatture Cotoniere Meridionali*, and her nickname is Giovanna La Carbonara. This is a woman who has led all the big strikes in her plant, one of the largest textile plants – and indeed, one of the largest factories – in Naples. Giovanna La Carbonara is also called Garibaldi because of the red blouse she wears when there is a struggle to be fought and won. And when Giovanna La Carbonara leads the other women into battle, security and victory are as good as guaranteed.

To talk with Giovanna La Carbonara is to hear politics and religious faith mixed together in the most simple and tranquil fashion imaginable. They are two aspects of the same moment in her life: on one side, the Party, on the other, God, Our Lady and the saints. She spoke – before we turned to the electoral campaign – of her visit to Lourdes and of how she and thirty-six other women of the quarter rented a bus and all went together to the shrine of the Holy Mother to bathe in the miraculous waters. She explains how they took a collection among themselves to buy a cloth gown which would cover their nakedness when they bathed in the stream at Lourdes. She was struck by the fact – so struck that she continued to repeat the details as if she was sure this would enlighten the minds of all who listened – that this cloth sack, or gown, got soaked every time a woman entered the water and bathed herself, but, as soon as the woman emerged and the sack was removed, it suddenly became as dry as a bone. For our militant proletarian comrade, this undoubtedly represents a miracle. I ask her if she doesn't think that all this could perhaps be due to some atmospheric phenomenon, maybe the way the air circulates in the place where the women bathed. She is almost offended by this suggestion and responds that this is absolutely impossible, that such a thing could only happen by grace of a miraculous intervention, for only a miracle could dry out a heavy cloth sack within the space of a few minutes, which is all the time it takes for a woman to come up out of the stream and pass the sack on to another person. Her story has made me think, among other things, of all the dirt and filth that must be accumulated in that bathing place, but it is clear that I dare not argue with Giovanna La Carbonara. And, once she has carefully explained how one bathes at Lourdes and how many concretely miraculous things those waters contain – as proven definitively by the sack – she turns, with equal fervour, to an examination of the problems of the electoral campaign and the things necessary to obtain a victory for the P C I.

Maybe this whole business with the sack is more believable because there is some kind of parallel with the miracle of San Gennaro's blood: that too is a physical, or rather, chemical phenomenon which men and women can witness in person, which they can, in short, 'verify'. In one case, a wet sack suddenly dries; in the other, blood which has been dry for centuries suddenly liquefies. And when they see a chemical-physical phenomenon take place before their eyes, the women cry 'Miracle!' But this is hardly their fault. The biggest newspaper in Naples (a regressive, sensationalist rag it is true, but which still has the largest circulation in the city), a true organ of misinformation, had banner headlines three times in a single month on the Miracle of San Gennaro. I saved one of the articles with its headline, which runs across the top of the entire page in large block letters and reads 'Scientific Proof of the Miracle of San Gennaro'.

Giovanna La Carbonara, who will do an excellent job organizing the electoral propaganda for the Party in her quarter, shows us, with great pride and emotion, the new telephone which has just been installed. One of her nieces has just become a nun, and Giovanna had the phone put in so that she could speak with her, every now and then, in the convent.

Or take this example, which just happened at San Carlo alle Mortelle, an area in the territory of the Montecalvario Section of the Party, the umbilicus of the Neapolitan 'belly'. A new electoral campaign headquarters was opened here, and I went along to inaugurate it. We were all talking about the problems of the Party and the activists, when it suddenly came to light that fifty comrades, part of the Party's 'organizational cadre', had abandoned our organization and joined the Jehovah's Witnesses, a religious sect which preaches the imminent coming of a new God-King. I am absolutely amazed. I ask the comrades what sort of activity the Witnesses go in for, and they explain, quite calmly, that they preach the coming of a new world. They go around telling all the other comrades that there is nothing left to do except to await death peacefully, for the world will be destroyed in the year 2000 anyhow. They tell me about one of their ex-leaders who, now a preacher, travels through the streets of the quarters, Bible in hand, reading the Psalms at the top of his voice. He invites his ex-comrades in the P C I to join him. And the section secretary at Pompeii recently became a Baptist. He will resign as secretary, but he has asked to keep his post as communal councillor.

The mass conversion at San Carlo alle Mortelle is not a product of ignorance, for I remember your comment that no phenomenon can be purely and simply a result of people's ignorance. It grows out of economic conditions. By going more deeply into the matter, I learned that the Jehovah's Witnesses, with headquarters in one of the most elegant districts of the city (Parco Margherita), are loaded with money. Its adherents, in a city of extremely poor people, are largely recruited from among the unemployed. And the sect tries to recruit Communists because they are used to propagating ideas and can add something to the techniques of their 'new calling'. When a poor proletarian out of work joins the sect, the family immediately begins to enjoy a new kind of salary. People tell me about ex-comrades who are now able to support, at least minimally, their families of seven children; many of the fifty new converts, all things considered, would prefer to be Communists, but things are more secure for them as Witnesses. As members of the sect, they enjoy many short-run benefits, and while this may be a limited perspective, it is one which provides them, in concrete terms, with a respite from poverty. With the Communist Party, there will be a long wait; with the Jehovah's Witnesses, there is no wait at all, because a guaranteed salary immediately begins to arrive in the home.

Gramsci and the Party

Re-reading Gramsci's speech to the Central Committee of the PCI in May 1925, I found certain issues which still have great relevance today. This speech was one in which Gramsci outlined what the main lines of discussion should be at the important Lyons Congress, and dealt with all the principal points around which the new leadership had focused the struggle which it was now bringing to a conclusion against Bordiga, and especially against certain positions of the Trotskyist opposition in the Comintern. What really caught my eye was the discussion of the 'bolshevization' of the Party and its organization into cells. Gramsci said:

The crises which all of the parties of the Communist International have undergone from 1921 to the present, i.e. from the beginning of the period characterized by a slow-down of revolutionary momentum, have shown that the general ideological composition of the communist parties was not very solid. We have seen the parties switch back and forth from the right to the extreme left, with not only very serious results for the party organization, but with the additional result of a general crisis in the relationship between the parties and the masses. . . . In Western Europe there is an increasing tendency to construct a division of labour between the working class's union organization and its political organization. Within the unions, the result has been an increased influence of pacifist and reformist tendencies, i.e. an increased influence of the bourgeoisie over the workers. For the same reasons, the activity of the political parties has increasingly shifted towards parliamentary activity, towards forms, in other words, which cannot be distinguished at all from bourgeois-democratic forms of activity.

During the War, and immediately afterwards, in the period just prior to the creation of the Communist International and to the splits in the socialist camp which led to the creation of our party, reformist tendencies consolidated their dominant position in the unions. A general situation was thus created which placed the communist parties of Western Europe in the same situation in which the Bolshevik Party found itself, in Russia, prior to the War. . . .

Gramsci's comments bring back into focus his own masterly efforts to give our Party roots in a *soviet* or *factory council* experience – our Party which had indeed been born as soviets and factory councils, accompanied by a great libertarian Marxist inspiration. Under no circumstances, as he affirms in this report, was the party to be ambiguous in its choice between Leninism and reformism.

Maria Antonietta

Dear Louis,   *Naples, 14 May 1968*

Today my electoral itinerary takes us to Parete, which is a truly extraordinary place, meriting study for its unique characteristics: it is a town made up entirely of *braccianti*,[1] where the PCI gets 46 per cent of the vote. The comrades from Parete come to get me in Giugliano, which is a large commercial centre of about 30,000 inhabitants. I am very happy to leave Giugliano, for the speech has been very poorly organized: cars keep weaving through the crowd, traffic police are continuously blowing their whistles to regulate the chaotic flow of vehicles, and the net result is that I have to speak in a veritable vortex of noise and confusion. Among the people who gather in front of the platform are several who are quite obviously intoxicated. I first realise this when I begin to speak about the question of our relationship with Catholics. I try to stress that we are Marxist-Leninists, and Marxism-

1. Agricultural day-labourers. (Trans.)

Leninism is based on historical materialism, which is a science, and on dialectical materialism, a philosophy. Our dialogue with the Catholics, I say, is not based on a confusion of ideologies or of faiths, but on common goals that all men can work for together, on common concrete demands. I thought I was quite clear in spelling this out.

But at this point, a voice from the first row interrupts me: 'Tell about those whores, those women who go to the Church to get —— by priests.' Now usually I am quite capable of responding to any and all interruptions; but what on earth can you say to something like this? I decided to restate the problem in simpler terms. But this person caught on right away, and continued to make explicit allusions to the relationship between 'devout' women and priests. It sounded like something out of Pietro l'Aretino. I quickly came to the conclusion that no headway could be made and that it was better to let the whole thing slide. So I changed topics.

The speech went on like this, with one interruption or confusion after another. Diabolical little kids climbed up on the metal supports of the platform, banging incessantly on the pipes with their fists or with sticks. I can assure you that the noise this set up was much louder than my poor voice. And I had already been left a little confused on this whole issue of *voice* after being interrogated by the Giugliano comrades the day before at the Federation. They began by telling me how they wanted X and Y; not me (X and Y are the most popular speakers on the list). Finally, they 'settled' for me, but on condition that I had a voice and could speak for at least an hour and a quarter. I told them that I don't have a very strong voice, but that I could speak for even longer than an hour if need be. And this is in fact another oratorical gift that I forgot to tell you about in my earlier letter about speechmaking. One of the things that is considered of the utmost importance here, in addition to how well one's voice carries, is how long one can speak. One of the most positive things that can be said about someone is *He spoke for two hours!* But if you ask what this celebrated speaker said in that period of time, you get very vague responses. 'Everything,' they will say, 'he dealt with every major problem.' But the thing that is stressed most is always that he spoke for two full hours. Hence speeches become a race against the clock, but in the opposite sense from what is usually meant in sports: it is more like an endurance contest of some kind, as with cross-country skiing or long-distance walking.

In my opinion, however, the best speeches are the concise, synthesized ones. In France I learned to shorten things as I wrote, and to simplify my syntax – all those phrases spiralling on like corkscrews which we learn from Ciceronian prose at school. One can, obviously, speak for two hours; but I am convinced that one hour is really too much, and if I speak any longer than that I will end up either repeating the same things over and over again, or else just restating the same things in different ways. But it is also important to remember, where the topic of public speeches is concerned, that two hours is roughly the same time that a feature film lasts. Political speeches are a form of staged entertainment in the poor towns of the South, not only because of their intrinsic nature, but because the people do not have the money to go to the cinema, or else there are simply no cinemas or theatres available. In the outlying areas of the province, on Sundays, the women bring their chairs to the piazza and form a semi-circle around the speakers' platform. Inside this makeshift corral their children play, safely within sight of their mothers. This is precisely what happened to me last Sunday at the Ina-Casa; as I tried to speak, the children all played ball and hide-and-seek under my trembling rostrum. The advantage of this kind of situation is that the mothers are usually quite favourably disposed towards the orator when they feel secure about their children.

Another thing that is extremely important to this kind of audience is the old 'give and take'. Comrades in the audience will take notes on all the insults and injuries hurled against the Communists by earlier, non-Party speakers. They give you this note when you arrive to speak, and everyone waits to hear your responses, so they can see if you can 'take care of yourself'. As the electoral campaign draws to a close, they want to hear powerful phrases from you, as in Racine's plays; they want refrains with flaming epithets, for these are signs of the strength of the Party against its enemies and indications that it fears no one. The kind of audience that interrupts you generally wants the power of the meeting to consist in direct aggression against the class enemy. And this is a clear indication of sentiments of class struggle being expressed.

I end up speaking for a full hour at Giugliano, just as the comrades there had wanted. I still try to develop some arguments, with everything brought right up to date: the latest events in Paris, the students, the general strike, etc. But I realize how incredibly difficult it is to try to follow a logical train of thought in this inferno of noise: the people talking, the motors and horns of the cars and buses, the police whistles, and all the rest of it. Finally, I stop and simply pass the microphone over to the local candidate, who is as powerful as Tarzan: he takes the microphone, holds it like a baseball player holds his bat and does not let go of it again.

Beneath the stage, the comrades from Parete are already waiting for me. They are angry, saying that the whole organization of the meeting here at Giugliano was extremely shoddy and lamentable. They take a pretty dim view of the traffic, the general disorder, the confusing interruptions, and the absence of a quiet environment in which one could speak. 'Come on with us to Parete,' they say, 'you'll see how different it is there.' I am somewhat suspicious at this, given that self-admiration is not exactly a rarity in the Mezzogiorno. But I am wrong. Parete, which is only two kilometres from Giugliano, is really a totally different world. It is already 9.30 in the evening, yet the people are all waiting for me at the entrance to the town, with a band and all the women and girls at the head of the crowd. We get out of the car and walk through the crowd; I am surrounded by the comrades who brought me, and they sing my praises without interruption. I am wearing a red suit, and this seems to get the women in the crowd all excited. 'Viva Antonietta Macciocchi, who is all dressed in red', they shout. Obviously they interpret my clothing as a symbol of my political faith and my personal beliefs, and they like it. I arrive on the stage, more carried along by this wave of enthusiasm than as a result of my own powers, which, in any case, are steadily weakening by now. I put my notes aside, as I do when I feel that there is already a congenial and direct link established with the comrades. There is, moreover, another element which works in my favour; this small piazza is marvellously silent, although completely filled with people. They listen quietly and thoughtfully: it is like the amphitheatre of a people's university, when the 'professor' who rises to speak is a capable, serious person who has a deep respect for his listeners. Truly, it is another universe. In this town of day-labourers, I can deal with the major themes: socialism, the contradictions of imperialism, the crisis of social democracy, the unity of the Left. These are topics which, if discussed in another place, would soon lead to complete boredom on the part of the listeners.

Instead, for the first time, I am able to analyse, in front of these day-labourers, why Vietnam, today, must be the starting-point for any discussion of the struggle for socialism. What is Vietnam? What does it represent? It is the focal point of the crisis of imperialism, I say, and this is the case because it is there that all of the theories of capitalism's abilities to 'absorb' socialism have been proven false. In Vietnam capitalism has not absorbed or hegemonized anything at all: it has fought, and continues to fight, a war which it is losing. And, at the same time that capitalism shows its impotence on the international scene, a crisis is developing inside the system as well. Both in America and in the countries which represent its network of alliances, the crisis is growing and social-democratic solutions, and with them the social-democratic parties, are being eroded and discredited, for all they ever did was fight in the name of a so-called 'American ideal'.

Imperialism's crisis is the crisis of social-democracy. The alliance with social-democracy is something that has to be re-thought all the way back to its basic assumptions: it is, after all, a line and an analysis which have not been questioned since 1936. This alliance business no longer has anything to do with frontism, or with the policy of 'popular fronts' or any other, more respectable front. Now the question is to carry on struggles on ever more advanced terrain and issues, struggles which will throw the old capitalist and social-democratic arrangements into a serious crisis which will help open the way to a different alternative, that of socialism. I tried, as I talked, to sketch out the path to socialism, with the whole network of alliances and with the intermediate objectives which it would require, in an attempt to outline our own model of a revolutionary strategy.

When the speech was finished, the *braccianti*, who had listened attentively right up to the last word, broke out into a rhythmic chant of 'Ho! Ho! Ho Chi Minh'; the names of General Giap and Che Guevara could also be heard. In the Chinese Cultural Revolution – which speaks a clear revolutionary language to the youth of the West – the masses are realizing the value of popular self-government, and the specific values of communist freedom and equality which can only be re-confirmed in a socialist society. When I refer to the Cultural Revolution, even though I only do so in passing, it truly seems as if 'China is near'.

I remember something else you once told me in Paris: It is quite possible no longer to have need of a 'guiding state' like the USSR, but what is not possible is to do away altogether with international examples of revolution to offer to the masses, examples which can inspire and fascinate them. And the example, today, is Vietnam. This only re-confirms that whoever wants to raise the question of the revolution has to come to terms, in some way, with the idea of a revolutionary model. We have had the October Revolution, the Chinese Revolution, the Cuban Revolution and that of the Democratic Republic of Vietnam. Today, for example, it is impossible to talk about socialism without some reference to the issues raised by the Chinese Revolution. A revolution begins with a model, and then it evolves its own strategy. The Chinese Revolution, for example, began with the Russian model – but we have also to see how it found its own original path, and we have to determine the ways in which the thought of Mao differs from that of Lenin.

In this 'red' centre, I become fully aware of the enormous inter-national value of every great revolutionary experience. I hear a *bracciante* chanting '*Ac-ci-rim!*' instead of Ho Chi Minh: in Neapoli-tan dialect, this means, 'Let's kill them'. He makes quite a significant transference: from Ho to the war with America to the Vietnamese who kill marines to the *braccianti* who can put an end to the domination of the bosses by killing them.

Once I have come down from the platform, I go along with the com-rades to the section, which is named after Che. Against an illuminated backdrop is written, in red letters, 'Section of the PCI at Parete: Ernesto Che Guevara'. My curiosity is aroused and hence, even though it is already midnight, I decide to stop in for a visit.

My first observation is a highly personal one, and it concerns the Party: it is completely normal that, in a party like ours, you find a section named after Che. On the other hand, it is also completely nor-mal to find, as I did last night at Acerra, that a picture of Stalin hangs on the wall of the section. This, to me, represents proof of a certain freedom of expression and debate inside the PCI. (At Acerra, which is a big *bracciante* centre, my discussion with the comrades after the speech was once again a totally political one: the role of Stalin; the Twentieth Congress and its inability to spell out the real causes of the distortions in Soviet society; the State, which has swallowed up the CPSU and taken its place; and Khrushchev's peaceful coexistence, as a moment of retreat, or at least stasis, before imperialism.)

The *bracciante* centres of the South seem, at times, to be on a much more advanced level than the urban centres in terms of discussing problems of revolution. In the city, the discussion is always more restrained. It is characterized by numerous silences and reservations, and at times it is as if the working class felt itself disregarded or humiliated.

Of course I can only judge on the basis of the two rural centres I have seen: Parete and Acerra. It is necessary to study the whole issue in much greater depth: the poor peasants of the South are a decisive revolutionary class; we must, however, construct an organic connection between them and the working class – which in the South is limited in size and scattered in a few urban centres. I would divide the Party, or the movement, in Naples into three rough categories (if this is not too arbitrary, when my experience is limited to an electoral campaign): (1) An intelligent and combative working class exists, but it is one which does not exercise as fully as it could its role of leader of the oppressed. It does not enjoy a solid link with the dominant mass of the population, the sub-proletariat and the very poor. The silence of the working class in the face of this situation is a very serious political fact. (2) Concentrations of peasants and day-labourers, where the revolutionary potential is so high that all that is needed is a detonator to touch off the explosion. But this group also lacks a political connection with the vanguard, the workers. (3) The enormous mass of a potentially explosive sub-proletariat, which at times seems to be the dominant force in the Party (some in the Party even see the 'common people' as the motor force of the revolution). But even the most combative elements in the sub-proletariat do not consider the workers as the leading force of the revolution. Some even see the proletariat as lost altogether, and feel that the working class has been integrated by the ruling classes. Some even conclude, in a confused way, that the future of the workers is tied directly to the success of neo-capitalism.

These three elements, in a rough way, comprise the Party and its situation in Naples and her province.

I am now back in the PCI section, 'Che Guevara'. In terms of its social components, Parete makes an interesting case study; it is almost a laboratory microcosm. There are 6,000 inhabitants, of whom 426 are members of the PCI. There are 700 *braccianti*, 500 of whom are members of the *Lega bracciantile*.[2] The Party, as I have already said, gets 46 per cent of the vote. The group that heads the section is under thirty years of age. A communal clerk, Orabona, is the secretary of the section; small and dark with a huge pair of glasses, he leaps around like

2. The PCI-dominated Day-Labourers' League. (Trans.)

a conductor when he speaks – and he speaks very well. The vice-secretary is a *bracciante*, Alberto Bolivo; his nickname is 'Pico della Mirandola', which reflects his exceptional memory. There is a continual exchange of top leaders: this is effected at assemblies of the membership which are held every six months or, at most, every year. As they say around here, no one 'gets encrusted' in his position in this section.

We all sit around the table and start to talk. When I first speak up, I am surrounded by dozens of faces, mostly *braccianti*, and almost every single one of them quite young. I begin to question them, to go through that act of *psycho-political listening* which is always so useful. This is the way things went: I start off by asking, 'Why have you named this section after Che Guevara?' Their response is that it happened 'by popular acclaim: we held an assembly and the proposal was put forward by the Directing Committee; it was immediately passed unanimously.' I then ask, 'But what does Che Guevara represent to you?' One comrade: 'He represents the incentive to struggle; he is a symbol of justice.' Another youth adds, 'He represents the ideal in the struggle against capitalism.' Yet others: 'He is the model of what a communist leader should stand for.' 'He represents selflessness and courage, which moved him to abandon a secure position of leadership in order to throw himself fully into the fight for socialism.'

At this point in the discussion, I interrupt with questions which are purposely provocative and polemical. I ask them if they have considered this fact: 'Don't we have to reflect a little about Che's call for "Victory or Death"? *For victory is always something that belongs to the revolution, while death is what happens to individuals.* And the two things do not always fit together so smoothly, because the death of the individual does not always guarantee the victory of the revolution. If we have to die, we should do so when it is necessary. But simply to die in order to affirm that the victory of the revolution *is possible* is to do nothing more than to deprive the revolution of its leaders.'

I put forward another argument. 'Guerilla warfare cannot replace a popular movement, i.e. the role and the organization of the masses. It can, of course, represent one of the forms that this movement takes. But the Chinese and Vietnamese have shown that guerilla warfare cannot replace the revolutionary organization of the masses.' I then asked the comrades if they felt that the revolution in Latin America could be repeated under the same circumstances as it occurred in

Cuba. I said that I seriously doubted that the Cuban experience could be reproduced both because of the way the Cuban revolution developed and also because of the kind of leadership it enjoyed.

Here are the answers that the *braccianti* gave: 'There is a lot of fatalism in what you say, comrade, a fatalism which sees the failure of Guevara's guerilla strategy in Bolivia as inevitable. In my opinion, however, Guevara carried out his particular form of guerilla warfare only after having first studied Bolivian conditions and after concluding that such an attempt in that place, at that time, could be successful. For this reason we should not speak of any sacrifice on the part of Guevara, because it isn't written anywhere that you have to die if you carry on a guerilla war. Guevara did not go to Bolivia to die; he went there to win.' Another comrade: 'I would raise another question, one concerning revolutionary morality. I think that Guevara wanted to provide an example for Cuba herself. By refusing to take the Ministry of Agriculture, he wanted to offer an incentive, a lesson, to Cuba. He wanted to be completely consistent with the moral position of a revolutionary, even if this consistency meant his death. He was, simply, a communist through and through; and a communist can never, not even for a moment, feel that he has become a bureaucrat. Maybe this is what Guevara feared most: for me, he stands as an example of the communist who struggles against bureaucracy. In terms of his revolutionary spirit, Che is a great example and a tremendous stimulus to action.' Another adds: 'Naming our section after Guevara also represents a polemical retort to Amendola's remarks about "pharmacy strategists". It is an open gesture of disagreement against the paternalism towards the young people shown by our leaders.' Another comrade notes that, 'The guerilla strategy that Guevara proposed is not valid for us, but as a form of struggle in Latin America. But perhaps my ideas on this issue are not really all that clear. For us, choosing Che's name for our section also represents choosing a method for carrying on the political struggle. One comrade, at the time, said, "I don't want to feel that I have wasted all my energies." In the face of a certain apathy on the part of the working class, in the face of some pretty cautious attitudes on our part, in the face of too much silence and the lack of a vigorous workers' response to capitalism, we need more men like Guevara in the Party today.' Another: 'When Guevara was a minister in Cuba, he was only a part of Cuban communism. But now he belongs to all the disinherited people in the world. He is now everyone's example of unselfish, revolutionary passion. In Cuba, he was only a communist; by falling in Bolivia, he comes to represent the proletariat of the whole world and all exploited people.' Yet another: 'I think there is a tremendous difference between what Guevara, as an historical personage, represents, and what our comrade has said about "Victory or Death". I do not think that we can make some kind of new Garibaldi out of Che. It wasn't romanticism that drove him to carry on the fight in Bolivia. He had a strategic plan which he thought would carry him to victory, not to death. Moreover, there are many elements in the struggle against the enemy over there which we simply cannot judge, for we do not have the essential information. Guevara, in other words, did not go to sacrifice himself, he went with the aim of promoting a victorious revolution in Bolivia.' Another comrade adds this: 'In Latin America there are only dictatorships. Something was needed which attacked this state of affairs, for the situation there is even accepted by the Latin-American Communist Parties. It was – and is – necessary to carry politics and ideals to a more mature level. Different political conditions exist all over the world: it is very different here from what it is like in Latin America. But this is just the point: Guevara was searching for a different road to socialism in Latin America, and it is completely untrue that his death should be seen as a defeat of this effort. In fact, Guevara's strategy for Latin America is really the way to victory, not defeat.'

I then interjected a truly malicious political question. The comrades had told me that they had had a great demonstration the night before, where the main speaker was Giorgio Amendola. So I asked the Parete comrades why they gave him such a big and warm reception – for if the Cuban leaders have attacked any Italian Communists lately, it has been Amendola. The answer they gave is very interesting. The secretary, Orabona, put it in these terms: '(1) We gave Amendola a popular reception because, in our opinion, mass enthusiasm gives the best results in terms of organizational ends and goals; (2) Because certain arguments inside the Party never really filter all the way down to the common voter anyhow; (3) and most importantly, the representative of the Party is a representative of all of us, especially in periods of struggle. When in battle, the Party closes ranks against the enemy, and it backs up every leader, even if there may not be much agreement with that leader's policies. In addition, the reception we

gave to Amendola is also an indication of the way our Party acts: this is the best guarantee that there is freedom of expression, and the freedom to disagree, for every militant. By receiving Amendola in this way, we are simply demonstrating what we mean by internal democracy in the Party, and how Amendola himself must respect it.'
Another comrade joins in on the topic of Amendola: 'I understood Amendola to say, in a meeting at Avellino, that two or three Vietnams would not really be helpful; what he thinks we need is a concentration of all efforts in the direction of Vietnam in order to resolve that war positively. I disagree with this opinion, and two or three others who were with me at that party meeting also disagreed. For me, two or three Vietnams is the best possible formula for waking up every citizen in the world to the fact that you can stop capitalism in its tracks. In any event, the big problem in the Party today is that of clarity: from the point of view of the political battle that has to be fought within the PCI, I am more for those who at least have the courage to state where they stand – and Amendola is one of these – than those who throw up a lot of smokescreens, so that you never know where they stand, left or right, and after a while you no longer even know what they mean.'

The discussion continues in this vein of absolute frankness, a frankness which would appal other communist parties. We speak about the idea of a 'single party of all workers' and about the dialogue with left-wing Catholics. The essential question comes up: which way should the Party direct itself? Towards trying to win back the social-democrats or towards winning over the huge left wing of the Catholics (especially large in terms of the votes it draws), which is, after all, comprised mainly of workers and peasants.

The 'Catholic Question' comes up again in terms of current developments. One of the comrades states, 'Comrade, I'd like to make a general criticism of the way our Party is conducting this campaign. We should be attacking the socialists with much more vigour, and this is something we should have done right from the beginning. It is wrong to think that more docility on our part can reconstruct the unity of the workers' movement. This unity will only come about when we communists force the electoral defeat of the other wing of the workers' movement, the socialists. They have to be beaten now, and history has to register their defeat for the future. This is the only "understanding" we should have in our platform, and this is what should guide our future actions. The social-democratization of our country, and the split in working-class unity, are things that the other European countries went through twenty years ago. But these things can be arrested and halted altogether if events are speeded up now, if the workers' and peasants' struggles become more powerful, and if the social-democrats' exercise of bourgeois power is shattered, immediately, under the shock of the masses. Our strategy has been based since the epoch of the Popular Fronts upon an understanding, an agreement with the socialists: they are seen as the fundamental force and ally for us. But is this strategy still valid today?' Reasoning which shows this kind of precision and such an acute class spirit makes it a lot easier to understand the way in which the unity of the workers' movement is not seen as a religious relic to light candles in front of (in the name of the Spirit of the Third International or the Popular Fronts). Instead, unity is seen in terms of being a more advanced and combative moment in the general struggle to liberate the masses from the 'Nessus's Shirt' of social-democratic mirages and illusions.

'But how much longer will we have to clap our hands?' a *bracciante* asks me before leaving. I do not know what he means. It is then explained to me that at the 'Che Guevara' section there are professional 'clappers' – just as, in the South, there are professional mourners for funerals. These clappers' are able to generate loud, sharp applause from hands so calloused that they are as hard as wood. By telling me this, they have let me in on a little internal secret, an organizational measure which helps generate waves of enthusiasm similar to the one that swept over me like an intoxicant when I arrived here. Opponents retreat in fear before that noise, and our own forces advance as if they were covered by supporting artillery. But how much longer will we have to continue clapping our hands? How much longer will we have to attack an enemy who, after each electoral campaign – in spite of all the sacrifices made and abilities employed – still stands before us as the strongest force in the country? It obviously has nothing to do with the dedication of our comrades, which is absolute. This is the question that lurks behind the Italian road to socialism, the path chosen for the Italian revolution.

Maria Antonietta

Dear Louis,   *Naples, 15 May 1968*

Sometimes I feel like all fifty of Danäe's daughters: the more water
they poured into the barrel, the less remained. You wrote that I
should go to the factories and use factory cells as a base for organizing
small-scale meetings between myself and workers. But there is a small
problem involved here: for years now, there have not been any Communist cells or organizations at all in the factories; the result is that
the entire workers' struggle, and all of the issues revolving around the
workers' conditions, have been delegated to the *unions*, which in turn
are often disparaged by the workers on account of their 'softness'.[1]
The relationship between the Party and the working class has been
eroded over time, and the number of workers who join the PCI has
steadily declined. The Neapolitan Federation, which has 34,560 members, has lost 5,600 members in the past two years. The social composition of the membership shows that, over time, the proportion of
workers has declined, there are very few peasants, there is an extremely
marked decline in the number of women who are members, and there
has been no notable entry of youth into the Party. Membership turnover is very high. Each year a large number of members enters, only
to leave the following year. A new influx of Communists occurs each
year; the recruits mix among us and then leave after twelve months.[2]
The CGIL, which had 65,000 members here in 1963, today only has
55,000. Even more distressing in an already bleak picture is the fact
that the largest drop in CGIL membership has come in the industrial
sector.

   With this general loss of workers from class organizations, most
notable in the unions but equally serious in the Party, we are not stingy
with slogans like 'more power in the factories'; nor do we shy away
from declaring the factory to be the main focal point of the clash for

   1. Official PCI statistics show that, from a peak of 11,500 workplace cells in
1954, the number had declined to 3,236 by 1968. While all organizational and
membership figures show a drop in that period, factory cells, by far, represent the
area of party organization which shows the most severe decline. (Trans.)
   2. This high turnover rate is noticeable throughout the entire Mezzogiorno.
Whereas roughly 5.5 per cent of the membership of the PCI in the North and
Centre consists of new recruits each year, the figure is close to 14 per cent for the
South. Since the *absolute* number of members has declined or, at best, remained
static over time, it is clear that this phenomenon has a disruptive impact on local
party organizations. (Trans.)

'real democracy', the place where we can wrench 'conquests' from the ruling class which will undermine their power position and bloc of forces. But all of these slogans – which we call *intermediate objectives* – seem to me to correspond to little that is real in what we do, in the Party, and in the unions. The workers, in fact, are highly critical of the PCI, and the absence of an organized presence in the factories – an undeniable fact – is quite often seen as evidence of a *retreat* in the face of the class enemy. We are faced with a serious political gap: How do we define the relationship which should exist between the working class and its political organization, between the workers' movement and its political leadership, between, in short, Party and social praxis?

The problem of the Party in the factories cannot be resolved with technical measures, work plans, dislocations of personnel from the apparatus, and things of that nature – because the gap grows out of a *political* problem: how to formulate, promote, and maintain, in the plants, a permanent mobilization against the system? How to organize, in the factories, *real* forms of power? As a result of this problem, the Party is unequipped at all levels of the factory to direct the struggle and to create the movement from the base. Our only presence is as one wing of the unions. But, as Gramsci noted long ago, we need to build from the base, creating a link between rank-and-file action and the hegemony of the Party, between the political experience of the masses and the synthesis of the political party.

So I can only speak with the workers by standing outside their plants at 6.30 a.m., catching them before they enter. Since the PCI is so weak inside the factories, no comrade has the authority to have you admitted at lunchtime. And you can completely forget about asking the unionists from the CGIL to try to get you inside: they don't even want to hear about this, and they tell you that that kind of activity is 'politics', and the union can have nothing to do with politics.

Speaking with the workers, I realized that their entire link with the Party is restricted to occasional visits to the sections, for sections are the only centre of organized political life we possess, as a party. For years, we have not had any 'street cells', even though this is a problem much less serious than our lack of factory cells. I do not know if things are any different in the North. The young workers say that even when they do go to the sections, there is nothing for them to do. They say that 'the old men play cards or endlessly discuss the same old issues and disputes'. Their conclusion is: '*If there's no politics in the sections, what is the point of going there?* No one studies, no one discusses politics, *there aren't even any books to read.* Now that the campaign is going on, it is a different story, because the electoral struggle fills the sections up, people go to listen to speeches, you can even learn some interesting things in some speeches, and then of course there is the fact that you have a concrete objective to work towards, the election itself.' One of them tells me how, before the election, he used to go to the PSIUP meeting-place in his town, the reason being that that was the only place where one found a group of young people 'talking about what is going on in the world'. They even had books and magazines there.

So, as I said, the only way to meet workers is to wait for them as they enter or leave the factories. But even this is extremely difficult, especially if you want to talk with women. They are usually in an even greater rush than the men, and, if the Manifattura Tabacchi is any example, they take advantage of their few free minutes before work to buy fruit and vegetables from the stall in front of the factory gates. The women workers of the Manifattura are almost all middle-aged – between thirty and fifty. According to the statistics, there have been no redundancies in this group: the working women in this age group numbered 64,600 in 1959, and they were 64,527 in 1967. This means that the most substantial chunk of the female proletariat in Naples is in fact middle-aged, while the others are very young and, indeed, often under-age. Those who are fired in droves are the women aged from fourteen to thirty, preferably when they marry or become pregnant. By the time they are thirty, the bosses reckon that resignation takes the place of combativity and the female workers become inoffensive in terms of both political and trade-union militancy.

The women arrive in the factory aboard dusty, dirty old buses which come from as far away as the provinces of Benevento or Salerno. This means that they are on the bus for as much as four hours a day. When they get off the bus, they buy fruit and vegetables to take home with them – home being fifty or a hundred kilometres away. They often refuse our leaflets, saying, 'We don't have the time to read anything.' As I listen to them speak among themselves, I realize that their lives are made up of dreams, of *escapist fantasies*, via a myriad illusions and most concretely via the lottery. A number of women are thronging around one who has just won 25,000 lire (with the combination 6-51-47), and the excitement and envy is incredible. A street mandolin-player strikes up with 'O sole mio' and I give him some coins. Apparently it is more than he expected, for he swells with pride and starts telling me how he is a real gentleman, don't I think it shows in his face, and why don't I come to meet him at Torre Annunziata, where the whole town knows him because he plays in the procession of the patron saint. The man with the fruit cart is furious with me all this time, because I have drawn the women's attention away from his business in that half-hour 'market'. Finally, to shut him up, after the women have gone I buy three kilos of fruit from him – and I have no idea at all what to do with it. He says to me, confidentially, 'But why do you always come here to make propaganda? What we need are facts. We need the revolution. . . .'

Every once in a while I manage to enter a worker's house, I succeed in striking up a friendship with one of the working-class comrades, who speak with more political clarity, like the one who said to me, 'Look, socialism is life's only goal.' He invited me to dinner – it was a feast day at his house. I thought he had a wife and children, but when I arrive I realize that he is a bachelor who lives with his mother, father and two married sisters. The whole family communicates across a terrace which serves as a hallway for the three rooms and kitchen, all of which open on to it. No doubt in anxiety over the visit of the Lady Communist, the mother of this working-class comrade has installed a gigantic table in her bedroom: she seats me and the comrade at either end of the table, like the lords of a manor. The mother and sisters then serve up an eight-course meal, consisting of a sea-food antipasto, macaroni, stewed meat, roast meat, fried fish, dessert, wine and fruit. Arturo I. speaks all the while of the Party and his bitter feelings about its absence from the factories and, hence, its lack of direct contact with the proletariat. What especially disturbs him is that this is all going on while a new situation is developing in society and the level of political consciousness is growing everywhere. At the same time, he sees the '*reformism* of the unions and the social conformism of the Party' as being in increasing contradiction with reality. In his opinion, youth, the workers and the people will vote *en masse* for the P C I, but they are not signing a blank cheque, they are voting *for a change*. In the unorganized youth movement, among secondary-school and university students and young workers, Longo's meeting with a number of spokesmen for the student movement has turned the whole situation around. Within the span of one month, the slogan for the elections that predominates among the young has changed from *scheda bianca* (blank ballot) to *scheda rossa* (vote red).

The Communist Youth have become 'inspired', and their unexpected wave of enthusiasm is helping carry along the electoral campaign. Day and night, in front of schools and factories, they are there. They arrive in the most far-flung areas, armed only with megaphones, calling on everyone to unite in the great electoral contest, which they see as a chance to challenge the entire system. Arturo asserts that 'The fathers, grandfathers and uncles have, for one reason or another, always ended up giving a qualified "yes" to the idea of structural reforms as representing socialism. What has changed is this: the young people respond with an emphatic "no". They have learned to say no.' Arturo has had a complex life, and is in many ways unlike the others. He came to communism for idealistic reasons, stemming from a total view of life. He became a manual worker after working as a *magliaro*[3] – a *mass* profession in the sub-proletariat. In fact, his father is still a *magliaro*. Arturo says, 'I already had some communist ideas and sentiments. But after having sold some rags to a poor peasant woman, saying they were pure wool – and seeing her lift her mattress to take out her last 2,000 lire – I underwent a crisis of conscience. I couldn't continue in this fashion. I wanted to become a worker so that I could become a communist, as I like to say, who lives out his principles in the way he conducts his life. I am not yet married because there is no one in town who will consent to a civil ceremony. She might be the most beautiful woman in the world, but I always say: a civil ceremony or no ceremony at all. She cries, and the whole thing ends there. . . .'

All around us, in the industry of the large nuptial chamber of the father and mother, there are piles of rolled rugs and boxes of sets of knives, forks and spoons. I tell about the time I was hoaxed, when I bought what I thought was a silver service from a young man who claimed to have been abandoned by his fiancée. It turned out to be made of tin. Arturo looks at me, almost in agony, as if to say, 'You managed to fall for a grade-A hoax, the one reserved for real idiots.' Now the father himself arrives; he is an old man who looks like Picasso, and he speaks to me with great style and smoothness, like a person accustomed to the most complex human relationships imagin-

3. See note on p. 42.

able. When he speaks, it is always 'Paris, France', 'London, England', 'Geneva, Switzerland'. These *magliari* have their general head-quarters in London, Paris, Berlin and Bonn, just like NATO. Arturo's father goes all over Lazio and Campania selling fake carpets: they are called 'Persian', but they are actually made in a town near Reggio Emilia. He also peddles 'silver' which is really made of tin. In his youth, he travelled in Venezuela, France, Belgium and North America. He speaks two or three dialects, and, in his youth, he spoke foreign languages. Sitting there among the heaps of rugs and silverware, he tells of a number of great adventures he has had. Now he only travels with others, for he has grown old. It is a long time since he ate oysters at Pigalle.

These *magliari* have meeting places in the large cities of the North, called *posteggi*. Let's say that one of them arrives in Milan. He will go to this *posteggio* and change his clothes: sometimes they dress up as truck drivers, at other times as clerks from a famous textile firm. Hearing all this, I tell myself that these people need as great mental resources as a nuclear physicist. And it is all done just to scrape together an income; to bring back here, to the rooms that open on to the terrace, enough for the family to live on.

Arturo looks on with shame and embarrassment. This *magliaro*-father of his obviously upsets him very much, for it is written all over his face. He keeps his head down and refuses to take part in the discussion. He acts as if the two of us were being in some way contaminated by certain stories, or challenged in our 'pure' choice of a communist life.

I see before me the relationship of the proletariat to the lumpen-proletariat shifted from the societal level to the inside of a single house, a single family. In a way, the common distrust that characterizes the relationship is much more disturbing to witness on this level. For, even though relationships are obviously more complex, with family ties, habit, affection and desperation all mixed together, the fundamental hostility between worker and lumpenproletarian remains, even though the two may also happen to be father and son. I try to question Arturo about the alliance between proletariat and sub-proletariat in Naples, for example, given that it represents such an essential political problem in the struggle for socialism here. But Arturo I. looks at me from very far away, as if I were ingenuous, a romantic, *one who does not know*. And he is quiet, completely enclosed in silence.

The father goes on with his stories, and he tells how a *magliaro* 'speaks' various languages, knowing a few words but faking the rest of it. He also describes how Neapolitan carpet vendors quite frequently disguise themselves as Arabs in Rome and no one ever seems to be aware of this camouflage. I am utterly fascinated by all these stories. But the comrade at the other end of the table does not share my enthusiasm, and he is very relieved when his father finally leaves, permitting us to resume our purely political discussion.

In Arturo's opinion, the Party should promote and encourage struggles both inside and outside the factories, without continually raising the question of demarcating the respective spheres of competence (autonomy) of party and union. In his opinion, 'political strikes should be considered one of the Party's legitimate prospects'. The unions and the Party should not represent two parallel lines, destined never to meet. Furthermore, in reality, action in the factories follows the sole existing line, and that is the line of the unions. This results in an inability to go beyond the day-to-day claims of the workers' wage struggle, under the stimulus of the Party inside the factories, on the level both of political formation and of the industrial struggle itself. To Arturo, the unions are infected with reformism: he recalls how the CGIL just recently approved the Government's truly pitiful pension proposal, with the result that millions of pensioners and workers took to the streets and went on strike, with the ultimate effect of forcing the union to backtrack.

Arturo does not know what 'intermediate objectives' is supposed to mean, and he asks me what they are, given that we are always talking about them in our speeches and in the Party press. And when I explain that the expression should mean precisely what he has in mind about workers' power in the factories, workers' assemblies and even the role of the Party in the workplace, he is greatly relieved. We part, finally, as dear friends, and I make the rounds of the flat's four rooms to say goodbye to Arturo's family. They all come out on to the terrace, very politely, and they all, babies included, wave goodbye to me for a long time as I leave.

Recommendations, Affiliation and Paternalism

I found an interesting study by Gustavo Jacono, who has the chair of psychology at the University of Naples, on what he calls the *affiliative orientation* of southern workers. The study offers a good perspective from which one can understand a whole variety of phenomena which characterize the relationship of the southern worker to his society – phenomena I have already described in other letters on the workers. According to Jacono's hypothesis, *work* is a cause of severe frustration, since the human problems so notable in southern factories are typical of an affiliative orientation (i.e. towards other people, rather than towards the job). Hence, among other phenomena, we witness a strong *lack of faith in one's own merits and abilities in terms of being qualified for the job,* which contributes to the whole vicious cycle of seeing *recommendations* as necessary for everything. Naturally, once the cycle is established, one is put into dependent relationships, which only further reinforces *paternalistic* forms of interaction. *Recommendations and paternalistic relations* – I have applied this scholar's psychological findings on another level – are two elements which, as we have seen, characterize associative and often even political relationships in the South. The same is true for *affiliation,* or *belonging* to the group or following of a powerful person.

A question you frequently hear in Naples is: To whom do you belong? when someone wants to know how high up on the social ladder your *affiliation* is located. (A not inconsiderable risk in this general environment is that the Party itself, at certain times, can appear as a gigantic affiliative mechanism, and that *recommendations* and the consequent *paternalism* can play a negative role in the organization.)

The southern worker, to return to Jacono's study, is found to have a *very high degree of adaptability to the most varied jobs and tasks.* This makes it highly likely that the widespread affiliative orientation (towards other people and structures) found on the job, in addition to the *recommendation,* can be interpreted as general attitudes towards authority inculcated by a southern child's mother and by the society in which he lives. On the other hand, without some kind of well-defined orientation to tasks and efficiency, it is extremely difficult to accept the discipline and tolerate the frustrations in human relations which are so typical of these manipulative activities. Jacono says that the efficiency motivation of a firm's *management* is lower than that of the average worker. A general examination of affiliation motivation might lead to this finding: that the firm would tend to promote those who are primarily concerned with being accepted and who know how to get on the good side of the top level of management; in any event, the primary orientation would clearly be towards *affiliation* rather than *efficiency*. Training programmes for *both* workers and management, in Jacono's opinion, should not have the development of ability and knowledge as their primary aims, *for the southerner generally acquires these skills quite rapidly*. Rather, training should focus on the assimilation of attitudes, motivation and a more appropriate general orientation toward the work situation. He goes on to say:

> *There is a recurrence, in the affiliative orientation, of a subjective configuration of needs, motives and mechanisms quite similar to what Freud describes as typifying orally fixated subjects (the need for dependence, nutrition and support; the presence of ego-defence mechanisms . . .). The general influence of the environment on the determination of this syndrome is better understood and examined in the light of Erikson's work, i.e. by a study of the institutions, educational methods, idealized norms, and sanctions and incentives present in southern culture which relate to the formation of the individual. Further light could be shed on this issue if an extensive study were made of the most culturally favoured solutions which come into play during the 'crises' of childhood and adolescent development.*

(Proceedings of the Fourteenth Congress of Italian Psychologists: Naples, October 1962.)

For anyone who is conscious of the place that Freud, after Marx, deserves as a fountainhead of the *new science*, these are working hypotheses which should not be cast aside lightly in any serious analysis of southern Italian society.

Maria Antonietta

Dear Louis, *Naples, 15 May 1968*

I return to Naples, to Piazza Municipio, which is the Plaza de Toros for the *corrida* of Neapolitan poverty. There is a show here every day and, though the actors change, capitalism's scenario in Naples is always of an unequalled violence. Today there is a group of unemployed workers, originally from the shipyards. Some months they work, others they don't, depending on the jobs the city finds for them:

one time some street repairs, another repairing broken pipes, etc. 'Can't you do anything for us?' mumbles an enormous man with a metal 'button' in his throat, out of which, from some profound depths, whistle words and breath together. He is old and fat, with a misshapen face which seems to be decomposing. How can he possibly work? But 'work' is an imprecise notion that a Neapolitan spends his entire life chasing, attempting to grasp, to define. This man praises some pro-Chinese groups who came along and bought the job-seekers coffee when they were camped out for the night. How about us?

Suddenly one of the workers bursts away from the rest of the group like an arrow, and hurls himself head-first on to the paved street, directly in the path of oncoming traffic. The cars brake hard and long to avoid him; he lies unconscious in the middle of the street and, for all I can tell, he is bleeding as well. In order to launch himself out there the way he did, he used a great big black umbrella as a vaulting-pole, and it now lies some distance from him, broken in two. I look at the mutilated umbrella, doubled over on itself like a collapsed marionette; then I look at the man, lying stiffly, his arms straight out, his whole body wracked by extended spasms. 'He is having an attack,' the others say. I think to myself that this is probably his 'happening' to dramatize his search for work. The 'happenings' of the Naples unemployed are tremendously varied and fantastic, but the authorities take a pretty dim view of it all. I know a man, Antonio R., who dived under the car of the president of the Communal Council with three babies in his arms. He of course was arrested immediately. I met Michele B., also unemployed; as a sign of desperate protest, he covered himself with petrol in front of the Council, which was holding a meeting in the medieval salon of the Maschio Angioino. He was going to demand work, in the most unequivocal terms possible. But, even though he set fire to himself, he remains unemployed, and all he has to show for his troubles are the scars from his third-degree burns.

I leave the unemployed in the street and, with my little delegation of comrades, I enter the building of the city government to try to find work for them. I go to the deputy-mayor, the same little Socialist, Porzio, of whom I have spoken before, who always receives me immediately – full of apprehension, protected by his massive walnut desk.

On the wall of the office, for the first time, I see a large painting: Gioacchino Toma's 'The Holy Inquisition'. I am struck dumb. The painting reproduces the exact scene I have just seen down the street:

an emaciated man is stretched rigidly on the ground; he lies below the Tribunal of high priests who, fat, lean, red, black, are discussing whether the repenter should live or die. They look at him, point at him, and interpret the Truth from huge copies of the Gospel. 'It's exactly like that man in the street', I say to Porzio. A communal councillor from our delegation turns to the deputy-mayor and says, 'Look how upset M.A. is.' My emotion has now obviously become some sort of test of the seriousness of the situation. Porzio peers at me with his tiny eyes and clearly is thinking. 'Can she be serious?' But then, even if I am serious, what can someone like me know of Naples, for after all I am a foreigner, come all the way from Paris. . . .

I think that all these people are cynics who no longer believe in anything, who are used to everything, so what difference does it make to them if some man should pass out on their doorstep? Now a big discussion starts up over what can be done for the unemployed. After an exhausting display of shilly-shallying, the deputy-mayor agrees to a subsidy. Not work, for God's sake! And even for this little bit of charity there will have to be a discussion in the Communal Council, the prefect's approval, and a whole bureaucratic machine will have to be put into motion before ten or fifteen thousand lire can be given to the man who has passed out, or the man with the button in his throat, or the human torch.

I go on from the deputy-mayor's main-floor reception room all the way up to the sixth floor of the Town Hall, for a new problem has developed. A 'parents' agitation committee' has come to protest about the Minucci Intermediate School: there are only three large halls to hold a total of six hundred students. In the suffocatingly hot and humid office of the socialist Assessor of Public Instruction, there is a tightly-packed crowd; everyone is on his feet with the exception of the assessor, who, visibly nervous, is seated at his desk. In order to win the dispute over the school with the socialist assessor, the agitation committee has hired a lawyer for the occasion. Perhaps they think that having a lawyer is better than having a union. They have brought this lawyer along (he, by the way, is also seated) out of the touching belief that such a person will know how to find the 'right arguments' to increase the number of halls, to clean up the schools and to provide a regular education for their children.

'The children,' begins the lawyer – who speaks for all of them – 'have to stand one hour and sit one hour in rotation because there are so few desks; this goes on all day long, even though there are three separate sessions.'

The assessor is silent.

'The three halls that the school has been loaned in Via Cavallino are all situated below street level. The walls are green from underground mould and fungus. . . .'

The assessor is silent, and looks attentively at his fingernails.

'The students find rats in their desks. . . .'

'And what do you expect me to do about rats?' the assessor finally explodes; 'They are dying because we put down poison; the Commune has undertaken this expense. Do you mean to say that this is not a good thing?'

'Headmistress Lumumba not only will not listen to the parents' complaints, she will not even receive them in the office. . . .'

Here an exasperated parent chimes in: 'Headmistress Lumumba is protected by the DC, that is why she does anything she pleases.' To see the headmistress, favourite of the Neapolitan Christian democrats, carry around a great name like Lumumba makes me laugh a little to myself.

I turn to the lawyer. 'Perhaps I can do something? I am from the Communist Federation.'

Now that my credentials have been presented, the lawyer says in front of everyone, *'We don't want any politics coming into this,* this is no place for the parties. . . .'

I think he is afraid that someone is trying to undercut him and take the bread out of his mouth, so to speak. At first the families nod in agreement with the barrister, but then some mothers and fathers accompany me outside the assessor's office and tell me about the incredible iniquities that the children in intermediate schools have to undergo in a class society.[1]

Teresa Rizzo, mother of six children, with one baby in her arms and the others hanging on to her skirt, is again blocking traffic in front of the Town Hall. On her own, she made a placard saying 'I Want a House!', which she is holding up. She comes from Piscinola, and since her house has been declared dangerous, the proprietor wants to evict

---

1. The demonstrations of the Naples intermediate students in December 1968 were among the most massive in all of Italy. For example, in the sit-in in Piazza Mancini, there were numerous clashes with the police, leaving about a hundred people wounded or arrested.

her. She is desperate because she has systematically been excluded from any assignment to the new popular housing projects. She has already, on one occasion, tried to commit suicide in front of everyone. The police arrive, and take her away.

As I write, I have opened, at random, Goethe's *Voyage in Italy*, and this is what I find written on Naples: 'I understood perfectly how someone could go out of his mind over Naples, and I remembered with great emotion how deeply my father had been moved by the same things I was now seeing for the first time. It is said that once a person has seen a ghost, he can never again regain serenity. In my father's case, it might rather be said that he was never again capable of being completely unhappy, because he was always able to remember Naples. I look, quietly, as is my habit, limiting myself only to opening my eyes very wide when the beauty I witness goes beyond the bounds of anything I could have imagined.'

I, too, can only open my eyes wide, because that is all that I have time for as I run the race of this electoral campaign. And the race is just about over: the final demonstration will be in Piazza Plebiscito. As long as he was alive, i.e. up to and including the general elections of 1963, Togliatti used to give the concluding speech of the campaign here in Naples. And he used to give the speech here in the vast semi-elliptical harmony of Piazza Plebiscito, in front of the former Bourbon Palace, whose massive façades contain the statues of the most powerful rulers to dominate Naples over the centuries: Roger the Norman, Charles I of Anjou, Alfonso I of Aragon, Charles V, Charles III (of the Bourbons), Gioacchino Murat, and, finally, Victor Emmanuel II. From the Norman monarchy to the birth of the Kingdom of Italy, the history of Naples is as rationally represented here as is the French experience represented in the Place de la Concorde, with its ring of powerful women seated all around it to guard the history of France.

Can you imagine a speech in the Place de la Concorde, with a red platform ten metres high, complete with a red curtained backdrop, and the square absolutely jammed with people? That is the way you have to imagine this speech at Naples, and the success of the undertaking was a sort of 'sign' as to how the whole election had gone. Togliatti himself did not shy, in his own way, from seeing certain 'signs' which boded ill for the Party at one of these great gatherings. It occurred in 1952, when we suffered a big defeat in the local elections: not only did Togliatti have the misfortune to be brought to the piazza quite late, as people had already begun to leave, but the platform was so sloppily put together that it was in a state of collapse. Togliatti took up his pen with carefully reasoned fury and wrote what follows in *Rinascita*: 'Let's imagine a large city, with a population which is a little suspicious and even believes, let us say, in the evil eye. If you hold a speech there and the stage collapses, do you think you will lose votes? Yes, you probably will. At the very least, you give your opponent the opportunity to say that if you are incapable of building a platform for a speech in a main piazza, where one of your most noted figures is to speak; if you bring this speaker to the square an hour and a half late, with part of the audience gone and the rest ready to leave, then it is obvious that (whatever the real causes) you are going to pay for your errors when the votes are added up.' (I leave to your imagination the consternation that this note – signed 'P.T.' – must have caused to the secretary of the Naples Federation, who in fact was fated to lose his position not too long afterwards.)

Now, in 1968, the Federation is divided into two distinct camps over the issue of the speech in Piazza Plebiscito. There are those who want to hold the speech anyway: since Togliatti died in 1964, we obviously cannot hold it with him, but we can provide speakers from our own list. Then there are those who say that without Togliatti it is impossible to schedule such a speech in Piazza Plebiscito. I am all for going ahead with it. But those who oppose the gathering are considerable in number. Finally, our *capolista* himself, after a series of stormy telephone calls, personally assumes responsibility for the success of the speech. As the decision is made, news of the strategy which will be followed begins to slip out through half-closed doors: finally, all three of the top *capolista* are set as the featured orators. But there are a lot of long faces around the Federation in spite of this, and the blackest predictions are heard. Perhaps – and the fact that I am a 'foreigner' means that I must consider things that are outside my realm of understanding – part of this negative evaluation derives not so much from a political analysis of the situation but, unconsciously, from a fear that the famous 'evil eye' might be cast on future electoral returns if things do not go well, as Togliatti pointed out himself. Even Croce was convinced of the existence of the *jella*; as he said in a quip which is famous even among us Communists: 'I don't believe in it, but it is true.' And Dumas had the following to say about the two-pronged power that reigns over Naples' destiny: 'Her enemy is the Evil Eye, and her protector is San Gennaro. . . . If San Gennaro had not been in Heaven for a long, long time, the Evil Eye, long ago, would have annihilated Naples; if the Evil Eye had not been on earth for a long, long time, San Gennaro would, long ago, have made Naples the Queen of Earth.' He adds that, 'the Evil Eye is an incurable illness'.

I, personally, have thrown myself into the preparations for the gathering in Piazza Plebiscito. Every evening, for a number of days now, I have ended my talks with an invitation to the crowds to come, dressed for a holiday, women and children included, to put fear into our enemies' hearts and show the Party's strength by filling that piazza to overflowing. I feel that mass organization ought to be the most effective tactic, even against the evil eye.

Maria Antonietta

Dear Louis,   *Naples, 16 May, midnight*

The gathering at Piazza Plebiscito was a success, a great triumph, in fact. From early morning, the women prepared their evening meals so they would be free to come to Naples in the evening. The oldest among them put on red blouses. The mothers put red carnations in their little girls' hair. It was raining like mad at first (evil eye?), but then the rain stopped and everything was calm and serene. I arranged for a chartered bus for the women of the area around the Cantieri Metallurgici of Castellammare, after having held a small meeting there. I was only sorry that Geppina, a formidable organizer in her own right, was unable to come: she said that tomorrow is the feast day of San Pasquale, her husband's patron saint, and she even went so far as to ask me for the flowers from my speech so she could give them to her husband. But my spirits rose when the crowd began to arrive and fill up the piazza – not, perhaps, as they had done for Togliatti, but certainly for, from what I can judge, a big and successful demonstration. By the time night fell, the crowd was sizeable. One comrade rigged himself up in what I thought was a marvellous invention: with bulbs, battery and switch, he had a luminous hammer and sickle on his chest, which he alternately flashed on and off. In the blackness of the crowd and the piazza, we on the stage were dazzled by this unambiguous beacon, which seemed to light the way for us.

Up on the enormous stage, everyone sits around in little groups and talks, exactly as if they were in a café, and I realize that this habit of not listening to the speakers is a habit which carries over even when the most important people happen to be at the microphone. When the speech was over, I was invited to dinner at the home of the number one *capolista*, who was extremely courteous to me, almost appeasing in his behaviour. I note this fact because in Rome, right at the beginning, he almost attacked me with these words, 'Look, you, don't go to Naples and behave like an *ingénue*, like a big enthusiast, or expect any kind of welcoming committees. . . . I don't even know if the Federal Committee will accept you on the list.' But when the Committee, as I have written earlier, did accept me, he never brought the topic up again, though he did act as if he were very angry with someone else – as if someone had played a nasty trick on him. Indeed, I know with absolute certainty that our *capolista* – who is the most important political figure, irrespective of party, in all Naples – was far from over-joyed when the Committee chose me as a candidate. But in Naples, everyone is convinced that I am here by dint of his *direct personal intervention* and that my candidacy is the result of a secret agreement between the two of us. Hence I am always in Procrustes' bed, with my own human qualities irrelevant to everyone. Some try to stretch me out, others to shorten me, according to their own political position. A real mess.

Maria Antonietta

Dear Louis,   *Naples, 17 May 1968, morning*

The first *Red Train* went through Naples Central Station at 6.00 this morning. A *Red Train*, in our terminology, is a train full of emigrants who have returned to vote. I got up early this morning to see the first one come in, and sure enough, there it was, practically covered with red banners and flags, with hammers and sickles on most of the windows, along with 'Vote PCI', and the emigrant workers leaning out of the windows giving the clenched-fist salute. It is like seeing a revolutionary train, full of soldiers who have deserted at the front and who now have come home to take part in a popular revolt. I have been speaking of the emigrants during the entire electoral campaign. I have seen them in the north of France and also in Belgium: they live like animals and always remain foreigners. I told about how they do without a beer or a glass of wine so they can put the money aside, either to send home or else to pay their fare home; about how they come up out of the mines, as at Barbis, where 2,000 emerge with their faces so blackened by coal that you cannot tell Moroccans, Algerians, Tunisians and Italians apart.

But the Italians, I don't know how, were able to recognise me as *one of them* and all gathered around to chat: How are things going in the Party? And *l'Unità*? What is happening in Italy? Then they took me to visit their huts, which rattle to their foundations with every blast of the frigid north wind. They are like a colonial army at the service of European capitalism, mercenary troops who are used for the most menial jobs, taking the posts that the more advanced part of the European proletariat refuses to have anything to do with. And they find all the racism and chauvinism of the 'superior peoples' arrayed against them.

In Paris, the abusive term used for an Italian is *rital* or *macaroni*. In Switzerland they are called 'Italian pigs'. In Belgium, Italians comprise a much more compact colony – entire towns are Italian – and they have their own 'circles' where they can drink, play billiards and take their families on holidays. Those who have the most to do with the Belgians – especially in the Flemish areas – are the youths who 'go to bed with Belgian women'. This is no great joy to them, for the women are usually elderly widows or lonely old spinsters. But, in exchange, the immigrant receives a little bit of feminine attention, he gets to eat a well-cooked meal, and so on. The West Germans have real forms of xenophobia towards all these 'foreign populations', and so it happens that in places like Düsseldorf the shopkeepers will write contemptuously outside their cafés, 'No dogs or Italians allowed in this establishment'. The Italians who live abroad live as if in the trenches, waiting for the war to end. They are brave people, and they have no fear of the foreign bosses.

In Cité Montigny en Ostrevent, near Douai, I met Pierino, who comes from Guspini in Sardinia. The secretary of the PCF cell called him 'an almost perfect communist'. This was on the eve of the 1967 elections in March of that year, and the Italian immigrants, all or most of them communists, were organizing the electoral propaganda for the PCF, raising money for them and calling themselves together to do whatever was possible. But they had to be extremely careful, for in France a foreigner cannot even hold a position in the union or be on a factory shop committee. 'All it takes is one incident, one word, and they throw you out,' I was told. I remember one Sicilian who was telling the French comrades – he was still somewhere back around 1947 – about Italy, and it sounded as if he were talking about a revolutionary country. 'It's nothing here compared to Valguarnera, where we occupied the land and attacked the carabinieri with hoes. . . . If they didn't give the vote to women, Italy would be socialist. Here, everyone is against de Gaulle, but then they go and vote and put him back in office.' The Italians were going back over old events for the French, taking advantage of the electoral campaign to spur on a proletarian spirit against de Gaulle. Because of this, they were also exaggerating their own successes in Italy, telling about things more in terms of how they would like them to be, rather than how they are in reality.

Where is the Dante who will describe the inferno of emigration? Whenever I raise this question in a speech, I always sense a very strong emotional reaction in the crowd. During my five years in France I too, at times, felt like an 'émigrée'. And once a comrade who was speaking at the same meeting as I was, at Secondigliano, turned to me and said, 'Come on: you aren't really serious are you, when you speak of the emigrants in such sad tones?'

But I really am. This is a topic that really gets to me, and Nobécourt from *Le Monde* once said to me, after a speech, 'Don't you think you are a little chauvinistic, the way you talk about Italian emigrants?' But my emotional reaction is, on the contrary, the result of rational, class feelings. Italian capitalism has assigned to the South the role of a labour pool for the factories of the North, and especially for the factories of Western Europe. For an essential feature of its industrial development is that labour costs are extremely low. In the last five years alone, according to official statistics, 1,410,777 emigrants have abandoned the Mezzogiorno; to them should be added another two million who left earlier. The fields have been abandoned, and entire towns have no more young people at all; it is known, for example, that in Calabria three families in four no longer have any members younger than fifty years of age. The women, 'promoted' to the status of heads of their families, are in fact if not technically widows, with their husbands two thousand kilometres away. In Cosenza, 46 per cent of family heads are women, with the result that women are also the leaders in political and union battles, against the bureaucratic structures of the state and against the bosses.

Whole populations are by now entirely dependent on the resources of emigrants: one-quarter of the income of Calabria and Basilicata is furnished by money sent home by emigrants. Just recently, the semi-official agency *Italia* announced that the clandestine export of private capital abroad in 1967 was 795.7 million dollars, which is 273 million dollars (or 42 per cent) more than the year before. In the same year, 1967, workers who had emigrated sent four billion dollars back into Italy – a figure equal to the total reserves of the Bank of Italy. The 'stability' of the lira in Europe is in part based, therefore, on the compulsory emigration of millions of Italian workers and on the money they send back to their native land. The positive balance of payments and hence the 'Italian Miracle' can also be seen, therefore, to rest on pretty precarious foundations, which appear so robust only when one chooses not to look too carefully.

Italian capitalism is ragged, tattered and ferocious. Making the South into a well from which manpower can be drawn at will, capitalism has devoted the absolute minimum of resources for structural renewal there, for schools, hospitals or the provision of water. In this way capitalism gains doubly: it profits from the money which enters Italy via the emigrants, and it is able to restrict public expenditure and public services since the population of the South is destined to be expelled in any event. This is a supplementary form of exploitation which should be added to the usual analysis of capitalism's more organic forms of exploitation: it is a supplementary 'plan' for the exploitation of the South which helps shore up the entire mechanism on which the power of capital is based and by which it rules.

Take one of the things which is most humble and indispensable: water. According to the official statistics provided by the Regulatory Plan for the Provision of Water, more than a third of the South's inhabitants do not have sufficient water. The way you get water is by having demonstrations or disruptions. Then the tankers will arrive by order of the Government. At Cappella Nuova, a *bracciante* village which lies just behind Torre del Greco, a water tanker arrives once a month. And even this kind of thing only happens, more often than not, when the Communist city councillors nearly come to blows in the council, or else it happens when the city is being run by prefectural commission.[1] Only when forced into a corner does Italian capitalism send its mobile water tankers. Then one is able to drink for fifteen days, no more. It is as if water were some sort of intoxicating beverage which the Government withheld from the people for their own good! (And it is said that at Torre there are sixty billion lire in liquid assets in the banks; remember too that this city, after Turin, has the highest proportion of cars to citizens in all of Italy.) Lacking water, schools, sanitary services and work, the young flee Italy and go to Switzerland, France, Belgium, and they would even go to Hell – which many of them do – to avoid staying to rot in the South.

As I have noted before, by an old agreement at national level Italy is divided into wage zones or 'cages'.[2] As a result of these agreements, southern workers generally receive, by contract, 20 per cent less than workers in the North doing exactly the same job. In the construction industry, the difference can be as great as 30 per cent. Why should anyone stay in the South under such circumstances?

I walk alongside these trains crammed full of returned emigrants in the Naples Central Station. This particular group of trains comes from Germany and is going to Calabria. Our comrades in Emilia and Tuscany have done their job well: they have transformed the trains into a revolutionary convoy: decking them out with flags, symbols and slogans, distributing *l'Unità*, food and drinks. . . . Several of the emigrants, to make sure that their sentiments are not misunderstood, have pinned hammers and sickles made of paper to their chests. 'We have come back to vote Communist', everyone says – as if their intentions were not explicit enough from the electoral symbols that abound all around them.

1. In Italy, when a city or commune is unable to form a stable majority coalition (*giunta*) in the council to run local affairs, the state – represented by provincial prefects – establishes a non-party 'caretaker' administration under a *commissario prefettizio*. Although most frequently established only for the duration of pre-election periods, this form of administration, in some cases, lasts much longer than that. (Trans.)

2. Naples called a general strike on 9 November 1968 against 'wage cages'. Between October and November of that same year, there were another forty general strikes, in forty southern provinces, against the adjustment of wages according to the area of the country in which one lives.

I speak with a worker from Stuttgart in Germany: he is twenty-four and emigrated when he was seventeen; married, he has six children, one for every year, each one conceived on one of his return trips. 'Every year I come back with the hope of finding some work, for then I would never leave again. You know how we live abroad, you know how we are treated. . . .' Another returned many years ago, because there was a competition for three jobs as street sweepers for the city. He rushed home to see if he could get the job, but all the posts went to people 'protected' by the local priest. 'This is the last time that I come home,' he said. 'I'll vote for the PCI, but if things stay the way they are, what is the point of voting? I'll go and become a *German*.' This is the supreme insult, like saying to an observing Catholic that you were going to become a Muslim.

As soon as I say 'comrades', the emigrants turn to me, all ears; they want to know how the campaign is going and if we 'will make it' this time. Some of them are going to Apulia and Basilicata, and others are headed for Sicily and Calabria. An emigrant from Afragola tells me that in a town in Belgium, free tickets for the trip home were given out with the symbol of a shield with a cross on it stamped on them (this is the symbol of the DC). Many workers took these tickets and promised to vote for the DC, but they are going to vote for the PCI. 'It's the least we could do. After all, we save money this way.' I tell a young worker that I will be speaking this evening and I ask him if there is a message that he wants me to convey to the audience.'Tell them this: we want to come back, and people should vote against the people who force us to leave Italy; they should vote for the Communists. . . .'

But it is always the same: We are returning, we will vote for the PCI, but if things don't change soon, what is the point of it all? Next time we will not even bother coming back. There is a lot of passion and rebellion in their words, but there is also a good deal of discouragement. 'The vote is not enough,' says one who is barely twenty-one, 'the bosses are not going to give up their power because of some vote, don't kid yourself; only the revolution. . . .'

Those who get off the train rush to embrace their families and then hurry off to their sections. . . . That evening, they are around the platform of the electoral meeting. A building labourer, who had stood in the first row and waved his work visa, saying, 'I'm an emigrant, but now I have returned to vote', comes up on the stage with me when I ask him if he would like to say something. Once in front of the crowd, however, he is silent, tongue-tied. He can neither begin what he wants to say nor gain control over his ideas in any coherent fashion. Finally, he manages to say, 'Brothers, countrymen, vote for the Communist Party, vote so that we can come home, so that we will have a job to come back to. . . .' It is hardly a polished performance or even a complete sentence. It is more a lament than anything else, full of rage and impotent desperation.

Then I told the people in the crowd about my encounter at Barra with the mother of an emigrant. She takes care of the seven children of her son – who was born in 1923. He has worked only in Germany, because 'he has never had the pleasure of being able to bring home a piece of bread from nearby'. This old grandmother Oliviero, who lives at 254 Corso Sirena in Barra, is seventy years old. I met her a week ago. I met her while holding a meeting of women in someone's house; she was dressed in mourning and her neighbours were all trying to console and encourage her. It is a story like so many others. Two months ago, her grandson, who was twelve years old, died while his father was abroad working. Her son did not have the money to return home for the funeral. The old woman cries bitterly, and takes from her withered breast a little heart bordered in black with a small photo of a child in the centre. It is a faded photo of an incredibly pallid, already corpse-like young boy. She shows me the picture and then kisses it. Now her son will be able to return to Barra for the elections, thanks to the cheap tickets which are available at election time. 'This way, at least,' the grandmother says, 'he will be able to go to his son in the cemetery.' And once more she pulls out the little mourning photo, and once again she kisses it. She seems like a sinner who wants to be forgiven by the little grandson she was unable to keep alive, even though his father had entrusted him to her care, and even though she had raised six other grandchildren and raised them all well.

Maria Antonietta

Dear Louis,   *Naples, 17 May 1968, evening*

The electoral campaign officially 'closed' today. Closing suggests bolts and shutters, but here it meant the explosion of all the remaining energies of the Party, the electoral helpers and the candidates.

My colleagues on the PCI list tried to 'capture' as many closing speeches as possible. Some people had as many as six speeches in a row, spaced out like timed laps in a race: 5.00, 6.00, 6.45, from place to place, all the way up to midnight, when the 'final bell' rings and the tournament is over. I think that I was almost alone among the thirty-seven in that I had only *one* closing speech. And 1 only managed to get that one because the Torre del Greco section specifically asked for me in an official letter. All the other speeches that were assigned to me were literally taken away, one by one, by my colleagues on the list. I would get a telephone call: 'The section at Portici has eliminated your closing speech; Y. will speak with A.Z., instead of with you.' 'The section at Chiaia Posillipo wants you to know that your presence is not necessary,' etc. I make my final calculations and realize that I have never been sent to any of the Party's large popular and working-class sections in Naples – e.g. traditional centres of militancy and struggle like the 'Giorgio Quadro' section or the one at Ponticelli. I meet Y., a paragon of electoral consensus, but he sidesteps my question: 'How should I know why they replaced you at Portici? You'll have to ask them about it.'

During the fifty days of the campaign, Y. has always assiduously avoided even the most fleeting contact with me. He has not spoken with me and he even refused to have a political discussion that I requested just after I arrived. In fact, Y.'s mute dissent has been one of the burdens that I have carried throughout this campaign. He sees in me 'the symbol of bureaucratic imposition from the top', and views my whole case as an example of 'a lack of democracy in the Party'. Y.'s means of combating these offences has been to employ *competitive electoralistic tactics*, and he has not been the only one. I ask myself: Is this the way to carry on a political struggle? Isn't it necessary to go a little deeper than this? Is it acceptable that, in a political fight between one group and the other, preference votes should be used as a weapon? On the other hand, is it possible to have real struggles going on when there are no clearly declared political positions involved? I am really confused by all of this.

Sometimes I think that 'electoral cretinism' creeps into the political struggle inside the Party, with the result that clientelism and electoralism disguise themselves as differences in policy or strategy.

For reasons I have already mentioned, then, my only closing speech is held at Torre del Greco. But, when all is said and done, I am really glad to speak just once, for the following reasons.

By giving only one speech, I have two advantages. (1) I can prepare the speech carefully and well, rewriting it completely, and therefore making a *real discussion* out of it. This is only possible where one is able to grasp what is real and essential on a given day, in a given place, at a given moment in the overall struggle. I have already said how there are a lot of speakers who continuously re-chew the same words throughout the entire campaign, just like priests with the *Ave Maria*. (2) I have the time to visit and understand the town, to speak with the people and to have a precise idea of the problems that exist, who the people are, and what their ideas and orientations are. Every time that I speak, I try to put together the things I have learned since the start of the campaign.

Torre (with 90,000 inhabitants, the largest urban centre in the province after Naples itself) is a powerful and civilized town, with beautiful architecture, predominantly from the eighteenth century; the main streets are grandiose, befitting a city founded on maritime commerce. The aristocratic villas which are scattered along these green streets have a structural form every bit as noble as the villas for which Venice is famous. Work is mainly provided by the sea: the men of Torre del Greco make up the crews of the world's merchant marine, from deck-boys to captains. All of Torre is like a docked ship, and the rules and laws in effect there are the retrograde ones of the old seaman's code – for the sea is the men's 'factory'. Of the 30,000 men waiting to be signed on with a navigation contract, there are 5,000 seamen, men who really go to sea. The others are waiting to be 'called', and they spend long months walking the streets or hanging about in the cafés, trying to make ends meet.

Like Ulysses, the sailors of Torre travel on far-off seas, touch on unknown shores and learn other languages and customs. Their wives, their Penelopes, remain at home working on coral and mother-of-pearl while their husbands are gone for ten months every year.

I visit their houses. In the enclosed courtyards, the women have set up their 'factories'. Two or three, of various ages, will work together.

They have a small grinding wheel, which they use to make the mother-of-pearl into beads for necklaces, and tiny hole-punching machines: the needle has to come down hard and you need a marksman's eyes to do it right. The men, or at least those with no seafaring jobs, and the young boys work cameos – the ones with the heads of ancient Romans hand-engraved on them – and they have the hands and eyes of jewellers.

Just to describe the general conditions of exploitation is to sound as if you are exaggerating. I go to visit Nunziata Ghiara in her 'home factory'. Her face is covered with little chips of mother-of-pearl that have flown up during her work and stuck to her skin. Two of her daughters work beside her. In one of my hands, she puts the unworked product: it is squarish and sharp-edged. In my other hand, she places the finished pearl, after it has been passed countless times over the rapidly whirring grinder: it is perfectly round. She gets 13,000 lire for a kilogramme of 'pearls'. She cannot even say how many pearls make up a kilo: 'there are so, so many of them'. It takes four or five people working together two full days (and that means twelve hours a day) to make a kilogramme. Naturally, no one has social security, health insurance or pension rights. These women are workers in another form of 'shadow factory', exploited twice over: first by their middle-man, for there is virtually a local monopoly on pearls and coral, and then by the state, which refuses to give them workers' qualifications. It is extremely common for women to fall ill from silicosis at a very early age. When all things are taken into account, the women end up making about 800 lire a day.

I then go to speak with the women who work on coral. In the same courtyard, four girls with their benches side by side are bent over, putting tiny holes in the fragile coral branches: these, too, will be made into necklaces. They earn 3,000 lire for every kilo of punctured coral. In one day one girl produces 250 grammes, and the working conditions are identical to those I have just described: no insurance, no pension, etc. When I see them sitting there, bent over, the light playing in their eyes, I am reminded of Vermeer's famous painting of the embroideress.

Thousands of families at Torre live in this way. The men who do not escape to sea also end up enclosed in these shop-houses all day long. Michele Lombardo works on 'chunks' of sea-shell and carves them into elephants, fish and good luck charms which the vendor buys from him for 150 lire each. He and his son, working from dawn to dusk, manage to make about twenty of these pieces a day. When we go to Luciano Prete's house, we meet the three people who do the cameo etchings: Luciano and his two sons. The cameo is fixed to a little wooden backing like a cork or a seal. First Luciano prepares the mother-of-pearl – which is only about three square centimetres in area. Then the eldest son sketches out the profile of the ancient Roman, the youngest son refines the hair and the contours of the face and the father completes the job with the really fine touches and highly polished finish. Showing me his youngest son, Luciano Prete says, 'I put him to work with me when he was eight years old. Now he is ten. But I am trying to get him to finish elementary school.' (I don't know if this is true because, by now, on too many occasions I have seen fathers and mothers who are ashamed to admit that they pulled their children out of school and sent them to work at a very young age.) 'When he is thirty, he will be a worker like me, without insurance, without a pension, without any rights. This is a job that takes keen eyesight, you can only do it for a certain amount of time. And just about all of us that do this work have bronchial problems by the time we are thirty.'

Anna Mennelli works with two friends on coral of inferior quality, earning between 1,800 and 2,500 lire per kilogramme. Working together from morning to night, the three women cannot earn 1,000 lire apiece in a single day.

I continue my walk in the alleyways of Torre, going from door to door, and I think about what lies behind the famous Italian artisan enterprise: 'Coral Cameos Factory'. The name is written everywhere on the villa-jewellery shops which have sprung up around Torre. It is truly ironic how much exploitation is embodied in one of those tiny Roman heads scratched out in a cameo, or in a coral necklace, or in any of these products which are sold in shops in Paris, London or New York. Here, as elsewhere, there is a whole chain of artisans who create a 'bridge' between the person who works in his factory-home and the largest exploiters.

As I am walking in the street, an old woman calls out loudly to me, stops me and raises with me the question: Is it possible to block the hole in the street that the rats come out of? She shows me a great pit where the road has caved in, with sewer water bubbling at the bottom. 'All of the rats around here come in and out of that hole,' the old lady tells me. She seems like a madwoman. She has a rosary in her hand and speaks of a Universal Flood, citing the Bible (correctly, by the way). She says that the Apocalypse is coming for the human race, and finally she says that a new harmony and unity among men will come from the Ark. In the midst of this discourse, she suddenly interrupts herself and asks, 'Could you have something done about the rats? I am seventy years old and have a bad leg. I wrote to the City, but they said that you have to go in person to lodge a complaint.' Her name is Carmela Romano, and she is the Ophelia of Torre del Greco's problems.

In the streets of Torre, I also meet the head of the DC gang that controls the distribution and collection of shells and coral. He limps around like Mephisto, and speaks with great gestures in the midst of a band of bravos. He is simultaneously the local Director of the *Cassa del Mezzogiorno* and has a corner on the pearl, coral and malachite market. Since the coral 'banks' of Torre have long since been exhausted, a brother of his now sends him the primary materials from Mozambique. He distributes this to the engravers, who have to give him back finished cameos, and to the women, who give him back mother-of-pearl necklaces. Whatever is left over of the precious material, the débris, is given to lesser traders, who deal in it in their turn. As in the days of the pirates, sacks of shells from the African coast are unloaded for the capitalist of Torre and taken first to his house, in via Giuglielmo Marconi, where there are big sheds in which the goods undergo an initial preparation and are divided up for distribution. This firm – since *lo zoppo* (the lame man) is also a director of the *Cassa del Mezzogiorno* – is registered in his mother's name (the only proper thing to do under the circumstances). The comrades tell me about other feared brigand chiefs who, thanks to this exploitation, have become owners of fleets and now have ships which ply the coasts of Sicily, Sardinia and Yugoslavia, and fetch what is fished up there for the great coral and cameo entrepreneurs.

The workers themselves say that the solution to all this exploitation ought to be the creation of a cooperative. But the primary problem which arises is precisely the same one that I have already noted a hundred times where the small artisans in the centre of Naples are concerned: how to provide labour rights for this immense mass of underpaid men and women who work at home, and to whom the state will not grant the status of workers? In one sense, however, there is a difference between Torre del Greco and Naples, in that here the *intermediaries* (who, as in Naples, are often poor, miserable wretches themselves) show themselves openly: the worker is confronted by large monopolists, by real capitalists. Torre del Greco is like an immense cage that no one can flee. Male and female workers alike are bent over their machines twelve hours a day, but, since they officially have neither employers nor jobs, they also have no rights.

Everything that I learn in my trip around Torre becomes, in my closing speech, material to support my plea to put an end to all this human desperation. There are of course the broad and sweeping general political themes, but I only bring them up after describing their own exploitation to this crowd, which listens in a tense, desperate way to hear if there is a way out for them. I go on and say that capitalism carries in itself contradictions which give birth to new forms of struggle, to social protests and revolts and to new mass movements. And I point out to the woman who works on coral, the mother who cannot send her child to school, that *her* exploiter is the capitalist system and the parties that govern in its interest, the P S U and the D C.

Here I turn and dwell on the things that are going on in France at this very moment: the students, the occupation of the factories, the enormous general strike, Renault and the Sorbonne. I challenge the youth here to rebel, and they answer me by shouting: VICTORY . . . VICTORY . . . HO CHI MINH. It is a revolutionary crowd; the young wave red flags. *'They cannot continue; capitalism's grave is open and waiting in Europe'*, I say. And a cry responds, 'We've had enough!' I am interrupted by these cries many times. I try in words to get across the situation in France, with her youth and workers in revolt, insurgent Paris and the red flag over the factories of Billancourt and Flins. The vaunted 'consumer society' seems to be flying to pieces. The civilization of computers seems destined for an early death. I repeat one of the slogans of the French students: 'The proletariat will take up the banner of revenge from the weak hands of the students.' I tell them to wave their red flags, for the day of socialism's victory is near. My words end amid the explosion of hundreds of fireworks of all kinds. The platform seems to collapse under the upsurge of laughing and crying faces, unfurled flags, and flashes and explosions. It seems like a gaping hole suddenly opened up in the heart of the system, and that the whole capitalist structure is about to fall into the maw at any moment. A huge procession begins to form, and we are practically pushed to the head of it by the weight of the moving crowd. Aniello Cuciniello, the most popular Party leader at Torre and a leader of national stature for the maritime union, links his arm with mine. We move to the head of the march – the crowd is gigantic – and begin to move towards the centre of Torre. It is almost midnight. The electoral campaign is over. But the youths, all of them, flood in to the section. And there we continue to speak with one another. It feels like a revolutionary assembly. What a marvellous last impression of the electoral campaign. I see the excitement of the young people, I feel their desire and will to fight, and I know that we are stronger than anyone else.

I am perfectly aware that this crescendo by far exceeds the objective state of things. But this is precisely the way that so much effort and struggle on the part of the masses and the Party ends up just prior to the vote. In other words, the entire front registers a real movement forward, at this point everything is catapulted forward towards a new day which, in these circumstances, seems about to dawn tomorrow. Yet all this 'exaggeration' – both on my part and on the part of the public – has a true, political and idealistic root in reality. (It also reflects a certain style of philosophic practice, a 'wild practice', as you wrote in your essay on Lenin, in the same sense that Freud speaks of a 'wild analysis'.)

The electoral campaign is only one moment among many. The struggle continues, and the explosion, in Italy, cannot be contained: in the South, the preconditions are emerging for a fundamental, revolutionary upsurge. Discussions, speeches and assemblies have resulted in a gigantic politicization of the people.

19 May will be an important date, aside from any electoral or parliamentary returns. My electoral experience has taught me one thing conclusively: the people have a revolutionary drive. And no one can contain it for long.

Maria Antonietta

Dear Louis,   *Naples, 19 May 1968*

It is late at night, 1.00 a.m., the hour at which I have written most of the letters I have sent you over the last seventy days. I spent the day going from polling station to polling station, from the time the first people went to cast their votes at eight this morning. By declaring my status as a candidate, I am allowed, according to the laws governing elections, to go to any polling station and ask the electoral officer how many votes have already been cast out of the total number of voters in the area. I am also permitted to direct a few banalities at him, e.g. 'Is everything going all right? Have there been any significant incidents during the course of the voting?' and so on. Finally, before leaving, I may wish the electoral officer, the tellers and the list representatives well in their work.

I started my day off by voting. Since the law permits me to vote at any polling station in the Naples-Caserta district, I chose a place in Castellammare, for it is to this working-class city that I feel the strongest political connection, and it is here that I have learned the most and gained the greatest support during the campaign. Castellammare also represents for me the outpost of the enemy, for it is here that the head of the DC, Gava, has his stronghold; it is here that he humiliated the working class by taking the city away from it through an alliance with the fascists and monarchists; and it is here that the alliance between Christian Democrats and Socialists ready to collaborate with capitalism followed. And there is a supplementary, personal reason as well: Gava – this 'Attila of the *res publica*' – has filed a suit for libel and defamation against me and *l'Unità* after my denunciation of his activities as a corrupt DC notable. As I have already pointed out, my article really shook things up and so, burning with anger at this challenge, Gava went before a large crowd on the evening of the 17th to defend himself. The crowd whistled and shouted at him. After hypocritically beginning by saying that he had only the greatest respect for me both as a woman and as a cultured woman, he announced that he had filed suit, and that I would have to renounce my parliamentary immunity to appear before the magistrate if I wanted to defend myself. He also said that I was not wanted by the Party in Naples, that the other candidates saw me as a problem and an impediment, and that the only way I had got on to the list in the first place was through the manoeuvring of some of the PCI leaders. The day after his speech, all of his client newspapers splashed the news of the suit all over their front pages. Now, everywhere I walk I practically trip over red, pink and yellow leaflets – printed by the DC press – in which Gava appeals to the voters 'not to be surprised or taken in by this unprincipled communist slur and trick'. There are so many of these things in the streets that it looks like the aftermath of a big parade, with confetti lying everywhere.

That, in any event, is my special reason for wanting to vote in Castellammare. In fact, I went to polling station No. 1, which is the one that Gava has voted at for twenty years. I indicated the preferences that the Party had recommended for the Castellammare section: 1-4-16-25, putting down the numbers instead of the names. Number 1 is Amendola, 4 is Ajello, the worker, 16 is another worker, De Filippo, and I am 25. I thought about things before I indicated my own number. But I finally put it down, telling myself that one has to depersonalize issues as much as possible and, since my name was recommended, not putting it down would have simply amounted to petty-bourgeois snobbery.

The whole business of preference votes went anything but smoothly during the campaign. Preferences are not, from what I have determined, an expression of *direct democracy* or *consent from below*. The people who decide are the leading group in each section, who in certain cases engage in 'direct negotiations' with the recommended candidate. I told you how it works in the Federation: a group of comrades parcels out preferences, so many to this one, so many to that one. But these people themselves know that their influence is only relative. Here is what can happen. Last evening, at the section in Torre del Greco, a comrade came in with his own private set of preferences. My number, 'recommended' by the section and placed in order on a card along with the other three, was not to be found on this comrade's card. In fact of the numbers he had on *his* card (3-7-13-33), only the first had been recommended by the Federation for this section. In fact, his was a card furnished by another section. Perhaps because I was right there, someone asked him very politely why he did not have number 25. 'Who is 25?' he asked. They told him it was M.A.M. 'Oh, the woman? We have decided not to put the woman down; we have decided that we shouldn't elect her.' The secretary of the section reprimanded him in stentorian tones. I got terribly embarrassed and left without telling him that I was the woman in question. And then, in the store where I went immediately afterwards to buy cheese, there was another comrade with the same 'alternative' numbers. There is evidently a little organization that is working on changing the preferences and it is either working behind the section's back or else a part of the leadership of the section itself is acting against the Federation on its own.

I am writing this first post-campaign letter in a state of great calm. At the beginning of the campaign, you wrote a letter which had a profound effect on me. You told me to use the campaign as a means by which I could come to know the people, that I should not delude myself, and that I therefore should also be prepared to learn from my own 'defeats'. I now feel as if I have, in my capacity as a militant, waged a meaningful electoral struggle. By behaving in this fashion I have tried, wherever my own personal activities have been involved, to act consistently with a specific political orientation.

I do not think it is sufficient to differentiate yourself from social democracy. Instead, from within the revolutionary camp, there must arise, visibly, an image of the counter-society that we stand for, the new society that we represent. There must be a clear image of the possibility for man to develop his creative abilities to their outside limits. There must be an indication of the possibilities for a *new man* to emerge. This, to me, means that there must be a conception of a way of being and of carrying on the struggle which is able, in itself, to suggest the characteristics of the new society for which we are fighting. Indeed, we should not only suggest this new society's contours, but *affirm* them in the way we carry on our struggle for power. And even an electoral campaign should be viewed and evaluated through this severe lens.

I also do not think that the political struggle is fought by winning for oneself the maximum number of preference votes, at the expense of some other candidate. This is fine for the bourgeois, but not for us. A political struggle is fought by hammering out the correct theoretical and political positions. It is fought by struggling in imaginative ways, by clearly and courageously indicating the proper revolutionary path to follow, and by defeating all attempts to integrate us into the existing system of power – including this whole business of preference votes. For preferences, in all but a limited number of cases, do not represent a free choice of the people, but are gleaned as a result of the superior ability of a given individual to put certain organized nuclei of the Party to his personal use.

Hence, to be totally honest, it is quite likely that I am not going to get elected. If I do manage to get elected, it will represent a real victory, for it will represent an exclusively and uniquely political relationship with the electorate and nothing more. I would be very proud of this, for it would mean that all this effort of mine did not go unnoticed. It would not only represent a personal victory for me, but would also underline the *politicization* both of the party's rank and file and of its electorate.

Aside from Di Vittorio's daughter who is running for Parliament in Apulia, I am the only woman candidate that the Party is presenting seriously in the entire South. Southern Italy is very misogynist, Communists included. Women tend to attract thoughts that have to do exclusively with bed, embraces, procreation and the like. In *this* area, women get plenty of attention and credit. Moreover, there is the whole masculine myth here in the South (which you wrote about when you discussed possible reasons for the high birth rate), and this myth has a negative effect even on the party of the working class. The comrades themselves seem to suffer from many complexes, and to feel humiliated by a woman who is involved in politics. In the entire electoral campaign, with the exception of my first 'trial' meetings, there have been very few candidates who have chosen to speak from the same platform as me.

In the South, the comrades are barely even able to countenance the idea of a woman concerning herself with women's issues. Quite capable female comrades often end up being intimidated by the male comrades when they have to deal with general political issues. In 1953, Togliatti had to call a conference with the unequivocal title, 'Was it Right to Give Women the Vote?' to destroy, once and for all, the belief among many militants and leaders that women had caused our electoral defeat on 18 April 1948. Togliatti also had to point out that 'in any event, we can hardly consider the entry into our country's political life of more than half the population to be an "electoral problem"'.

The 'Woman Question' must be an organic part of the working class's political struggle. But woman cannot wait for a socialism created *exclusively by men* to end their oppression. Moreover, the relationship is dialectical: as long as women remain in a position of inferiority, they will run the risk of being considered nothing but useless ballast for the workers' movement.

My political presence clashes with the prevailing conception of the role of women, both in society and in the Party. But long years spent doing a 'man's job' (I was the only woman foreign correspondent for an Italian daily paper, and the only woman who edited a political weekly – *Vie Nuove*) have armed me well, enabling me to get out of the strait-jacket of 'woman's work' as it has traditionally been understood in the Party.

And so I landed on the shores of this strange Neapolitan world, a little like Minerva leaping fully armed from the head of Jupiter, an androgynous being. To allude to my coming from another world, people often start off a conversation by saying, 'You, a Frenchwoman. . . .' As I have written, I have sometimes suffered a lot from this kind of treatment, but I have been able to put it all, including the petty tricks and spiteful acts, behind me. Once this is done, one makes rapid progress. After two months, one's presence alone in a meeting is sufficient to impose, let us say, a new kind of woman and therefore a new kind of man-woman relationship, within the Party itself. But this is not easily accepted. When confronted with this challenge to traditional patterns, the man, your comrade in the political struggle, finds himself confronted with new worries and inferiority complexes.

My day in the polling stations has provided me with a whole range of reflections – even within the most obvious limits of an election in a bourgeois regime.

When you enter a polling station, the first thing that strikes your eye is a sort of tribunal which is set up in front of the voter: a large table with two lateral wings, behind which a group of officials is seated. On the table, right in the centre, are two urns which look exactly like two tiny coffins: they are certainly as inscrutable and contain as many secrets. In one urn are placed the straw-yellow ballots for the election of Senators; in the other go the light blue forms for Deputies. Behind the table are either two or four cabins, which face each other across a discreet distance. To one side go the women – and the examiner dutifully calls out 'Feminine' – and to the other the men ('Masculine'). They are like the beach-cabins you see at the seashore, but inside they are quite different, for the air in them is close and fetid.

The common people have a timid, circumspect air as they stand in line: they show fear of the atmosphere of universal judgement, fear of making some mistake. At the bottom of this whole electoral procedure is a sense of class inferiority: inferiority, with respect to the 'cultivated' bourgeoisie, of the 'uncultivated' popular classes. I make the rounds of polling stations 64, 65, 66 and 67 in Torre del Greco; the popular classes are in the majority. Even the ballots, ambiguous instruments that they are, support class differentiations: they are easily intelligible for the educated person, barely decipherable for the illiterate. Many of the women of the people remain for up to ten minutes in the booths, and at times they seem never to want to leave. The electoral officer says to one of them, from outside the curtain, 'What's the matter, don't you feel well?' The woman shouts back, 'I can't find the right hammer and sickle.' The representative of the DC list then sets up a great shout: 'Void ballot, void ballot!' 'Calm down, now,' says the officer in response. 'After all, there are four different symbols with the hammer and sickle on them!' And in fact this is true: there are four separate party symbols which have the hammer and sickle on them: the PCI (the one the woman wanted), the PSIUP, a local list of 'proletarian communists', and that of the unified PSI-PSDI.

Our party, to help the voters out, gives out facsimile ballots before the elections with the 'X' already marked against our symbol and, in the lined space alongside the symbol, the four recommended preferences with their list numbers. The women slip these inside the tops of their dresses before they go to vote, and then they pull them out once they are inside the cabins. There, they can accurately copy out the instructions even if they cannot read or write: first the 'X', then the numbers. Mothers who come with their families – they temporarily leave their flock of children out in the hallway while they enter the cabin – are all flushed and sweating by the time they emerge, so great has been their effort and anxiety. They burst out of the cabins like people who have been underwater for a long time, like coral divers. They do not know if they have done the *right thing* or not. And this doubt will stay with them for some time. 'I did as I was told', the comrades that I speak with will say nervously. They had earlier asked some militants how one is supposed to vote for the PCI, for they had desperately wanted to do so.

In every place I visited, I was struck by the initial disadvantage that, even from a technical point of view, an election represents for us. The ballots which are declared void are, in fact, in great majority those of the PCI. Some people, for example, to avoid making a mistake mark *all* the symbols that include a hammer and sickle. Some people sign their ballot. Some put their mark against one symbol, but then fill in the preferences against the adjacent symbol. Our own comrades who are acting as list representatives read the various regulations from a little notebook which the Party has had printed. But, since most of them are workers, they find it hard suddenly to become 'lawyers' and argue with the real lawyers and other professionals who represent the bourgeois parties in power. Moreover, these professionals treat the workers, despite their official standing as representatives, in a very high-handed and classist way. They use the most insulting phrases to shut the comrades up, including such things as, 'If you don't like it, why don't you just go home?' They practically call them ignorant to their faces.

Late at night, the Federation sends me to the polling station at Capodimonte to lend a hand to a working-class comrade who is having twenty-five ballots contested by the electoral officer. It seems that these people have all put their 'Xs' against two different symbols with the hammer and sickle. But since they also all filled in their preferences on the PCI list, next to our symbol, our representative – citing paragraph 70 of the electoral code – insists that in such cases the vote goes to the symbol which has the preferences indicated on its list. He is absolutely right, for the paragraph says precisely that. But the electoral officer, who happens to be a judge, treats him like a convict. So the comrade went to the phone and called for reinforcements. Several of us leaped into a car and roared across the entire city. But by the time we arrive, we find our comrade, desperate, in the middle of the street. The electoral officer has simply closed the polling station and refused to record the teller's objection. It is as if he had simply slapped our comrade in the face. The latter tells us how it went: 'He told me, "Look, you, my work is finished, and you can do whatever you want, I don't give a damn. Your complaint is not accepted; if you like that, fine, if not, that's too bad, but get out of here."' In these long, pettyfogging arguments, our comrades quite frequently come out on the losing side, just as it is usually the ballot of the poor or the illiterate which is annulled.

Certain electoral officers change their tone and tactics when they find themselves challenged by people who belong to the upper classes. At station number 10 at Torre del Greco, I witnessed the following scene: a young, elegantly dressed blonde presented her voting certificate, but she had no other identification to verify that she really was the same person named on the certificate. She is, however, accompanied by another, older woman, who vouches for her identity. So the officer, in accordance with the law, begins to ask 'questions appropriate to the circumstances' in order to ascertain if she was indeed the owner of the certificate. 'When was she born?' he asks the older woman. The answer gets both the month and the year wrong. Now, under such circumstances, the officer has the right to call in the police and accuse them of *suspected fraud*; but instead he is all sugar with this distinguished woman. All he says is, 'I can only allow you to vote if you return with a document that corresponds to your electoral certificate.' And the woman simply walks out.

On the other hand, in a polling station right next door to this one, a poorly-dressed old man is also without any documents. When he is questioned, he states an age thirty years older than that indicated on the form: he says he is seventy and the certificate says forty. It is obviously a typographical error. The electoral officer, who is a fascist, a local M S I leader, suddenly assumes the role of Defender of Justice; he starts a terrific row, shouting at the top of his lungs and calling for police intervention, and suspends the whole voting operation in the meantime. I arrive in the midst of all this confusion and chaos, and a *carabiniere* refuses to let me enter. After insisting, I succeed in getting inside, where the fascist electoral officer wants to throw me right out again. But finally, after a face-to-face exchange, he leaves things as they are. He then turns to the *carabiniere* marshal and demands the arrest of the old man for attempting to defraud the public. But the marshal knows the man, knows his name, and is able to confirm what he has been claiming all along. He says that it must be the date on the certificate which has caused all this trouble, but this is not the old man's fault.

Nevertheless, the fascist screams: 'Either you arrest him or I will suspend all voting operations!' At the same time, he turns to me and says, 'You are superfluous and useless here; there is no further light that you can shed on this issue.' I respond, 'The light I can shed is that you are abusing your powers and treating voters like convicts.' I am furious, but quite calm, at least externally. And the marshal, for his part, wants anything but to arrest the old man. Finally the dispute is settled with this outcome: the poor old man runs off terrified, and you can be certain that he will never go now to the Town Hall to get the certificate corrected. On the contrary, after this experience, he will probably avoid the whole issue, for he now has evidence that you can get into a lot of trouble if you vote. Voting must now seem to him to be a trap which can land you in jail if you are not careful, and he is sure to feel this way for the rest of his life.

The D C 'grooms' its electorate in those permanent schools, the parishes. Ballots which are annulled are most frequently those cast by people who want to change the world that oppresses them. On the night of Friday the 17th, just prior to my speech at Torre del Greco, Aniello Cuciniello gave a public lesson in the main square on how to vote.

He took the two ballot forms in his hand, and began by saying, 'Now listen carefully: when you go into the polling station, the electoral officer will give you two ballots, one straw-coloured, the other blue.... This is the straw-coloured ballot, and you mark this one to elect senators. For those of you who are not able to read the names, put your mark on the hammer and sickle. And this is the blue ballot.... Pay attention and don't make any mistakes.... Be sure, before you go home from the polling station, that the electoral officer has put your ballots in the urns.'

He goes on like that for half an hour. I get bored listening to him. But the audience stands there all attention, with eyes and mouths wide open, listening carefully. I realize that many of the people in this dense crowd (they are packed in so tightly that I think a dropped coin would never reach the ground) are not sure that they know the correct way to vote – for the party to whose rally they have come with red banners and such fighting spirit. For between this powerful determination and the actual mechanism of voting, parliamentary democracy has opened a huge gap, a gap based on class. In ten different polling stations, I see exactly the same scene: women comrades, with fearful eyes, recognize me but say nothing at all, just smile. For they have been told that in the polling stations the party representatives and *carabinieri* watch carefully to make sure that no one expresses any political ideas or propagandizes in any form. I think of all the ballots which will be annulled, with all these hammers and sickles which whirl in a St Vitus's dance before their eyes; with this supreme tribunal of the polling station, like the highest Court of Appeal, which admits them into its presence, identifies them, gives them ballots as if they were holy wafers, shuts them in cabins, etc., etc.

The comrades have managed to pull off miracles simply in terms of teaching the women to vote, just to *vote*. Yesterday we went around from house to house, clambering through the back streets first of Torre del Greco and then of Castellammare. We visited barber shops, bakeries, fruit vendors, etc. In each place, we took out our facsimiles and, in the back of the shops, we would teach people how to vote. Those who obtained this 'instruction' then went on to teach others.

And, from the unbelievable number of problems we encountered yesterday on our rounds, I at once realize that there will be many, many invalidated, annulled and problematic ballots today.

It may seem like a silly, minor point to you, but the mechanics of voting, for an old, illiterate proletarian woman, a person who has never handled a pen or picked up a newspaper, represents a real trap. The ingenuity of the comrades was sharpened to the maximum by this challenge. Salvatore Petrucci, a sailor, had this amazing idea for teaching the women of his quarter to vote for the PCI's symbol. He asked the first woman, 'Which hand is it that you do not eat with?' The woman responded, raising her left hand, 'This one'. Then Salvatore said, 'All right, that is the side of the ballot, the one towards the hand you don't eat with, where you will find the hammer and sickle. It will be all the way over on the side of the hand you don't eat with. Put your mark against that symbol.' He went over and over this set of instructions, but the old woman did not really seem to grasp his instructions on how to find the symbol farthest over on the left. She would keep raising her left hand, but then she would falter and simply leave it suspended halfway up, not knowing what to do with it. Comrade Petrucci leaves her near a twelve-year-old, to whom he gives the following instructions: 'Make her try it all day long, and by this evening she will have learned it.' And, sure enough, by evening the old woman knows where to make the mark: *on the same side as the hand you don't eat with*. There are hundreds of thousands of women just like her in the South.

Even the soldiers who stand on guard at the polling stations vote for the PCI, as I learn by questioning them politely. They are the sons of southern workers, peasants and *braccianti*, and they speak of the poverty in their home towns. One soldier says ironically, 'With my vote, I discharged my debt of gratitude' – i.e. to the Government.

At polling station 68 the electoral officer is an old sea wolf, with a face literally cooked brown by the sun. He leaps to attention as soon as he sees me, and all he can say is this: 'All they send me in this place are old men; I wish I could have seen just one beautiful girl since this morning.' At station 69, even the *carabiniere* on duty seems to have voted for us. I try to imagine the reality that these people, sons of the people, have in their hearts and how different it must be from the protection of the bourgeois order that their uniforms symbolize. Yet the Government uses the sons of the people in its police operations. And so I keep thinking of an old slogan, *Soldiers, Workers, Peasants* as the police, the *carabinieri* and the soldiers in the polling stations find ways to strike up conversations with me.

Maria Antonietta

Dear Louis,   *Naples, 26 May 1968*

We have won an impressive electoral victory. These letters, which began with a large gathering at the Metropolitan Theatre, now close with another large gathering in the same spot.

That first meeting was an uncertain prologue, and this last one represented the final development and resolution of the entire plot. We all found ourselves, once again, in the same place where it all began, but this time everything was different: the audience, the atmosphere, the scene up on the stage – everything was changed, as if it had literally been turned inside out or given a fresh coat of paint which rendered it all but unrecognizable. Longo, the secretary of the Party, came to Naples to emphasize the great advance of the PCI here; this in fact is his first public appearance since the elections a week ago. Even within the context of the great progress we made all over the country – we gained 800,000 votes, raising our percentage of the total vote from 25.3 per cent to 26.9 per cent, with a total of 8,555,131 votes – the figures for Naples represent our greatest step forward in the entire South. In addition, of the great proletarian cities Naples now for the first time comes directly behind Turin and Genoa and ahead of Milan, in terms both of percentage and of votes cast.

In Naples, our Party gained 30,000 votes and 4.5 per cent, going from 155,134 votes (24.3 per cent) in 1963 to 183,628 votes (28.8 per cent) in 1968. In the province as a whole, the PCI obtained 373,332 votes, or 27.7 per cent. In the city itself we are now separated by barely 7,000 votes from the DC, whose total in the province fell 1 per cent compared with five years ago (from 35.8 per cent to 34.9 per cent, i.e. 470,990 votes), whereas nationally it increased. But the DC still does have its coffers filled by 470,990 votes in Naples and, above all, in the rest of the province. This is partly due to the fact that the Right – the Monarchists of Lauro, their electoral bosses, their *clientele*,

their *camorra* associates who share control with the Christian Democrats of the port and all the various markets (fruit, fish, meat, etc.) – has
gone over almost lock, stock and barrel to Gava. This of course ensures
the continuation of a connection between local power groups and the
Government and central institutions of the state. The Socialist Party
lost 5.4 per cent, obtaining only 65,000 votes in the city as opposed
to 95,000 in the last elections. In Naples and her province, social-
democracy has begun a downward slide, dropping from 209,970 votes
(16.7 per cent) in 1963 to 154,412 (11.5 per cent) in this election.

This popular denunciation of the Socialists extended to all of Italy
in similar proportions: the PSU lost 1,527,778 votes, and received
29 less seats in Parliament than in 1963. The great surprise of these
elections was precisely this very high price paid by the Socialists for
their policy of continuously giving in to the demands of the ruling
class. It must be said that *even the Left* – with the PCI very much
included – believed that *the entry of the Socialists into the Centre-Left
majority* was going to result in an electoral success among the masses,
among the 'ignorant people', supposedly won over or corrupted by the
prospect of seeing themselves represented *in power*. Instead, this
turned out to be an erroneous prediction: the masses slammed the
door in the face of the social-democratic entry into the corridors of
power. The collapse of the Socialists, along with the fall of the spokesmen for the bosses (represented by the DC) make Naples' results
quite exemplary.

I provide so many crude statistics because, in this instance, there is
probably nothing which really communicates a better sense of what
went on. The political heart of the victory was provided by two elements, a proletarian resurgence and the vote of the young people. And
in the Metropolitan, the representatives of these two groups were
there tonight, with elated, beaming faces, some of them almost overcome with the joy of the occasion, out there among the sea of red flags
and the rhythmic chants of *vit-tor-i-a!* which seemed to make the
whole place explode. This was not simply the 'natural' disposition to
enthusiasm of the southern character; rather, at a time like this, you
get an inkling of what, for the people, *the conquest of power* might be like.

For five days running now, there has been a veritable Bacchanal of
happiness and celebration, with parties, speeches, marches and so on in
all of the areas where we did exceptionally well. At 9.00 this morning
you should have seen Piazza Plebiscito, with wave upon wave of

comrades, literally marching in formation to the theatre behind the banners of their respective sections; they looked exactly like victorious troops, receiving well-earned cheers from the crowd, flowers thrown in their path and kisses from the women. Everywhere, people stopped on the pavements to watch what was going on. The comrades sold *l'Unità* to everyone, and such was the elation that they even went into the most elegant cafés in the centre of town. We all took turns buying coffee for one another and called out greetings across the rooms, so that each of us drank about five coffees apiece before even setting foot in the Metropolitan. Several people came up to me, saying, 'Congratulations, comrade, on being elected Deputy.' For in the midst of all the incredible things that have happened in these days, it also happens that I have been elected – by a narrow margin, it is true – and am now an '*Onorevole*' (Honourable Member), which is the pompous and obsolete title by which we will be addressed in Parliament (an incredibly rarefied title when you consider the electoral mechanism).

Today the Metropolitan was absolutely crammed full of the people who, in this campaign, emerged as the Vietnam Generation: the youth. Students, workers and the children of workers and unemployed, an entire movement which is part of the Party but which is also outside the Party, and for whom *the* important political fact of their lifetime is the defeat inflicted on the American Cyclops by the tiny Vietnamese nation. The three intensive months of campaign activity were enough to bring the profound politicization of young students and workers to light, and to reveal the political potential this movement contains. This phenomenon is destined to make its weight felt inside the P C I, in the very fibres of the Party and all its organizations. Within the P C I there is already opposition to the *Old Party*; although we are not yet fully aware of it, it is fundamental, rooted in objective reality and sooner or later is bound to surface. Out in front of me, the theatre seems like a field of poppies in the wind, so abundant are the red banners and scarves being waved by the young people. And this scene gives me the distinct impression that we will not be able to rest for a very long time on the laurels of this victory, for things look as if they are going to proceed from here in rapid fashion. In terms of students, Naples is a lot like an Italian Nanterre. The recent student demonstrations were 'invented' in Naples, with the occupation of the Faculties of Agriculture and Architecture in *December 1967*. These acts led to the occupation of the entire university and to the sequestration of the Rector – which was the first truly rebellious act. And it all took place a long time before the students at Nanterre began to sing 'Dansons la Grappignole' to their deacon, Grappin. But everyone has always obscured Neapolitan events. Not even in the flood of documents now being published on the student struggles do you find mentioned the fact that it was Naples students who first touched off the big rebellions which later followed in Trento, Turin, Milan and Rome. This, too, is a sign of the total lack of political rationalization which is inevitably found in the South, like a kind of self-destruction. Yet I myself was able to reconstruct, with little difficulty, the degree of political imagination and originality which this first movement contained, as well as its impact. And I did this just a few days ago, using the 'oral history' method, getting my information from one of the people who is now up on the stage with me, the F G C I secretary, d'Alò.

The Party's greatest progress was in the large workers' centres. At Castellammare, to take a typical example, we went from 31.3 per cent to 42.9 per cent, with a net gain of 5,000 votes. The D C suffered a sharp blow, so sharp in fact that the notorious Gava himself barely managed to hold on to his Senate seat. I catch sight of Saul Cosenza in the audience, all dressed up in a white shirt and a tie, and his son Matteo who is with him has three red carnations in his buttonhole. We exchange long-distance greetings. I also see Comrade Di Martino, large and angular, who at seventy – dressed, as he always is, in a very correct dark suit – looks more like a professor of Latin than a worker at the Italcantieri Shipyards of Castellammare. He is the former head of the factory's shop committee, and he was summarily fired at the time of the demonstrations against General Ridgeway. In fact, local persecution and blacklisting of Di Martino went so far that his children all had to find jobs far from Castellammare. Is it presumptuous of me to assume that some of these comrades might have been deeply moved by the election results as they learned of them in the section at Castellammare? The young comrades let their emotions carry them out into the streets, where they snake-danced, with red flags, past D C headquarters, which had all its windows shuttered as if for a wake. There the comrades held a fantastically joyful celebration over the enemy's body.

It was from Castellammare, in fact, that we had the first indications of the extent of our victory. Early on Tuesday afternoon the phones started to ring at the Federation, and they did not stop for two days and nights. The very first message was that with half the votes counted, the P C I was 3,000 votes ahead of its 1963 level. Then came a call from Fuorigrotta (a workers' centre as well, this one the home of Italsider), 2,400 votes ahead of last time; then Gragnano, the little bakery town, with 3,700 votes, a full thousand more than in the last elections; then Resina with 1,250 more votes, then San Giorgio a Cremano, up by just over 2,000. In the senatorial college of Torre del Greco, the P C I became the largest party, going from 42,736 to 45,547 votes: this advance cost Rubinacci, the D C Minister of Scientific Research, his seat. He was the only important minister to lose in all of Italy, the only one to have the doors of the anterooms of power slammed in his face.

And that is how the whole count went; in the same way that eating one cherry inevitably leads to taking another, we found one victory following another, inexorably. On the telephone, the comrades who called up to report were often so excited or moved that you couldn't understand anything they were saying.

Finally, from Naples, we began to call the results in to Rome, to Party Headquarters and to *l'Unità* – where the figures had already been obtained from the Interior Ministry – and there was universal shock and joy at the great leap forward of this unhappy city, whose vote – is it finally clear? – was a *class* vote, a vote for political rebirth, a workers' vote and, finally, as the figures clearly show, a vote of the younger generation. Of the three million-plus young people between 21 and 25 years of age (you can only vote for the Senate if you are 25 or older), 1,338,000 voted for the opposition lists on the Left. Out of 31,785,389 valid votes cast on 19 May, we and our ally the P S I U P (which got 1,414,043 votes on its own in the elections for the Chamber of Deputies) got about ten million votes between us. This is a clear vote in favour of socialism, and it shows the commitment to socialist ideals of the generation which has just entered political activity. Hence it is not simply a *vote*, but a *political choice* they are making, and it does not affect only a single election, but an entire political perspective.

To clarify this point, I will give you an example from Castellammare which, in microcosm, serves as an excellent example of how the vote of the younger generation went. Out of 33,242 votes cast for the Chamber, the P C I got 16,235, a truly striking advance to 42.85 per cent compared with 31.3 per cent in 1963. I would have loved to see the expression on Gava's face as he discovered that we had become the largest party in this proletarian city. And the DC's decline at Castellammare was greater than elsewhere, going from 33.6 per cent to 31.6 per cent. But Gava, as I have already said, managed to become a Senator again, even if only by a hair's breadth and in spite of his decline of 1.6 per cent (from 30.9 to 29.3 per cent). For the Senate, we and the PSIUP got a total of 14,916 votes, which means that, for the Chamber, the PCI on its own got more than 3,000 additional votes, thanks to the voters below the age of 25 who cannot yet vote for the Senate. Hence a lot of our success was due to the youth; these figures could be repeated for every place in Italy where we moved ahead significantly.

And our advance was also notable in the old centre of Naples. I will only tell you about some of the sub-proletarian quarters which I have been discussing constantly in these letters, and where I invested so much time and interest. At Arenella, we went from 4,988 to 6,230; at Avvocata, from 6,020 to 7,818; Barra: 7,941 to 9,171; Miano: 4,007 to 5,644; Mercato: from 2,983 to 4,032; Montecalvario: from 5,268 to 5,779; at Piscinola we went from 2,996 to 4,065; at Poggioreale: 6,098 to 7,209; San Carlo Arena: 11,796 to 15,517; San Ferdinando: 3,078 to 3,655; at Secondigliano, we passed from 7,841 to 11,622. I could go on and cite even more statistics, but I don't want to drug you with numbers. Just one last fact: even the Parete section managed to increase its already incredible percentage.

By now, I can recognize many faces in the crowd, and I can even call many of them by name, names learned in both the positive and negative aspects of my experience. Let me try to proceed step by step for a moment and give some kind of order and chronology to what has been going on since Tuesday night. From the first bits of information, like seismographic waves, it was clear that things were going in our favour and that the results would be clear and unequivocal. The result, which we now find ourselves forced to face (and this is its exquisitely political value), is the orientation of the masses, which have become in a manner of speaking a collective intellectual, uniting their reactions to the elections, synthesizing and interpreting them. We find, at the side of the students and workers, those Neapolitan intellectuals who are located in the new centres of social tension, the schools, the universities, the courts, the public administration. Fed up with the machinations of the state apparatus, for the first time they are expressing their disaffection and rebellion against the corrupt ruling class that governs Naples; all these figures out of a Gogol story are finally sick and tired of bowing down before the all-powerful.

These are whole strata of citizens who have been aroused to struggle by the tremendously important events which are shaking the entire West and the old equilibria of the world. They are often more aware of the importance of these events than are we Communists. We in fact are so often wrapped in the cocoon of an ancient structure that we really have little, if any, contact with these developments. Not all of this victory, then, is a result of our own actions. The thing which is really at the heart of this victory is, as I have written so many times, the triumph of the ideals of profound opposition to the old class society; the aspiration to overturn this society (and not simply to correct it or see it improved); it is, in general, what we call a drive for socialism. The French students shout that the beach lies beneath the roadway, as they tear up paving-stones around the Sorbonne and throw them at the police. Here at Naples too the roadway has been torn up, a roadway of humiliation and capitalist exploitation, the paving-stones have become votes, and lying underneath them we too have found a beach, our renewed hopes for victory.

Here in the Metropolitan, I am no longer sitting among the candidates, but among the elected. My election was greeted with stunned silence, which reveals a lot. All the people in the Ambassador's Hotel congratulated me and one member of the staff, who recognizes me by 'those same shoes that you leave outside your door at night', said to me in sincere tones, 'We were sure that you wouldn't make it. You were so quiet. You never went around promoting yourself, and you didn't even ask us to vote for you. The people who wanted to get elected went to a great deal of trouble to advertise their list-number. But you never said anything. And here in Naples people do anything, stoop to any depths, to get themselves elected: friends, relatives, personal groups, connections, luncheons, meetings, receptions and so on.' He makes me understand, making lavish use of examples, how somebody who has managed to become a Deputy (of course it is understood here that we are talking about the social-democratic and bourgeois portion of the spectrum) finds his personal position so instantly improved that an oil well might well have just been discovered in his backyard. Election means an enormous qualitative leap, a flight to the moon, a total change in one's life, ease and wealth, now that the controls of public power are in your hands. As Gava's case teaches, you can start from zero, or almost zero, and become a financial power of the first magnitude. I explained to the porter that *with us* it is a different story, even in terms of salary, since a Communist Deputy gives the lion's share of it to the Party every month, just as journalists on *l'Unità* do (and I think, in terms of proportions, that the journalists, given their national labour contracts, sign away an even greater proportion of their earnings). I explain to him that we are left with roughly what a specialized technician in the North might earn.

This question of how much a Deputy earns is an important matter that the people ought to be informed about. But I do not yet have the exact figures which would enable me to demonstrate how our Party is different, and talking to this man I promise myself to get those figures in the future since I believe that this is the way things should be done in a party like ours. I think that we, as the PCF does, ought to publish regularly exactly what a Communist Deputy earns in a month.

In the rest of our talk, I try to impress on the porter that my election shows that the *really* important thing is to create a direct political link with the masses, to carry out a correct political activity, both inside and outside the Party. For the people – the working class above all, and also the youth, the new intellectuals and others – are fundamentally honest, in a real and genuine sense, and ultimately judge us on our ideas and our ability to transform these into reality. This has nothing to do with the old forms of electoralism.

I can also tell you a little more about my own election, in rough terms at least, on the basis of the figures given out during the formal ceremony at which we were proclaimed Deputies. This solemn ceremony took place the day before yesterday in the famous Castel Capuano, the Hall of Justice, immediately the magistrates had finished sorting through the hundreds of thousands of preference votes to piece together the electoral mosaic. It was, as the French would say, *un travail de romains*. My election is due to the fact that a number of workers' centres gave me their preference votes. Out of the 24,000 *preferenze* that I got, Castellammare and its environs contributed roughly 8,000, and Torre del Greco gave me 3,000; both of these are places where the Federation had 'recommended' my name. I do not have many other specific figures at my disposal, but it seems pretty clear that without these workers' votes, I would not have been elected. In fact, even with them, I only came in ninth out of ten Communists elected on our list (which includes not only Naples but Caserta as well). In the sub-proletarian quarters of the city, which I have written so much about, I got another ten thousand votes.

Our three *capolista* are on the stage of the Metropolitan, and the preference votes won by them can only be described as an avalanche. The first comrade on the list got 131,469 *preferenze*; the second, 78,380; the third, who passed to second, 94,829. These extraordinary figures are, I would wager, not even imaginable in the rest of Italy where, the farther North you go, the greater is the tendency to vote strictly for lists, for party programmes, and much, much less for individuals.

Now Longo rises and prepares to speak. Even before he opens his mouth, the crowd in the Metropolitan salutes *his personal triumph*. And this is neither pure formality nor simply a pragmatic recognition due the titular head of the Party. What is it that this crowd so sincerely applauds in this man, I ask myself, that goes beyond even the victory of his party? For me, there is no doubt at all. It recognizes his ability to break with old habits and schemas. Longo has proven himself in the last few years to be a man capable of making significant policy choices. He showed this when he, personally, assumed the responsibility, in the face of Soviet opposition, of proposing to the leadership of the PCI that Togliatti's famous 'Yalta Testament' should be published. He also demonstrated these capacities during this electoral campaign by going personally to Prague – and in so doing, he sacrificed personal appearances and preference votes – in order to get a better comprehension of both the immediate and long-term significance of developments there. And, finally, he also demonstrated these abilities of his when, last April, he invited a number of spokesmen for the student movement to have a direct dialogue with him in his study – against the opposition of a good part of the leadership of the Party. But the students came, and they spoke for four hours, with Longo listening to everything, not getting upset when he heard serious criticisms launched against the PCI and its policies. It was this exchange which led him to write an article in *Rinascita*,[1] in which he explicitly stated that a Communist Party should not see politics as beginning and ending solely in terms of its own structure and policies, but should instead be conceived as a party through which the working

1. The article, 'Il movimento studentesco e la lotta anticapitalista', appeared in *Rinascita*, 3 May 1968, pp. 13-16. (Trans.)

class organizes its advent to power thanks to a new historic bloc of forces, including new allies: youth and students. This gesture of Longo's freed the Party from what might have become a rigid stance towards the student movement, and prevented the crystallization of an attitude of out-and-out condemnation or 'excommunication'. I also think that this gesture laid the groundwork for freeing the Party, at the base, to move in the direction of a real alliance with the new generation of political activists.

'I wanted to be here,' Longo began, 'to emphasize how very proud the comrades of Naples must be to have achieved an advance of over 4.5 per cent in the city, attaining a percentage as high as that of Turin (24.6 per cent), and falling only a bit short of Genoa (31.3 per cent).' Genoa is the scene of the most impressive gains in the entire country. I notice that Longo does not mention that we have passed Milan, where the PCI obtained 23 per cent of the votes. Longo proceeds in his precise, uncluttered style: 'A common element in the elections was the increase of our vote in the proletarian cities: we did better wherever social tensions and the general struggle have been most acute. We advanced in the South wherever we were able to understand and direct popular protest against the conditions of inferiority that are imposed by the DC and the Centre-Left.'[2]

After Longo spoke, our *capolista* launched straight into a number of burning issues and said roughly this: 'We older comrades can only offer one thing to the young people who brought so much enthusiasm, self-sacrifice and optimism to this victory: tenacity, continuity and perseverance in the struggle. Together we are a well-trained Party, capable of overcoming the ills and vices of the South – *trasformismo*, the cultivation of personal followings and so on – and together we are a united Party, one that discusses and then acts, breaking the vicious circle between verbal extremism and passivity. . . .'

These are very appropriate comments, and the challenge and polemic contained in them is recognized by a good deal of applause from the youth. But – looking out over this young crowd – I am also forced to question, and I try to imagine what the attitude of the Party Centre 'of Rome' (as we say here) would be if – unexpectedly – there was to develop a new local leadership in Naples which openly criticized the way the Party is run at present; if the conditions were to be

2. In spite of the general advance made by the PCI nationally, its vote in fact fell in many parts of the South and Naples was, in some senses, an exception. (Trans.)

created for a profound renovation of the Party – for these are also the conditions for creating, here in Naples, a real policy. I am not optimistic about this. The problems I have become involved in are hardly new ones, they raise numerous delicate questions of responsibility and would inevitably create a lot of 'guilt complexes'. All in all, there are undoubtedly sectors of the Party which would be perfectly happy to see things continue just as they are; who would not be averse to tolerating certain distortions and harmful practices in silence. It amounts to an involuntary, but habitual, *omertà*, which goes through two separate but connected phases. The first thing is to castigate the functionaries for their defects (as the *capolista* is doing right now). The second is to close ranks behind the apparatus and praise its devotion as soon as the apparatus itself runs the risk of being the object of criticism from the rank-and-file – criticism whose repercussions would be far-reaching indeed, infringing the whole principle of the *continuity of the leadership*.

Looking at the leaders of the Federation, in fact, you can see that, with good reason, they have a satisfied air about them today. After all, they feared a defeat and here is a tremendous victory, in which their own sacrifices and efforts have certainly played a part. Even the problem of what to do with me, which had bothered them a good deal, has been pretty satisfactorily resolved, and the agreement they came to with the 'Centre' has been respected. But in spite of this, I still cannot really convince myself that the way they view things will, after today, become any more profound, and tomorrow things will probably begin from exactly where they left off prior to the elections. I also ask myself if now I will be permitted to occupy a humble political space in this complex and 'closed' world where very special laws exist – laws which often impose themselves over the kind of laws that ought to govern a party which is a revolutionary vanguard.

What, in fact, will I be able to do as an elected representative? Will I be able – this is the first thing that comes into my mind – to bring with me into Parliament some picture of the dramatic reality of Naples; to use Parliament as a platform from which to denounce the situation forcefully? What do I even know about this Parliament, this foreign planet? I *do* know something about the Party. What will my future as a militant be? On the one hand, I am quite clear: I will work at the base of the Party, where I have encountered so many revolutionary forces. In fact, for us there is really no other option than that of direct action with the masses, direct contact with the people. This is the only way to defeat the pseudo-revolutionary flatteries of the salon radicals: the experience of the non-communist French Left teaches us that not getting involved at the base only leads to the inevitable separation of a group of intellectuals from the masses, from reality, and they, in the end, get more and more involved with themselves, ending up in satisfied contemplation of their own navels. On the other hand, I feel the overwhelming need for direct political action, an urgency to make a direct contribution to changing the present state of affairs in the most profound fashion possible, and hence to work side by side with new political forces.

But when and where will I get the chance to take part in a political struggle? What if I find myself alone in this? I tell myself that – even if I am alone – I will fight all the same. I can no longer look out over a crowd like this and see it as just so many people. These are human beings, and real communists. In the last seventy days, the result of my shock, my sharp reactions, my (often frenetic) research, has been a violent – and rational – passion for Naples. I really love this dramatic city and its people, whom I have come to see as having been systematically betrayed.

I don't know why, but all at once I remember a passage from Descartes (I can't check whether I am quoting it accurately): 'In order to arrive at the Truth, one must, at least once in one's lifetime, do away with all received opinions and reconstruct, from the very beginning and from the very foundations, the entire system of everything one knows. . . .' In this city, one encounters candour about as frequently as one encounters concreteness. Have I, then, been capable of discovering the truth? I can hardly be sure, but I have tried. In Naples, the capitalist system can be seen with the naked eye, a dinosaur in action. And the Party can also be seen with the naked eye. Here, there are no nuances, no skilful mediations, no sophisticated intermediaries.

But it would be a serious mistake to slip into the catchword, 'This is the way Naples is' – which might even contain a suggestion of racism – because, in reality, *this is the way the system is*, with all its primitive exploitative violence. Everything that *we say about the domination of this system* can be seen here, where the system has been carried to its logical conclusions. 'The bourgeoisie has no pleasure except that of degrading all pleasure.' Some of those beautiful slogans of the Paris uprising are still buzzing in my head. 'Well said,' I think to myself as I look at the youth here. Then there is another one as well: *Be realistic and ask for the impossible.* . . . In my pocket I feel a thick sheet of paper and cannot recall what it is, until I suddenly remember that it is the photocopy of a document given to me by a citizen. It is the reproduction of a card sent to him by the Audit Office, printed on both sides, saying the following: 'You are hereby informed that your inquiry into the matter of your military pension has been filed and will henceforth be referred to by its case number, 735602'. If this is a photocopy, it must mean that the citizen in question made up several of them, to distribute among all of our recently-elected candidates. It is my first 'recommendation', the first gesture that qualifies me in my new capacity as a Deputy. And it can hardly be seen as a minor episode, here, in the theatre, today. I get up, more out of guilt than anything else, and go over to P.A. to ask for some information, figuring that if anyone knows, it ought to be him: he has been a scrupulous Deputy for over twenty years. He whispers (in order not to disturb the speeches) that when he was elected in 1948, the file numbers were at 300,000, and that by now the examination of cases has reached dossier number 600,000; it will take at least five more years to get to *my number*. Hence, unless I can exercise some impossible kind of influence on the president of the Audit Office, it will be five years before my 'recommendation' will even be heard. I calculate: five years, and the War over for twenty-three years, and the *Special Section for War Pensions* at dossier 600,000. . . . There is time for another war. What should be done? Certainly I will try to 'push' this request forward, but that is no real solution; trying to solve the problem in this fashion would be like trying to bail out the ocean with a bucket.

Naples and the South are crammed full of people crying out for houses, work, pensions, etc., and they always approach the problem as if it were something for which they have to be 'recommended', rather than something they have a right to demand. The distinction between a right and a recommendation, since it concerns not single individuals but masses of people, whole populations, enables the system to avoid its most serious responsibilities, and enables it to maintain a *faceless*, unresponsive character. There is on the one hand the one who is in need, and on the other hand there is the one (man or party) who can intervene in favour of *the needy* with a 'recommendation', and there is, finally, the fleeting concept of public or state authority, seen as a beehive of offices in Naples and Rome, where everything is possible for the influential man: he can get a flat allocated, a war pension, a subsidy. . . .

There are two fundamental dramas in Neapolitan life, work and housing. And for the latter even more than the former – remember that 200,000 Neapolitans live in *bassi*! – the *recommendation* is decisive. Housing is at the centre of all the squalid trafficking and corruption, so much so that you still can find – as I have during the past few days – that the vast majority of flats allocated by the city in the course of all these years are in the hands of respectable bourgeois, not the poor. For example, if you look over the blocks of flats in Via P. Castellino and Via Marconi, you will find them occupied by the well-off and even by DC hierarchs, all of whom pay 30,000 lire a month.

Even those who most easily qualify for housing, those with the highest priority-rating, go out of their way to get their recommendation, which is seen as the only protective device they have. They do not even really hope to get a flat by it, but rather to avoid being for ever deprived of one, and thus at least for the future to protect themselves against the fraud which undoubtedly operates against them. As I am thinking these thoughts, I see, in the first row, the woman from the 'shanty-dwellers' of the Arar camp – a *bidonville* in an advanced state of collapse – who, in the May-day march, had her own shanty lifted bodily on to an uncovered van. Then she, her husband and their three children stood at the windows of this house being dragged along like a snail's shell, with all of its doors and windows thrown wide open to reveal everything inside. From this vantage point, she screamed out at the crowd along the entire length of the march: *This is how you live in Naples!* There are 540 shanties just like hers to be eliminated; they are occupied by thousands of people who do not have even the money necessary to pay the rent of the *bassi*. From far off, the woman sees me and we smile at each other.

Often we Communists, rather than try to break this vicious circle of misery (and, for example, come up with a denunciation of building speculation which goes right to the heart of this modern Plague of Naples), run off to present our own recommendations. We bring the shanty-dwellers to the Town Hall for a little subsidy, given that there are no *houses for them*. We exert our little bit of pressure on the municipal *Giunta* for housing allocations. All the unions will be there, too, including the CGIL and, in the public's eyes, they are all equally involved in the whole business.

Everyone recommends everyone else, ourselves included: we make recommendations and we recommend each other in turn, prying a few lire from the Prefect or the Mayor and making them turn this pittance over to the homeless, who in turn will go away happy because at least now they can eat for a little while longer. But it all starts up again in a week or a month, because the whole sub-soil of Naples is corroded and caves in every time it rains, bringing houses down with it. The homeless have faith in us as they would in a powerful organization to which they feel themselves associated, and which, after all, leads them victoriously to the Town Hall after their houses collapse around them and manages to wring some money out of the municipality – money which, of course, belongs to the people (and is doled out 30,000 lire at a time). For in fact the Commune of Naples, that exceptional centre of deals and 'simony', by virtue of the *special laws* regularly passed for it (*100 thousand million lire* from the last appropriation are still in the municipal coffers), is actually extremely rich. By begging, it manages to save a great deal of money, which it keeps in a special fund for the more serious cases of popular unrest, for natural catastrophes, etc. I have been informed that of the one billion lire allocated for public housing (Gescal, etc.) between 1963 and 1972, to date only 151 thousand million have been spent, while the sharks of the building trade circle jealously around the remainder to make sure that not a mouthful of their prey escapes them. And this is typical of the way that Naples lives: capitalism pays the barest minimum to ensure that a truly productive structure is never allowed to grow. It pays to preserve the parasitic character of the city, which is necessary to its own equilibrium halfway between progress and regress. This, I tell myself, is the synthesis I have come up with after this campaign. Capitalism has invented, for the masses 'marginal' to the productive process in Naples and the South, a whole system of relationships which in many ways is similar to the relationship between the US and the so-called 'third world'. Reacting to needs generated by the role of imperialism in entire continents, capitalism decides to 'exclude' or 'push aside' enormous masses of human beings, increasing their alienation or even tearing away from them any hopes of things ever changing for the better. All this is done so that monopoly capital can keep large markets (here we see the rationale for the construction of Alfa-Sud, which at most will reabsorb the 15,000 workers who lost their jobs in industry in 1967, and whose real aim is to foist economy cars on these disinherited people) and a ridiculously ill-paid workforce (just look at the emigration problem in the South – and the resulting influx of foreign currency sent home by the emigré workers).

The entire dynamic of capitalist exploitation has its *raison d'être* in the system itself, in the dichotomy between superdevelopment and underdevelopment, and all these letters that I have been writing are not only aimed at describing the real conditions of the lives of the people, but also at coming up with an answer to *the* decisive strategic question: how to smash the system's mechanism of accumulation in Naples, in the South and in Italy. The characteristics of Naples' 'tertiary' economy can only aggravate the general picture, especially as the industrialization process in the North reaches more and more advanced levels, and as the whole national economy is integrated into the Common Market. This system, concentrated in the Paris-Brussels-Hamburg 'triangle' will push the 'peripheral' cities into an even more dependent role in terms of their designation as cities which are to be distributors of services. And as those characteristics intensify, so too will their 'charitable' relationship with capitalism grow even more dismal.

The workers' revolt which is shaking France to her roots at this very moment gives the lie to those who have spoken so often of the integration of the workers into the system, and who even go so far as to claim that workers in an advanced capitalist society thrive like 'rats in cheese'. I think the same lie has been exploded, with these elections, here in Naples, and this seems even more true if we look to the future. I also think of the knowledge I have gained of the powerful working class here, and of the admiration I have come to hold for it. But this proletariat – which is the city's most exploited, most homogeneous and most revolutionary class – must learn to extend its activities into all of the popular strata and rid itself of every residue of sectarianism (whose origins go all the way back to Bordiga). It has to wash away the permanent stain of its separation from and hostility towards the sub-proletarian strata of the people. I have already pointed out how complete the confusion on this issue can be; while the sub-proletariat dismisses the workers as capitalists, the workers have nothing but silent scorn for the sub-proletariat. Only then can the proletariat achieve the necessary level of strategic consciousness that will enable it, as Lenin said, to go with its revolutionary vanguard *among all the classes of the people, sending the detachments of its army in all directions.*

I can only see our leaders from behind as they look attentively out over the audience, for I am seated in the last row of chairs on the stage. But I wonder if they are fully aware of the Party's problems – and the way these problems have been developing in the midst of everyone's self-satisfaction (or total indifference). I wonder if they are aware of the Party's responsibility for these problems. Is this a problem that only concerns Naples? I think that, even in our language, there are objective obstacles to the renovation of the Party and to what is called the *restoration of Marxism*. We say, for example, as our *capolista* is doing at this very moment, *Let the youth go forward*; but then we add almost instantly afterwards that 'youth is not determined simply by chronology'. Or else we come out with a hypothesis for a new physics of politics by which 'we change ourselves while remaining the same'; or else we trot out our old formula of *renovation with continuity*, which is very much like Lavoisier's 'nothing is lost, nothing destroyed'. All of these ingenious formulae, assimilated at all levels of the Party, show, in effect, how incredibly difficult it is to change anything.

As, brick by brick, I place all these fragments of ideas together, I feel that I am climbing on to the shoulders of an imminent future, where things will have to be different from the way they are now. I ask myself: what is the Party like, today, in other parts of the South, let's say in Sicily, and in the rest of Italy as well? I really do not know very much about those other places. And what I have written to you is perhaps boring and has certainly been rushed. But I think nevertheless, that I would happily read letters like these, written from *inside the Party* with the same kind of spirit that has gone into writing them. For this reason I think that, when I come to Paris at the end of these 'events' which in many ways already appear to be of great historic importance, I will give you this mountain of paper that I have accumulated, day by day, and almost hour by hour.

The celebration has ended, and we sing the 'Internationale'. Longo, who really is a very sensitive man in spite of his reputation of being as hard as nails (Croce once maliciously asked if it were true that when Longo was the commander of the Garibaldi Brigade in Spain during the Civil War he really had, as was rumoured, raped . . . 2,000 nuns!), who hates lies and obfuscations, who is used to leaving his door open to anyone, Longo appears to be deeply touched by the triumphant joy which is erupting all around him here in the theatre. And this, too, is the Party. There are pure men at every level of the apparatus, uncontaminated combatants whose defining characteristic is their dedication to socialism and to the revolution; and, because of this constant principle of their lives, they are capable, come what may, of rediscovering intact their 'style of work' as revolutionaries. This is the real patrimony of the Party, the apple of its eye. And it is this that makes us the best part of this society in which we live.

But the problem which faces us is political and theoretical. How can we bring the Party back to what Lenin called a certain 'style of work', a certain form of political direction from the top down, in the context of a struggle which is a struggle for socialism?

I will end this now. One day I will even pick up where I leave off. Finishing these lines in a great rush, I still keep thinking how I will be in Paris – another Paris, another France – in two days; and I think of how every great revolutionary event in France has had a direct political impact on Italian history. For this reason I ask myself: where are we, then? At what point are the revolutionary forces of Western Europe, as red flags wave over the Renault factories in France?

Maria Antonietta

Dear Louis,   *Naples, 1 July 1968*

I am sending you the letters written while you were sick, my final contributions to our correspondence project, which was to be written 'without any plans for publication'. The letters might benefit from a set of conclusions, but I think that it is their lack of any conclusions that makes them interesting. In them, I have tried only to record certain facts and moods, for three basic reasons: (1) because this was a way of establishing a political connection with you, who helped me put the things I saw in a larger context, and who also spurred me on to carry on a *political* election campaign, something that would have an enduring political impact on me; (2) because some of the things I witnessed seemed to me to be significant if one wishes to examine more closely the reality of the Party and the people of the South, and in particular of Naples; (3) because these letters – although they are incomplete and often schematic – were written before the historic lesson of the French 'events'. Re-reading them now, they seem to me, without my having intended it, to bring into sharper focus the whole question of the relationship between the revolutionary party and the masses, the party and the working class, the Party and youth, the Party and mass movements – the key questions, perhaps, that *'les événements'* raised for the workers' movement in the West, cutting through every mystification that the so-called 'post-industrial societies' could erect. On the walls of the Music Amphitheatre of the University of Nanterre I saw a graffito which, ironically, struck at the heart of 'my' Neapolitan reality: 'To see Nanterre is to live. Go to Naples and die with the Club Méditerranée'.

Numerous episodes are still missing from the letters, episodes which might help clarify how, beginning with theory, I managed to find a guide for action. And for all those who claim that Marxism today is an absolute abstraction, and who speak of 'laboratory Marxism' when they refer to works that lay out Marx's ideas with scientific rigour, all I can say is that your letters are the best kind of response to these accusations.

You already know the electoral results, in broad terms. I came to Paris at the end of May – you were still in the hospital (on whose main gates was written, 'Unlimited General Strike') – and the first thing you asked me, since you were already quite well-informed about the PCI's advance, was, 'Well, did they elect you or not?' I had been so caught up in the 'events' that I had forgotten to tell you, or to write anything about it. You were pleased and a little surprised; you too had thought that the undertaking was a difficult one, and you too had written off my election as unlikely. I didn't bring you these letters then, not only because I hadn't typed them up, but also because I wanted some time to think about what they said, and meant. In other words, I wanted to be able to give them to you only after I had a chance to think about them in some quieter moments.

There are several images that are still burned into my memory. Not accidentally, the most vivid of these have to do with the incredible outburst of joy that followed the news of our victory. You would have thought that we had taken power.

The workers' celebration at Castellammare, which lasted the whole night of 20–21 May, seemed, as soon as the results were made public, like a celebration of the Liberation – only as if this time the people had been liberated from capitalism. Imagine what a Neapolitan Bastille

Day would be like, and you will get some idea. I will never forget the night march, with all the torches and placards, and people in their night-shirts at the windows. 'Bandiera Rossa' was being sung at top volume, and everyone was up, either watching or participating. The line of marchers seemed endless: at the very head of the line was a swarm of Vespas, with their silencers removed and with the young riders standing up on them and shouting out news of our victory; right behind them came, all together, those who had been elected, along with other comrades, both workers and leaders of the PCI section.

But anyone aware of the line-up of forces which still exists in Parliament could not but feel depressed even at that moment. I suddenly felt very melancholy, for I knew that the bourgeoisie always finds a way to rob the people of an electoral victory. Hence I was silent, closed off, incapable of communicating: yes, they had won, but precisely because of this the hour of the decisive showdown was brought closer. And how were we going to continue the fight? But I did not want to be a kill-joy, so I just kept quiet.

At the moment that the votes are cast, the comrades seem to believe that you can overturn the whole world with ballots. This is not really all that surprising, since an electoral campaign does raise all of the great issues and most idealistic choices of the proletariat: socialism, proletarian internationalism and the battle against imperialism and capitalism.

Another, more depressing memory: two days before the election, a worker at 'Avis' of Castellammare, Adolfo Gallinaro, died. He was forty-five years old and had five children. It all happened on account of one of those completely paradoxical, but all-too-common (for us), work injuries. His arm was crushed by a machine and was duly bandaged by the factory doctor. At first he just asked for a few days off, but then, when it became clear that he had been seriously hurt, he filed a request for an early pension on the grounds that he was now a civil invalid, for he felt weaker and sicker and knew he could not work again. The doctor said that this was quite impossible, with such a minor injury, and soon stopped even taking off the bandages. The illness lasted two or three weeks. Gangrene spread inexorably under the bandages. The coffin, in his house, is covered with red carnations, put there by his comrades from the factory. Adolfo Gallinaro's widow goes over to a dresser and, from under a plaster dog, takes out some ballots and walks towards us. She is tense and seems a little intimidated by the clarity of the message she delivers: 'It was his last wish: he told us all to vote for the P C I . . . On Sunday, come and take us all to the polling station.' This, in its own way, is a true worker's testament. The vote transcends the ballot paper, in the sense that the vote manifests the highest aspiration of all: a will to socialism. Day after day, in countless ways, it has become clear to me that this electoral campaign, in May 1968, was the manifestation – just as the 'events' in France were a manifestation, if in an extremely different way – of an irresistible movement of the working class and the young people towards social-ism, in the heart of the Western world. This is essentially what these general elections reveal. Otherwise two things would be completely impossible to explain: (1) our ability to take such an important step forward, without having even one-tenth of the money or other means that the class enemy has at his disposal; and (2) our relative failure in local elections (even following on the heels of political victories) in the South – for these are always characterized by a low level of politiciz-ation and a high degree of localism.

The other image which is fixed in my memory is that of the death of another comrade, a worker from Sant'Antimo, Raffaele Tarantino, the father of ten children. He was struck down by a heart attack in the course of an argument with the electoral officer in charge of a polling station over whether a number of ballots could rightfully be attributed to the P C I. This death, in a manner of speaking, is certainly a sym-bolic one. An electoral battle has its obscure heroes in our Party.

The battle drains, to the last drop, the combative energies of the militants, of the comrades, of the rank-and-file, of sympathizers, and even of those who – and they are the great majority – disappear from the sections for the rest of the year. During an election, the Party goes through an unexpected season of organizational vigour and inexhaust-ible political labour. In the course of the electoral struggle, vast amounts of personal sacrifice, intelligence and initiative are poured out by thousands of simple comrades. The Party is like a great tree which, dormant for a long time, suddenly sprouts branches, leaves and fruit on every limb. It is the contact with the *reality* that surrounds it which fertilizes the P C I.

But then, once the election is past, it is as if a long, hard winter has set in, and the Party falls dormant once more. I went back to a few of the largest sections: with the tension of the elections dissipated, I found them quiet, turned in on themselves, tired. Once the joyous moment of victory has passed, there comes, once again, the realization that a long hard struggle is ahead, a struggle which moreover presents no clear prospects for changing the balance of forces which still so strongly favour capitalism. An English journalist from the left wing of the Labour Party was in Castellammare on the night after the elections and – with a meticulous, accountant's mind – he and the comrades calculated that to obtain a parliamentary majority, the PCI, if it maintained the same proportional advance in every election, would have to wait until the year 2008. The parliamentary road to socialism is as long as the road to Mars. And maybe this realization also contributes to the political lassitude in the sections.

I am well aware of the fact that this bunch of letters I am sending to you raises much more serious problems than it solves. But still, I think that these letters are far from useless in that they propose, re-propose and underline facts and issues which are unavoidably linked to our future, as militants and as a revolutionary party. I am not an external witness to events in the Party; I am intimately tied to its history and I participate fully in its daily ups and downs. I try to approach problems from the inside, using the technical means of political investigation and writing everything down, *hic et nunc*. I know that, on account of this method, the lack of historical 'background' can seem a disadvantage. All I can say is that this lack is deliberate, since I only intended, from the outset, to live seventy days of an electoral campaign among the masses and within the Party, at a moment that was not amorphous, but *typical* of a party like ours. And the only historical point that was absolutely necessary to bear in mind, for this, was the creation by Togliatti, in 1944, of the 'mass party'.

I also believe that there is quite a dose of political optimism in these letters – because the letters show the enormous combative potential which exists in the working class and in the people; they show how terribly far ahead *of us* the masses are – as you wrote in February, long before the explosion in France; and they also show the immense resources we will have at our disposal if we only manage to penetrate among the people, not in the limited and qualified period of an electoral campaign, but in a concerted, conscious attempt to carry forward a revolutionary strategy.

If the electoral success at Naples is seen as a workers' resurgence – as it clearly is, in a sense that goes far beyond the mere voting figures –

then it is easy to see that *new times* are upon us, there is a need for *new* organizational forms and *new* forms of struggle. This is why we need a critical examination of just what the Party is, as the indispensable and irreplaceable guiding organ for every revolutionary struggle; the permanent element of mass mobilization, capable of expressing and embodying a *mass line* and a continuous, mass-based, internally democratic life. Bureaucratic forms, which Lenin fought against in the last years of his life (primarily on the basis of his political intuition and therefore, unfortunately, never spelled out systematically), and electoralistic deformations in the Party (which I have hinted at in these letters, and which represent defeats for the masses) are only parts of a much more general and important issue: the link between the Party and the working class, the link between the Party and the masses.

It has become clear, in the light of everything that is going on in the West, that a Communist Party cannot have a charismatic relationship with the working class. The question that arises is: How can the Party become a valid instrument for guiding (in the proper sense) the revolutionary struggle? What are its genuine leadership abilities with regard to the working class and its allies? How ought the Party to be represented in the movement, when students and workers are organizing themselves in completely new forms of struggle – inside the factories, outside the factories, in the schools, outside the schools – and when the Party is denied an *a priori mandate*? It is true that there are some phenomena on our left today that recall Lenin's *Left-Wing Communism : An Infantile Disorder*, but it is useful to recall as well that Lenin wrote that certain 'opportunistic errors' could cause a vacuum on the Left which in turn gives rise to these characteristics.

The central question, today, is that the whole of the old magisterial design for a party with certain characteristics – and we Italian Communists are the architects of this design – is called into question by the entry on to the political stage of large masses who are not organized by the Party. It is called into question by the spontaneous extension of a socialist spirit provoked by the capitalist system's contradictions. What is going on all around us is the enormous growth of revolutionary forces, and hence the challenge to this type of party, a challenge that develops at the base of the Party, among the young and among the most clear-headed militants. The relationship of the Party to the masses must be re-evaluated. We must address ourselves, on both a theoretical and practical level, to the question of what, exactly, a Communist Party – its cadres and its structures – should be, and how it can leave room for voluntary political forces and actions.

There is, in fact, a contradiction between the entrenched professionals in the apparatus – who get a mandate based on faith as much as anything else – and the continuous call for political volunteers. These volunteers are automatically put in a *de facto* position of inferiority with regard to the apparatus, because they have no way of influencing the Party line. (Even the Party's financial autonomy, to say nothing of its ability to broaden its areas of influence and activity, depends on the entry into its ranks of thousands of new cadres, who do not draw salaries and who hence look on militancy in the PCI in a very different way from those who are full-time party functionaries.) The kind of apparatus which has been created – with all the attendant bureaucratic incrustations – risks becoming an obstacle to the very influx it purports to desire. I saw this process occur time and time again in the campaign, when not only did new forces appear, but leaders of a new type also appeared, forged in the heat of struggle. And the kind of bureaucratic establishment we have also makes it nearly impossible for these new leaders to gain influential positions in the Party.

Another thing that needs rethinking is the reason or reasons for the continuous decline of membership in the Party. The difference between our organized forces and our electoral strength continues to grow at the expense of the former. In fact, as absurd as it sounds, there seems to be a negative relationship here: at Naples, *we have never had, with such low membership* (34,560), *such a high number of votes* (373,332). Similarly, the perennial fluctuation and turnover of members, who enter and leave the PCI with alarming rapidity, is connected to the internal structure of the Party, which is becoming progressively more closed. Of course, it would be unfair to say that the leaders of the Party do not know these things, or to imply that they do not worry about them.

The problem of the Party is, as Lenin has taught us, that of its strategy: 'Without revolutionary theory,' he repeated again and again, 'there can be no revolutionary movement. . . . Only a party guided by a vanguard theory can fulfil its function as a vanguard in battle.' Perhaps this is the key to understanding how it is that, after the impressive growth of the Party in the elections, in the following period –

except when great political and social struggles break out – our organization takes on again an internal life which is to a great extent stunted and stifled. It falls back into a bureaucratic routine, guided by a calendar of events, with a few fixed highlights: the celebration of certain dates, the month of the party press, the recruitment drive, local elections and so on. Most of the time, the implementation of directives comes to be seen as little more than the carrying out of orders which come, periodically, from the Centre to the provinces. This kind of work keeps the functionaries occupied a good deal more than does any original reflection on what is going on around them: what is *their own* reality like at that moment? what are *their own people* up to at the moment? what is important about that *particular* point in history, etc.? The directives offer the functionaries *a pre-interpreted Truth.* And, during these periods, the Federations often operate like normal office buildings, with fixed hours, and many leaders do not take the trouble to listen to or understand the very people to whom we make our appeal. And even less frequently do they seek these people out in their own territory.

It thus often happens that we hold interminable meetings where everyone conjugates problems with the verb 'to speak' instead of the verb 'to do', and nevertheless ends up going to bed with a clear conscience, convinced of having *done* everything necessary and possible. We claim that the functionary of the apparatus is a professional revolutionary. This, indeed, is a noted Leninist principle. But the question, I suggest, is to see, *at all levels of the Party*, when and under what conditions the functionary is transformed from a *professional revolutionary* into a *professional bureaucrat.* The relationship between Federation and centre is based on the principle of *loyalty to the line of the Party.* This is a pretty broad conception, but in its most vulgar interpretation it becomes the principle of *uncritical loyalty to the leadership.* Often this leadership is seen as primarily preoccupied with preserving its own power – which is certainly to do it an injustice – and the repercussions on the attitudes of the apparatus are just what you would expect. You find leaders being vilified in the privacy of the corridors, but exalted in public. On the other side, the accusation of *trasformismo*, when used by a leader, can serve as a Sword of Damocles hanging over the head of anyone foolish enough to express *an opinion* which differs from the particular vision of reality which that leader might have.

In this context, even if we are not a church, the vice of *double truth* (or *duplicity*) discredits, at least in some cases, the democratic life of the Party. There is Official Truth, but there is also the truth of real internal relationships. In a party as complex in its internal workings as ours, where loyalty is not taken lightly, and where the Official Truth of the Party is, by definition, revolutionary, I think you need half your energy simply not to fall victim to the worst characteristics of the Party itself, so that only the other half remains to fight the class enemy. In Paris, I worked 'like a machine' because I could channel all my energies in one direction and did not have to disperse them on two fronts. What will I do now? This is not a personal problem, but a general one: how can we restore 100 per cent capacity to the Communists, to channel all our energies against the class enemy?

Meanwhile, new needs for action and political struggle are welling up in the masses, as, little by little, the people get increasingly exasperated (these letters are clear evidence of this exasperation) and as capitalism, faced with increasingly serious contradictions, which it is increasingly unable to resolve, takes a double tack. On the one hand it lashes the workers mercilessly, while on the other it suggests – in a clear attempt to blackmail and intimidate – that it is intending reactionary adventures and *coups d'état*.

If, at the end of these letters, I had to say what is *the problem of problems* I would say: It is the *problem of the Party*, which, in turn, is inextricably tied to the problem of its *political line*. More concretely: What must we do to transform the enormous charge of energy that the Party releases during an electoral campaign into a *permanent* revolutionary charge? Even if I have no answers to this question, I have tried, in these letters, to single out a few of the most important issues that will have to be faced. The main issue is that the problem concerns *the entire party* and not just a part of it. There is not, in fact, a *better part* and a *worse part* of the Party, those *with a mandate* and those *without a mandate*. The Party is every one of us, and the concept that the person with more power in the Party is right is a false concept, as is the assumption that someone who is a member of the apparatus must naturally be *more of a communist*.

The whole party faces the same problem, even if in the apparatus or at the top levels in Rome there is a good deal of difference over what is the best solution. There is no doubt that there are serious differences in the leadership. But I do not believe that you have to find the right answer in what one or another individual leader proposes. The PCI is not like the DC, where one person backs Rumor in the hope of modifying the position of Fanfani while another backs Moro to pressure Piccoli and – through this interplay of conflicting pressures, involving tightrope acts and ruses worthy of the Florentine Court during the Renaissance – comes up with one government or programme rather than another. This method not only solves nothing, it risks creating a space for hypocritical clerics, like Stendhal's Julien Sorel, and ending up, after all the classifications of various forms of *dissent*, exactly at the point of departure. Or else ending up mulling over, in a pathetic way, *the best use to which dissent can be put.*

Moreover, the term 'Left' – which in France covered so many different operations that at a certain point the students involved in the revolt began to speak of 'right-leftists' – often serves only to confuse. It must be made clear, once and for all, that 'leftists', or better, 'true communists', are not identified by their self-proclamation but by their revolutionary praxis. And the PCI has an overwhelming quantity of true revolutionary militants in its ranks, above all in the working class; these men and women are its real patrimony, as I wrote you in my last letter. But, as I have also said on other occasions, there are also very many militant revolutionaries *outside* the Party and we have to do everything possible to bring them into the Party. This has to be done, not to create *factions*, but in order to rethink our entire revolutionary strategy, with full respect for democratic rules. In a Communist Party, there cannot be a Left and Right *tout court*. In fact, these are bourgeois, social-democratic definitions. What can exist are *deviations* of the left or right. And the only distinction possible in the Party is between the communists in the Marxist and Leninist sense of the word and the others – who may be protagonists either of left or of right deviations.

The pressing issue in the PCI is to win the whole Party over to one line instead of another. And the only way you can convince the entire Party is to wage a political battle that *involves* the entire party. Some comrades seem to think that we could make more headway by following the path of the DC or the Socialists, by instituting tendencies or, worse still, organized factions. But I simply cannot agree with this, as I have already said. This approach really closes off options at the very moment that the really pressing need in the Party is that of getting all its militants to participate in the important choices and decisions. So in my opinion, it is the logic of factions and pressures that we must reject. ('The Revolution must be made in men's minds before it can be realized in fact' is a slogan that I saw at the Sorbonne, and, if not interpreted in a 'moralistic' or anarchic way, this does not, in fact, seem to me to be a bad way to approach certain important political questions.) So what we need to do – and it is not an easy task – is to get the whole Party involved in a great clarifying debate.

It will have to be a long and bitter battle, no doubt, but it must also be a coherent and honest one. For it is the masses, after all, who will decide its outcome: and hence it is before the masses that *all problems* will have to be put, with a maximum of clarity. In this sense I think it might also be useful to us to study in much greater depth the Chinese 'Cultural Revolution' and the reasons that it has had such a deep effect on the young masses of the West. And we should also study the extremely different and even contradictory forms that this influence has taken. In the same spirit, we must probe in much greater depth the reasons for the sclerosis of the Party in so many of the socialist countries of Europe, and for the disheartening narrowness of the concept of Leninist democracy under socialism. This means that it is especially important to study what has happened in the country of the October Revolution, the Soviet Union, in order to understand the gulf between restricted élites who decide everything and the gigantic majority which accepts (or submits to) their decisions.

These are only ideas, sketches of ideas, rapid annotations. But I believe that this is the direction in which we must move. I repeat: the whole Party is faced with the same problems; the whole Party, therefore, must participate, in the first person, in the search for solutions.

And here I am, finally, at the end of my correspondence. I am sending you raw material, but its roughness and lack of definitive solutions are compensated for, I think – if only modestly – by the fact that these letters comprise a living document of the reality of the Party and the people in a given, limited time period: two and a half months in the spring of 1968, at Naples, during the course of an electoral campaign. Now that it is all put together, I find that it has a very strong effect on me, even just skimming through it. For this reason, I will tentatively raise the question with you: what should we do with it? I will leave the answer up to you, after you have had the chance to read it all.

Maria Antonietta

Dear M.A.,   *Paris, 21 August 1968*

I have just finished reading your letters (from 7 May to 1 July), and they have deeply moved me. (How did the strike at the Ambassador's Hotel go?)[1]

Your manuscript represents, in its own right, an impressive and concrete vindication of the best-known principles of our doctrine, and it further shows the 'enormous resources' we have at our disposal when we make the effort to carry out political work correctly. I am speaking of the resources of that magnificent working class that 'adopted' you, because it recognized you as one of its own – i.e. it recognized itself in *your actions*.

You are kind enough to ask me what thoughts are inspired in me as I read what you have written. From a certain point onwards, everything functions perfectly well on its own, and I do not see anything I could add to what you have written. Your experience, *transcribed – described* in your particular style, is an impressive document, incredibly full of life and at times very amusing. By the way, have you kept your articles on Naples (the ones you speak of in the letters, and which seem to have earned you so many enemies)? I think you should give rapid and serious thought to using them along with the letters. The letters can be published as they stand.

Has the P C I written anything by way of an analysis on the May–June events in France? I think that was just the first stage of a process that is going to take a long time to play itself out, with many ups and downs,

---

1. The strike failed. No rise or improvement of any kind was conceded. In the succeeding months, a number of people were fired in retaliation for their role in the strike; the official excuse given was that the hotel was overstaffed. Now that it has been determined that there will be no regional pay-scales in Italy (the infamous 'salary cages'), the remaining workers are waiting for their wages to be brought up to parity.

but during which the struggle is going to be continuous. The big question now is: which parts of the working class really wanted, politically, to go beyond the material benefits which were won? Some things were, of course, simply the effect of an instinctive class reaction, a contagious spirit of defence and solidarity against repression, and so on. But certainly the younger workers (less caught up in the old habits of loyalty-discipline, less burdened by the weight of a family and 'freer' economically) were ready to go very far indeed in a political sense. As for the older workers, it is hard to know whether they did not think that things had gone on long enough, for the moment (provisional). But next time, they too will probably be willing to go further.

The results of the elections should not be misunderstood; no one here, from what I can tell, even in the highest positions of authority, is so very sure of what these results might mean. To be sure, the results were overwhelming – but at the same time they are extremely fragile, for it is clear that the elections did not answer the real question that was raised in May. The elections only succeeded in *shifting* the focus of the question, and hence what they answered was something quite different from what was originally asked. You might even say that the elections make up a part of the 'lesson of reality' concerning the parliamentary road.

Louis

Dear M.A.,   *Paris, 20 September 1968*

The better I am able to see (in spite of the fog that still remains), the more convinced I am that your letters deserve to be published. 'Diary of a Communist Candidate in Naples'. All you need is the right formula. The formula of 'Daily Letters' already comes pretty close to what I mean, since it allows you very great freedom.

As for the person to whom the letters are addressed, it should be possible to reduce his role to that of the wall off which a ball bounces, or of an older, very close friend who begins by writing certain things, but then, little by little, disappears from the scene because he has nothing more to say, and can only listen, just as you listened to the things that people told you. The essential thing is what *you* have discovered; it is to let the people speak themselves, as you have in your letters.

The question is quite simply a political one: is it politically correct to publish these letters? I think the answer is *yes*, it is. Many militants, and not only in Italy, are interested in what goes on in a city like Naples, which, with its unemployed sub-proletariat, the domestic industry of its super-exploited 'housewives', and its advanced proletariat in large-scale industries, offers a surprising *picture* of the historic forms of capitalist exploitation. All those who speak of 'industrial society', 'consumer society', 'the new working class', etc., will be obliged to look this reality *in the face*. If one does not understand, concretely, what the sub-proletariat is, how can one possibly understand, for example, what is going on with the sub-proletariat, black and white, in the United States?

Louis

Dear M.A.,   *Wednesday, 22 October 1968*

I am writing this immediately after your telephone call, just to offer a few suggestions. Firstly, fill in the letters with numerical details, i.e. whatever statistics are available (even if they are only on the overall population of Naples, the proportion of proletariat, sub-proletariat, etc.); *make use of* the statistics worked out by the bourgeoisie (this is how Marx and Lenin proceeded).

Please take my advice: do not touch anything, neither in the broad outlines nor, especially, in the 'tone' of the letters. They are marvellously alive. What you should do (in the text or in the notes) is insert as much concrete information as possible. And round the letters out with all the facts and memories that you must be carrying in your head but have not had the time to write down. Re-reading my own letters, I think that they hold together well enough for the purpose they serve. But the important thing is *your* letters: even if you add things to them, you have to keep their 'tone', their 'spontaneity', and their 'emotion', for these are irreplaceable and cannot be duplicated.

I will take up my first point again: for the French edition, you ought to add, as a supplement to the letters, a kind of preface which flatly states all of the facts available through statistics, and you also should have, in the front of the book, a good socio-political map of Naples which includes the city quarters and outlying areas that you had contact with during the campaign. Finally, you should add what our economists call 'socio-professional' statistics for the city and for the individual quarters, etc. At least for French readers, this seems to me to be necessary.

One should be able, within the span of a few pages, to inform oneself rapidly on the geography of Naples, the social composition of the various quarters, their population and social conditions, the locations of the largest factories, etc. Moreover, if the material is available, it would be a good idea to provide a *historical* perspective on all these elements: the social variations, innovations, etc., in the area around Naples over the past fifty or a hundred years. Going back in time can be very useful, because it can give some idea of the *specific forms* that 'capitalist development' took at Naples and of the *tendencies* of capitalist development there. In sum: the maximum amount of facts and data of an objective nature. Do this quickly, and do it well.

Louis

Dear M.A.,   *Paris, 30 November 1968*

Now that I have been able to re-read all of your letters in a calm fashion, let me add a few more suggestions that might help make their publication as smooth as possible.

Aside from what I wrote in the letter of 22 October, I think it would be a good idea if, at the end of the correspondence, you added some thoughts that put everything you have described into a national, and then international context. In this summary, you should mention the split in the international communist movement (for you speak on several occasions of militants who became 'pro-Chinese'). I think that this 'horizon' of the political crisis of the international communist movement is frequently present in what you come up against in your own experience. For example, the simple fact of the 'traditional' style of Italian electoral campaigns, the kind of relationships which exist between the voters and their elected representatives . . . a hundred particulars in your letters show that you found yourself up against a 'tradition' and a 'style of work' inspired by a relatively *conformist*, if not *reformist*, ideology; this might explain the creation of 'pro-Chinese' groups.

Do not forget that, when world-scale events are involved, politics can be 'contagious' and have 'long-distance' effects. These effects will occur in a more or less disconnected way, of course, but they will be felt nevertheless. All the great bourgeois revolutions (1789, 1830, 1848), and the Russian Revolution, had a 'long-distance' impact in this way, producing more or less disconnected effects at first – but real effects in the end. To take only one example, that is plain for all to see (and without wanting to give the 'student movement' a role which it does not merit), it is all too clear that the Cultural Revolution acted on the students 'from a distance'. We will have to see where the Italian working class stands in this respect, in terms of both the immediate and far-off future.

Even without going as far as this, it seems to me that your experience could serve to test a number of Marxist-Leninist principles, which relate to the most 'sensitive' (i.e. *fragile*) points of the 'unity of theory and practice'. You know that, in its most general form, this unity has been realized and is realized every day in the unity of Marxist theory and the workers' movement. This unity exists in organic fashion in a revolutionary proletarian *vanguard party*. To say this is to repeat the obvious, but it also indicates an initial difficulty concerning which I would greatly like to have some more information: Why does the P C I *officially declare itself* a 'mass party' and not a proletarian 'vanguard' party? To raise this question no doubt means to allude to certain historic difficulties the Italian party has had to face, first under Fascism, then in the War and Liberation. But I am curious as to how any solution to these difficulties can continue to be proposed – and accepted – more than twenty years *after the Liberation*, in the form of the expression, 'mass party'.

Perhaps it is necessary to pose the question in less direct fashion, and ask ourselves: In what way does the Italian Party realize its union with the masses (both revolutionary and potentially allied) in a 'mass line' and in a mass 'style of work'? These two notions are, from a Marxist-Leninist viewpoint, fundamental.

Everyone knows that every political party has to have a political line, but not necessarily a *mass* revolutionary political line. A Communist Party must have a 'mass' revolutionary political line, one which assumes a completely original and unprecedented kind of relationship with 'the masses'. Gramsci demonstrates that Machiavelli, in earlier times, had a kind of presentiment of this relationship. What we need today is something which goes far beyond a simple presentiment of the problem.

The Russian and Chinese Revolutions allow us to be more specific. A mass revolutionary political line must unite, in the closest possible fashion, 'theory and practice': in other words concrete analysis of the concrete situation (carried out by applying Marxist science in concrete political investigations) and 'the masses', who are, in the final analysis, the only ones who can make history.

The simple realization that the masses also are part of the *concrete situation, and hence appear two times in the formula* of 'unity', makes us aware of how complex the problem is. Concretely, a mass line means doing two things simultaneously. On the one hand, you have to pay the most careful attention to what the masses (most of all the 'fundamental' urban and rural proletarian masses) *have in their minds*, as a result of their material, ideological and political conditions of existence. Then you have to relate this ('subjective') content to the (scientific) class analysis of the society as a whole. This supposes that once this dual analysis has been made, the Party – in constant contact with the masses and constantly informed by Marxist-Leninist theory – then offers to the masses the *political line* that it has thereby elaborated: that it explains this line to the masses in such a concrete way that the masses are able to recognize *their own will* in the line proposed to them. Listen, analyse, explain. And pay the most careful attention to the way the masses react during this complex process.

This is a very complicated 'practice' that represents an extremely sensitive and fragile link in the unity of theory and practice. It is not only a process of *understanding*, but also a question of a *savoir-faire* of a very special type which requires the most careful attention.

Lenin and Mao call this *savoir-faire* a 'revolutionary style of work' or a 'mass style of work', which must continually be rectified. One must make certain that contact with the masses is never lost, and that this contact is *revolutionary*, i.e. does not take the form of simply following in the wake of the spontaneous ideology of the masses (which frequently – take the example of the Naples sub-proletariat – can weigh them down), but is a 'step ahead' of the masses (Lenin), in order to help them free themselves from their spontaneous ideology and recognize themselves in the line that is proposed and submitted to them.

Louis

Dear M.A.,   *15 March 1969*

I promised, when I saw you last summer, in the heat of July, that I would write something on the events of May and on the Student Movement. I see now that this was, in many ways, a foolish promise to have made. For how could anyone presume to speak of 'events' of this kind without having a minimum of *objective* documentation at his disposal? How can anyone presume to speak of an important historic event without that minimum of objective information which would allow one, if not to carry out in full, then at least to outline 'the concrete analysis' of the 'concrete situation' that produced the May events?

Given my forced withdrawal, due to illness, I did not have that necessary information last summer. Today, I still only have a few things on the 'Student Movement'. I am lacking the really *essential* material: *what, exactly, happened* in the working class and among the broad strata of (non-proletarian) employees who together made the portentous *May general strike*. The articles which have appeared in *l'Humanité* and a few other scattered reports only furnish the most general elements of an analysis.

Under such circumstances, anything I can say can only be very schematic, crude, and perhaps even fundamentally incomplete. I originally hoped to send you my analysis in the form of *theses*. Instead, what I have are, at best, *hypotheses*.

But these qualifications do not mean that we should wait indefinitely, i.e. wait until it is possible to carry out a truly Marxist historical study or (which really amounts to the same thing) a truly Marxist political analysis (a concrete analysis of a concrete situation). We have to say what we can. We should of course be careful, but we must say something. We have to do this in order to submit our hypotheses to the criticism of our comrades, so that something more than hypotheses will result and, above all, so that we will be able to see things a little more clearly in the post-May situation. For something of great importance happened in May, something of the greatest importance for revolutionary prospects in the 'capitalist countries of the West', something which *must* have repercussions on our policies, or else our policies will risk being 'dragged along' by events. And I do not mean by the events of May, which now are a part of the past, but by present and future events which, one day, are going to go far beyond those of May.

This, then, is how I will proceed. I will put forward two *Facts*, one *Thesis*, and at the same time one *Hypothesis*.

By *Facts* I mean incontestable facts, historic facts in the strongest sense of the term, i.e. *constituent* facts of the national and international conjuncture.

By *Thesis* I mean a demonstrable political or theoretical proposition.

By *Hypothesis* I mean a political or theoretical proposition which I cannot demonstrate conclusively, either for lack of space (one cannot go on forever in a letter), or else for lack of information that could only be provided by objective sociological inquiries 'in the field'.

I will follow a *relatively* arbitrary order in what I am about to write. It is, primarily, a *pedagogical* order, though subordinated to the primacy of politics. Consequently, my Facts (Facts I and II), my Thesis (Thesis I) and my Hypothesis (Hypothesis I) will be presented in a *mixed* order.

The pedagogical order of the argument requires that I begin with that which presently *dominates* current *interpretations* of the May events. Hence

FACT I

The *absolutely determining* role in the events of May was played, in the final analysis, by the general strike of nine million workers. The mass participation of university students, secondary school students, and young intellectual workers in the May events was an extremely important phenomenon, but it was *subordinated* to the economic class struggle of the nine million workers.

This brings us to the first fact: in the comments and interpretations currently being put on the market in our capitalist countries, the relative order of importance of these two phenomena (the general strike and the 'student' actions) has been *completely reversed*.

This is not the case with our communist parties, and in particular the French Communist Party. The PCF presented things in their real order: the primacy of the general strike over the student actions. This is correct not only because it reflects the real relationship of forces in May, but also because it conforms to the Marxist-Leninist thesis of the revolutionary character of the working class, and *of it alone*. By 'revolutionary', we mean: not subjectively revolutionary (= petty-bourgeois revolutionary declarations) but objectively revolutionary (revolutionary actions which culminate in the proletarian Revolution).[1]

In contrast, this reversal is found in all bourgeois and petty-bourgeois publications, including the majority of Student Movement publications. Aside from de Gaulle's imprecations, which directly attacked the 'totalitarian' working class, and aside from a few manifestos of the Action Committees, these publications all push the general strike into the background: *no one mentions it any more*. They simply erase from history the greatest workers' strike in the history of the world. What is brought into the foreground, in its place, is the Student Movement, the barricades of the Latin Quarter, and so on, as if, given the importance of these phenomena, History could be made by petty-bourgeois students, 'who lead the working class towards the Revolution. . .'.

I know that some students do not fall into this bourgeois trap. At least they do not do so *in writing*, where they clearly recognize the primacy of the May general strike over the May student actions. But it is not enough to write down a correct Thesis: it is also necessary for this Thesis to pass from the heads of the limited number of 'conscious' students who write it into (a) their own actions, and then (b) the concrete line of action of the Student Movement as a whole.

---

1. Let us be careful about these terms, subjectively revolutionary and objectively revolutionary. The first designates subjective *intentions*, the other objective *capacities* of individuals or groups in terms of the proletarian revolution. These terms should not be confused with the distinctions introduced by Lenin, when he defines a situation as a revolutionary one when there is a conjunction of *objective conditions* (a shattering economic–political–ideological crisis) and *subjective conditions* (the Party, its line, its link with the masses) which must *measure up to* the objective conditions for the proletarian revolution to triumph.

Now I would contend that the present concrete line of action of the Student Movement contradicts *in practice*, with a few notable exceptions, this correct Thesis. The line of action of the Student Movement reflects the 'ideas' of the Student Movement, in other words the ideas of the vast bulk of the students. And the vast bulk of the students still believes that the actions of the students played the *determining* role in the May events.

The mass of the students live in a dream based on a misunderstanding. On the grounds that (and this is an historico-*chronological* fact) the savage repression of their 'barricades' served as a 'detonator' to the general strike, the mass of the students thinks that they were the *vanguard* in May, leading the workers' actions. This obviously is an illusion. It confuses chronological order (the barricades came *before* the 13 May demonstration and therefore *before* the general strike), the role of 'detonator' or 'the single spark that lights a forest fire' (Lenin), with the historical (non-chronological) role which *is determinant in the final analysis*. And in May it was the working class, and not the students, who, in the final analysis, played the determining role.

To the extent that the Student Movement (French, German, Japanese, American, Italian, or whichever) *does not recognize this fact* in theory (in its writings) *and*, above all, in practice (in its 'line' and in its forms of organization and action), its interpretation of the May events simply merges with the bourgeois and petty-bourgeois interpretations of May. The students' interpretation is only – in a linguistic form appropriate to the variations of ideology in the student 'organizations' (libertarian, neo-Luxemburgist, Guevarist ideologies) – the pure and simple *demarcation* of the bourgeois interpretations.

The students must become aware of this fact: that they are contributing objectively – in their own way, of course, and in spite of the subjectively revolutionary intentions of the best of them – to the bourgeoisie's reversal of the real order of things, i.e. to the passing over in silence of what, in the final analysis, played an absolutely determining role in May, that is, the general strike of nine million workers.

In order to convince the students of this reality, which they have not recognized, I will make two observations for their benefit. Both these observations refer to *the occupation of the Sorbonne*.

The students reoccupied the Sorbonne and raised the red flag over it during the 13 May demonstration. That they were able to reoccupy and then 'hold' the Sorbonne for such a long time was due, it is clear, first, to the presence of hundreds of thousands of workers on the 13 May demonstration and, secondly, to the massive general strike which broke out thereafter. This general strike mobilized the bulk of the repressive apparatus of the state on a front which represented a much greater danger to the bourgeoisie than did the 'student front'. And, without this strike and mobilization, it is most unlikely that the occupation of the Sorbonne would have lasted more than a few days, at most.

This same occupation presented an objective 'problem' to the students. But because they were too confident in a strength they thought was theirs alone – and which, on the contrary, derived essentially from the power of the general strike – they never gave it a moment's thought. For an occupation, even if only an occupation of the Sorbonne, cannot be improvised. Now, even if the students had no experience with factory occupations (and this is understandable since these events were their first test 'under fire'), there were men who were already experts in the practice of occupation. I am of course referring to the workers, who, having 'inaugurated' this form of struggle in 1936 and extended and refined it on numerous other occasions since then, had not forgotten what they had learned. The proof can be seen in the exemplary success of the factory occupations in May–June 1968.

Instead of simply going to the factory gates to 'offer their help' to the workers, the Sorbonne students should *at the same time* have asked the militant workers of these factories to come to the Sorbonne to teach them how to carry out an occupation effectively; how to defend the Sorbonne against the intrusion of undesirable elements and police agents, who instead – as is well known – were able to come and go as they pleased; how if necessary to defend the Sorbonne against the assaults of the repressive forces. Then the occupied Sorbonne might have become one of the most significant terrains of the class struggle in May, where the *fusion* of student actions and the workers' struggle could perhaps have begun to take shape. Here too, things have to be clearly stated: the students thought that it was the workers who needed them, while in reality it was the students, novices in this form of struggle, who needed the most 'help', in the form of advice and support from the working class.

We can see from this example what the practical consequences can be – indeed, always are – of a correct, or erroneous, estimate of the relative importance of the forces involved in an 'encounter'. If the encounter of 13 May has, *essentially*, had no sequel; and if, after May, such a sequel – which will come one day – seems, provisionally, farther off than ever; this is due, at least in terms of what we are discussing here, to the false evaluation of the real order of importance of the forces involved.

For this reason, things must be put in proper perspective. It is for this reason that the following Thesis is important.

THESIS I

What is commonly called the 'May Events' was the result of the objective encounter of two types of action:

1. The action of the economic and political class struggle of the mass of French workers and employees: i.e. the general strike of nine million men and women that lasted a month. This action of the masses was the *historically determining* element, *in the final analysis*, of the 'May Events'.

2. The actions of the university students, secondary school students and young intellectual workers, for whom the repressive acts of the Government and police provided the spark for a magnificent explosion. (These repressive acts were objectively 'clumsy', from a bourgeois point of view: since May, the politicians and the representatives of the bourgeois state apparatus have 'caught on' and now they behave accordingly, i.e. with more proper bourgeois manners.) The explosion reached its high point on the barricades on the night of 11 May, and afterwards in the occupation of the Sorbonne, the Odéon and other pillars of culture.

What happened was an historic *encounter*, and not a fusion. An encounter may occur or not occur. It can be a 'brief encounter', *relatively* accidental, in which case it will not lead to any *fusion* of forces. This was the case in May, where the meeting between workers/ employees on the one hand and students and young intellectual workers on the other was a brief encounter which did not lead, for a whole series of reasons I will mention very briefly and very generally, to any kind of *fusion*.

An encounter which is, or becomes, a long encounter must necessarily take the form of a *fusion*. This did not happen in May. Developments since May confirm this thesis: the fusion of the workers' movement and the actions of students and others is still not objectively on the agenda. For it to be put on the agenda the non-proletarian youth will have *to come a very long way* from where they presently are, and the Workers' Movement (yes, it too) will also have to move a certain distance. As long as this distance is not traversed by both sides (and each side must cover, on its own, the distance in front of it), the fusion of the two will not be on the agenda. And in the meantime, the Workers' Movement will follow its own path and the non-proletarian youth will follow *its* hesitant route.

Starting from this Thesis I, we can give some order to the *chronology* of things by subordinating it to *History*. The encounter took place, in the proper sense of the word, in the immense demonstration of 13 May, to the cry, ten years after de Gaulle's coup d'état, of '*Ten years is enough!*' It was, to be sure, a *political* slogan, in that it was directed against de Gaulle, but it was also a defensive, negative slogan (*against* de Gaulle). In the huge column one could also hear some isolated shouts, mainly the anarcho-syndicalistic cry of the CFDT: '*Workers' Power!*' And then there were a few shouts from the *groupuscules*: '*Serve the People!*' '*Support the workers!*' In addition to the defensive political slogan ('*Ten years is enough!*') there was also a powerful expression of proletarian internationalism: '*Down with US Imperialism!*' '*The NLF will win! Victory for Vietnam!*' But if we want to examine what the mass political slogans ('Down with imperialism', 'Ten years is enough') *concealed*, we find, on the march of 13 May, slogans of the *economic* class struggle: '*We want rises! No more redundancies! Guaranteed jobs! No more timed production! Stop the crackdown on the unions!*', etc.

The most extraordinary thing in the extraordinary encounter which this procession of hundreds of thousands of workers, university and secondary-school students and young intellectual workers represented was the *objective discrepancy* between the slogans which predominated among the workers, and the slogans which predominated among the students and intellectuals. The students and intellectuals (with Sauvageot and Geismar at the head) were asking not just for a change of government ('Ten years is enough', 'Down with de Gaulle!'), but, simply, for 'the revolution'. This 'revolutionary' call subsequently took the form, on occasion, of the anarcho-syndicalist slogans (which represented a synthesis of the anarchism which was dominant at that point among the students and the revolutionism of the 'doctrinarians' of the SNES-SUP and the UNEF): *'Workers' Power! Student Power! Peasant Power!'* But the immense mass of workers had very different aims in mind, which took the form of defensive political slogans: 'Ten years is enough!' and, massively, slogans of the *economic* class struggle.

Who stopped to think about this discordance? Yet it was this which dictated the entire tone of everything that followed the May events (in both a *chronological* and an historical sense). It above all conditioned the form of all subsequent encounters – which rarely succeeded, and were more often either fragmentary or, frankly, non-existent – between the workers' actions (the general strike) and the actions of the students and intellectuals.

For their part, the students occupied the Sorbonne, the Odéon, etc., which they turned into bases of ideological (and, they thought, political) agitation. Workers, mainly young but also some older ones, came freely to the Sorbonne and the Odéon. Naturally, among those who also came were social misfits and members of the lumpen-proletariat, who found food and shelter, as well as the chance to sublimate their own personal tragedies (the 'Katangese').[2]

The students, for their part, all sought to outdo each other in their burning desire to 'serve the people' and 'help the workers', and in this spirit they went to the gates of the factories to offer their services. In the beginning the gates opened for them almost everywhere, but later (with certain exceptions, for example Flins, *where there are no gates*) they remained closed, to the great disillusionment of the student militants. In some cases (Flins, Cléon, Nantes, Sochaux), the students were able to participate directly in the violent battles provoked by the intervention of the CRS in the factories. One young student even died, drowned at Flins, and two workers were killed by rifle fire at Sochaux (where the CRS also left a number of their own men on the ground).

But as a general rule the mass of workers did not respond to the enthusiastic invitation of the students. There was an all-too-apparent gap, and consequent lack of understanding, between the utopian (ideological-'political') hopes of the students and the immediate demands of the workers.

2. Certain of them claimed to have previously served as mercenaries in Katanga, and constituted themselves as a defence-force for the Sorbonne in case of police attack. (Trans.)

Some students, in a rather too simplistic fashion, discovered the reason for this in the 'betrayal' by the leaders of the CGT and the PCF. This is simplistic because it is not a Marxist-Leninist explanation to believe in *the determining role of leaders* when a mass movement of these proportions is involved. The truth is that the entire working class, and not just its leadership, was not, in general, at all disposed to 'follow' the suggestions of the students, which were based more on a dream-experience than on an understanding of reality.

The working class felt that it ran the risk – given the manifest inexperience of the students in the class struggle – of being dragged into what has to be called, for lack of a better word, an uncertain adventure.

It is for this reason that the working class continued, on its own, to follow its own path, informed by its own experience. This, of course, was not and could not be the path indicated for it in a flurry of proclamations by the student 'leaders', Geismar, Sauvageot and later Herzberg – proclamations echoed publicly and with glee by the bourgeois radio and press. (The bourgeoisie is not as stupid as the student 'leaders' thought.) (Incidentally, Geismar and Herzberg were not even students, but rather teachers and researchers: Geismar was a member of the PSU and Herzberg – who was immediately expelled – was a member of the PCF.) It is also for this reason that the working class looked so surlily on the great meeting of the PSU (Unified Socialist Party, which at that time should really have been called the *University* Socialist Party) at Charléty. Thus the working class in practice resolved its own problems alone: first of all the problem of its demands; then, also, in some cases, the problem (which was absolutely secondary from the point of view of the existing situation) of its relationship with its own leaders. This second problem, in any event, is its own business and has nothing to do with the students. The students ought to get this simple fact into their heads, even if it is hard for them to understand it.

The working class went back to work. It often did so in an atmosphere of victory, with its banners raised. In other cases, it had to face often serious problems with certain union leaders. And then everything fell back into the normal order of things. But some things had changed. Wages had been temporarily endowed with a greater purchasing power. The unions had won basic civil rights inside the factories (at the Citroën plant, this was really a great victory). And, *above all*, the working class now had etched in its memory (and this is a *definitive* inscription) the knowledge that the bosses, the Government and the state apparatus had been thrown into stark fear overnight by the action of the masses, that action was therefore possible, and that such action, one day, could lead to something that the working class has heard spoken of – since the Paris Commune, since 1917 in Russia and 1949 in China: the *Proletarian Revolution*.

When the working class had gone back to work, the students 'continued the struggle' with the famous slogan, *'This is only a beginning, continue the struggle!'* Beginning of what? And what struggle?

When I ask these questions, it does not mean for a moment that *nothing at all* had begun. On the contrary, something very basic had begun for the university students, for those in the lycées and the technical schools, and for the young intellectual workers, but something which is only the barest *beginning*. Beginning of what? The students think it was the beginning of the revolution. In the long-term sense, of course, this is true, but then, this beginning was not something they achieved: it is the achievement of the working class which did not wait until May to 'begin the struggle', which indeed it has been waging for more than a century. If this is so, what, then, has begun for the students? 'Continue the struggle!' Well, the struggle continued, or rather in reality it declined and, in the coming months, it will, at least in France, move more and more towards the complete *disintegration, at least in the student milieu,* of what the students call, in overly ambitious terms, the 'Student *Movement*'.

This disintegration has already begun in France. It first took the form of a proliferation of *groupuscules*, and currently it takes the form of an anti-*groupuscule* ideology (of a neo–Luxemburgist kind) embodied in the ideology of the Action Committees. This disintegration will continue and become even more pronounced. We can count, moreover, on the (bourgeois) intelligence of E. Faure[3] to contribute to it with all his might, at least in the universities.

'This is only a beginning. Continue the struggle!' Beginning of what? What struggle? This leads to the next question: *what does the term 'Student Movement' mean?*

3. The Minister of Education at the time. (Trans.)

Hypothesis I

I would like to begin with the observation that, at least in France and Italy, but also in Germany, Spain and the USA, the 'Student Movement' carries a title which does not accurately indicate what it is in reality.

In this respect, May 1968 in France was a kind of scientific experiment, a verification-test in which many hitherto hidden facts came to light. Above all, the following fact: if the students, in the strict sense, had supremacy and the principal role, at least at the start of the events, they also had the tendency to pretend not to recognize the active presence of other strata, *more important than they*. In the first place, school students: the *lycéens* and the pupils from the technical schools, and even from the upper grades of the elementary schools. Then, above and beyond the school students, there were large and highly differentiated strata of young 'intellectual workers': young doctors, lawyers, artists, architects, engineers, journalists, low- and middle-level white-collar workers, technicians, teachers, researchers and so on.

The fact is that the too-vague and unilateral, and hence inaccurate expression *'Student Movement'* covers a whole series of activities which converged in May, generated by *various strata* of young students and *various strata* of young intellectual workers. This great diversity explains many things which occurred in May, both convergences of action (e.g. the stupendous posters of young artists and architects) and clashes and even divergences. Amid this great diversity one common element prevailed. A common ideological source dominated this mass, of petty-bourgeois origins: *petty-bourgeois ideology was dominant*. But this same diversity helps explain the different variants of petty-bourgeois ideology that were expressed during May: the *dominant* libertarian anarchism, but also Trotskyism, anarcho-syndicalism, Guevarism, and the ideology of the Chinese Cultural Revolution. It should be said that the direct influence of Marcuse, which was so significant for the student youth in Germany and Italy, was *practically nil* in France.

Another observation. The title 'Student *Movement*' lends itself to a good deal of ambiguity in the light of what I have just said. To be sure, the students tend to call their actions a 'Movement', which is understandable from the point of view both of their intentions and of their admiration for the Workers' Movement. But it is difficult to give them *full rights* to this title. For in my opinion, if a movement like the Workers' Movement deserves its title, that is because it is the Movement of *a social class* (the proletariat), and furthermore of the only *objectively revolutionary* class. The university students, secondary-school students and young intellectual workers do not constitute a class, but rather 'middle strata' with a petty-bourgeois ideology. Moreover, they are not objectively revolutionary even if some of their members may become authentic revolutionary militants (Marx and Lenin were, precisely by their social origins, petty-bourgeois intellectuals). That the 'Student Movement' is not a real Movement, i.e. a *united* movement, was made clear in May by the conflicts and serious divergences in both initiatives and actions, and by the fact that the Student Movement, in some cases (e.g. at Charléty), let itself be led by the ideologues of a political party, the P S U, whose basic orientation was not a student one.

Having said that, and without wishing to deny our student comrades the right to call themselves a 'Movement' – since this expresses their aspiration for *unified* action and a *unified* organization which will go beyond scholastic and professional institutions and experiences and attack the whole structure of the capitalist state – it is essential to put this movement into proper perspective. The following *fundamental fact* must be taken into account: this is not a movement which concerns one or two countries, but practically *every capitalist country* and even a number of socialist countries. It began fifteen years ago, made some notable advances, and then had some spectacular failures in a number of countries (who still remembers the magnificent Turkish student movement, crushed by the local fascist dictatorship?), before culminating in May 1968 in France.

A long-lasting international movement, born in 1955 and alternating victories and defeats, regressions and then spectacular recoveries right up to the present day. What, then, is this event without historical precedents, an event which certainly is *irreversible* notwithstanding its inevitable defeats, which, having begun, may and certainly will meet with future failures, but *will not stop again*?

To explain it, on the basis of my limited knowledge, I will present the following fundamental hypothesis: this international movement is one of the spontaneous forms of the class struggle, waged – generally

in utopian-leftist forms – in a *petty-bourgeois environment* and provoked, in the final analysis, by the crisis of the present phase of
imperialism, *the phase of its death-agony.*

It is not terribly difficult to find evidence for the impact of the
international anti-imperialist class struggles on the birth and development of this Movement. To name only the most significant, let us
remember the effect on young students and intellectuals of the war in
Algeria, the Cuban Revolution, guerilla war in Latin America – where
'Che' met a heroic but politically costly death – the prodigious and
victorious struggle of the Vietnamese people against the aggression of
the world's greatest military power, the Chinese Cultural Revolution,
the violent revolt of black Afro-Americans in the large cities of the US
and the Palestinian resistance. These anti-imperialist struggles have
met with an extraordinary receptivity among the contemporary youth
of our countries, including young workers (let us not forget that in
France it was the proletarian and peasant youth who were mobilized
for the Algerian war, that it was they who paralysed Salan's 'putsch'
and made his officers hesitate and that they have not forgotten this
lesson).

Naturally, this receptivity would not be so profound if the suc-
cession of events which have punctuated the years from 1930 to 1960
had not *shaken bourgeois ideology to the point of rendering it extremely
fragile and vulnerable.* Mussolini's fascism; Hitler's Nazism; the
Spanish Civil War and the defeat of the republicans under the blows
of international fascism; the Second World War; the revolutions that
resulted from it in Central Europe, but especially in China; the
political and at times social liberation of the countries of the 'Third
World'; the 'victories' as well as the defeats (Korea, Vietnam!); the
direct political and military interventions of the United States, which
has become *imperialism's only international gendarme* as a result of the
weakness and contradictions of its 'allies'; in short, the public demonstration of the political and ideological impotence of the bourgeoisie's
gigantic economic and military forces – all these events have reduced
almost to nothing, if not entirely annihilated, the power, still impressive today, of traditional bourgeois ideology.

This is an historic fact of primary importance, which it would be a
very serious error to undervalue, this little-mentioned but open defeat
of the dominant ideology, which is the ideology of the dominant class.
It is a defeat which extends around the *entire world.* This defeat has

created a vacuum, a wide-open door, which leaves Marxist-Leninist ideology virtually hegemonic, even if petty-bourgeois strata in revolt seek the way to Marxism-Leninism in 'infantile', utopian, ideological forms. After all, we know that utopianism (anarchic, anarcho-syndicalist, neo-Luxemburgist and generally 'leftist') is only an *infantile* disorder which will be cured if, as Lenin said, 'it is properly treated'.

We should not, therefore, be too surprised that the combined effect of the prestigious examples of the victorious struggle against imperialism, on the one hand, and of the void opened by the virtual defeat of bourgeois ideology, on the other, should have opened up a vast battlefield for the *ideological revolt* of the student and intellectual youth.

In addition to this, if one considers the tendential development of the economic crisis of imperialism, which affects the material existence not only of the increasingly exploited working class, but also and perhaps especially, for the first time, directly that of the *petty bourgeoisie*, even in its relatively well-off strata (intermediate cadres, engineers, teachers, researchers, etc.), one will not find it surprising to see one's own children, distressed by the unemployment that they know is waiting for them, hurl themselves directly into the battle. Politically, economically and ideologically, the death-agony of imperialism has created the conditions for an attack by petty-bourgeois youth on certain capitalist apparatuses of the State, first among these being the apparatuses of ideological indoctrination, where bourgeois ideology now shows its incurable weakness: the educational system.

My hypothesis, therefore, is that the 'Movement' of the young students and intellectuals, on both a national and international level, must be considered as *an ideological revolt* (N.B.: an ideological revolt is not, in and of itself, as the students too readily believe, a political revolution) *which first attacks the apparatus of the educational systems of the capitalist countries.*

For now, this is the stage at which things are. But I think that if one knows where things come from and in what historical depths they have their roots, one can reasonably predict where they are going, or in any event where they are tending, and where they will indeed end up, after numerous and often serious vicissitudes.

This in fact is not the first time that the capitalist countries have been a theatre for the ideological revolts of their young students and intellectuals. The revolts of the 1920s, surrealism in Western Europe and the Proletkult in Russia, were also ideological revolts. But, for reasons which relate to the world situation of that time, the strength of imperialism and the power of bourgeois ideology – or for other reasons (in Russia) – these movements did not fulfil their promise. They never got beyond the stage of infantile disorder, at least not in Western Europe.

Is it necessary to remind ourselves that masses of youth were also mobilized, with great enthusiasm, into the 'ideological revolt' of the fascist movements in all of Europe and Japan before the last War? But that revolt, odiously exploited by the fascist leaders whom the big bourgeoisie had adopted as political leaders to fight against the working class, was distorted and made rotten by the horrible methods of the fascists, and then massacred in the wars of aggression of the Axis powers.

Things are completely different today. Fascist movements today have practically no chance at all of recruiting *legions* from among the student youth, in spite of the very real, objective and even imminent dangers of a neo-fascist reaction by the ruling class. The bourgeoisie had better resign itself to the fact that it has definitively lost its ideological hold on the best of its young people. It is because of this fact that we can say, with no fear of being mistaken, and notwithstanding the inevitable defections (which at times can be dangerous, however, on account of the objective anti-communism of certain of their elements), that the world-wide ideological revolt of students is objectively and definitively *progressive*, and that it already plays a *positive role* which cannot be ignored, of course at its own level and within its own limits, in the international class struggle against imperialism.

The whole problem, the crucial problem, that the Student Movement *must* face and which it has not yet faced save in largely mythic terms, is this: *under what conditions, within what time-span, and after passing through what tests, will the Student Movement succeed in establishing a lasting juncture with the Workers' Movement and finally merging with it?*

At this point it is necessary to introduce a second fact.

FACT II

This fact requires a lot of courage to face squarely, because it is serious. And, precisely because it is so serious, it has not yet really been faced squarely.

It is something which, in terms of the international class struggle, is deplorable, but, unfortunately, it is an incontestable fact. *Our Communist Parties had momentarily – we hope – but effectively lost ideological and political contact with the students and young intellectuals.* The fact that efforts have been made since May to re-establish contacts are simply the proof and absolute demonstration that this contact effectively did not exist in May in France. I think that the same thing is happening in other countries. The fact that Longo judged it indispensable to receive *personally* a number of 'leaders' of the Italian student movement is also proof that the Communist student organizations were not able, on their own, to ensure in a normal way the contact which they had lost.

The fact is that in May the Union of Communist Students (UEC) was completely overwhelmed by the events. The young masses – students, intellectual workers and even a number of workers – followed other leaders, not the leaders of the UEC; they fought under other slogans, not Communist ones. They followed Cohn-Bendit and his '22 March' group, which was not even an organization; they followed Sauvageot, who represented a National Union of French Students (UNEF) which was such a ghost-organization that it had not even had a president since the former one resigned; they followed Geismar and then Herzberg, secretaries of the National Union of Teachers in Advanced Education (SNES-SUP); some even listened to Barjonet at Charléty, where the PSU, which presided over the meeting, could not get Mendès-France to speak, even though he was present. They did not follow the UEC, nor the directives of the PCF or the CGT, except in the great demonstration – which had no sequel – of 13 May. There, it is true, they participated with enthusiasm, but they were following *the working class* rather than the PCF or CGT. *En masse*, they did not even go along with their own *groupuscules* which, for the most part, were literally crushed by the Student Movement of May.

This is a serious and impressive fact, which deserves not only reflection, but also, above all, precise documentation and a more profound analysis. (For how is reflection possible without facts and without an analysis?)

Why have the Communist Parties, who after all are represented among the students by their own organizations, lost practically all contact with the student youth, to the extent that they were left behind by the latter's spontaneous actions and ideology in May?

I only raise the question here, not having the necessary information to risk formulating an hypothesis. Certainly, for France, it is necessary to go back to the effect of the Algerian War on the students, for it was due to this and its aftermath that the UEC suffered two very serious and damaging splits, both of which damaged it greatly and considerably weakened both its membership and its following. We must certainly also recall the influence of the Chinese Cultural Revolution, and the scissionist slogans which the CCP directed at the movements outside China. But all these are only *partial elements* in a general *system of causes*, and this system must be analysed both in its details and, most definitely, as a whole, for it concerns not only the youth of a single nation, but the youth of the bulk of the capitalist countries, and also of certain socialist countries.

Whatever the ultimate causes are for this loss of contact, one thing is certain: it helped in no small measure to push the youth revolt into what is imprecisely termed *leftism*. The term is imprecise because it is necessary to specify the various forms which this leftism takes – some of them mutually antagonistic, as the divisions which today reign between the remnants of the *groupuscules* and their ex-adherents amply prove. It is also necessary to specify that what we are talking about here is *petty-bourgeois* leftism, and not the *proletarian* leftism that Lenin wrote about in *Left-Wing Communism*, a work which is too often cited indiscriminately. It is also necessary to specify that, while Lenin thought that proletarian leftism was 'a thousand times less dangerous than Right doctrinairism' for the revolution and relatively easy to cure, as an infantile disorder of the *Workers'* Movement, Lenin's formulas cannot be applied directly to the leftism of the *petty-bourgeois* students.

We can safely assume that petty-bourgeois leftism, although 'infinitely less dangerous than Right doctrinairism' and even less dangerous than proletarian leftism, will nevertheless be *infinitely more difficult* to cure than proletarian leftism. For it is evident that the petty-bourgeois do not have the 'natural' remedy of 'proletarian class instinct', but on the contrary have a 'petty-bourgeois class instinct', which is incredibly difficult to transform into a 'proletarian class position'.

All these specific conditions render necessary a very special kind of 'treatment' for this intellectual and student leftism. As Lenin said of youth movements in 1916, they 'must be given every assistance. We must be patient with their faults and strive to correct them gradually, mainly by *persuasion*, and not by fighting them.'

But how can we truly define even a line with respect to the complex leftist ideology of the youth, without first of all having satisfied certain absolutely indispensable conditions for not simply advancing into the unknown of an ideological revolt without historical precedent, an ideological revolt which, for all its errors, arrogance and vain defections, is *unquestionably progressive as a mass phenomenon*. For let us make no mistake, this is a true and proper mass movement, a petty-bourgeois one, to be sure, *but a mass one.*

The indispensable conditions, in my opinion, are the following:

1. First of all, employing whatever forms of sociological (economic, political and ideological) analysis are necessary to understand the specifics of what occurred in the sensational May general strike, it is essential to re-establish the historical order of things: hence to *assert the historical primacy of the general strike of nine million workers* (which swept away the ideology of Marcuse and his cohorts) *over the actions of the student and intellectual youth.* This analysis will have the immense advantage, if it is really detailed, not only of enlightening the working class about its own forces and resources – and hence about its prodigious powers of revolutionary intervention – but also of educating the young students and intellectuals as to the *reality* of the working class and the Workers' Movement, of which they necessarily have only a distorted idea, notwithstanding the contacts they have had with some young workers (*some* young workers are not *the* working class). This analysis must also bring out *the almost total abstention* in May of the rural proletariat, the poor peasants and the smallholders, whose demands and anger are nevertheless well known. Why did they abstain? To answer this, one must necessarily go beyond a national frame of reference and refer to the international context, to imperialism and the international struggle against imperialism, and to the very difficult conditions created by the split in the International Communist Movement, the reality and component parts of which cannot be ignored.

2. It is also essential to undertake a profound study of the national and international causes which lie behind the *ideological revolt of the students and young intellectuals.* This analysis will have the immense advantage of enlightening the youth about the causes which have set them moving; about the *necessity* of the events that they have ex-

perienced as 'freedom'; about the difficulties of the blind alleys (*impasse*) in which they are floundering and will continue to flounder. It will make them understand the limits and errors of the spontaneous forms of petty-bourgeois ideology which governed their historical actions in May; and it will prepare them to unite with the working class, to recognize the principle (affirmed with incomparable clarity by Lenin) of the latter's *leadership* of the revolutionary struggle, and to confront, in precise terms, the problem which at present torments them: the problem of the *necessity of organization* (because they sense, and some of them even know, that no political action is possible without *organization*). Furthermore, such an analysis will enable us to make the workers understand the causes and the sense of the ideological revolt of the student and intellectual youth, and also the causes of the utopian reactions of the students, which, with good reason, disconcerted the workers and made them generally wary – if not actually distrustful. Naturally, an analysis of this nature will have to be carried out, as I think I have made clear, on both a national and international level.

3. Lastly, it is essential to undertake a thorough-going analysis of the reasons which led to the abnormal *loss of contact* (practical, ideological and political) between the majority of Communist Parties and the youth. Here too we must get to the bottom of things – even if this means bringing in reasons of an international nature, since the phenomenon is one which transcends the framework of any one nation – provided that we do identify the specifically national causes of the phenomenon. Without this, the attempts currently being made by our Parties to re-establish links with the student and intellectual youth run the risk of filling the void which was so fatal in May with methods and a line arrived at *au jugé* (by guesswork) – i.e. of filling it as best one can, which means not very well. Of course, the results of this final analysis must find their place – perhaps a limited one, but nevertheless an undeniable one – in the analysis of the reasons for the massive rise of all the various leftist ideologies which, without appropriate and patient treatment, risk holding sway *for a long time to come* over the aforementioned youth.

I apologize for sending you such a long letter, promised so long ago. But all this time was needed in order to formulate anything more than simple value judgements or simple factual descriptions concerning May. That is why I am sending you this letter anyway, ten months after May and eight months after the end of your electoral campaign. I know that many of my suggestions are extremely precarious, and there is no doubt that in many cases I have been mistaken. All I ask is that the error be demonstrated to me.

I would be very happy if this letter, the first I have written to you knowing it would be published, provokes some analyses which will give us a more clear understanding of the May events. For May 1968, which saw a general strike of unprecedented proportions, represents the *most significant event in Western history* since the Resistance and the victory over Nazism.

Louis Althusser

Appendix:

Discussion of the *Letters*
in the Party Press

This second edition conforms exactly to the first. The only corrections have been those of a typographical nature. The only thing that is new in this second edition is this appendix in which the reader will find, in the chronological order in which they appeared, the writings which dealt with this book in the Party press, *l'Unità* and *Rinascita*. That is, these are reactions from inside the PCI.

The articles reproduced were written by Mario Gomez d'Ayala (the vice-secretary of the PCI's Regional Committee for Campania and a member of the Central Control Commission), Luca Pavolini (a member of the Central Committee and the Editor-in-chief of *Rinascita*), Alessandro Natta (member of the Party's National Executive and head of the Press and Propaganda Commission), Lucio Lombardo Radice (member of the Central Committee) and, finally, an editorial note from *Rinascita* in reply to Lombardo Radice's letter.

Many other letters about the book were sent by militants and by readers to the Party press – and not published. Of those of which I received copies, I here reproduce only one, with the consent of its author. This is the letter sent to *Rinascita* by Sebastian Matta, and I feel it is worth including because of the particular position it reflects.

M.A.M.
September 1969

Naples: The Reality of the Party[1]

CONCERNING AN ATTEMPT AT
SOCIO-ECONOMICO-POLITICAL RESEARCH

Dear Editor,

Reading the recently-published correspondence between Comrade Macciocchi and the French philosopher Louis Althusser has brought a few thoughts to my mind, which I feel compelled to share with you. This sharing is all the more urgent given that, as recent reviews in certain dailies inform us, this book has made a number of papers 'tremble with admiration'. Which papers? To cite only a few: *La Stampa* of Turin, the *Gazzetta del Mezzogiorno* and the *Corriere della Sera* (where Indro Montanelli professes his 'respect' for 'these crises of conscience of true militants').

I do not care to enter into the literary merits of the volume, and I feel just as ill-qualified to discuss the cautious counsel offered to our comrade by the French communist philosopher. If *l'Unità* feels it necessary to undertake such an analysis, it has both the qualified personnel and an appropriate cultural page. What moves me to intervene here is my experience of the Party in Naples and my knowledge of the lives of the workers of the city and of the province. I think I am also qualified to say at the outset that my own experience – I was a Deputy for ten years and a Senator for five – gives me an idea of what an electoral campaign is and what a communist parliamentarian does. I can for instance state unequivocally that election to Parliament does not represent the *climax* of a career, and even less is it a sinecure.

I took part in the last elections not as a candidate, but as a member of the Naples Federal Secretariat, and my own experience and this particular perspective allowed me, I think, to understand a few things that seem to have escaped the author's notice. One would probably find that Althusser could also benefit from hearing things from such a perspective – then he might not persist in the belief that everyone in the Party is only concerned with getting himself elected. I can think

1. From *l'Unità*, 10 June 1969.

of at least five comrades who would be eminently qualified to provide such a perspective, they being the men from Naples who have risen through the ranks of the Party, occupied the post of Federal Secretary, and who now are members of the Central Committee and even, in some cases, the National Executive of the Party.

I would like, then, to consider some of the frequently expressed judgements of Macciocchi on conditions at Naples, on the problems of the state and development of our Party at Naples, on the formation of its cadres and on its relationship with the masses. As a result of the research of our comrade, aided immeasurably by the precious counsel of a philosopher, it seems to me that the image emerges of a party (or at least its leaders) which, if not totally blind, is at least acutely near-sighted, markedly decrepit and, above all, incurably infected with an electoralistic virus. Ours is apparently a party which has not really come much farther than where it was twenty years ago when, as Comrade Macciocchi recalls for us (not without a number of inaccuracies and confusions), the Congress of the Democratic Front of the South was held at Pozzuoli in an atmosphere of flaming political passions and the peasants of the area, struggling to abolish the most humiliating forms of servitude and to secure a decent labour contract, marched in procession to Naples and there gave the chickens and other payments in kind which the landlords extorted from them (over and above the heavy rent on their land) to the hospitals or to the children's committee.

But, according to our comrade, things are in fact worse today than even those days twenty years ago; for, since then, the problem has become that much more acute, and everything is now further complicated by the bureaucratization of our cadres, by the sclerosis of our apparatus, and by the electoralism which runs rife throughout the Party. This image of the PCI deserves to be discussed thoroughly, not in response to the commentators of *Il Tempo* or *La Stampa* (whose unanimous praise for the book certainly cannot make Comrade Macciocchi very proud), but rather to set our whole position on the state of the Party in proper perspective. It simply is not true that these past twenty years have been spent almost in vain, even if it is true that along the difficult path we have come there have been (inevitable) errors, insufficiencies, reticences and delays in our analyses, in our political options and in our actions. For example, a good deal of the 'original' research carried out by our comrade on the forms of super-exploitation, home labour and the workers' and peasants' condition has for years been a part of our patrimony of experience. Quite apart from the scale of our successes in practice, such research has represented one of the Party's main fields of study and initiative. For a long time now, our sections and other levels of the Party organization (the City Committee, our parliamentary representatives and others) have established a dialogue with certain strata of the population – and here Macciocchi's long absence certainly did not aid her perspective. The kind of relationship these elements of the Party maintain are hardly clientelistic: our dialogues have gone deeply into matters such as housing, health, hygiene, civic institutions and other general and specific problems of the economic and civic conditions under which the working class and the popular masses have to live. And our actions have affected these issues.

The presence of the PCI in these struggles, the sacrifices made by so many comrades and our own, albeit modest, ability to direct and orient popular struggles (hardly in tones modulated to those of the 'goldfinch'!) are all responsible for the manifest expression of popular support we obtained on 19 May, support which seems to have stunned our comrade. Moreover, the idea of asking the masses about their problems is hardly a new form of research; we have been using it since the first meetings for the rebirth of the South, in both the cities and in the countryside. And it has often proved very useful, not only in terms of the facts we learn of the denunciations these enable us to make, but also because this kind of activity gets the masses involved, in a political sense, in the choices that are made and helps them participate in the definition of both the objectives and the forms of our struggles.

Our Party is in the factories both in traditional organizational forms and also in new forms; we maintain contact with the working class in every way that our experience suggests would be fruitful. In this regard, it would probably be a good idea to let Comrade Althusser know that, in Naples, the PCI continuously – not only during electoral campaigns – promotes important meetings outside the factories on themes relating to the workers' conditions. This would make clear that the kind of meetings we, for the last twenty years, have called 'household encounters' are in fact nothing other than the type of meeting that Comrade Macciocchi experienced for the first time, with such enthusiasm, during the 1968 electoral campaign, in the company of the comrades from Torre del Greco, Acerra and the 'quarters' of Naples.

Our links to the working class are hardly as weak as Macciocchi suggests. We have discussed not only short-term issues with the workers, but also fundamental questions of social change, and we have met with them inside and outside the factories. The PCI often ties together political initiatives and parliamentary debate, on the one hand, with struggles and demonstrations in the cities and factories, on the other. We have done this for the reform of the pension law, for the principle of showing 'just cause' in sackings, and against the abolition of rent controls. In the countryside of Acerra or the Nolano, together with the peasants, we have drawn up plans for social struggles which involved the defence of the soil, and which attacked the very heart of the reclamation, contractual, and landholding systems in the fields of this area. If we have not done all these things, to what then do we owe the gratifying flood of votes that have been showered on us by the workers of Castellammare or Torre Annunziata, by the labouring classes of Naples and by the peasants in various zones of our province?

We have also had some notable successes on a purely organizational level. This is seen most clearly in the most recent figures on membership in the large and small factories of both the city and the province. Our cell in the Navalmeccanica Shipyards has 360 members; even more modestly-sized cells like those in the factories like CMI, SAFOG or Saint Gobain, show that our Party's organizations can grow. Hence *something* seems to be happening, if we are to accept that the 1968 electoral success was due, to a not inconsiderable degree, to efforts undertaken by our Party, to its link with the masses, to its prestige, and also to those characteristics which differentiate it from all the other political forces in Italy.

The sections of the book which most grieved and even embittered me are those dedicated to the active and passive electoralism of Neapolitan Communists. No one has ever tried to hide the fact that a party with tens of thousands of members, one which obtained close to 400,000 votes in these elections, is not immune from certain forms of contamination or even degeneration. But it is hardly justified – especially in a Party militant – to take a few marginal phenomena and generalize them, drawing from them one's basic conclusions.

It is also unjustifiable to conclude, because some people respond affirmatively to the urgent demands of certain strata of the population, that a Communist parliamentary representative therefore does little more than solicit 'dossiers'. A party linked to millions of voters, who find themselves in countless difficult situations, who are assailed from all sides by every conceivable kind of problem – such a party can hardly deny its attention and solidarity, its human and civil support. Hence it cannot refuse to intervene, wherever possible, in the form that our comrade defines, almost with disgust, as 'dossiers'. Wouldn't it be much more strange if Communist parliamentary representatives completely cut themselves off, between one election and another, from the voters and did not consider them worthy of attention, just because they too are assailed by thousands of personal problems? What really counts, in the performance of this and other tasks, is the honest, disinterested way they are carried out, and the fact that they should not detract from the essential job of a Deputy in parliament.

Within the confines of the research conducted by our comrade, I suggest that an examination of the curriculum of all the Deputies of the district would have been highly illuminating, and might well have provided her with some useful facts which she then could have had the French philosopher ponder. An examination like the one I am suggesting would have found our Deputies and Senators present on the benches of Montecitorio and Palazzo Madama, involved in the debates on the central themes of social and political reform in Italy.[2] It would have shown them informed by and linked to the masses, pushing ahead in the struggle for the South. It would also have shown them outside the halls of Parliament and present in front of the factories, in the countryside, or in the universities, whenever and wherever the popular struggle was at its peak; or else it would have found them in the decision-making or administrative organs of the Party.

I am convinced that if our comrade had been able to participate in the long debate that took place in the Party in the preparatory period prior to the '68 elections (when the Party decided she would be elected – as she was), she would have sent very different and much more useful information to her interlocutor. She would also have come to some different conclusions, recognizing marginal episodes for what they are and putting them in their proper place. She would also have learned how the renewal of political leaders and parliamentary representatives takes place in the PCI, without any humiliation or personal recriminations, and in full awareness – gained in open discussion – that any changes are political acts carried out with only the

2. In Rome, Palazzo Madama is the site of the Senate, Montecitorio of the Chamber of Deputies. (Trans.)

interest of the Party and the optimal performance of its revolutionary role in mind.

I understand how it was not easy for our comrade – conditioned as *l'Unità*'s Paris correspondent to spend so much of her time in contact with ministers, party leaders and men of culture, letters and philosophy (though these are very important assignments as well) – to guard against the danger of hurried generalizations and first impressions in her unexpected renewal of contact with Italian conditions. But I think that more caution in her judgements and more reflection on facts and persons would have greatly aided her comprehension of the complexities of Naples, to say nothing of the complexities of our Party. For, after all, the PCI did succeed in electing, and almost in the precise predetermined order, its Deputies and Senators; it also utilized to the fullest the forces of its parliamentary delegation, once they were freed from their tasks at the national level.

More caution also would have permitted her, finally, to be more generous towards 'comrade A., who died of a heart ailment', a few years ago. It would have forced her to recognize that this comrade, while he was severely criticized in 1958, was a worker who was sacked following his role in factory struggles in Naples, who fought alongside the bricklayers of the city right up to the last day of his life, who fought alongside the workers and militants in the 'Mercato' section, who fought alongside the Calabrian peasants during the period of land occupations and who fought alongside the citizens of Sant'Antimo, who, not surprisingly, still have very fond, grateful and vivid memories of him.

M. Gomez d'Ayala

A Candidate in Naples [1]

This book of Maria Antonietta Macciocchi's (*Lettere dall'interno del PCI a Louis Althusser*, Feltrinelli, Milan 1969, pp. 361, 1400 lire), certainly cannot be said to have been helped by the provocations quickly penned by editorialists of the ilk of Gorresio or Montanelli, who seemed, predictably enough, to feel as if they had just been invited to a wedding reception; nor could the book benefit from the excesses of Jacques Nobécourt of *Le Monde*, who did the author no big favour by lumping her together with the Encyclopaedists, Stendhal, Malaparte, Roger Vailland, Italo Calvino and Jeanne Moreau. None of this helps us to maintain, for better or worse, a proper sense of proportion.

The origins of the book are, by now, well known. Macciocchi, a candidate of the PCI for the Naples-Caserta district in the '68 elections (immediately after returning from a long stint in France as the *Unità* correspondent there), recounts her experience in the electoral campaign as it unfolds to the French philosopher Althusser. He writes back, from afar, with counsel and suggestions.

The result is a vivid description of Neapolitan reality, seen through the eyes of an expert journalist, with much emphasis on detail and the revealing fact: this is especially the case in her treatment of the dramatic sub-proletarian reality of the 'belly of Naples', the winding alleys, dead ends and *bassi* where 'mature' capitalism is not contradicted, nor negated, but instead shows its other face, which is just as important as the more pretentious, technological façade. The author succeeds in rendering very effectively this terribly confusing jumble, with the teeming centre of the city on the one hand and, on the other, the strong worker-class nuclei in the city and in the urban centres that surround Naples. All in all, this is one of the most singular social mixtures in the world, of extreme analytic and political interest: the

1. From *Rinascita*, 13 June 1969.

living denunciation of every theory of development imposed mechanically from outside and unlinked to a view of dynamic processes of profound changes which have the masses as their protagonists. And, in my opinion, the best parts of the book are those where Macciocchi closely criticizes not only the old and new feudal structures of the Christian Democrats, led by the Gavas, with their accompanying corruption, speculation and clientelism, but above all those groups she calls 'Southocrats' (by analogy with technocrats and Eurocrats): the Compagnas, the La Malfas, *Nord e Sud*. Naples is their failure and their shame.

Much more perplexing, however, is a contradiction that runs throughout much of the book. I refer to the contradiction between the 'parachuted' nature that the author continually attributes to herself – 'parachuted' from Paris into Italy, Naples, the PCI Federation, the electoral lists – and the rapidity and finality of a whole series of conclusions about the political problems of the city and, in particular of the PCI. A bit of presumption is not, in a journalist, a mortal sin; it is, at most, venal. Her 'discoveries' may be something that someone else has already found out, but they are important enough to be communicated and diffused. But the whole issue becomes much more delicate when it involves the life and activity of an organization as complex and historically determined as the Communist Party; it becomes all the more delicate when the context of the Party is one as intricate, difficult and tortuous as that of Naples. In such cases, caution is *de rigeur*. And, too often in this book, caution is not respected. To undertake an analysis of the crisis, or, better, of the actualization of the mass party, in theory and practice, is not only legitimate but necessary. But then this analysis gets totally lost in a series of petty electoralistic episodes which lack any generalizable value. This was amply proved by the electoral success itself, which in Naples was especially striking and which surely did not happen purely by chance.

I would certainly caution against any triumphal celebration of our success. The Party's problems, particularly in the South, exist in abundance, and we have to discuss them without any false inhibitions, for they must be faced. But we are neither explorers nor memoirists, for these are just new ways to fall into the old, justly condemned trap of illuminism or, worse yet, sensationalism or exhibitionism. The letters which comprise this book claim to be written 'from inside the

PCI'. But an analysis from 'inside' implies the ability not to consider oneself a privileged, isolated individual, but rather to be an integral part of the complicated whole, rich in history, full of energies for renewal, that is the Italian Communist Party.

Luca Pavolini

Concerning M. A. Macciocchi's book[1]

Dear Editor,

As you have undoubtedly noted by now, a critical comment on Comrade Macciocchi's book in a report on the deliberations of one of the commissions of our Central Committee and a review in *Rinascita* (one, I might add, that was calm and even good-natured) were enough to make all the columnists of the 'independent' press and even many intellectuals of the Catholic Left cry 'scandal!'. They saw only anathema and condemnation hurled by Communist 'bureaucrats' against the interesting, vivid testimony supposedly represented by the exchange of letters between two communists, Macciocchi and Althusser. This anything-but-disinterested 'concern', and the squalid game of overdoing the praise and eulogies hardly surprises me. But we communists can never allow accusations to run rife which confuse condemnation and excommunication with criticism. Comrade M. A. Macciocchi believed that she was exercising a right when she published a volume on *her* electoral campaign in Naples in 1968. No one, to be sure, can prevent any of us from putting forth his own opinion with equal freedom, even if it is a harsh, severe opinion.

I personally dislike saying unpleasant things, but to remain silent at this point might seem to indicate embarrassment or tolerance for a book which I personally feel is a cultural misfortune and a political error.

Let us be completely clear: Comrade Macciocchi has *harmed* neither the Party nor its organization in Naples, for the outcome of the election, the examples of objectivity and personal sacrifice on the part of leaders of the PCI, including parliamentary representatives not standing again as candidates – and Gomez has already said this in *l'Unità* – are the most adequate response to the image (supported to a certain extent by Macciocchi's letters) of a Communist Party divorced from reality, bureaucratized, infected by electoralistic and clientelistic

1. From *Rinascita*, 27 June 1969.

viruses. The *harm* that the book in fact does is to our assessment of the intelligence and seriousness of Comrade Macciocchi, and this in turn reflects – as the excessive reaction of certain near-ecstatic reviewers reminds us – on all of us in a harmful way.

The book's biggest problem is a failure to keep the affectation of its central character separated from an interesting electoral 'journey' in the Naples of 1968. Had the separation been maintained, the 'journey' might have appeared all the more interesting. One still, of course, might have preferred the author to be inspired more by the dry rigour of a Francesco de Sanctis than by colourful, vivid, personalized impressions *à la* Matilde Serao. (And references of this type are not at all forced, if we remember that we are talking about a work which shows off excessively, stringing together every literary reference imaginable, from Stendhal to Dumas to Goethe to Serao; *si licet* – but it seems appropriate to Macciocchi – *parva componere magnis!*) I am not trying to discredit the merits, qualities, work or dedication of Comrade Macciocchi. But I cannot help wondering if there is even one leader of our Party who would ever take it upon himself – unless, of course, he wanted to suffer merciless ridicule – to recount not only his own speeches but the novelty and audacity of his attack, in Castell-ammare or Naples, on the policies and clients of the Gavas! Or to have it suggested to him by the philosopher Althusser – who in turn gives the impression of viewing Naples as some mysterious extension of Darkest Africa – that perhaps at the base of the high demographic index of Naples lie social reasons more profound than 'ignorance', and that the solutions to these problems cannot therefore be anything as simple as the 'Pill'! There are too many discoveries that are not dis-coveries at all. *Myself in Naples, Myself and the Party, Myself and the History of the PCI*!

This is not to suggest that autobiography cannot be a form of historiography which is often extremely interesting and useful. But when someone tells me about a meeting with Togliatti around the time of the emergence of a new line, and all I get is how the protagonist – who was young then – was dressed or a pungent comment on Togliatti's wife; when the message of Togliatti is communicated as the all-too-obvious, 'Work, find things to do', well, then I just have to point out how vacuous these autobiographical contributions are and, even worse, I have to note how the key to the entire book is an exag-gerated presumption about one person's own importance. This presumption encroaches, from the first pages, on all of the book's observations, even those penetrating ones on the complex and contradictory nature of Naples.

There is another phenomenon which has to be seen within the context of this sweeping, all-embracing 'logic' of self-assertion (which, at times, can be quite disarming). But what I am now referring to is a rather petty fault, due I think more to a modish acquiescence to Althusser than to Macciocchi herself. I refer, of course, to the flirtation with extremism; the echoing of critical comments towards the P C I's line, which would have us guilty of emphasizing 'the defensive moment of political alliances at the expense of an offensive initiative of the working class'; the peremptory judgements on the obsolescence of both the theory and actions of the 'New Party' (and I prefer not to begin a serious discussion here of Comrade Macciocchi's effective grasp of this line, from 1944 on); and her habitual use of the Marx-Lenin-Mao triad! As I said above, not only do I think that much of this is homage paid to Althusser's analysis, but our French comrade himself offers the best rebuttal of his own position when he analyses the 'events' in France in 1968. It is also just as well that our comrade decided not to refer to Eleanora Fonseca Pimentel in her speeches, even though she was sorely tempted to do so!

Memoir writing is a difficult task in the best situations. It is especially risky for someone who is a professional politician. And M. A. Macciocchi's book goes against the customs of our Party not because it utters bitter truths, and not because it denounces, publicly, our failures and our delays, but because it is written from a blatantly individualistic point of view, with such obvious concern on the part of the author for personal recognition and self-affirmation.

The philosopher, from Paris, wisely suggests that the electoral campaign be approached as an 'occasion' to be grasped in order to understand what 'the People' is, and hence to be better able to carry out a political struggle. But Comrade Macciocchi is never able to hide – both in the book and even before she wrote the book – her self-consciousness about being a 'parachuted' candidate, and hence her doubts about how willingly the Party would support her and work for her election. Comrade M. A. Macciocchi, with this reaction, has shown that she does not really know the Party in which she has been a militant for all these years. But the 'discovery' that then must have been obvious even to her after 19 May seems to have been ignored;

this, ironically, is one 'discovery' that she did not reflect on at all. And *this* is her political error. She first of all has not understood that the Party in Naples, once it was presented with her name as a candidate, had every right to discuss, object, and decide on her merits – and certainly couldn't be expected to stand back with its mouth hanging open in abject admiration. She also plainly did not understand that the Communist Party in Naples is a serious organization which, once it took on a commitment, would honour it – as it did in her case. There is simply no way on earth that anyone in the P C I can see their own election as a personal victory, for no one is elected – whether in Naples or in Genoa – without a prior decision and the prior support of the Party. Finally and above all, Comrade Macciocchi made the mistake of not reflecting on her own experience and writings, in the wake of the election. She evidently could not resist the temptation of publishing a book that she had already written. My view of this may well be a prejudiced one, but I think that communist militants *are*, in general, prejudiced and we, quite simply, do not appreciate this fact. But to those who, outside the Party, expect to see sanctions, penalties or excommunications, we can say, quite calmly: *habent sua fata libelli.*

Alessandro Natta

Once more on M. A. Macciocchi's book [1]

Dear Editor,

I was very pleased to see that *Rinascita* did not consider its editorial comment on Maria Antonietta Macciocchi's book to be definitive (cf. 'A Candidate in Naples', 13 June) and that, in the issue of 27 June, there was a letter different in tone if not evaluation, written by Comrade Alessandro Natta. I feel that today it is *essential* to promote and facilitate public debates between ourselves on problems that affect the Party.

I will say immediately that I am not in agreement with Comrade Natta, particularly as regards the tone and negative spirit of his letter. 'The key to the entire book is an exaggerated presumption of one person's own importance,' writes Natta. But then when he attempts to justify his main assertion, he says a number of things which, frankly, are not very persuasive. The book 'shows off, stringing together every literary reference imaginable, from Stendhal to Dumas to Goethe to Serao'. 'I cannot help wondering if there is even one leader of our Party who would ever take it upon himself – unless, of course, he wanted to suffer merciless ridicule – to recount not only his own speeches, but the novelty and audacity of his attack, in Castellammare or Naples, on the policies and clients of the Gavas!'; 'when someone tells me about a meeting with Togliatti around the time of the emergence of a new line, and all I get is how the protagonist – who was young then – was dressed or a pungent comment on Togliatti's wife; when Togliatti's message is the all-too-obvious, "Work, find things to do" . . . !'

Dear Natta, this doesn't strike me as a calm way of criticizing things: everything you say can easily be turned around, and in fact it is turned around by anyone reading this book who doesn't have an axe to grind. Why shouldn't there be quotations from Stendhal, Dumas, Goethe or Matilde Serao? The simple fact that they are there

1. From *Rinascita*, 4 July 1969.

is in no way grounds for condemnation. And that the author 'shows off' in this regard is your impression, not a fact. The author's progressive discovery of the reality of Naples, of the Gavas' system of power relationships, of the sub-proletariat and proletariat, is a process which both interests and 'holds' the reader precisely because it involves him in actions which take place in the first person, and in discoveries which also occur in the first person (and they still are discoveries, even if someone else found out the same things earlier). The meeting with Togliatti at Salerno and the dress (red) of the narrator (who was young*er* then, and who is still young today) not only go together, but I would even say are necessary items to include in a first-person narration.

In my sincere opinion, egocentrism did not in fact appear to be the key to understanding the entire book. My *impressions* on this subject obviously are quite different from those of Comrade Natta. As I read this book, I felt grow in me 'a violent – and rational – passion for Naples. I really love this dramatic city and its people'. I, along with the author, also feel that both the city and its people have been 'systematically betrayed'. And, after just a few dozen pages, I felt true class rage exploding inside me: a profound feeling of solidarity with the Neapolitan 'plebs' and a lucid fury against the socio–economico-political system that continuously reproduces the sub-proletariat, all the forms of super-exploitation and the monstrous 'belly' of the capital of Campania. By means of our comrade's research, I gained a much fuller understanding of 'forms of super-exploitation, of home workers, of the mechanisms which keep salaries so low and of the general conditions of the workers and peasants'. I am well aware that all these facts are already 'part of our patrimony', at least to a degree (as Comrade Gomez said in *l'Unità*), but I am also aware of the need to go beyond those limits and generalize. Maria Antonietta Macciocchi did this, and in so doing she fully carried out her tasks as a militant journalist. For enriching my understanding to such a degree and, in so doing, for showing me how much is yet to be done, I wish to thank the author publicly.

As a Communist, I felt a great deal of pride well up in me as I accompanied the candidate, through her writings, to Naples, Castellammare, Torre del Greco and the agricultural centres in the outlying areas of the province. 'Vast amounts of personal sacrifice, intelligence and inventiveness are poured out, in the course of the electoral struggle, by thousands of simple comrades. . . . At all levels of the apparatus, there are pure, uncontaminated combatants and human beings, whose essential characteristic is their dedication to socialism and to the revolution. . . .' And, even more than in words of this kind, it is in the narrative of facts that one sees how valuable and great the Communist Party is in Naples: a party capable of bringing together, in spite of frictions, delays and reciprocal mistrust, workers and sub-proletarians, peasants, intellectuals and white-collar workers.

These, then, are *my* impressions and they are very different from those of Comrade Natta. I would have greatly preferred, however, a discussion *on the merits* of the book, and not a juxtaposition of impressions, tones and sympathy or antipathy. On the merits of the book, I think that I would have made certain criticisms which paralleled those of Natta (e.g. on the 'habitual use of the Marx-Lenin-Mao triad', which, however, as Natta notes, is much more Althusser's construction than that of the author). I would also have made some criticisms which differed from those of Natta and, even if less 'pungent', they would concern issues which perhaps go more to the heart of the book's faults. My major criticism concerns the tendency to mystify and mythologize the masses, 'who are so terribly ahead of us', and a vision of the rank-and-file of the Party as an autonomous entity with respect to the leadership.

I am glad that Comrade Natta – as is customary with him – places himself squarely in favour of open confrontation and debate, of 'the equal freedom' to 'express one's own opinion'. It is equally encouraging to note that his argument with the book centres on its individualistic slant and not 'on the fact that it utters bitter truths (nor because) it publicly denounces our failures and delays. . . .' For a choice of method seems to me, today, to be decisive: we must choose to discuss our problems publicly.

For this reason, let us concentrate our attention and our passions on the substance of issues; let us take advantage of every occasion to go to the heart of the issues and then proceed. Let us face, for example, *the merits* of one of the largest, most important issues in our Party: Is the 'Party of a New Type', the brain-child and product of Togliatti in 1944–5, adequate *today* to our tasks and situation? This is a problem which exists in fact, and it really does not matter if the judgement of Comrade Macciocchi is superficial or 'peremptory'. In any event, do we really want to claim that problems which are central to our collective and individual lives can be debated without errors, bitterness and a degree of unilaterality?

Lucio Lombardo Radice

EDITORIAL POSTSCRIPT

It is not Comrade Natta's impression or opinion, but an objectively verifiable fact that Comrade Macciocchi's book combines not only a description and analysis of Naples (which at times is penetrating and incisive, and at other times is heavy-handed and exaggerated), but also a self-satisfied recounting – at times at 'the risk of ridicule' – of the author's electoral campaign, and her denunciation of the alleged 'real state' of the Party. Moreover, the individualism that Natta wrote about, and the sensationalism and exhibitionism that our Editor called our attention to, can hardly be ignored by anyone who reads the book – not in the spirit of a critic with 'an axe to grind', but with that measure of severity that one must bring to an enterprise so politically transparent and ambitious.

There are, to be sure, matters on which there can be differences of opinion. This is the case with the varying interpretations of the merits of literary quotations and historical digressions; these issues are best left to the personal tastes of each reader. On the other hand, it takes all the generosity – as a militant and as a reader – of Comrade Lombardo Radice to see in this book a celebration of the Party! Given the emphasis, in Comrade Macciocchi's letters, on the description of negative characteristics in the PCI, given the emphasis put on these facts, given the way they are attributed to a presumed general process of decay and decline in the Party, we really have a hard time imagining how many readers – whether comrades, friends or enemies – could possibly have come away from the book with the same positive 'impressions' as Comrade Lombardo Radice.

Be that as it may, we thought it appropriate to publish Lombardo Radice's point of view. But we really cannot see that there is any basis for a further discussion. This is not because there is nothing to discuss about the Party and its policies – this, at least, should be clear! There is, in fact, much to be discussed in terms of whether the PCI is 'adequate', and in what sense, to the situation and tasks of today. But a discussion of these issues must occur within the context of a serious elaboration and confrontation of analyses and theses, and is not at all served by an ill-intentioned, clamorous parrotting of certain criticisms.

From a Friend of the Party

Dear Editor,

I am not a member of the Party and I do not know if I have the right to ask that this letter be published. But I am a friend of communists, and I am very much a friend of the Italian Communists. Longo, Amendola, Pajetta, Napolitano, Guido Fanti and the comrades in Bologna can all attest to this.[1] I have attended the Party's congresses, coming specially from France to do so. I admire the PCI for its ability to be both very Italian and very internationalist. I have always felt at home among Italian Communists and I want to continue to feel that way.

I bought Maria Antonietta Macciocchi's book in Paris, and I know that many revolutionary friends from Latin America bought it as well. When I had finished reading it, I wanted more than ever to be an Italian Communist. It is a beautiful book. I learned many things from it, about Naples, about workers and about the sub-proletariat. It provided me with yet another proof of the importance of the working class taking charge of the future of sub-proletariat and the poor, not only in Italy but all over the world. I think that the PCI can and should make this line its most important contribution to the world revolution.

While on a trip to Rome, I read the pieces in *Rinascita* on this book and I found them very strange. I am not even speaking here of the insinuations and barely-masked insults: these are disgusting things that remind us of other epochs. I would just like to say a few things. Why is Maria Antonietta called an 'exhibitionist'? If exhibitionism means revealing yourself, revealing your own ideas and making others reveal their ideas, then I accept that Maria Antonietta was an 'exhibitionist'. *Exhibitionism*, in this case, is the richness of the creativity of a consciousness. A creation, and its creator, grow out of imagination;

1. Giancarlo Pajetta is a member of the PCI Executive and head of its Foreign Affairs Commission; Giorgio Napolitano is also a member of the Executive and head of the Cultural Commission; Guido Fanti is mayor of Bologna and similarly a member of the Executive. (Trans.)

they use imagination to awaken their own contradictions and to address themselves to the contradictions of others, in this way encouraging the maximum possible number of points of contact between themselves and others. Hence the whole Party ought to be much more 'exhibitionist', i.e. it ought to reveal its own ideas much more frequently, and make all members of the Party reveal their ideas. This should not be done out of some general notion of democracy, but it should be done because a great revolutionary party like the PCI needs to stimulate and awaken all ideas. And the thing the Party should fight against is the flabby megalomania that sits immobile and expects homage to be paid to its inflexible truths.

I also read in *Rinascita* that Maria Antonietta described *her* electoral campaign. I find this perfectly appropriate. I am, so they say, a painter, and I know that you cannot say anything worse about a painter than that he seems like another painter. Why should one candidate be like another one? The important thing, for a painter and for a candidate, is to demonstrate your own emotions and your own personality within the broader context of an ideology and a programme. This Maria Antonietta has done, and she has done it very well indeed. Her emotions permitted her to speak and encouraged others to speak. She spoke to me and made me feel much closer to the Italian Communists. She made the women, the workers and the sub-proletarians of Naples speak, and in so doing she made them express their own emotions and individuality. What is wrong with this? I find this kind of activity essential for a revolutionary party. I also read in *Rinascita* that Comrade Lucio Lombardo Radice is 'generous' because he saw, in this book, new links with the Party and new stimuli to go out and struggle. I do not know Lombardo Radice and I therefore cannot know if he is really a generous person. But I too, after reading the book, felt myself to be even closer to the Italian Communists. I therefore accept being called generous.

I hope that this letter will be published. If this happens, then my friendship for the PCI will be even stronger. This is a friendship, by the way, that friends of mine in Paris and even Rome often reprove me for. But it is a friendship that I have always defended because I have always found the PCI to be very intelligent and very open. Maria Antonietta Macciocchi's book has proved me right in my defence of the PCI. Does *Rinascita* want to prove me wrong?

Matta

Printed and bound by CPI Group (UK) Ltd, Croydon, CR0 4YY

22/04/2026

02095406-0009